ORGANIZATION D

C.S.G. Krishnamacharyulu

Director
RVS Institute of Management and Computer Applications
Karaikal
Former Professor
Department of Management Studies
Sri Venkateswara University, Tirupati

Lalitha Ramakrishnan

Professor and Head
Department of Management
Centre Head, Pondicherry University, Karaikal Campus
Karaikal

PHI Learning Private Limited

Delhi-110092
2014

₹ 350.00

ORGANIZATION DEVELOPMENT
C.S.G. Krishnamacharyulu and Lalitha Ramakrishnan

ISBN-978-81-203-4803-5

The export rights of this book are vested solely with the publisher.

Published by Asoke K. Ghosh, PHI Learning Private Limited, Rimjhim House, 111, Patparganj Industrial Estate, Delhi-110092 and Printed by Star Print-O-Bind, F–31, Okhla Industrial Area, Phase I, New Delhi-110020.

To
Our youngest sister, who transformed our lives
Vasanthalakshmi, Chilakamarri
her husband
Srinivas, Vangala
and children
Manoj & **Nitya**

Contents

PART ONE: PROFESSION

PART TWO: FOUNDATION

PART THREE: PROCESSES

PART FOUR: TYPES OF INTERVENTIONS

PART FIVE: FUTURE TRENDS

Preface

Managers today are facing the challenge of operating in a dynamic environment characterized by increasing complexity, scarcity and diversity. Faced with the challenge, managers are seeking the help of consultants who can offer solutions, not only for short-term, measurable, tangible performance improvements but also for long-term capacity building and organizational transformation. In this context, the theory and practice of Organization Development (OD) has become all the more significant. We find today, many certified consultants offering a wide range of services and many universities offering OD as an elective or a specialization paper.

Objectives

In this book, an attempt is made to explain the concepts, describe the tools and discuss the applications of OD, with the twin objectives of (i) documenting the emergent theoretical frameworks and current practical approaches, adopted by OD practitioners who have firsthand experience in designing and implementing OD solutions, and (ii) provide a guidebook for young students of management and social sciences aspiring careers in the field of human resource management and capacity building of institutions.

Structure of the book

The book consists of 15 chapters organized into five parts labelled as Profession, Foundation, Processes, Types of Interventions and Future Trends.

Part One deals with issues relating to the profession of OD. The two chapters in this part provide theoretical framework for OD, explain the growth of OD profession and discuss issues that determine the nature and quality of client-consultant relationships.

Part Two lays the foundation to the practice of OD by discussing the four themes in four chapters—Organizational design, Organizational Climate, Organizational Culture and Organizational Change.

Part Three explains the two key processes of OD viz., organizational diagnosis and action research in two separate chapters. Various models of organizational diagnosis and the process of action research with its variants are examined with the help of illustrations

Part Four is devoted to the description of various types of interventions. It comprises six chapters that explain techno-structural, strategy, planning, training, role, team, learning and large scale interventions in detail with examples.

Part Five of the book consists of only one chapter that explores the future trends in OD profession. Also, it provides a bird's eye-view of the ongoing research in the field of OD by presenting, in brief, a few select research works on OD interventions.

Pedagogical tools

We have strived to make the book comprehensive by including major conceptual and operational themes on Organizational Development. Each chapter opens with a vignette describing the role played by the consultants in different situations and closes with a chapter end case for readers to apply the concepts learned in the chapter.

For exercising in the intellectual gymnasium of OD, each chapter offers challenge in terms of one web assignment and one mini-project. Further, every chapter provides review questions and discussion questions for students to undertake discussions and prepare for their examinations.

We hope the book will be a helpful guide to management students and young practitioners in acquiring knowledge of consulting and enriching their skills in applying it. We look forward to receiving valuable feedback from students, teachers, managers and practitioners.

C.S.G. Krishnamacharyulu
Lalitha Ramakrishnan

Acknowledgements

Though we cherished the desire to write a book on OD, the inspiration to do it has come from PHI Learning. We are thankful to the editorial team who worked with us and co-created this book.

A textbook of this kind cannot be complete without the support and contribution of freelance writers, researchers and practitioners. We have drawn cases and information from the websites of consultants and research papers published in different journals. We are extremely grateful to all those consultants who have supported our work by providing permission to use website information about their services and cases. Among them are: Potentia, Culture Strategy, Human Dimension, OD Alternatives, OD Network, Clarity Consultants, Clariy consulting, Samuday Psycon, Accelera consulting group, Mincu & Associates, Future Search, TQM International, Confianzys Consulting, and Centum Learning.

We have used information from papers in the journal of Hospital Administration (AHA), Vikalpa and TMC Academy Journal. We thank the respective authors and managements of the journals for according permission for such use.

Our special thanks are due to Mr. Sushanta Banerjee of Samuday Psycon, and Mrs. Sunita Raut for contributing cases for the first two chapters. Mrs. Sunita Raut provided a range of services she offers and Prof. Sri Ranganath Iyengar of Strategic Interventions India Pvt. Ltd (SIIPL), gave an illustrative account of the strategy interventions from a practitioner point of view. We are indebted to them for their kind gesture.

While every care is taken to acknowledge the sources appropriately, there may be some inadvertent lapses. If you kindly notify us, we will be happy to make necessary corrections, with due apologies.

We are deeply indebted to Prof. (Mrs.) Chandra Krishnamurthy, Vice-Chancellor of Pondicherry University, for being the main spring of motivation to us and many academicians like us and leading the transformation of the university from a national to international campus.

We thank Prof. M. Ramadass, Director, SEI & RR and Prof. R. Prabhakara Raya, Dean, School of Management, Pondicherry University for their support in our endeavours.

We are grateful to our colleagues Prof. K. Chandrasekhara Rao, Head, Department of Banking Technology and Prof. G. Anjaneya Swamy, Department of Tourism Studies of Pondicherry University for their encouragement.

We take delight in acknowledging the moral support we got from our children, Sri Krishna and Srivalli, who through their interventions have brightened our spirits during this arduous book writing project.

C.S.G. Krishnamacharyulu
Lalitha Ramakrishnan

Chapter 1

Framework of Organization Development

Learning Objectives

After studying this chapter, you will be able to:

- Explain the concept, nature, scope and significance of Organization Development (OD)
- Discuss its goals, values, assumptions and beliefs
- Trace the evolution of OD as a discipline and profession
- Know the competencies and career opportunities of OD practitioners

Vignette: In Search of Effectiveness

Unrealistic targets, disappointment with the board, Empire Building of functional heads, and a 900 member army looking for direction, led the CEO of a company to declare "in the next 18 months we want to grow as much as we have in the last ten years". The CEO invited Potentia, a well-known Organization Development (OD) consultant firm, to design a lean and agile organization structure that can be supportive to the growth envisaged and acceptable to the executives of the organization. Potentia leveraged the use of appreciative inquiry, and donned the role of a process facilitator to articulate roles, responsibilities and deliverables, and succeeded in creating a vibrant organization.

Pfizer recognized that in order to be successful, they need to work together as a global team to serve their customers. To reach that goal, Consultancy firm Clarity delivered team-building training classes in two-day sessions. These sessions addressed issues, such as how to interface with colleagues and employees, negotiation tactics and conflict management. Consultants facilitated, coached and guided the corporate participants using Pfizer-specific content and best practices for team building.

A financial services company lost an important international client because of a number of errors and incidents. Mincu & Associates was roped in to bring about process improvements. The consultant interviewed concerned organization members and composed a case study with

1

characters in situations typical to their real-life counterparts. In a two-day interactive workshop on Systems Thinking the senior management team members were asked to empathize with each character, and analyze how well each character can perform in the situation. This helped them understand how a small part of the big picture-inadvertently compounded the problem. They appreciated systems thinking, and decided to apply it to improve organizational processes.

A large global organization contacted Accelera consulting group to integrate a new enterprise software system to increase efficiency, decrease bureaucracy, and improve the employee experience. Accelera helped the company to identify and empower the project team to articulate project goals, determine the impacts to workflow and other downstream impacts of the change, decide the training required for employees, and develop measures to track progress and ensure sustainability. Change was implemented efficiently, with minimal work disruption and a higher than expected degree of employee support and buy-in.

These cases[1] illustrate the ways in which OD interventions can benefit client organizations. In this chapter, we will introduce the disciplines and professions of OD.

INTRODUCTION

In the globalized knowledge economies of today, majority of global CEOs plan fundamental change and expect new forms of innovation to drive growth, according to IBM study[2]. One of the most effective tools to promote successful change is Organization Development (OD), which has emerged as a discipline and profession during 1960s in India. With the strategic link with HR, OD can foster the development of healthy and productive organizations with competitive advantage[3].

ORGANIZATION DEVELOPMENT: DEFINITIONS

A survey of definitions on organization development reveals that there are minor variations in presenting the concept. To arrive at a standard and universally acceptable definition is neither feasible nor desirable. To develop a working definition, it is important to have an idea of the purposes, processes and techniques of OD to define it in clear terms.

Let us consider some of the important definitions given by various authors.

SHRM Glossary of Human Resources Terms[4] defines OD as organizational effectiveness improvement process.

The basic purpose of organization development is to increase an organization's effectiveness through planned interventions related to the organization's processes (often company-wide), resulting in improvements in productivity, return on investment and employee satisfaction.

A similar definition is offered by Beckhard[5].

Organization Development is an effort planned, organization-wide, and managed from the top, to increase organization effectiveness and health through planned interventions in the organization's processes, using behavioral science knowledge.

The definition of Cummings and et al.[6] is much similar to the above ones.

Organization Development is a process by which behavioral science knowledge and practices are used to help organizations to achieve greater effectiveness, including improved quality of life, increased productivity, and improved product and service quality.

Warren Bennis[7] defines OD as a response to change and education strategy.

OD is a response to change, a complex educational strategy intended to change the beliefs, attitudes, values, and structure of an organization so that it can better adapt to new technologies, markets, challenges, and the dizzying rate of change itself.

The definition by Matt Minahan and associates[8], though lengthy, emphasizes the system concept of organization, nature of interventions and goal of OD as a discipline and profession.

Organization Development is a body of knowledge and practice that enhances organizational performance and individual development, viewing the organization as a complex system of systems that exists within a larger system, each of which has its own attributes and degrees of alignment. OD interventions in these systems are inclusive methodologies and approaches to strategic planning, organization design, leadership development, change management, performance management, coaching, diversity, and work-life balance.

Another lengthy, definition given by French, Bell and Veena[9] includes essential components of OD.

Organization Development is a long-term effort, led and supported by top management, to improve organization's visioning, empowerment, learning and problem–solving processes, through an on-going, collaborative management of organization culture, with special emphasis on the culture of intact work teams, and other team configurations using the consultant–facilitator role and the theory and technology of applied behavioral science including action research.

The above definitions reveal only minor variations in identification of the elements of OD. All of them agree on many aspects related to aim, approach, process and outcomes. Utilizing the areas of agreement, let us define OD in the following terms.

OD is a discipline and profession, with focus on strategic organizational transformation process, in response to change, aimed at achieving sustainable individual, team and organizational effectiveness, through interventions based on behavioral science.

NATURE OF ORGANIZATION DEVELOPMENT

The term OD represents a process, a discipline as well as a profession. We will first discuss the characteristics of the OD effort, and then examine the features of OD discipline and the attributes of OD profession. The following characteristics of OD effort can be identified from its definitions.

Systems approach

OD is not designed to solve a single or temporary problem in an organization. It helps improve organizational effectiveness by focusing on the total system as well as its interdependent parts. It seeks to find solutions in the broader internal and external context of an organization, working closely with employees within and with stakeholders (customers, stockholders and community)[10].

Planned, long range initiative

OD is a planned system of change. It takes a long-range approach to change attitudes and systems to improve organization's problem-solving and renewal processes. It avoids the (usual) quick-fix. It is a long-time effort, spread over a long period, undertaken in a phased manner, often with the assistance of a change agent or catalyst. It is a continuous process as its goal is to create sustainable improvements in organizational effectiveness.

The duration of a consulting assignment is dependent on the following factors:

- Nature of initiative required—strategic, techno-structural, systems, and human process
- Size of organization and number of people-affected
- Scope of intervention—Comprehensive vs specific aspect of the organization
- Level of clarity about the organizational challenge—Certain or uncertain

A simple assignment may need duration of 3 months–12 months, on an average, to fulfill its avowed objectives, whereas complex assignments takes 1–8 years to achieve.

Strategic OD–initiated from top

Organization Development (OD) is an organizational improvement strategy designed to face the challenge of change. OD is recognized as a key factor in successful implementation of large-scale organizational changes, such as mergers, acquisitions, downsizings, and restructurings. Since OD seeks to bring about change in the organizational systems, process and people, for long-run effectiveness, it requires the initiative and support of the top management. The top management has to model it, not just espouse it. The OD process also needs the buy-in and ownership of workers throughout the organization.

Political

Almost all OD efforts are political in nature for two reasons[11].

1. The OD effort is centered around the political structure of an organization. The hierarchical structure of authority, status differences, and individual power strategies impact OD effort.
2. OD practitioners encourage collaboration and participation that enfranchise participants.

The OD practitioner needs to know where the political power bases are, who makes decisions, who has the most influence, and who needs to buy into strategies and can carry them forward to ensure their success as well as the success of the OD work[12].

Behavior-oriented

Organization Development employs tools and research findings of behavioral sciences to understand people, systems, and their interactions. It utilizes interventions supported by the knowledge drawn from behavioral sciences to bring about a change in attitudes and competencies of people.

While deciding the direction of change is critical, much more significant is managing employees' personal reactions is yet another. The successful and satisfying result is one that leaves employees feeling involved, recognized and satisfied and not disenfranchised, forgotten, and wounded.

Process-driven

Organization Development is a change process that can bring about improvements in various processes of an organization. It involves, three different phases:

1. Understanding of situations requiring change through inquiry methods.
2. Planning interventions and gaining acceptance of the people through educative approaches.
3. Bringing about desired change through administration of interventions.

Warner Burke[13] emphasizes that OD is not just anything done to better an organization; it is a particular kind of change process designed to bring about a particular kind of end result. Here are the different steps of the organizational development process. It is a cyclical process beginning with a problem and ending with a solution and its impact assessment on the system

1. Understanding the situation
   - Problem identification
   - Situational assessment
2. Planning interventions and gaining acceptance
   - Action planning/planning of the intervention
3. Administration of interventions
   - Implementing the intervention
   - Evaluating the intervention
   - Feedback

If feedback is found unsatisfactory, the process is repeated. OD is thus an unfolding and evolving series of events.

Collaborative effort

OD practitioners are a sort of change agents. However, in bringing about the desired change, they are neither external change drivers nor magicians. The critical part of any OD change intervention is ensuring that everyone affected by the change is included. OD practitioners are best served by realizing that they are not the change owners, but rather the vehicles for the change.

They are facilitators, collaborators, and co-learners with the client system, encouraging collaborative effort with focus on continuous learning through self-analytical methods to enable client organization to solve its problems on its own. OD exercises are undertaken in collaboration with human resource management and with the support of top management.

Goal-directed

OD is tied to specific goals that improve the stability and profitability of a company and their sustainability in the long run. It aligns the organization's systems with its people and increases organization health and functional abilities of the entire organization. In fact, the ultimate aim of OD practitioners is to work themselves out of a job by leaving the client organization with a set of right attitudes, and an appropriate action plan for further progress toward its own renewal and development[14]. In so doing, they positively contribute to the sustenance of socio-economic goals such as profitability, satisfaction of stakeholders and company image.

Value-laden

OD effort is guided by values relating their approach and functioning with the individuals, teams and organizations. The values embedded in the practice of OD are: quality of life, growth, empowerment, effectiveness, efficiency, excellence, freedom, responsibility, justice, cooperation, and integration.

Universal

OD principles and tools have universal application. It is practiced in a number of different types of organizations in both the private and the public sectors. However, it is viewed as industry related practice because the published material on OD has focused on applications in industrial organizations.

FEATURES OF OD DISCIPLINE

As a science and subject of learning, OD has the following characteristics:

Interdisciplinary Mix

Organization Development is an interdisciplinary behavioral science, drawing from many fields (see Table 1.1): behavioral sciences (anthropology, sociology and psychology), administrative sciences (management and public administration), economics, and education.

Applied science

OD applies models and tools drawn from its scientific knowledge base, to the real-life situations to bring about solutions to problems. OD has number of theoretical models of individual, group behavior and organizational systems, to solve a variety of practical problems. Indian Society for Applied Behavioral Science (ISABS) offers a one-year post academic certificate programme in Organization Development. The four-phase programme will equip candidates to design and lead planned strategies to handle change in their organizations. Course modules will focus on

TABLE 1.1 Contributions of Disciplines to OD

S.No.	Discipline	Contribution
1	Psychology	Motivation, personality, ego, attitude, and perception
2	Sociology	Leadership, group dynamics, relations, norms, status and roles
3	Anthropology	Values, culture, and evolution of humans
4	Politics	Power, conflict, authority, discipline and controls
5	Administrative sciences	Organizational structures, span of control, delegation, decision making
6	Economics	Manpower supply and demand, valuation of manpower, cost-benefit analysis
7	Education	Knowledge, learning, reinforcement, and training.

areas, such as organizational diagnosis, intervention strategies and methods, team building, and leadership. In addition, mentoring sessions are provided by an ISABS trainer.

Evolutionary field

Beginning in 1940s as an applied behavioral science with T-group techniques at operational level, OD has evolved into a multi-disciplinary mix to provide strategic solutions.

1. *Social solutions phase:* During 1950s and 1960s, OD principles focused mainly on the social side of organizations. The best known are T-groups, process consultation, and team building. The emphasis was on humanistic values promoting openness, trust, and collaboration.

2. *Socio-technical solutions phase:* In 1970s, new concepts emerged, focusing on human side of technology. The initiatives addressed issues like structural change, employee involvement, and work design. The emphasis was on quality of work life and productivity.

3. *HRM solutions phase:* In 1980s, Organization Development became a theory that many management consultants wanted to apply. Human resource development and performance management techniques, like career planning and development, reward systems and employee assistance programmes showed up. Besides, process control and total quality management came into focus. The emphasis was on empowerment of people, innovation and productive utilization of technology.

4. *Strategic management solutions phase:* During 1990s, strategic issues like organization design, corporate culture, strategy formulation and implementation, self-designed organizations, and trans-organizational development became important. The emphasis has been on right fit (people—organization—environment) and organic growth.

ATTRIBUTES OF OD PROFESSION

OD practitioners are recognized as professionals. The occupation of OD meets most of the requirements of a profession as explained here.

Science

OD is science with strong theoretical knowledge base developed by a good number of authors and researchers. It has a body of knowledge comprising concepts, tools and processes. Today, there is a proliferation of academic programmes. These programmes are focusing on developing consultants of external and internal categories.

Today, OD consultants are found with varied backgrounds with experience and training in organization development, organization behavior, psychology, education, management and human resources. Many have advanced degrees and most have experience in a variety of organizational settings. Often described as "change agents", they work with captains of the corporations, toward organizational renewal and effectiveness.

Art

OD is a skill-based occupation. OD practitioners work in a manner similar to medical practitioners who use knowledge-based skills for prevention and cure of diseases. The study of the organizational structures and design is similar to the study of anatomy and physiology, whereas the study of organizational behavior is similar to the study of psychology and sociology in human systems. Finally, the study and field of Organization Development compares to the study and field of medicine that deals with diagnosis and treatment or interventions.

Professional association

The India OD Network (IODN) is a professional development organization for OD professionals learning and practicing in the field of OD. The objectives of IODN are as follows[15]:

- To provide a forum that promotes personal growth, development and learning in a fun, enjoyable environment.
- To share, nurture and expand the skills of members to continuously improve business practices.

Code of conduct

OD consultants profess the values and ethical norms that govern their business conduct. However, this is not an isolated, individual exercise. Internationally, it is recognized that a code of ethics is important as evidenced by the following statement of the OD Institute, USA which developed an International OD Code of Ethics[16]. By providing a common reference for OD professionals throughout the world, they seek to enhance our sense of identity as a global professional community. The code development process began in 1981. It has support of most OD-oriented professional organizations, associations, and networks in the United States. It was also supported unanimously by the participants at the 1984 OD World Congress, in Southampton, England.

The purpose in developing an International OD Code of Ethics, according to OD institute, is threefold:

1. To increase professional and ethical consciousness among OD professionals and their sense of ethical responsibility.

2. To guide OD professionals in making more informed ethical choices.
3. To help the OD profession function at the fullness of its potential.

SCOPE

To make a clear definition of the scope of OD, one has to find answers to the following questions:

- Is it a separate discipline, or a part of HRM?
- Is it an alternative to T&D and HRD?
- What are the key functional areas and boundaries of OD?

Nexus with HRM

Until recent past, OD and human resources were considered as two distinct and separate entities, and hence, competing disciplines. They are separate, because OD has roots in social sciences and applied behavior, with values based on humanistic psychology, whereas the field of human resource is based on human capital theory, behaviorism and performance engineering[17]. They are competing, because both focus on development of human resources for enhancing individual and group effectiveness.

However, the metamorphosis that has been taking place in the nature of organizations and employment of people, has led to the present view that OD and human resources are, in fact, complementary, to promote and sustain organizational success. OD offers HR professionals a wealth of tools, models, theories and competencies invaluable for a competitive business environment.

The literature indicates that these two disciplines are melding together, with a growing collaboration and integration between OD and HR[18]. Like Training & Development (T&D) and Human Resource Development (HRD), OD is very much a subset of HRM. However, the total system focus and long-range change process of OD have necessitated a separate approach.

Training and development is the organizational activity aimed at improving attitudes, skills and knowledge of employees to achieve high performance and results. It is often referred to as 'employee development', and 'learning and development'. Human resource development is a process by which the employees of an organization are helped, in a continuous and planned way, to acquire capabilities to perform well in their present and future roles for their own and OD purposes. The mechanisms include: performance appraisal, counseling, training, and organization development interventions.

It is clear that HRD is broader than T&D as it is more focused on continuous development of people through appraisal and methods of improvements like coaching, mentoring and counseling. OD is broader than HRD as it deals with a gamut of "people problems" and "work system problems". It uses structural interventions that have organization-wide implications. As Warner Burke described it OD is a process of fundamental change in organization's culture and systems[19].

Broadened Scope

With evolution of the OD profession, its scope has expanded from operational issues, such as work efficiency, productivity, operational economies, team work and conflict management to embrace the strategic issues like growth, competitive advantage, organizational effectiveness, corporate governance and ethics. Today, OD practitioners work with managers at different levels, to counter changes and use a broad spectrum of interventions designed for individuals, teams and organizations. Table 1.2 shows the range of issues and typical interventions.

TABLE 1.2 Issues and Interventions

Category of interventions and issues	Level of management	Interventions
Strategic interventions related to innovations, growth, organizational renewal, competitive advantage and corporate governance.	Top management	Organizational transformation, Culture change, Mergers and acquisitions Integrated strategic change, Knowledge management, Organizational learning, Global strategic orientation, Ethics change management, Process improvement, Organization design and whole system analysis.
Techno-structural and human resource management interventions concerned with effective HRM policies and systems and structural effectiveness	Top and middle level management	Structural design, Downsizing, Re-engineering, Parallel structures, High-Involvement Organizations (HIO's) Total Quality Management (TQM) Goal setting, Performance appraisal, reward systems, Career planning and development, Managing workforce diversity, Employee wellness and stress management.
Human Process Interventions in relation to issues like leadership, team work, conflict management performance improvement and process improvement.	Middle and lower level management	Organization confrontation meeting, Intergroup relations, large-group interventions, Grid organization development T-groups, Process consultation, Third party interventions, Team building, and Work design.

GOALS

Broadly speaking, the goal statement of OD practitioners is creating and sustaining individual, group and organizational effectiveness and stakeholder satisfaction. Keeping this in mind, let us examine what OD practitioners have observed. Hurley and others[20] based on the responses 289 respondent OD practitioners listed the following values with which OD practitioners are associated.

- Increasing effectiveness and efficiency
- Enhancing productivity
- Creating openness in communication

- Empowering employees to act
- Promoting organizational participation

Marge Yanker[21] an OD practitioner has identified the following as goals of OD

- The health of the organization
- The organizational effectiveness
- The organization's capacity to solve problems
- The organization's ability to adapt, change, or of self-renewal
- The organization's ability to create a high quality of life for its employees

Thus, the goals will be focused on organization (effectiveness, health, self-renewal), team performance (effectiveness, efficiency, productivity) and team well-being (empowerment, participation, quality of life).

ASSUMPTIONS AND BELIEFS

Consistent with the Douglas McGregor's theory Y[22] which views people as active, responsible and leader type, who take initiative to perform, the present generation employees need recognition and opportunity for participation. Box 1.1 presents Y theory.

Some of the changes that have led to the above views are:

1. Development of organic systems in place of mechanistic ones.
2. Emergence of knowledge workers and skilled people.
3. Legitimization of human feelings (a movement from commodity to resources concept) inspired by the spirit of democracy.
4. Development of more effective "team management".

BOX 1.1 Theory Y assumptions of Douglas McGregor

- Work is as natural as play and rest.
- People will exercise self-direction if they are committed to the objectives (they are NOT lazy).
- Commitment to objectives is a function of the rewards associated with their achievement.
- People learn to accept and seek responsibility.
- Creativity, ingenuity, and imagination are widely distributed among the population
- People are capable of using these abilities to solve an organizational problems.
- People have potential.

Richard Beckhard[23] and others stated several assumptions about the nature and functioning of organizations and their implications to OD practitioners. Table 1.3 presents them.

TABLE 1.3 Assumption of OD Practitioners

Assumptions	Implications to Practitioners
The basic building blocks of an organization are groups (teams)	Focus on groups in change management. Invest in teams; adopt a team leadership style and train people in team decision-making
Reduction of inappropriate competition between the parts of the organization is a change goal	Develop a more collaborative team work with harmony and synergy
Decision-making is located at source of information	Avoid dependence on a particular role or level of hierarchy for decision-making
Controls are interim measurements, not the basis of managerial strategy	Place emphasis on goals for progressive achievements
Developing open communication, mutual trust, and confidence between and across levels is goal of healthy organizations	Streamline communication channels and train emp-loyees as good communicators. Groups that learn to work using open and constructive feedback are more productive
People support what they help create	Involve people in designing and implementing change programmes
People are capable and like to accept challenges	Ask, listen, support, challenge, encourage risk-taking, permit failure, remove obstacles and barriers, give autonomy and responsibility, set high standards and reward success

The beliefs held by different OD consultant organizations are given in Box 1.2.

BOX 1.2 Beliefs of OD Consultants

Samuday Psycon believes

- OD is not just doing anything.
- Every organization has a mind that runs it.
- Human beings have ability to "change by choice as *Atma Vidya Param Vidya* (self awareness is the mother lode).
- Though all members of the client organization are doing their best, when collectively they carry out OD guided reviews, they discover enlightening areas for improvements.
- Such improvements enhance simultaneously individual as well as collective wellness. *Atma Kalyan* (individual good) and *Sarva Kalyan* (collective good).

21st century Organizational Development Consulting believes

- An organization is made up of people.
- An organization is more than the sum of its members.

- An organization has a culture.
- An organization and its members are mutually dependent.

Clarity Consulting holds three beliefs given under

- People want to do great things.
- People have latent abilities to do great things.
- Greatness happens when you create an environment to support it.

Mincu & Associates is guided by the belief that the ultimate answers reside within the client organization itself. Rather than providing the answers, the role of OD consultants is to offer expert process that brings out the internal awareness and expertise and allow the client to learn to provide their own answers.

Source: Based on Samuday Psycon - OD Consultants—About Us
www.samuday.com/about_us. 21st Century Organizational Development Consulting,
www.manage2001.com/21odc.htm
Clarity Consulting: What We Believe, www.clarityconsulting.com/what.../3-beliefs-that-guide-our-work.
ph... and Mincu & Associates: Coaching, Consulting, Training
www.bonniemincu.com/.

VALUES

McLean has identified values like respect to individuals, concern for self-awareness, authenticity, empowerment and collaboration and regard for democracy and social justice[24]. Table 1.4 shows values and related behaviors of OD practitioners.

TABLE 1.4 Values of OD Practitioner

S.No.	Values	Behaviors
1	Respect and inclusion	Shows respect for the views and opinions of people and involves people in activities and decision-making
2	Collaboration	Creates win-win relationships among people involved in work
3	Authenticity	Encourages behaviors of people in accordance with their espoused values.
4	Self-awareness	Promotes self-awareness and interpersonal skills within the organization
5	Empowerment	Focuses on increasing autonomy and sense of personal power among employees
6	Democracy and social justice	Fosters freedom of thought and expression and justice to one and all

The International Code of Ethics[25] provided a comprehensive list of values which are of fundamental importance to OD professionals. As one can observe, they are much similar to those elaborated earlier. The list is as follows:

1. Quality of life
2. Health, human potential, empowerment, growth and excellence

3. Freedom and responsibility
4. Justice
5. Dignity, integrity, worth and fundamental rights
6. All-win attitudes and cooperation
7. Authenticity and openness in relationship
8. Effectiveness, efficiency and alignment of the subsystems in the larger system
9. Holistic, systemic view and stakeholder orientation
10. Wide participation in system affairs, confrontation of issues leading to effective problem solving, and democratic decision-making.

SIGNIFICANCE OF OD

The contribution of OD to the organization is manifold.

1. *Change readiness:* To remain competitive in today's global marketplace, organizations must change. To implement critical organizational change in domestic and global companies, Human resources managers seek the help of OD consultants or use OD interventions. OD helps create change readiness and change coping skills by establishing continuous learning processes.

2. *Learning and innovation:* Reflection, dialogue and bridge-building are skills that open doors to innovation and learning. OD helps develop such skills and establishes a climate that encourages individual and organizational learning as well as knowledge management. Learning not only promotes employee retention and career development but also supports innovation and knowledge management.

3. *Business goals and strategies:* When used as a key strategic HR tool, OD can give a long-term advantage by building climate and culture that is congenial for high performance teams to achieve, productivity and profitability. OD can assist top management in implementing growth strategies like expansion, diversification and integration by providing cultural transformation and development of new skills and attitudes among employees. OD can help top management in integrating different cultures especially in case of mergers and acquisitions.

4. *Human resource advantage:* The strategic link between OD and HR, results in the development of a healthy and productive workforce in any organization. OD encourages self-development, vision and integrity among employees. It encourages broad ethical thinking and cooperative and creative team work.

5. *Strengthens HR profession:* HR managers, who hone the OD competencies, enhance the strength of HR profession, and thereby, give additional benefits to their organizations. In the dynamic and competitive environment of today, HRM has moved from operational to strategic level and OD has become an integrated, strategic HRM tool.

6. *Improves organizational communication:* Organizations are today described as information processors and every manager is primarily a communicating centre. Effective functioning of employees requires free flow of communication through multiple channels and use of multiple media vehicles. OD practitioners help conduct communication audit and redesign media mix and improve communication skills of employees.

EVOLUTION OF OD

From a historic perspective, the OD field began about 50 years ago. The science of OD has at least four important streams. They are:

- Laboratory training
- Survey research and feedback
- Action research
- Tavistock socio-technical and socio-clinical approaches.

The Laboratory Training Stem

The stream of OD evolved in the year 1946, with the successful experimentation and use of T-groups by behavioral scientists. Kurt Lewin is regarded as the 'Father of OD'. According to Weiss, the credit for coining the term Organizational Development (OD) goes to Douglas McGregor and Richard Beckhard. In the 1950's, they coined the term to describe an innovative bottom-up change effort[26]. However, French and Bell opine that it had emerged from the writings of Robert Blake, Jane Mouton, Herbert Shepard, Douglas McGregor and Richard Blanchard.

Lewin founded the Research Center for Group Dynamics (RCGD) in 1945. His contributions included group dynamics, change process, force-field theory, and action research. RCGD colleagues were among those who founded the National Training Laboratories (NTL), which has been fostering the development of OD.

Laboratory training is learning from a person's "here and now" experience as a member of an ongoing training group. Such groups usually meet without a specific agenda. Group interactions bring to surface problems of leadership, structure, status, communication, and self-serving behavior. Group participants can learn such skills as speaking, listening and functioning as effective group members. Laboratory training was conducted in stranger groups, or groups composed of individuals from different organizations, situations, and backgrounds. However, the stranger labs posed the problem of transferring experiences to the actual situation back home. The problem was due to differences in cultures, the relatively safe and protected environment of the T-group and the give-and-take of the organizational environment with its traditional values. The failure of off-site laboratory training led to the use of on-site family groups—groups located within an organization and from this emerged the concept of organization development[27].

During 1952–1953, Robert Tannenbaum conducted "team building" sessions. The credit for conducting such sessions with CEO and the top executive team goes to Chris Argyris. In 1957, he was one of the first to conduct such team building sessions. Various contributions by different behavioral scientists[28] that have led to the present day OD are depicted in Table 1.5.

TABLE 1.5   Contributions of Behavioral Scientists to OD

Scientists	Contributions
Bradford, Lippitt, and Benne	Role playing, learning groups
Moreno	Psychodrama
Benne and Mary Follett	Integrative solutions to conflict management
Blake and Mouton	Managerial grid and win-lose dynamics of conflict management
Chris Argyris	Laboratory training, interpersonal competence and organizational learning
Robert Tannenbaum	Vertically structured groups—dealt with personal topics (self analysis, communication, interpersonal relationships and departmental socio-metrics) and organizational topics (policies and procedures, duties and responsibilities and deadlines).
Hebert Shepard and Robert Blake	Training through T-groups, organizational exercises, and lectures. Lessons learnt from experience: (i) Top management involvement is important and (ii) On-job application is must.

The Survey Research and Feedback Stem

Survey research and feedback, as a tool of OD was developed by Rensis Likert, Floyd Mann and others at the Survey Research Center (SRC) of the University of Michigan over a period of years. SRC was founded in 1946. Rensis Likert developed a five point scale for measurement of attitudes. Floyd Mann played a key role in development and use of feedback system. He called the process of feeding back data from an attitude survey to the participating departments, as an interlocking chain of conferences. He observed that the feedback would bring significant improvements[29]. Based on the experiences in Detroit Edison study, Baumgartel offered supporting evidence to the utility of feedback. The results of the experimental study lend support to the idea that an intensive, group discussion procedure for utilizing the results of an employee questionnaire survey, can be an effective tool for introducing positive change in a business organization[30].

The Action Research Stem

The action research literature refers to the difficulties of applying the conventional methods of research to bring about improvements within human and social contexts, e.g., in the domains of education, organizational management, social helping, and various other professional practices.

Action research facilitates "learning and theorizing by doing". It has two-fold concerns: (i) to contribute both to the practical concerns of people in an immediate problematic situation, and (ii) to contribute to the theory of social sciences.. Action research is known by many other names like participatory research, collaborative inquiry, emancipatory research, action learning, and contextual action research, but all are variations on a theme.

Kurt Lewin, first coined the term "action research" in the mid 1940s. He described action research as follows.[31]

"A comparative research on the conditions and effects of various forms of social action and research leading to social action" that uses, "a spiral of steps, each of which is composed of a circle of planning, action, and fact-finding about the result of the action".

The most common usage of action research has been a problem-solving mechanism in the context of making focused efforts to improve practice. Scholars concede that there are four common characteristics of action research[32]:

- an action and change orientation of action research based study
- a problem focus
- an "organic" process involving systematic and sometimes iterative stages, and
- collaboration among participants.

THE TAVISTOCK SOCIO-TECHNICAL AND SOCIO-CLINICAL STEM

The fourth stem of the knowledge tree of OD is the contribution of the Tavistock Clinic in England. The Socio-Technical Systems (STS) concept may be traced to the groundbreaking action-science studies carried out by Fred Emery and Eric Trist in Great Britain, in 1949, in a South Yorkshire coal mine. Eric Trist and the Tavistock Institute studied the English coal mining industry, where mechanization had actually decreased worker productivity. Trist proposed that manufacturing (and many other) systems have both technical and human/social aspects that are tightly bound and interconnected. Moreover, it is the interconnections more than individual elements that determine system performance[33].

The socio-technical approach challenged the mechanistic, authority-at-top organizations and proposed a novel organismic model that enabled autonomous work groups to assume responsibility for the entire work cycle. From a socio-technical perspective, a system is described in terms of both socially and technically mediated relationships. The approach provides an organizational context for knowledge sharing, learning and innovation and encourages work groups to collaboratively develop original work patterns[34]. The contemporary programmes such as Quality of Work Life (QWL) and Total Quality Management (TQM) programmes are examples of the socio-technical approaches.

Another important contribution has come from Northfield experiments[35]. The first experiment (1942–43), conducted by Wilfred Bion and John Rickman emphasized the relationships within groups and the relevance of the social setting to the patient. The experiments led to the development of group therapy and rehabilitation techniques.

New Generation Developments

The movement of organizations to the new information era from industrial era has led to the evolution of second-generation OD techniques as shown in Table 1.6.

TABLE 1.6   New Generation Techniques

Generation	Focus	Scope	Interventions
First	Adaptive, incremental change	Group level	Action research, team building, process consultation, survey feedback, intergroup problem-solving, socio-technical systems, job design, and participative management.
Second	Organizational transformation-paradigm shift	Multi-dimensional, multi-level, qualitative, discontinuous, radical organizational change	Organizational culture, Learning organization, Team building and performance (high-performance teams, cross-functional teams and self-managed teams), Total Quality Management, Visioning, Large meeting and Getting the "Whole System" in the room.

OD PROFESSION IN INDIA

In India, OD profession has made a beginning in 1960s and slowly gained the acceptance of the industry. Today, it has acquired a status of significance, thanks to the economic reforms that ushered in an era of change characterized by domestic and global competition.

A humble beginning

A group of Indian professionals trained at the National Training Laboratories (NTL) at Bethel, Maine, USA, introduced OD applications in training programmes. Grid programmes were used in the Small Industries Extension Training (SIET) Institute, Hyderabad, State Bank of India and in the Indian Institute of Management (IIM) programmes in the mid 1960s. However, OD could not catch the attention of industry and it remained dormant for more than a decade.

A break

In the mid-1970s, for the first time OD was embraced by industry. Larsen and Toubro utilized OD as a formal and structured programme of the HRD department. It was expected that the change process would get institutionalized and more OD specialists would be developed.

It was expected that other corporate organizations would take cognizance of OD and its benefits, but it did not happen as the corporate sector in the country was in a very protected and regulated environment[36]. Hence OD remained mostly in academic institutions. A few specialists were found making use of training based interventions like T-Groups.

The new wave

The scenario has changed in the post liberalization period. Every progressive company has been forced to seek change. As a result, the following changes took place:

1. HRD movement: The concept of HRD was proposed as a comprehensive approach to the development and use of individuals, teams, and the total organization through several systematic ways. A large number of organizations have started HRD departments. The work on HRD made new strides with the establishment of the National HRD Network founded and guided by Professor T.V. Rao.

2. *OD focus of MNCs:* The Multinational Companies (MNCs) in India have promoted organization development as a critical competency for business leaders and managers. As a result, we find today, there is an increasing number of applied behavioral scientists and T-group trainers.

3. *Institutional networks:* Various professional bodies, such as (Indian Society for Applied Behavioral Sciences (ISABS), Indian Society for Individual and Social Development (ISISD), Indian Society for Training & Development (ISTD), and the HRD Network, are promoting growth of OD professionals.

4. *OD education:* Organizational Development course is offered as an elective course in Human Resource management group at many business schools throughout India. In addition to master's degree options, some institutes offer bachelor's degree programs, graduate certificates and doctoral programs in organizational development. Indian Institute of Organization Development (IIOD) is an OD consultant and educator in India. Box 1.3 shows details of OD courses at IIOD and Institute of OD.

BOX 1.3   OD Courses in India

IIOD offers a comprehensive OD Certification program in collaboration with Institute of Organizational Development, USA. The OD Certificate Program is designed for those individuals who are new to the OD field or currently practicing in the field of OD and for those in HR/L&D/Change Management roles. The OD Certificate Program is being offered as classroom and online programs to meet the needs of the participants.

It consists of eight foundational courses: Introduction to Organizational Development–Theory and Practice, Organizational Development Consulting—Core Competencies, Ethics & Values, and Process Skills, Organization Systems and Dynamics, Organizational Analysis and Design–Diagnostics and Assessments and Interventions, Group Development and Processes, OD Facilitation Skills, Organizational Behavior and Change and Change Management: Planning and Implementation.

It offers a Talent Management Certificate Program that can prepare you to meet the Talent Management challenges in organizations.

It offers an online OD Certificate Program (ODCP) for those interested in advancing in the field of Organization Development. The ODCP program offers participants an opportunity to learn the role of the OD Consultant. Participants attend 8 monthly 3 hours sessions online. Participants work in teams with others to complete assignments, goals, and activities. Participants receive 48 continuing education credits for completing the program. The programs are offered globally, with partners in the US, India, and Africa.

Centre for Organisation Development, is a recognized doctoral research centre by Osmania University and the Government of India.

Source: www.iiod.in , www.institute OD.com and www.codhyd.org/ - - .

OD ROLES AND COMPETENCIES

The Society for Human Resource Management (SHRM) identifies six roles[37] of OD practitioner.

1. *Credible activist:* Combines credibility and activism often referred to as "HR with an attitude."

2. *Culture and change steward:* Facilitates culture changes through the development of disciplines and implementation of strategy.

3. *Talent manager/organizational designer:* Practices effective techniques that combine talent management and organizational design.

4. *Strategy architect:* Participates and actively supports an overall strategy that maintains an organization's sustainability.

5. *Operational executor:* Understands and executes an organization's operational strategies to support its business goals and people.

6. *Business ally:* Contributes to the success of the organization by understanding the business of the business and planning change as the organization evolves.

Much research has been done on Organization Development competencies. The list of competencies provided by Rosset[38] and Worley and Feyerherm[39] are illustrative of the important ones. Table 1.7 shows them.

TABLE 1.7 OD Competencies

Researcher	Type	Competencies
Rossett, A. (1998)	Interpersonal competencies	Ability to remain neutral, have a tough skin, is courageous, naturally inquisitive, respectful, trustworthy and analytical with a commitment to application. Must be good communicators and effective leaders with strong interpersonal and team-building skills.
Worley and Feyerherm (2003)	Knowledge competencies	Organization design, organization research, system dynamics, history of organization development and change, and theories and models of change.
	Skill competencies	Managing the consulting process, analysis and diagnosis, designing and choosing appropriate interventions, facilitating and process consultation, developing client capability, and evaluating organizational change.

OD CAREERS

Organizational Development professionals have two options:

1. Becoming employees in large organizations interested in OD interventions, or consulting organizations.
2. Setting of a consultancy firm and act as external consultants to organizations.

Professional and Organizational Development (POD) careers generally require a bachelor's, master's or doctoral degree in Organizational Management and Development or a field with applicable coursework, such as labor relations, psychology or education. Box 1.4 presents some job offers and specifications.

BOX 1.4 Jobs in OD

Director of Organizaton Development & People for CAFOD

Job purpose: To ensure that CAFOD's approaches to organizational working and people management enable CAFOD to deliver its mission and strategic framework "Just One World". To lead Organizational Development and People division in taking this forward, especially in delivering effective HR approaches both in England and Wales and in our international offices, and in leading on programms of organization change and development, supporting a culture of achievement, accountability and learning.

Job scope: The post holder will line manage the Head of HR and the Head of Organization Development, leading a team of 18 staff and 3 volunteers.

Accountability: The post-holder is a member of the Corporate Leadership Team (CLT), reports to the Director and works closely with other Directors and CAFOD's Board, including the HR Committee.

Organizational Development Consultant for Abt Associates India Pvt. Ltd. New Delhi
Minimum 15 years experience in organizational development and or strategic planning for agriculture/agribusiness based organizations or enterprises. Has to work with a prominent Indian Industry membership organization to assist it with the design, establishment and strategic positioning of a Center of Excellence for Food and Agriculture.

OD Manager for Cadbury India, Mumbai
Reports to Vice President—Human Resources, Experience Minimum of 7 years.

The Organization Development Manager would play a lead role in delivering an effective performance management mechanism, talent management, development of (functional) career pathways.

Organization Development (OD) Consultant for a Reputed Company
Key Skills: Organization Development; Experience: 4–10 years experience; Qualification: B.E. with P.G. ... reengineering, Change management initiatives or who has thorough knowledge in HR and OD.

OD consultants recruit for manning their ongoing HR & OD assignments. A job offer from "People Power" is given here.

HR Officer for People Power a OD Consultant at Kochi
Specification: Any Graduate; Any Specialization PG–MBA/PGDM–HR/Industrial Relations. We are looking for an MBA (HR) with 0–3 years experience in HR/OD, PMS, etc., ability to cope with pressure and challenges, good interpersonal and relationship management skills, willingness to travel, ability to learn quickly.

(Contd.)

BOX 1.4 Jobs in OD (*Contd.*)

Job description: The current requirement is for an experienced HR Professional to work on hard core HR/OD assignments at our client's sites at Kolkata/ Bokaro and includes traveling also. The job involves providing HR solutions as per requirements of specific clients.

Center for Organization Development, Hyderabad, takes Research Associates (Lecturer), Assistant Professor (Reader) and Associate Professors. The suitable person/s will have Ph.D. in Business Management, Public Administration, Psychology or Sociology, HR with specialization in strategy, structure, and behavior in organizations. The center offers an attractive remuneration package and a congenial learning environment. Designation and remuneration will be decided on the basis of a candidate's qualification, experience and competence to contribute to research and training activities.

Source: Organizational Development Professional: Job Description and Info ...portal.com/.../Organizational_Development_Professional_Job_Description _and_Info_About_a_Career_in_Organizational_...

SUMMARY

In the present environment of change, OD has a crucial role to play. It has grown to be a distinct discipline and profession and OD consultants are hired to improve and sustain organizational effectiveness. Based on systems approach, OD effort is a planned, long range, strategic, initiative supported by top management. It is a behavior-oriented, process-driven, collaborative, goal-directed with political implications. It is value-laden, and universal. The characteristics of OD discipline are: interdisciplinary-mix, applied science and evolutionary. It is regarded as a science and art guided by professional association and code of conduct. It has broad scope with issues ranging from group effectiveness to organizational renewal.

The goals of OD are focused on organization (effectiveness, health, self-renewal), team performance (effectiveness, efficiency, productivity) and team well-being (empowerment, participation, quality of life). OD practitioners assume that people are capable of taking initiatives and responsibility and prefer involving them in change process. They observe values like respect to individuals, concern for self-awareness, authenticity, empowerment and collaboration and regard for democracy and social justice.

The benefits of OD are many. It makes organization ready for change, by creating learning and innovation abilities, contributing to business goals and strategies and strengthening HR systems. OD has evolved in four phases: Laboratory training, Survey research and feedback, Action research and Tavistock socio-technical and socio-clinical approaches.

Various professional bodies, such as (Indian Society for Applied Behavioral Science (ISABS), Indian Society for Individual and Social Development (ISISD), Indian Society for Training & Development (ISTD), and the HRD Network, are promoting growth of OD professionals in India. OD field offers two type of career opportunities–jobs as OD experts and independent OD practitioners.

EXERCISES

I. Review Questions

1. Explain the meaning of OD.
2. What are the characteristics of OD work?
3. Identify the features of OD profession.
4. List the attributes of OD discipline.
5. What are the key values of an OD consultant?
6. List the assumptions of OD practitioners.
7. Explain in brief the benefits of OD to organizations.
8. What are the milestones in the evolution of OD?
9. Sketch the growth of OD profession in India.
10. Name the competencies required of an OD practitioners.
11. What kind of jobs an OD specialist get?

II. Discussion Questions

1. Explain the concept, nature scope and significance of OD.
2. Is OD a profession? Explain the growth of OD consultancy as a profession in India.

📖 MINI-PROJECT

Visit any two local business or service organizations and find from them whether they have utilized services of OD consultants. If yes, find out their experiences. If no, inquire reasons for not using the services. Make a paper for presentation in the classroom.

🖰 WEB ASSIGNMENT

Develop a paper on OD Consulting Skills Development programs. Gather information about Indian Institute of OD, NTL, and Strategic Development.

(www.iiod.in/programs.html, www.ntl.org/inner.asp?id=207&category=3 – and

www.strategicdevelopment.com/simulations.php?simulations..).

CASE STUDY

My Experiences with OD Education

As a mother of a three month old son, expatriate wife and having worked for six years in both India as well as Sweden with Leadership Training, Competency Development and Change Management, I wondered what I would like to do when I go back to work from my year-and-a-half long generous Swedish maternity leave.

I Chose OD

Organizational Development seemed to be the logical next step. I scanned the horizon and found that OD consultants in India, Sweden, Jamaica and US were atleast 10 to 15 years senior to me. I wondered what could give me the same seriousness that people attach with age. I figured that a certificate from a reputed international body in the field of Organizational Development could help.

I Chose NTL

I zeroed in on NTL Institute of Applied Behavioral Sciences, USA. Some of the deciding factors for me were my familiarity with the institute through ISABS, India, where I am a professional member. I knew NTL members and appreciated their level of competence, professionalism and commitment to the field of OD. The values that I practiced in my life matched their espoused values. I am listing them here:

Social justice manifested through inclusion, equity, access and opportunity for all people and the elimination of oppression; experiential learning; ethical use of power; creation and dissemination of new knowledge and practice; diversity, continuous learning, colleagueship and service and organizational excellence and quality.

In addition, I believed that NTL's approach to learning, i.e. increased awareness to self through facilitated group dialogue is the critical building block to any change and development at personal and organizational level. I registered for the NTL Institute's OD track which included a series of six one week programs at the end of which I would be given an OD practitioner certificate.

Focus on Tools

My focus as I went to attend these programs was to learn the technique of how to do it. I wanted tools in my kit. I mechanically went about collecting them. I tediously kept the course material. I made tabs so that when the opportunity came I would be able to pull out the appropriate model, the relevant exercise and use it.

Waiting and Frustration

Meanwhile I started a proprietorship firm in Sweden and started looking for assignments. I got assignments; however, they were training assignments. I was truly disappointed from an OD perspective even as I enjoyed doing the training work. My Swedish stay lasted for an year, and I got a chance to move to India a year-and-a-half back. I continued to do training work for an international organization and started meeting practicing consultants. Training work was easy to find and consulting work difficult. I felt my frustration, rising for not being able to get anywhere despite an expensive education, international certificates, and an increasingly heavy and sophisticated toolbox.

Realization and New Focus

A self-focused program at this stage helped me get in touch with my deep seated sense of incompetence. I had done four out of the six courses and knew that some paradigm has to shift before I took the next two courses. I had a sense that it was my mechanistic focus on tools and my plummeting confidence that hampered my progress. I had two choices—One, accelerate and get the OD certification done, and Two, stop and get to the depth of what was really happening and get an answer from there. I decided to pause in my OD certification program.

The Mind Cocooning

Once I stopped, there was a real vacuum. I started to focus on maintaining my psychological, physical, spiritual health and continued to be keenly aware of my sense of being stuck as well as my desire to be unstuck. I started a private limited company. I and my business partner started doing work with executive coaching, intercultural management, and personal and executive leadership development. All the work falls in the area of coaching and training.

The pause was two years long during which it seemed that there was no real progress on my OD consultant front. Suddenly, one day I decided to book my tickets, and finish my OD practitioner certification. It seemed like the right time to do the two courses that I had left.

Knowledge after the Pause

The full extent of the value of the pause in my OD education did not become apparent till I went to the last two courses. I did things and said things which went beyond the tools and techniques that I had focused on so much. I was able to integrate my life experience into the work I was doing. The only way I can describe that experience is to say, "In those moments I was OD." I now call it the mind cocooning process at the end of which the butterfly of knowledge emerges. I finally understood Mahatma Gandhi's words, "Be the change you want the world to be."

I believe that only this kind of integration leads to true and clear knowledge. I will list the different kind of knowledge I believe is critical for an OD practitioner:

Knowledge of Self, Knowledge of own past experiences with organizations; Knowledge of own competence level, Knowledge of philosophy behind different OD practices; Knowledge of current trends in OD; Knowledge of different OD tools and techniques; Knowledge of influence of culture on OD; Knowledge of the market, and Knowledge of OD practitioner networks.

The Certificate

I got the certificate and it is an artifact which I do plan to frame it expensively to adorn the walls of my India-based office. It will be difficult to carry them around. My new integrated 'I', however, is with me all the time.

Questions for Discussion

1. Examine the logic in the 'choice making' processes of the narrator. Are they in conformity with the rational choice making model?

2. From the case, identify the values and knowledge framework of OD consultants.

3. What barriers do you find in the way of the narrator—a training expert becoming an OD consultant? Can we generalize them?

4. What kind of mindset is needed for one to be a successful OD consultant?

Source: Adapted with permission from: My experiences with OD education Sunita Raut- Nyqvist Introduction ... www.odsummitindia.org/content/html/.../Sunita%20Raut.pdf (with permission) You can contact Sunita at sunita@valueaddedthinking.org or sunita_rautnyqvist@hotmail.com

REFERENCES

1. Adapted with permission from: http://www.potentia.in/casestudies9.html, http://www.clarityconsultants.com/case-studies.asp and Organization Development,www.bonniemincu.com/organization and Organization Development 101 | Accelera **Consulting Group**, www.acceleraconsultinggroup.com/.../organization-development-101...

2. IBM Business Consulting Services (2006), Retrieved April 10, 2007, from www-03.ibm.com/press/us/en/pressrelease/19289.wss.

3. Dunn, J. (2006), Strategic human resources and strategic organization development: An alliance for the future? *Organization Development Journal*, Vol. **24**(4), pp. 69–77.

4. SHRM Glossary of Human Resources Terms, www.shrm.org.

5. Beckhard, R. (1969), *Organization Development: Strategies and Models*. Reading, MA: Addison-Wesley, p. 9.

6. Cummings, Thomas G. and Orley, Christopher, G. (1993), *Organisation Development and Change*, West Publishing: St. Paul, MN.

7. Bennis, Warren G. (1969), *Organisation Development: Its Nature, Origins, and Prospects*, Addison-Wesley Publishing: Reading M.A.

8. Manhattan, M.M. and Associates (2005), Silver Spring, Maryland, quoted in 'What is Organization Development?' available at managementhelp.org/org_chng/od-field/OD_defn.htm.

9. French, Wendell L., Bell Jr. Cecil H. and Veena (2008), *Organisation Development*, New Delhi: Pearson Education.

10. McLean, G.N. (2006), *Organizational Development: Principles, Processes, Performance*. San Francisco: Berrett-Koehler Inc.

11. Richard Arvid Johnson (1976), *Management, Systems, and Society: An Introduction*. California: Goodyear Publishing.

12. Margulies, M. and Raia, A.P. (1984), *The Politics of Organization Development*, In Richard L. Hill (Ed.), *The Best of Organization Development.* (pp. 90–93). American Society for Training and Development: Alexandria, VA.

13. Warner Burke W. (1994), *A Process of Learning and Changing*, Reading MA: Addison-Wesley.

14. Hersey, P. and Blanchard, K.H. (1993), *Management of Organizational Behavior* (6th ed.), Englewood Cliffs, NJ: Prentice-Hall, Inc.

15. India OD Network—IIOD, www.iiod.in/od_network.html

16. The International OD Code of Ethics—The Organization Development ... www. odinstitute.org/ethics.htm

17. Yaeger, T., and Sorensen, P. (2006, Winter), Strategic Organization Development: Past to present, *Organization Development Journal*, Vol. **24**(4), pp. 10–17.

18. Jelinek, M. and Litterer, J.A. (1988), Why OD must become strategic. In W.A. Pasmore & R.W. Woodman (Eds.), *Research in Organizational Change and Development*, Greenwich.

19. Warner Burke, W. (1994), *A Process of Learning and Changing*, Reading, MA: Addison-Wesley.

20. Hurley, Robert F., Church, Allan H., Warner Burke, W. and Van Eynde, Donald F. (1992), Tension, Change and Values in OD, *OD Practitioner*, pp. 1–5.

21. Marge Yanker, Organization Development Overview owww.trainersdirect.com/.../OrgDevlpmt.htm—United States

22. McGregor, Douglas (1960), *The Human Side of Enterprise*, New York: McGraw-Hill.

23. Beckhard, R. (1969), *Organization Development: Strategies and Models*, Reading, MA: Addison-Wesley, p. 9.

24. McLean, G.N. (2006), *Organizational Development: Principles, Processes, Performance*, San Francisco: Berrett-Koehler Publishers Inc.

25. The International OD Code of Ethics—The Organization Development ... www.odinstitute.org/ethics.htm

26. Weisbord, Marvin (1987), *Productive Workplace: Organizing and Managing for Dignity, Meaning and Community*, San Francisco: Jossey-Bass Publishers.

27. Arvid Johnson, Richard (1976), *Management, Systems, and Society: An Introduction*, California Pacific Palisades, Goodyear Pub. Co.

28. Benne, Kenenth D., Bradford, Leland P., Gibb, Jack R. and Lippit, Ronald O. (Eds.) (1975), *The Laboratory Method for Changing and Learning: Theory and Application*, Palo Alto: CA: Science and Behavior Books.

29. Mann, Floyd C. (1962), Studying and Creating Change in Bennis, Benne and Chin (Eds.), *Planning of Change*, New York: Holt, Rinehart, and Winston, pp. 605–613.

30. Baumgartel, Howard (1959), Using Employee Questionnaire Results for Improving Organizations: The Survey (Feedback) Experiment, *Kansas Business Review*, 12, pp. 2–6.

31. Lewin, K. (1946), Action Research and Minority Problems, *Journal of Social, Issues*, Vol. **2**(4), pp. 34–46.

32. Peters and Robinson (1984), quoted in 'Interface between Action and Research', Silver Jubilee Conference of the IAWS, Lucknow 7–10 February 2008, available at www.soppecom.org/pdf/IAWS_First_report-ST4.pdf.

33. Quoted in Socio Technical Systems (STS) {Strategos} www.strategosinc.com/socio-technical.htm.

34. Trist, E.L. (1981), The Evolution of Socio-technical Systems: A Conceptual Framework and An Action Research Program, Ontario Quality of Working Life Center, Occasional Paper No. 2.

35. Tom Harrison, Bion, Rickman, Foulkes and the Northfield Experiments, available at www.jkp.com/catalogue/book/9781853028373.

36. Studies of Indian Organizational Developement At Present– Seeds India, 19 Apr. 2011 www.seeds-india.com/.../studies-of-indian-organizational-developement-at-present.html

37. SHRM (2008), HR, OD Competencies Complement Each Other, www.shrm.org/.../. CompetenciesComplementEachOther.aspx

38. Rossett, A. (1998), *First Things Fast: A Handbook for Performance Analysis*, San Francisco: John Wiley & Sons Inc.

39. Worley, C.G. and Feyerherm, A.E. (2003), Reflections on the Future of Organization Development, *Journal of Applied Behavioral Science*, **39**, 97–115.

OD Practitioners and Challenges

Vignette: Clarity Hired for Clarity

Walter Dorwin Teague Associates was set up, in 1926. It is well-known for its design expertise in areas, such as aviation, consumer electronics, and consumer lifestyles. Teague has worked with its clients on products, such as the Boeing 787 interior, the Hewlett-Packard TouchSmart PC, and the Xbox 360 Wireless Racing Wheel. The company believes in innovation and excellence as a way of growth and development.

Change needs: Intensifying competition, increasing sophistication in technology, changes in customer preferences and rising growth opportunities, have made Teague to seek organizational renewal. Teague decided to conduct a detailed organizational assessment to understand better where the company needed to focus most to improve operations.

Consultant chosen: The company decided to hire an external consultant to conduct this assessment with an unbiased perspective when obtaining information. The company chose Clarity, an experienced Organization Development consultant with requisite skills in organizational analysis, process reengineering and realignment efforts.

Problem identification: The areas for the assessment included leadership, decision-making, business processes, organizational communication, and inter-department coordination, for improvement. Assessment of best practices for organizational structure and work dynamics is also included in the areas of assessment.

Support: Clarity is given complete freedom for undertaking this exercise. To gather preliminary information, the consultant held interviews and discussions with key executives in the company, including the Chief Executive Officer. The executives promised support and assured that they were open to both positive and negative feedbacks. Enthused by this support, the consultant developed an unbiased assessment and devised an assessment plan.

Discovery process: Following the assessment plan, the consultant organized interviews and focus groups to obtain accurate information from employee groups. An important finding was the existence of two unique cultures—one that emphasized cutting-edge technology and new approaches and one that emphasized a more traditional approach.

Communication processes: Senior management favoured open communication. As such, feedback was given to each participant. Information about overall results was shared with all employees of the organization. The information sharing process and open approach improved the participation and overall quality of the information.

Recommendations: After completing the inquiry, Clarity made specific recommendations to senior management. On the request of Senior management, Clarity helped Teague implement the recommendations and track their results[1].

The above case, vividly describes what goes on in consulting. In this chapter, we will examine various aspects in consultant-client relationship and related challenges.

INTRODUCTION

OD practitioners improve the effectiveness of an organization by applying knowledge from the behavior sciences and other related disciplines. In India, there are good number of consultants offering a variety of services. Organizations requiring improvements have wide choices in selecting consultants as well as interventions. However, care is necessary in choosing consultants and techniques, and also in effecting smooth implementation of the interventions.

WHO CAN CONSULT?

Victor Pryles[2] in his book, "Anyone can Consult" points out that "consultants come in all sizes and with all manner of backgrounds". A consultant is an expert at recognizing problems and shaping solutions to those problems. OD consultants, may be described as change agents and Organizational transformers, who customize OD models and methods to organizations seeking to change and achieve high levels of economic and human performance. OD consultants are those who have rich knowledge of behavioral sciences and preferably OD certification. Until about a decade ago, the title consultant was more or less limited to retired diplomats and top corporate officers, recruited more because of their contacts, rather than their practical knowledge. In other words, until recently, the consultant's position was more honorary than actual.

With the growing demand for consulting, independent consulting has become one of the fastest growing businesses in the country. A welcome development is women have broken the glass ceiling and have entered the field of OD consulting.

TYPES OF CONSULTANTS

Consultants in human resources area, who claim practicing OD, can be classified as given under:

Types Based on Service

OD consultants are different from HR management consultants in that the client is the total organization, not just the management team. They help enterprises integrate and align their human, managerial and organizational systems for high performance in an environment of change. Though some consultants call themselves OD practitioners, they may be catering to HR services depending upon the clients and their requirements.

Based on the nature of services offered HR consultants can be as follows:

1. *Organizational development:* The practitioner offers a wide range of services that help change organizational behavior at group and organizational level. The interventions will be for a period ranging from one to five years.

2. *Survey and feedback:* The practitioner is a specialist in getting information from customers and employees using surveys.

3. *Human resource policies:* The practitioner looks at rewards, benefits, sexual harassment, discrimination, and other issues; may overlap with Organizational Development.

4. *HRD consultants:* The field of compensation involves extensive knowledge of legal issues and results of comparative compensation surveys. Appraisal is used largely for development, and it can be a 360° feedback to be more effective.

5. *Training and development:* The practitioners focus on communication and soft skills development, personality development, or skills development in functional areas.

Categories of consultants

Nees and Grenier proposed five categories of consultants[3] as follows:

1. *The mental adventurer:* Consultant analyzes problems at macro level, such as long-term scenarios for Human Resource Development, and provides advice on future trends in developing human system of enterprise.

2. *Strategic navigator:* Consultant recommends courses of action-based on his rich quantitative understanding of the market and competitive dynamics.

3. *Management physician:* Makes recommendations from a deep understanding of the internal dynamics of the client organization.

4. *System architect:* Helps clients working in close cooperation in redesign processes, routines, and systems.

5. *Friendly co-pilot:* Counsels senior managers as a facilitator rather than as an expert, and has no ambition to provide new knowledge to the client.

Models of Consultants

Schein has identified three models of consultation[4], which are similar to the last three models of Nees and Grenier.

1. *Purchase of expertise:* Clients are expected to provide an independent perspective on problems of organization. The relationship is limited to a buyer-seller relationship without any attachments.

2. *Doctor-patient:* The consultant is expected to diagnose the organizational problems and prescribe solutions. Emphasis is on building a strong relationships and trust with the consultant.

3. *Process consultation:* The consultant is expected to be a facilitator assisting in transformation process. Emphasis is on building a strong relationships and trust with the consultant.

Types Based on Occupation

OD consultants can be either a full-time employee with a given organization, or a proprietor or an employee of a consulting firm. The employee is referred to an internal consultant and the other as an external consultant.

SERVICES OFFERED BY CONSULTANTS

Consultants offer a wide range of services as shown in Table 2.1.

TABLE 2.1 Services of OD Consultants

Consultants	Services
Samuday Psycon, New Delhi	Organization imagery assessment, visioning, organization design, team formation, team strengthening, collective leadership at the top, developing internal leaders and leadership processes, leading and managing change, leadership coaching, executive coaching, and Intra team resolution
OD alternatives, New Delhi	Leadership, team effectiveness, executive coaching, organizational DNA workshops, attitudinal and mindset change, and human side of change
Potenita, Hyderabad	Top team effectiveness-Executive coaching, team building and organization climate
OD consultants, Hyderabad	ISO certification, business excellence, training capsules, sustainability reporting, and management services

As an Organizational Development consultant, Sunita describes her life work as "To light the spark in people so that they explode and dazzle the SKY". Box 2.1 presents the range of services Sunita offers.

BOX 2.1 Consultancy Services of Sunita

She is very clear that every moment she lives is a movement towards the life objective. So, her work does not start when the client signs a contract and finish when she delivers the project. Even a two minute interaction with someone in the airline queue leads to her lighting that spark. She also understands that everyone is not a firework and some people will not respond to the spark she provides. She is fine with that.

Business Review: Operating for sustainability is at the core of organizations. The way people work in the organization, interpret their role, and define what they do at the workplace is intricately connected to this. Unraveling this connection is a very critical part of Sunita's work. She discovered that for an organization that manufactures railway signals and spends 60% of turnover in sourcing raw material, strict performance criteria in the procurement function and long-term strategic thinking is critical. Mostly clients do not pay for this work, sometimes this may happen even before the first meeting with the client.

Assessing People Business Gaps: There are always gaps between what the business wants and what the people working for them deliver. The gap presents a variety of needs for creating interventions to address specific capability gaps that the organization has, or moving people so that both the people and business benefit. For a Metro Operating Service organization that had to win upcoming Metro operating tenders she found a Business Development Director, who can work in solitude as well as independently. Without this person the operation would collapse. This work may also happen before the client pays for the assignment, and in fact this work will fill the details of the solution that the client will eventually buy.

Strategic Recruitment: Finding the right leader for the business can be the single most important factor in changing the direction of the entire organization as well as the operative culture of the organization. Sunita worked with a Cosmetic company to find a Marketing Director who will be the living incarnation of their brand values, the face of this company to the outside world.

Capability Assessment: People perform roles in organizations and each role has a certain capability requirement which is partly static in nature and comes from a functional point of view, and partly dynamic in nature and this comes from the business point of view. Sunita was contacted by a product life-cycle software organization. For the organization that planned 30% year on year growth in the next three years, it was critical to have sales people who are capable of closing business deals of 10 times the value that they were used to today.

Team and Group Facilitation: For an OD consultant, this is perhaps the area where the maximum volume of work comes from. For any number of reasons especially when faced with a new situation the team performance drops. Sunita has supported a project team of an electrical equipment organization when they moved to a matrix structure.

(Contd.)

BOX 2.1 Consultancy Services of Sunita (*Contd.*)

Business and Executive Coaching: This is the second area that is growing very fast in India. An individual may require a personal dialogue to clarify their objectives and find ways of moving towards them. Sunita has worked with incoming expatriate managers as an intercultural coach. She used her life experiences of living and working in several countries along with her skills of working with people to develop her own model of coaching in this area.

Credits: sunita@valueaddedthinking.org or sunita_rautnyqvist@hotmail.com

---

DEFINING CLIENT SYSTEM

It is important to know the client system and who the client is. Schein points out that any helping or change process always has a target or a client[5]. However, identifying the client is not always easy. It can be ambiguous and problematic. He has distinguished six basic types of clients as follows:

1. *Contact clients* are the individuals who first contact the consultant with a request, question, or issue.

2. *Intermediate clients* are those individuals who facilitate interviews, meetings, and other activities during the problem definition phase.

3. *Primary clients* are the individual(s) who have authority to own the problem and pay the consulting bills.

4. *Unwitting clients* are the outside members of the client system who will be affected by interventions without any knowledge of the ongoing interventions.

5. *Indirect clients* are the outside members of the client system, who are aware of the impact of interventions.

6. *Ultimate clients* are the community or the total organization or any other group that the consultant cares and seeks to promote its welfare in all interventions.

The consultant, or the consultant team, has to be clear as to who the client actually is because different types of clients may well have different needs, expectations and influences.

CLIENT–CONSULTANT RELATIONSHIPS

Turner[6] argued that until late 1970s, consultants tended to work more as suppliers to the client. In 1980, a radical change took place and relationships in consulting have become partnerships with mutual respect. He provided a continuum of relationships as shown in third column of Table 2.2.

TABLE 2.2   Client-consultant Relationships

S.No.	Type of consultant	Relationship continuum	Nature of relationship
1	Purchase of expertise	Providing information to a client	Seller–buyer, transactional
2	Purchase of expertise	Solving a client's problem	Seller-buyer, relationship marketer
3	Physician	Making a diagnosis, which may necessitate redefinition of the problem	Expert-novice, strong relationship, transformational
4	Physician	Making recommendations based on the diagnosis	Expert-novice, strong relationship, transformational
5	System architect	Assisting with implementation of recommended actions	Mentor-mentee relationship strong relationship, transformational
6	Process consultant	Building a consensus and commitment around a corrective action	Strong relationship, transformational
7	Process consultant	Facilitating client learning	Strong relationship, transformational
8	Process consultant	Permanently improving organizational effectiveness	Strong relationship, transformational

CONSULTING PROCESS

An OD consultant works with organizations in a systematic way following a process. Though the process is very much same, analysts have different approaches in explaining it. Some divide it into four steps, and some others into six steps.

4-Step Model

Organization Development Consultants[7], USA devised a four step model that represents the four key decision areas–intake, project agreement, implementation and evaluation as shown in Figure 2.1.

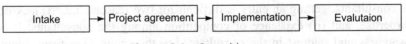

Figure 2.1   Consulting process.

Step **1:** *Intake:*   In this step, a consultant meets with or finds a client and engages in discussion on problem-situation. Jointly with the client he determines, the issues that require interventions.

Step **2:** *Project agreement:*   This is a critical step in which a project agreement is finalized with the client. The areas of agreement include: goals, nature and type of interventions, time schedules, resources, and approach to be adopted in implanting interventions.

Step 3: Implementation: The third step is the actual implementation of the project. It involves measures like meetings, coaching, training, on-going consultation, etc.

Step 4: Evaluation: This is a complementary step to implementation. In this evaluation of services in terms of expected impact will be done. Evaluation is for both short- and long-term benefits.

6-Step Model

The general model of planned change outlined by Cummings and Worley[8] consists of six phases as outlined in Table 2.3.

TABLE 2.3 Six Phases Model of Consulting

S.No.	Phases	Activities
1	Entering	Establishing rapport, identification of problem/opportunity, and creating interest in consulting
2	Contracting	Discussing term and conditions and entering into an agreement
3	Diagnosing	Making in-depth analysis and knowing the dimensions of the problem
4	Intervening	Designing interventions, getting involvement of people and monitoring implementation
5	Evaluating	Mid-process and post-implementation feedback and verification of results
6	Sustaining change	Helping management team in taking steps to consolidate and benefit from changes in the long run

EXTERNAL CONSULTANT AND CLIENT RELATIONSHIPS

How do external consultants make an entry and execute OD interventions? What kind of issues they face in the process of consulting? Adopting the 6-phase model suggested by Cummings and Worley, we will now examine the process of external consulting[9].

Entering

For external consultants, getting an entry is difficult for two reasons, i.e., (i) lack of awareness about the expertise, and (ii) existence of competition among the consultants. It is important to create awareness and interest in the consultant. For this, consulting firms adopt marketing strategies. The common ways used by externals to obtain clients are:

- Establishing credibility—attending professional meetings and public speaking
- Creating interest—making cold calls

To be effective, consultant should overcome two barriers in respect of two important aspects in relationship: (i) language and (ii) problem understanding. Externals should become familiar with the jargon, to communicate with the client. In presentation of the problem, client speaks more about symptoms and fails to see the problem. Consultant needs patience to listen and analytical skills to separate symptoms from problems.

Contracting

The purpose of contracting is to clarify goals, roles, ground rules and the use of resources. Agreement serves two purposes—to guide both the parties in cooperation and conflict avoidance and resolution. The contract mainly spells the following:

- *Expectations*, i.e., goals and expectations of client
- *Actions*, i.e., duration of consulting and nature of interventions
- *Resources*, i.e., details of resources to be committed for the intervention
- *Confidentiality*, i.e., guarantees for the confidential treatment of data as generated by participants.
- *Withdrawal clause*, i.e., circumstances under which either party can withdraw, usually indicating that the relationship can be terminated at will.

External consultant relies on letters, proposals and legal contracts.

Diagnosing

This phase involves the collection and analysis of data, preparation of feedback and action planning. External consultant uses data collection tools like questionnaires, observation, and face-to-face interviews for data gathering. However, it is an iterative process and will be followed by the client.

Data collection requires support from employee. Rapport building is easy for well established consultants; their prestige and status as a paid consultant, help develop rapport and trust quickly. Assurances of confidentiality further smoothens the process. Finally for authentication and ownership, a meeting is to be structured to ensure that the appropriate members, with the appropriate power and motivation, authorize and advise the consultant to use data.

Intervening

In this phase, based on the issues generated as a result of the feedback session and joint diagnosis, activities are designed. For success of this phase, commitment of people and availability of required resources are prerequisites. As laid down in contract, management has to meet all the conditions. Consultants should involve people in intervention process. Sharing valid information encourages free and informed choice on participation. As people take ownership of planned activities, commitment grows.

Evaluating

Evaluations of interventions are conducted mid-stream to allow for course corrections, and at the end to monitor the extent of the change project's realization.

Evaluation measures include:

- *Qualitative measures*—Satisfaction of employees and client organization
- *Quantitative measures*—First pass yield, cost, delivery, or safety or referrals

Generally, the evaluation phase receives the least amount of attention. It is not unusual for an external consultant to shy away from it altogether.

INTERNAL CONSULTANT AND CLIENT RELATIONSHIPS

We will now examine how the internal consultant approaches the OD consultation[10].

Entering

As an insider in the organization, the internal consultant spends less time on entry. The internal consultant will have problems of awareness only when he is new to the job. Those, who have put up service in the organization, will be aware of the empathetic and apathetic employees as well as the sources of power. Already familiar with the culture of the organization, they can easily align their approach to the style of the organization. There is negative side too.

- Internal consultant may not be interested in the project assigned by the senior manager for two reasons. He has no liking to such interventions or he considers the suggestion of the senior manager not appropriate.
- Some of the managers may be less helpful due to internal politics.

The senior managers and consultant, should discuss and must make the best of a bad situation, delivering the required results on time in a conscientious and courteous manner.

Contracting

This is equally important for internal consultants. Due to familiarity, much work is contracted verbally. However, having everything on paper is desirable. Regardless of familiarity, it is important for the consultant to have a personal contract with the client organization. The contract should cover the following four areas.

1. *Confidentiality:* The consultant and senior manager must decide on the degree to which the entire change process will be open.

2. *Delivery of bad news:* In this area, the internal consultant is particularly vulnerable. When negative messages regarding style, power and control is delivered he can be subject to client retaliation. In extreme situations, the client may abandon the change project altogether.

3. *Consultant's role:* The internal consultant is expected to be a change agent. He may also be asked to drive the project on behalf of the senior manager.

4. *Client's personal involvement:* Busy managers will offload anything they can. However, success requires involvement of senior manager and other key managers. The exact nature of the manager's involvement must be defined.

Diagnosing

Though the process and tools may not differ between internal and external consultants, the nature of work differs. The factors responsible for the differences are:

1. *Status of the consultant:* The position, the reporting relationships, membership in the power network, and relationship with superior affect the role of an internal consultant.

2. *Trust in the consultant:* Internal consultant is known to employees. Based on their experiences and observations if employees consider him reliable and capable, they help him in diagnosing the situation.

3. *Power of the consultant:* Internal consultant has legitimate power, by position and authority, which external consultant cannot have.

Open process simplifies the change effort. However, few organizations can embrace open change processes. Managers may find it embarrassing to receive negative feedback about their styles and controls from their colleague, here the internal consultant.

Intervening

Organizational issues and interventions do not differ between the internal and external consultants. One key difference is that of free and informed choice. In change projects, the mobilization of people to support OD interventions will be done as follows:

1. *Penetration:* Some change projects begin with testing the waters of opportunity, hoping to gain support and commitment slowly and gradually from all members. Some may be successful in generating enthusiasm for change and some others may not.

2. *Imposition:* Senior manager or management team insists on the change project regardless of members' interest. In place of voluntary participation and free choice, there will be assignment of work or roles, and forced choice.

In either case, consultant gains support through collaboration, cooptation and obligation. They conduct meetings to share information. But they are influenced adversely by the interference of managers. Meetings with stakeholders tend to be of two types:

1. *Work sessions:* Everyone knows that they are coming to brainstorm, discuss, analyze, anticipate and solve problems.
2. *Ceremonial:* Players meet to commit to each other their willingness to support a change effort.

Senior internal consultants do not take the face value of the assurances and commitment pronounced by the players. They try to know people and their politics. They will do all preparatory work offline. They meet all the key players individually and will come to know their needs and concerns. They build rapport with them and design change project in a way that addresses their needs.

To go public with the change project before these steps are accomplished tends to create political issues. Meetings will be ceremonial, with high sounding lip talks. After initial euphoria, what happens is the slow derailment of the project.

Evaluating

There is no significant difference between the internal and external consultants regarding evaluation of interim activities and project termination. Both are interested in success, of course for different reasons. For internal consultants, success means possible pay rise and promotion opportunities. For external consultants, client satisfaction, award of new projects, word-of-mouth referrals, are the possible rewards. Internal consultants, being an employee will be with the organization even after the completion of the change project. This leaves him in a stressful condition with the following end results:

- Compliments: "Wow! He did it" kind of praise for successful completion of the project
- Apprehension: "I think it is going to be messy" kind of comments
- Pleasure: The pleasure of watching the institutionalization of projects, and playing a role in monitoring the activities which sustain and ensure a change project's success.

INTERNAL VS EXTERNAL CONSULTANTS

Having understood the consulting process of both the internal and external consultants now we can identify the differences in their work. Table 2.4 portrays them. Internal consultant has a world distinct from the external one. His internal position is an advantage in terms of understanding problem, working out relationships with people and institutionalizing change. On the other hand, external consultant can be more professional and less political, in designing and implementing change interventions.

TABLE 2.4   Differences between Internal and External Consultants

Phase	Aspect	Internal	External
Entering	Finding clients	Ready access to clients	Finds clients through marketing
	Relationships	Already established	Builds relationships
	Communication	Knows company jargon	Learns company jargon
	Project analysis-effort and time	Easy understanding of problems and root causes. Does not require much time	Problem–analysis exercises are necessary. Time consuming
	Project selection	As per management direction	Based on own judgment
	Remuneration	Pay: Part of the job	Fees-negotiated
Contracting	Agreement	Informal	Formal
	Project continuation	Must complete projects assigned	Can terminate project at will
	Out of pocket expenses	No such problem	Guard against out-of-pocket expense
	Information	Open or confidential	Confidential
	Risks	Loss of job or unpleasant relationships	Loss of contract
	Expected role	Third party change agent and also driver	Third party change agent or pair of hands

(Contd.)

Phase	Aspect	Internal	External
Diagnosing	Source of prestige	From job rank and reporting authority	An outside expert
	Image	Existing one–good or bad; can build new image like external consultant	Through interactions and presentations can build quickly
	Familiarity with organizational members	Knows people already; however, has to know them in the new context	Meeting first time. Takes time to build mutual understanding
	Sharing diagnostic information with managers	Restricted sharing due to political sensitivities; restraint necessary to save job.	Prudence necessary to avoid project termination on one side and achieve success in project on the other
Intervening	Information base	Valid and true information	Valid and true information
	Free choice and internal commitment	May not be possible due to political influences and manager interferences	Insists on voluntary participation for internal commitment
Evaluating	Individual success criteria	Rely on repeat business, pay rise and promotion	Referral as key measure of success
	Institutionalization	Oversees institutionalization	Entrusted to management team

MAKING CONSULTING EFFECTIVE

What are the major problems of internal and external consultant? How can they make their roles effective?

Internal Consulting

We will now examine the problems faced by internal consultant and identify the ways of overcoming them. Table 2.5 shows the problems and measures that make internal consulting effective[11].

TABLE 2.5 Making Internal Consulting Effective

Areas	Problems	Guidelines
Client perception	Can be positive or negative depending on previous experience	Hold one-to-one meetings with key persons related to the project.
Client expectations	Lack of proper understanding of issues among senior managers	Develop credible and impressive analysis and presentation of situation
Role	Role confusion—Whether third-party consultation, facilitating, counseling, leading a project or performing as a team member	Establish role clarity in the agreement

(Contd.)

Areas	Problems	Guidelines
Confidentiality of information	Apprehension among employees that the information will be used against	Ensuring conscientious use of data
Relationships	No reference groups or like skilled and like minded people to support. Feeling of isolation	Work with different departments and show empathy to build relationships
Career path	Satisfied clients push the internal consultant to leave behind the third-party role by offering a management position—usually of various functions such as OD, HR, T&D, etc.	Make a conscious decision as to whether to safeguard the individual contributor status or secure management opportunities
Force field	Influenced by power centers and culture of organization. Departmental jealousies and envy because of the pivotal position of the consultant and association with senior managers	Establish good rapport and strong relationships. Develop a credible reputation in order to minimize the possible adverse impacts of departmental jealousy
Project completion	Institutionalization requires sustained interest and monitoring	Strengthen relationships with people and key managers and monitor the progress
Client satisfaction	Lack of patience to wait for long-term benefits and willingness to appreciate good work.	Maintain emotional balance. Explain the progress and results to people concerned. Show the future picture.

External Consulting

Like the internal consultants, external ones also have their own advantages as well as disadvantages. Table 2.6 presents the problems faced by external consultants and also guidelines to make consulting effective.

TABLE 2.6   Making External Consulting Effective

Area	Problem	Guidelines
Client perception	Positive in case of reputed ones. Dubious attention in case of new comes	Establish credibility by displaying your knowledge and interpersonal competence. Use systematic procedures
Client expectations	Lack of proper understanding of issues among senior managers	Develop credible and impressive analysis and presentation of situation. Establish trust
Power to influence	Less cooperation from employees and political games by managers who are against the change	Ensure top management involvement. Provide clarification on various issues to managers
Solutions	Difficulty in convincing management team if solutions are expensive and long-term in nature	Make a clear presentation of the proposal containing solutions, schedules and budget

Area	Problem	Guidelines
Confidentiality of information	Apprehension among employees that the information will be used against.	Ensuring conscientious use of data
Relationships	Resistance to change	Encourage employee participation and educate and train people
Force field	Influenced by power centers and culture of organization	Establish good rapport and strong relationships
Project completion	Institutionalization requires sustained interest and monitoring	Train managers in monitoring and evaluating progress.
Client satisfaction	Lack of patience to wait for long-term benefits and willingness to appreciate good work	Explain the progress and results to senior managers. Show the future picture

POWER AND POLITICS IN OD CONSULTING

Organizations are social systems designed for people working together to achieve common goals. Henry Mintzberg premises that organizational behavior is a power game in which various players, called influencers, seek to control the organization's decisions and actions[12]. Organization Development has been criticized in the past for not taking into account the complexities of organizational power and politics while designing and implementing development and change programs. This criticism was essentially valid in the past but is not relevant in the present-day context[13].

What is power?

Power is the ability of an individual to influence the beliefs, emotions, and behaviors of people, whereas politics is the art of acquiring power. Though power has a negative connotation for most people, it is through the use of power that things get done in the world.

Two faces of power

Salancik and Pfeffer[14] view organizational power as a good thing. According to them power in the hands of the critical problem solvers helps the organization cope with the various realities it faces. David McClelland[15] distinguishes between the two faces of power—positive and negative.

- The negative face of power is characterized by a need to dominate others, whereas the positive face of power has a socialized need to initiate, influence, and lead.
- The positive face of power earns respect to people and assists them in reaching their goals, whereas the negative face of power helps individual to pursue individual agendas and self-interest in an organization without concern to achieve common goals.
- The positive face of power seeks to empower self and others whereas, the negative face of power seeks to dominate and control others.

How is power exercised?

An organization has many potential influencers, such as the board of directors, the managers, the top executives, the employees, the unions, suppliers, customers, regulators, and so forth. Power is used by these persons to enhance their own survival through control of scarce critical resources, through the placement of allies in key positions, and through the definition of organizational problems and policies.

How is it derived?

Power is a personal possession or attribute in the social context. It is also a legitimate feature in the organizational context. Mintzberg[16] maintains that exercise of power requires three things:

- Sources of power
- Will and skill (Influencer)
- Context for exercising power (organization)

According to Mintzberg, the five possible bases of power are: (i) control of a resource, (ii) control of a technical skill, (iii) control of a body of knowledge, (iv) legal prerogatives-being given exclusive rights to impose choices, and (v) access to those who have power based on the first four bases. In addition to a base of power, the influencer must have both the will and the skill to use it.

John R.P. French and Bertram Raven[17] suggested five sources, or bases of social power which are as follows:

- *Reward power*—Power to give something positively valued by the other
- *Coercive power*—Power to give something negatively valued by the other
- *Legitimate power*—Power based on position
- *Referent power*—Power based on attraction or feeling of oneness others have with power holder.
- *Expert power*—Power based on knowledge or information needed by the other.

What is politics?

Politics may be defined as the art and science of acquiring power in the pursuit of individual agendas and self-interest in an organization. Since organizations are social systems characterized by power, we have to accept that politics is a way of life in organizations.

Politics—A double-edged sword

Organizational decision-making is not only a rational process, but also a political process. Organizational actors play politics in order to achieve organizational goals, while satisfying their needs driven by self-interest. It can cut both ways. It can make organizations democratic or dictatorial. According to Aristotle, politics stems from a diversity of interests. Obviously, in modern organizations, the diverse work groups bring to the workplace their own interests and needs and pursue them. Competing interests can be reconciled in different ways. Domination and integration are the two polar points on the continuum of conflict resolution methods.

Politics based on democratic principles will promote integration and win-win solutions in different contexts of conflict. Politics of this kind promotes human values, and enhances individual dignity. Conflicts will be looked upon as sources of new ideas and innovations and constructive mechanisms of Organization Development. Conversely, politics based on self-interest, will create authoritarian systems, and diminish human values and subvert organizational processes and goals.

Influences on OD consulting

OD practitioners need to be aware of political complexities in which they operate. According to Broom and Klein[18] there is paradigm shift in the OD belief systems regarding politics. Table 2.7 defines and contrasts them. The new paradigm sees power as an enabling process and politics as a joyful game for well being of all the participants.

TABLE 2.7   Paradigm Shift in Perceptions of Power

Views on	Finite paradigm	Infinite paradigm
Power	Power is scarce. It is a zero-sum game. No one can win in the long run. The purpose is to establish who is winner and who is loser.	Power is abundant. It is a positive-sum game. Everyone wins. The purpose is to maintain the game and the players
Workforce diversity	Being different is viewed as dangerous; conforming to and collusion with authority is the route to safety. Differences are used to determine who wins and who loses. Changing people is a strategy of choice	Being different is valued and safe; conformity is a matter of personal choice. Authority is a matter of function, not superiority. Differences are cause for curiosity and learning. Changing systems is the strategy of choice
Diversity management	Diversity leads to adversity. Partnerships and teamwork are difficult because of distrust and hostility. Collaboration is difficult, provisional, and short-term	Diversity leads to learning and synergy. Partnerships and teamwork are supported by curiosity and learning from differences. Ease of collaboration is only a matter of practice
Doing	Doing is more important than being. Speed is essential. Knowing what you are doing, often with little real data, is preferred over being seen as ignorant. Doing to others is valued over doing with others	Being is seen as the path to effective doing. Taking time is essential. Ignorance is valued as a necessary precursor to curiosity, learning, and increased knowledge. Doing with others is valued. Doing to others is not
Politics	The paradigm of choice when survival is a moment-to-moment issue. A self-fulfilling prophecy because potential partnerships are temporary and limited. A game to be played very seriously when individual or group identity is perceived as at stake	A game to be played well and joyfully as no one's survival is at stake. A self-fulfilling prophecy because potential partnerships are secure and unlimited. The paradigm of choice when growth and learning are primary goals

Source: Based on Broom and Klein (1995), Power, The Infinite Game, Penssylavania: HRD Press, and Greiner, Larry and Schein, Virginia (1988), A Revisionist Look at Power and OD, The Industrial and Organizational Psychologist, Vol. **25**(2), pp. 59–61.

Strategies to enhance power

Larry Greiner and Virginia Schein[19], argues that in modern pluralistic organizations, power is a common phenomenon. If used constructively and responsibly, power and OD are not incompatible. Their effective combination represents high road to organizational improvement. How can an OD practitioner reconcile OD and power? Greiner and Schein suggested the following approaches:

1. *Power enhancement approaches*
   - *Networking with powerful*—Building own power base and establishing links with power centers
   - *Gaining political support*—Through fair means enlist the support of key power-holders

2. *Power neutralization strategies*
   - *Assisting in a political problem-solving*—Assist powerful to find solutions to substantive issues in an a political, managerial processes.
   - *Transforming for power equalization*—Change negative political structures into positive ones to bring about power equalization.
   - *Supporting powerless to gain power*—Upholding the interests of those with less power, who are affected by interventions.

Guidelines to working in political environment

Cobb and Margulies[20] caution that OD practitioners can get into trouble if they prefer political role to facilitator role. The practitioner is not a political activist or power broker. His role is limited to that of a facilitator, catalyst, problem-solver, and educator. Though OD practitioners are not power brokers they should be competent in political arena. What should OD practitioners do to gain positively from power and politics in organizations?

French and Bell and others[21] suggest the following ground rules:

1. *Become a desired commodity both as a person and professional:* Demonstrate competence to gain respect and acceptance. Cultivate and nurture multiple relationships with power groups and individuals close to power corridors.

2. *Make OD program itself a desired commodity:* OD interventions enhance the positive face of power and help establish democratic traditions and values such as power equalization, trust, openness, collaboration, individual dignity, and competence. Make intervention results-oriented and involve people using educative strategy.

3. *Make OD program a valued commodity for multiple powerful people in the organization:* OD program become a valued one when it has sponsorship, preferably multiple sponsorships in powerful places. The recognized maxim is to get top level support for the program.

4. *Create win-win solutions:* Use effective conflict management techniques to develop constructive, stable relationships.

5. *Mind your own business which is to help someone else solve his or her major problems:* OD consultant is hired to help managers in solving organizational problems and increase its effectiveness. As such, the program belongs to managers and not to OD consultants. If there is political trouble, managers have to defend it.

6. *Mind your own business which is to be an expert on process, not on content:* OD consultant has to be a catalyst and supporter of the intervention processes. He has to offer his expert advice on processes like goal setting, intervention design and implementation and people involvement. Two major reasons for the consultant to stay out of expert role are: (i) Expert role creates a sense of dependency in the client. This is undesirable. The client has to on his own make critical managerial decisions relating to interventions and keep working even after the interventions (ii) If consultant assumes expert role, he has to own the solution and defend it if required. In fact, it is the client, who has to own the solution and defend it.

7. *Mind your own business because to do otherwise is to invite political trouble:* OD practitioners have to be aware of their roles and limits of authority or power. If they side step, from their role of facilitator, catalyst, problem-solver, and educator, they will be entangled in political battles.

ETHICS FOR OD PRACTITIONERS

Simply put, ethics refers to doing the right thing. Ethics includes the fundamental ground rules by which we care others and environment. Values that guide how we ought to behave for example, respect, honesty, fairness and responsibility, when presented in statement form are called moral or ethical principles. These principles are documented as a code of ethics for ensuring professional behaviors. OD consultant works with three types of people (i) client organization (managers) (ii) employees of the client organization and (iii) other OD consultants in the field. To be ethical in his dealings with people, an OD consultant will require an understanding of ethical problems and a commitment to ethics.

Being Ethical

To begin with, OD consultants must realize that they there is a significant difference between the theories of OD and what happens in reality[22]. In real life, ethical dilemmas arise, which are intimidating and intriguing. The ability to resolve ethical dilemmas depends on the OD consultant's ability to choose his or her values and standards consciously, ability to clarify ones personal values and how to apply these values systematically.[23]

1. *Ethical sensitivity:* It is important, as such, for one to learn and develop ethical sensitivity as one way of developmental process. Ethical sensitivity can be developed through establishing one's beliefs and values. Sensitivity can be sharpened based on experience gained through facing ethical dilemmas.

2. *Fairness in dealings:* The simple way of resolving ethical issues is to remember that one should not use other people for their own benefits or for their own purposes.

3. *Sharing with colleagues:* Another best way is to discuss ethical problems when they arise with other consultants.

4. *Following a code:* Following ethical code of associations or institutes of OD professionals.

Unethical Dilemmas

According to one study, there are 39 common dilemmas; however only 13 of them are conspicuous by their repetitive occurrence[24]. These dilemmas according to the frequency of their occurrence are:

Illusion of participation, skip the diagnosis, inappropriate intervention, stretch the limits of competence, coercion, political pressure, informed consent, client has misled the consultant, misuse of information, violate confidentiality, priority of interests, role of expectation and Conflict with co-consultant.

We will discuss ethical issues of consulting under three heads:

* Consultant—client relationships in various stages of OD process
* Consultant—employee relationships in intervention design and implementation
* Consultant—consultant relationships in professional work setting

In all these relationships, consultant is responsible to two institutions:

  (i) Client organization—the interests of stakeholders
  (ii) Profession—the community of consultants who take an oath to deliver services abiding by certain code of conduct.

Ethics in consultant–client relationships

Ethics is subjective. What is right to one consultant is wrong to another. To be ethical, a consultant should upholdvalues like truthfulness, honesty, integrity, trust, quality and expertise and think of common good. Keeping this in mind, consider the following behaviors of consultants. While the first three are clear unethical practices, the fourth is a controversial one. It is also evident that the unethical behaviors fall into two categories: (i) Those motivated by self-interest and (ii) those forced by situation or people with power.

* To have a good relationship with the client, a consultant adopted the client's perspective on all issues and did not voice any disagreement.
* To save time and money, consultant did not conduct enough discovery (or "diagnosis") and implemented actions.
* On the request of some managers, a consultant incorporated false, negative information about one manager.
* To help community, a consultant revealed in public, some information that is guarded as secret by the client.

Table 2.8 shows the unethical aspects in the consultant and client relationships. It also presents the possible steps a consultant may take in such cases[25].

TABLE 2.8 Ethical Issues in Consultant and Client Relationship

S.No.	Ethical issues	Description	Comments	Measures
1	Exaggeration	Consultant overstates his competencies and resources to secure project	Lying and cheating a client is unethical	Be honest. Avoid such false representation
2	Promising unrealistic outcomes	Consultant makes an overstatement of the outcomes of intervention to the client to secure contract	Making promises in order to gain a client contract can be great, but it can reduce credibility of the consultant	Be truthful. Display integrity. Provide realistic outcomes with system perspective
3	Skip the diagnosis	Client insists on skipping diagnosis	It may cause loss to organization	Negotiate with the client
4	Misrepresentation of data	Consultant provides distorted data to support the interventions he likes to propose	Suggesting solutions in self-interest is deception. It harms the interests of the organization	Be truthful. Keep client interest above self-interest
5	Inappropriate intervention	Client asks for an intervention that is not appropriate	It will be a waste of resources of organization	Use action research and negotiation
6	Stretch the limits of competence	Consultant tries a new intervention that is beyond proved competencies	If the consultant hides information that he is trying it for the first time, it would amount to deception	Be open. Let the client know your talents in trying new intervention
7	Political pressure	Political ideas and power group influences may distort OD process	Organizational good is more important than individual good	Take independent actions and use action research. Some use negotiation and indirect response
8	Client has misled the consultant	Consultant is asked to design interventions without providing full and right information	Acting without proper information is unfair to the organization	Respond to this through confrontation and action research
9	Priority of interests	Whose interests are more important to the consultant–managers or employees?	Balancing is important keeping in mind the interests of organization	Use action research and negotiation
10	Role of expectation	Consultant is caught between self-perception and client's perception of his role	Working without role clarity may lead to disappointment on either side	Use negotiation and confrontation.
11	Collusion	Consultant agreeing with client to ignore or sabotage the interests of some managers	Getting involved in organizational politics is detrimental to the interests of organization as well as consultant profession	Be straightforward and stay out of politics

Ethics in consultant-employee relationships

Table 2.9 presents the ethical issues in the consultant and employee relationships and suggests the responses of a consultant. There is a long history of management consultants being used to eliminate or demean jobs. In the past, work study was used to get maximum out of workers without passing on the benefit of extra production. Even in the heyday of job enrichment and empowerment, many companies tried to push power upwards instead of downwards.

TABLE 2.9   Ethical Issues in Consultant and Employee Relationship

S.No.	Ethical issues	Description	Comments	Measures
1	Illusion of participation	Giving impression that employees are involved while employer has already made up his mind	This is unfair and dishonest	Convince employer to organize meetings to elicit employee views
2	Coercion	Employees are forced to participate in an OD intervention without their will	This is against human values, such as free choice, dignity, responsibility and respect	Convince client. Use negotiation, or action research to gather more information
3	Informed consent	Employees are drawn into an intervention without getting informed consent from them	Asking for blind following is against human values	Use action research, negotiation and indirect response methods
4	Misuse of information	Consultant is asked by the client to reveal information for using it in HR decisions	This is against the confidentiality assurance and unfair	Refuse to divulge information. Make an agreement on this aspect
5	Violate confidentiality	Client insists on sharing employee information without any intentions	This is against the confidentiality assurance and unfair	Refuse to divulge information
6	Priority of interests	Whose interests are more important to the consultant–managers or employees	Balancing is important keeping in mind the interests of organization	Use action research and negotiation

The various tools used by OD practitioners can easily be subverted or made ineffective in the wrong hands. Some examples are:

1. *The fad or fly-by-night initiative:* A change program starts with wide publicity and enthusiastically involves people, takes their time and energy. Suddenly, it disappears because managers are not interested in it. Such exercises are waste of time for everyone involved.

2. *The untold success:* An OD project takes off with big publicity and produces good results. The employees are however, kept unaware of the success.

3. *The false front:* Often, consultants and managers start out their discussion of a major project by saying that nobody would lose their job as a result of the initiative. But the end result is termination of many in the name of rightsizing.

Generally speaking, the ethical consultant can do many things to make the lives of employees and managers better and he should strive to do that. The important values in consultant-employee relationships are: freedom, dignity, honesty, cooperation, integrity, confidentiality and expertise.

Ethics in consultant–consultant relationships

Table 2.10 shows the potential ethical issues a consultant faces in two situations– when working on a project, and when in professional competition. The important values that guide consultant are: integrity, tolerance and expertise.

TABLE 2.10   Ethical Issues in Consultant and Consultant Relationship

S.No.	Ethical issues	Description	Comments	Measures
1	Conflict with co-consultant	Disagreement between co-consultants on project	Conflicts harm the interests of client	Resolve through negotiation, or confrontation
2	Defamation	Making negative campaign to tarnish image of competitors in the field either openly or discreetly	Reduces credibility of profession. It boomerangs and harms the consultant indulging in such negative act	Be truthful. Preserve your integrity and dignity. Stay above jealousies and envy

Ethical code of conduct

It is important to establish mission, vision and values, to ensure fair practices that minimize one's liabilities as a consultant. The values can be an inner compass in the midst of the confusion that is typical in an organizational change effort. Here are some important ethical guidelines for consulting during organizational change.

1. Never, do anything that harms your client.
2. Never, do anything that insults or injures employees and their interests.
3. Never, side step from your professional approach of OD.
4. Never, disclose client information unless the client permits or law requires doing so.
3. Do not make client dependent on you.
4. Do not be dependent on client. Use our own judgment and expertise.
5. Make conflicts constructive for the good of parties involved.
6. Do not go beyond your own expertise.
7. Treat others the way you want them to treat you.

One of the important tasks of the educational institutes and association of consultants is developing a code of ethics or conduct of conduct, for all consultants to follow. Box 2.2 presents the International Organization Development Code of Ethics (1991).

BOX 2.2   The International Organization Development Code of Ethics
(December, 1991, 22nd Revision)

As an OD professional, I commit myself to supporting and acting in accordance with the following ethical guidelines:

Responsibility to Self
- Act with integrity; be authentic and true to myself.
- Strive continually for self-knowledge and personal growth.
- Recognize my personal needs and desires and, when they conflict with other responsibilities, seek all-win resolutions of those conflicts.
- Assert my own economic and financial interests in ways that are fair and equitable to me as well as to my clients and their stakeholders.

Responsibility for Professional Development and Competence
- Accept responsibility for the consequences of my acts and make reasonable efforts to ensure that my services are properly used; terminate my services if they are not properly used and do what I can to see that any abuses are corrected.
- Strive to achieve and maintain a professional level of competence for both myself and my profession by developing the full range of my own competence and by establishing collegial and cooperative relations with other OD professionals.
- Recognize my own personal needs and desires and deal with them responsibly in the performance of my professional roles.
- Practice within the limits of my competence, culture, and experience in providing services and using techniques.
- Practice in cultures different from my own only with consultation from people native to or knowledgeable about those specific cultures.

Responsibility to Clients and Significant Others
- Serve the long-term well-being, interests and development of the client system and all its stakeholders, even when the work being done has a short-term focus.
- Conduct any professional activity, program or relationship in ways that are honest, responsible, and appropriately open.
- Establish mutual agreement on a contract covering services and remuneration.
- Deal with conflicts constructively and avoid conflicts of interest as much as possible.
- Define and protect the confidentiality of my client-professional relationships.
- Make public statements of all kinds accurately, including promotion and advertising, and give service as advertised.

Responsibility to the Profession
- Contribute to continuing professional development for myself, other practitioners, and the profession.
- Promote the sharing of OD knowledge and skill.
- Work with other OD professionals in ways that is exemplary what our profession says we stand for.

- Work actively for ethical practice by individuals and organizations engaged in OD activities and, in case of questionable practice, use appropriate channels for dealing with it.
- Act in ways that bring credit to the OD profession and with due regard for colleagues in other professions.

Social Responsibility

- Act with sensitivity to the fact that my recommendations and actions may alter the lives and well-being of people within my client systems and the larger systems of which they are subsystems.
- Act with awareness of the cultural filters which affect my view of the world, respect cultures different from my own, and be sensitive to cross-cultural and multicultural differences and their implications.
- Promote justice and serve the well-being of all life on Earth.
- Recognize that accepting this statement as a guide for my behavior involves holding myself to a standard that may be more exacting than the laws of any countries in which I practice, the guidelines of any professional associations to which I belong, or the expectations of any of my clients.

Source: Code of Ethics—The ISOD, www.theisod.org/index.php/.../code-of-ethics/9-uncategorised.

HIRING CONSULTANT

Expert consultants are hired as a pair-of-hands to do something that cannot be done in-house, because of routine pressures and resource constraints. These consultants are hired based on two considerations—(i) the person with right experience, skills, style, and fees that is reasonable. We will now look at the different factors that influence the hiring of a consultant.

1. *Experience:* Should we hire a successful one or a fresher? Generally, it is the name or sales ability that influences hiring decisions. But one should not jump at the conclusion that the successful consultants are always the best. Very busy consultants, over-the-time, may become complacent with success and may spare less time to our organization. Further, they may be very expensive. As such, depending on the seriousness of the problem, choose the right one.

2. *Skills:* Before hiring a consultant, make sure that you do not have the competencies inside the organization. External consultant should provide value-added services worth the money paid to him. Check the credentials of the consultants carefully. Make calls to their past clients and ask for information on the interventions they did for them and know the results obtained. Some consultants may be more skilled in selling their services than in actual consulting work. Look behind the sales spiel to judge how skilled and honest the consultant is.

3. *Style:* The OD consultants require a great deal of contact and collaboration with people directly involved in the intervention. As such, consultants with participatory style who value people and their ideas are to be hired for successful OD interventions. Some consultants stay too distant from front-line employees. An aristocratic consultant who fails to work with company executives is likely to be less effective. Even processes such as the balanced scorecard, which are top-down in nature, involve front line people eventually.

4. *Results of earlier intervention:*   In case of rehiring a consultant, the results of previous experience should be considered. The OD consultant is a change agent and helps people in the organization to learn how to solve their own problems. If there is no learning from the work that was performed, then the consultant must not be hired back again to do the same thing.

5. *Fees:*   The costs can be broughtdown without losing the value of intervention. Some useful ideas are:

- Handle many parts of a project yourself, and only tap their skills wherever necessary to keep the bill down to an affordable size.
- Consider a process consultant. He makes employee team work more effective. This arrangement can be the most cost-effective consulting method, and can help you to use your resources more effectively.

IMPLICATIONS OF OD FOR THE CLIENT

What are the implications of OD for the client? The implications are discussed with reference to the decisions involved: (i) deciding to change, (ii) hiring consultant, (iii) awarding project (iv) implementation of project, and (v) completion of project.

Implications of Decision to Bring About Change

Top management has to prepare their organization before embarking on a change project.

Change as a way of life

The OD deals with constant change and helps develop organizational capacity to learn—at the individual, team and organizational levels. When this becomes a way of life for the organization, the organization becomes flexible. It will then be like the mast of a sailing ship that naturally adjusts to the changing winds. Create change readiness in the organization.

Empowerment of employees

For OD consulting to be effective, three people related initiatives are important:

- First empower employees to do their jobs to the best of their ability. That requires pushing authority, responsibility, and information downwards.
- Second is empowering employees to change the system. Since systems are designed by people, they should be asked to fix problems. It helps create employee ownership of change and encourages innovation.

- Third is providing a clear vision to people and helping everyone to understand the organizational strategy. This is the primary role of the organizational leader. This initiative avoids wasted effort due to duplication of work, and conflicts that arise due to working at cross purposes.

Implications of Decision to Hire a Consultant

When an expert is hired, an obligation to provide an opportunity to the consultant to design and deliver solutions is given. However, top management has to ensure that consultant works with right perspective and right style.

Right perspectives

Two perspectives—people and systems—are important for successful consulting. Encourage consultant to take both the perspectives.

- *People perspective:* Using an OD lens, the consultant should be able to detect signs of dysfunction, resistance, or a lack of trust within the client system. Paying more attention to these people issues can often mean the difference between a project's success and failure.
- *System perspective:* The expert consultant should also consider taking a whole systems perspective when diagnosing the system. Is the present problem a symptom or a real problem? Is it really the issue at local level or is it something larger within the entire organization that needs to be addressed before a sustainable solution can result?

Right style

The personality and style of an OD consultant is as important as his or her experience and expertise. OD consultant must be a person who can work within the client's corporate culture. He or she must be able to sit on the boundary of the organization as an interested, objective, informed observer. He or she must provide accurate, informed feedback—the mirror in which organizational members can see themselves clearly. He or she must be credible to everyone. Choose the person with right style.

Implications of Decision to Award Change Project to the Consultant

Once project is awarded to a consultant, the client system has to lend support to him in playing his role of designing intervention, facilitating change process, securing involvement and commitment of people and evaluating progress and results.

Right intervention

The ever-increasing range of tools, processes, and interventions can easily overwhelm anyone looking for OD solutions. Give a child a hammer, and everything will need hammering. Likewise, consultants try to sell what they have in his tool-box. An expert in surveys will recommend surveys, and an expert in mergers and acquisitions will suggest mergers and acquisitions.

Watch out for one size fits all products, and people who try to sell services that are not required. Choosing a wrong intervention is worse than doing nothing. It can disappoint people, lower their faith in management, waste company's resources of time, money, and energy. Discuss with consultant and choose right intervention.

Right process

Effective process requires involvement and ownership of people. Meetings, team building and group decision-making are important to create involvement and ownership. Support consultant in organizing interactive and educative sessions.

Right communication

The consultant must also use appropriate and excellent communication techniques to help the organization understand and operate on the data collected. He or she should speak the language which management team and employees can comprehend. Provide support to consultants in communication activities.

Right integration

OD consultant must be a catalyst, providing a special presence that encourages and supports the people in the organization. Without benefit of participation in early planning, the OD practitioner can only develop band-aid solutions for the issues. Knitting together diverse and sometimes warring sub-cultures is a challenge. OD consultants require power strategies and support to meet the challenge. Play active role in integration efforts[26].

Right evaluation

The results of OD consulting must be consistent with the expectations. It should also be cost-effective. For this, right criteria of evaluation are to be developed and incorporated in the agreement for management and consultant to apply in mid-course and at the end of intervention. To win appreciation, consultant should deliver the best value to the organization. It is important to provide solid measurable results that are tied to business objectives along with the best practices of OD consulting that incorporate people issues, and systems perspective. If the intervention does not make business sense, it will appear much less important to the organization, no matter how much it has directly contributed to an increase in overall productivity. At the time of entering into agreement establish criteria for evaluation.

Implications of Project Completion

What kind of responsibilities management will have on completion of project? OD is an initiative sponsored by top management with an intention of transforming organization—in part or as a whole. Table 2.11 presents the expected changes.

TABLE 2.11   Transformation of Organization

Issue	From	To
Data base	Limited and local	Expanded, organizational wide
Influence process	Superior dominating employees	Equally and mutually influencing
Informal system	Separated from formal system	Integrated with formal system
Response to change	Passive due to submerged data	Active due to unfolding data
Conflict resolution	Win-lose, cooperation	Win-win collaboration
Leadership style	Authoritarian or bureaucratic or transactional	Democratic, participative and transformational
Response to environment	Resistance to change	Change readiness and adaptation

It means there is a new organization with new elements and processes. Client has to make an effort to institutionalize the change and stabilize the new organizational processes.

OD IN GLOBAL CONTEXT

As organizations go global, OD has to assist global human resource management. The differences in climatic conditions, cultural values and traditions, language, quality of life and work life pose a major challenge of adaptation to the employees. HR managers require support from OD professionals with new set of cross-cultural sensitivities and competencies, to prepare employees for overseas positions. We will now examine the challenges faced by global OD practitioners.

Language challenge

Language differences will be the first major barrier. When working with HR professionals of different countries, OD professionals have two options:

- To speak the native language of the HR professional
- Use an interpreter

Otherwise, misunderstandings arise, and the OD progress will be hampered.

Values challenge

OD practitioners require an understanding of cultural values of the HR professionals and people with whom they work in different countries. Differences in values, attitudes and social etiquette require careful consideration, understanding and assimilation. For instance, the field of OD, originated in the United States was founded on values of social equality, democracy and human dignity, which are acceptable in democratic nations like India. But they are not always accepted globally.

Research strongly recommends that professionals should have cultural empathy, flexibility, patience and a sense of humor. Without such qualities they cannot design appropriate interventions for both global and local workplaces[27]. The research of Hofstede provides a framework for cultural sensitivity. He differentiated national cultures using four dimensions: power distance, uncertainty avoidance, individualism/collectivism and masculinity/femininity[28].

Integration challenge

It is equally important to consider how best to integrate different national cultures and values with others. Three key issues are: (i) the strength of the value set; (ii) the presence of subcultures; and (iii) value change. In other words, the degree to which most people accept values as desirable and legitimate, the presence of contradictory values within the general values set and the acknowledgement that value change is an evolving process, are often slow to take hold.

Work ethics

Further, not all cultures have the same work ethics. In certain countries, taking a long meal or mid-afternoon break may be an integral part of the culture. Finally, in some countries, corruption is taken for granted as a cost of doing business. The HR professional will have to come to terms with his or her own values regarding the feasibility of working in environments with vastly differing ethics and values.

Quality of life

Differences in levels of economic development and the resulting quality of life and work life differences may impose certain limitations to the practice of OD. Differences may manifest in seven key areas as shown in Table 2.12.

TABLE 2.12   Quality of Life Variations with Economic Development

Key areas	Variables	Advanced nations	Backward nations
Skills	Level of employee and management skills in decision-making and implementation	High due to growth in technical, scientific and management education facilities and achievement orientation in society	Low due to lack of facilities and affiliation motives in society
Staff	Size and composition of staff	Knowledge and skill levels high but limited numbers; High manpower costs	Low skills and knowledge. Availability of cheap labour in large numbers
Style	Leadership styles and employee participation in organizational affairs	Participative style of management. Mentoring and empowerment of people	Paternal or autocratic style. Guiding and caring people
Strategies	HR practices like selection, placement, development, appraisal motivational and reward systems, etc.	Strategic, competitive and innovative	Operational, reactive and adaptive
Systems	Degree of sophistication in operating technology and information systems	High-tech capital intensive systems	Low tech labor intensive systems

Key areas	Variables	Advanced nations	Backward nations
Structures	The level of bureaucracy, and corresponding lack of flexibility in organizational design and functioning	Bureaucratic or charismatic family organizations	Organic and virtual organizations
Shared values	Work and profit ethics	Work is a play and achievement driven. Profit and social responsibility balanced	Work is a means for livelihood. Profit dominates social responsibility

These issues are less likely to be encountered in more wealthy countries. In underdeveloped economies, where there may be little knowledge of contemporary management and business practices in the local workforce, OD may primarily be used to address community and/or social issues. Finally, to be effective in global OD and OD, HR professionals have worked together for integration of values and determine the most appropriate OD interventions.

Global OD interventions

Typical global OD interventions include global learning programs, expansion of cultural self-awareness, cross-cultural team building, virtual team building, expatriate job assignments, story telling/sharing and organizational blending.

SUMMARY

In India, we have a good number of consultants offering a variety of services. With the growing demand for consulting, independent consulting has become one of the fastest growing businesses in the country. OD consultants are different from HR management consultants in that the client is the total organization, not just the management team. Nees and Grenier (1985) proposed five categories of consultants: mental adventurer, strategic navigator, management physician, system architect and friendly co-pilot. Schein (1990) identified three models of consultation—purchase of expertise, doctor-patient and process consultation. Schein (1997) has distinguished six basic types of clients—contact clients, intermediate clients, primary clients, unwitting clients, indirect clients and ultimate clients. Turner opined that relationships in consulting have become partnerships with mutual respect.

OD consultant works with organization in a systematic way following a process which is explained in different ways. A four step model says intake, project agreement, implementation and evaluation explains the process. Cummings and Worley divided the process into six steps: entering, contracting, diagnosing, intervening, evaluating and sustaining change. There are differences in internal and external consulting. The internal consultant has advantages of being insider in knowing problem and involving employees. The external consultant commands more respect for his expertise and neutral position.

Power and politics are part of organization. OD practitioners need to be aware of political complexities in which they operate. They can enhance power by networking with powerful and gaining political support. French and Bell (2000) suggested some ground rules. According to practitioners ethics is important for professional success. OD practitioners have to uphold values which guide the profession, and stay ethical despite pressures from clients. Expert consultants are hired as a pair-of-hands to do something that cannot be done in-house. It is important to choose one with right skills, style, and exposure at a reasonable price. Hiring OD consultant imposes certain responsibilities on management. They include preparing organization for change, supporting discovery and interventions and evaluating project.

As organizations go global, OD has to assist global human resource management. The differences in climatic conditions, cultural values and traditions, language, quality of life and work life pose a major challenge of adaptation to the employees. Typical global OD interventions include global learning programs, expansion of cultural self-awareness, cross-cultural team building, virtual team building, expatriate job assignments, story telling/sharing and organizational blending.

EXERCISES

I. Review Questions

1. Who can be a consultant?
2. Explain a classification of consultants.
3. Mention the services offered by OD consultants.
4. Provide a classification of clients.
5. Describe in brief OD consulting process.
6. Explain external consultant process and consultant-client relationships.
7. Explain internal consultant process and consultant-client relationships.
8. Distinguish between internal and external consulting.
9. How do you make consulting effective?
10. Explain power strategies of OD consultant.
11. How do consultants face politics?
12. List any five ethical issues of OD consultants.
13. Identify the factors that influence the hiring of a consultant.
14. Mention some global OD interventions.

II. Discussion Questions

1. Explain internal and external consulting processes and discuss the advantages and disadvantages of internal consulting.
2. Discuss the influence of power and politics on consulting. How do consultants operating in an environment of politics?
3. Examine the ethical issues confronted by OD consultants.
4. Explain the concept of client. What is the implication of OD to clients?
5. Explain the OD challenges in the global context.

📖 MINI-PROJECT

Conduct a study on values of MBA students and make a presentation based on the analysis and findings. Use the questionnaire given under for data collection. The study aims at finding out the values that you consider important for you to become an OD consultant. Choose the values that are most important to you, the values you believe in and that define your character. Kindly circle the number on the 3-point scale of importance to represent your view.

Scale: 3–Important 2–Somewhat important 1–Unimportant.

S.No.	Values	Scale		
1	Caring	3	2	1
2	Courage			
3	Creativity			
4	Friendliness			
5	Honesty			
6	Achievement/success			
7	Equality			
8	Fairness			
9	Reliability			
10	Autonomy			
11	Loyalty			
12	Punctuality			
13	Dedication			
14	Conscientiousness			
15	Team work			

🖱 WEB ASSIGNMENT

Consult reference given under and other useful websites and develop a paper on "OD consulting in Public and Private Sectors".

Porous Boundary and Power Politics: Contextual constraints of ......
www.csend.org/component/docman/.../28-20081121-un-od-docpdf

CASE STUDY

The Journey of A Consultant

A few key experiences of disappointments in my engineering plus management education and training ended up orientating me towards the way people and organizations work. It remained a private despair until I saw the world of experiential learning. The first experience at a

Self Awareness Laboratory (at that time it was called Sensitivity Training, in IIMA) was a revelation of a lifetime and suddenly opened up a new vista and a goal worth dedicating myself to. Although there was no established career path in the field, the journey into the world of Organization Development and personal growth had begun.

My first job was with the Indian Space Research Organization (ISRO) Ahmedabad in the capacity of a Social Scientist with knowledge of management tools and techniques. I am thankful to the then intellectual culture as it provided a fertile ground for nurturing my interest in the social sciences in general and developmental communication in particular. The popular term we had learnt then was sensitivity training. It was not an established profession in the 70's. A few personal experiences led me to believe that there is much more than meet the eye, in the world of human experience. After five years in ISRO, I found a job as a Faculty Member at ASCI (Administrative Staff College of India), Hyderabad where I could take up consulting assignments as well as engage in the College's curricular work in the area of human processes. In order to ensure that exigencies of income and employment did not detract me from the central pursuit, I actively remained engaged with building up an institution which subsequently became the ground from where Sumedhas took birth (www.sumedhas.org). In 1980, I left ASCI and started the consulting practice. A guiding light and inspiration all through this part of the journey was our illustrious teacher Prof. Pulin K. Garg of the IIMA. This pursuit, of building up intellectual capital by engaging in pro bono public work became the central backbone of my professional engagement with the world. In other words I also did consulting.

Early Assignments

Early consulting assignments were mainly focused on conducting stand alone programs that dealt with human processes. In those early days, client organizations came in largely with intent to improve the sociology of co-operation, in other words create reconciliations and settle low level high cost conflicts that plague the world of management using the special insights available in the applied behavioral sciences in contrast to then extant modes of settling disputes.

The first OD assignment came in 6 years after I began the practice. In 1984, I was called in by a client to increase the levels of collaboration in the top management team. This was the first time I was privy to the organization as a whole, not restricted to an individual program chosen by the HR department. After a year of engaging with OD, the client organization's performance had improved remarkably as decisions were flowing smoothly since several of the persistent conflicts had been resolved. The bottom line was showing very healthy figures.

I remember inviting one client to begin costing the OD exercise so that at the end an ROI may be crystallized. The request was immediately turned down. The GM (Personnel) apprehended that the whole exercise may only be a cost. In some ways at that early stage of OD's maturing in the corporate firmament, it was seen largely as a welfare cost. Very soon in the practice, it became clear that OD cannot be sold. All attempts at push failed, pull was the only way it worked in the market place. Credibility through conceptual soundness, intellectual capital, effective ethical practices and an undying subscription to articulating hard truths were the main attractors for the "pull" to work. The client had to experience deep confidence in order to call in the consultant. The consultant had to be ready as well for this confidence to be examined from time-to-time.

Knowledge Foundations

My grounding originally was in what was called unstructured lab work. As an outsider to the client groups it was very easy for me to believe that an adequate dose of personal growth should solve all problems. New methods had to be developed to focus on sectoral aspect, such as role taking, leadership, and conflict management. A new journey had begun. My stint at ASCI introduced me to the world of structured exercises and sectoral agreed upon areas of confrontation. A very early recognition that dawned on me was very few individuals have a view of the organization as a whole, not very different from the old adage missing the woods for the trees. Therefore, we as the outsider must gather data to build up the picture of the wholeness of the organization. Changes, in parts, create unforeseen impacts on several other parts. Unless the OD exercise responds to the wholeness as well as requisite partial needs it will not create the right new alternatives.

Clearly knowledge was following practice. I for one certainly feel grateful to the clients for helping me learn. Learning was at several levels at once. At the core was an evolving universe of learning about myself-my own motivations and vulnerabilities. It followed with discovery of new responses. There was a series of learnings of the spectrum of human response to situations. The core knowledge I had started out with, was the distinction between experienced reality and constructed reality. Insights formation, I found, had an interesting and curious pattern. The beginning is always a small flash; small because almost always it had an air of familiarity with it, as if the awareness was already there. Soon bits and pieces from unexpected sources would get attracted, and like crystal formation, a cogent insight would get built up. Insight formation seemed to have a life of its own, not quite a distinct voluntary effort that I was making. The seed was like an attractor and just as a magnet pulls the iron filings, together the seed became a sapling.

Cybernetics and history were converging with social psychology, psychotherapy and later even fractals. Therapists had used systems theory to develop extraordinary insights into human communication, paradoxes and existence itself. Slowly, the apparently diverse sources of knowledge and human processes were coming on to the same field. It was bewildering, for it completely befuddled any answer to the question what am I? No answer was sufficient. I have recently found to my relief that the word experientialist is present in the dictionary.

The practice clearly led me to work with social and organizational phenomena as well as individual processes. The connection lay in studying experience itself and phenomena themselves. Over the years it has become clear that the eastern sources of understanding human perspectives, especially at the individual level are a potentially very rich source of insights that have helped my practice. These help understand and intervene in the unfolding of phenomena in organisations especially conflicts with long histories. These have become a huge and beneficial addition to the knowledge and learning from the classical social sciences. The contribution of management sciences to the world of OD is limited to understanding the economic implications of behavior in organisations. To remain relevant and continue to enjoy my work, I have to admit, that I must remain a student forever, and be willing to learn from anyone and everyone.

Questions for Discussion

1. Identify the factors that were facilitating and discouraging in the progress of the consultant.

2. What kind of knowledge and values the consultant has acquired through practice?

3. Based on the experience of the consultant, what lessons can you draw for beginners in the field?

Source: Sushanta Banerjee, Founder and Principal Consultant, Samuday Psycon, http://www.samuday.com/resources/pebbles_on_a_beach.html, and Co Founder, Sumedhas Academy for Human Context, http://www.sumedhas.org

REFERENCES

1. Adapted with permission from: Case studies–Clarity Consultants, www.clarityconsultants.com/case-studies.asp

2. Pryles, Victor, Consulting: Expanding the definition, 1, April 2006... www.upublish.info/Article/Consulting--Expanding-The.../24154

3. Nees, D.B. and L.E. Greiner (1985), Seeing Behind the Look-Alike Management Consultants, *Organizational Dynamics* 13 (Winter) pp. 68–79.

4. Schein, E.H., (1988), Process Consultation: Its Role in Organization Development, 2nd ed., Vol. **1**, Reading, Mass: Addison-Wesley.

5. Schein, Edgar H. (1997), The concept of "client" from a process consultation perspective: A guide for change agents, *Journal of Organizational Change Management* (1997), Vol. **10**(3), pp. 202–216.

6. Turner, A.N. (1982), Consulting Is More Than Giving Advice, *Harvard Business Review* 60 (September-October), pp. 120–129.

7. Consulting Process, (14 Dec. 2009), ... www1.umn.edu/ohr/orgdev/conpro/index.html

8. Cummings, T. and Worley, C. (1993), *Organization Development and Change*, 5th ed, St. Paul, MN: Addition-Wesley.

9. Cummings, T. and Worley, C. (1993), *Organization Development and Change*, 5th ed., St. Paul, M.N.: West; Dyer, W.G. (1989), *Team Building: Issues and Alternatives*, Reading, MA: Addison-Wesley; Argyris, C. (1970), Intervention Theory and Method: A Behavioral Science View, Reading, MA: Addison-Wesley.

10. Beckhard, R. and Harris, R.T. (1977), *Organizational Transitions: Managing Complex Change*, Reading, MA: Addison-Wesley; Block, P. (1981), *Flawless Consulting*, Austin, TX: Learning Concepts; Nadler, D. (1977), *Feedback and Organization Development: Using Data Based Methods*, Reading, MA: Addison-Wesley.

11. Lacey, Miriam Y. (1995), Internal consulting: perspectives on the process of planned change, *Journal of Organizational Change Management*, Vol. **8**(3), 1995, pp. 75–84; Kleiner, A. (1992), "The gurus of corporate change", *Business and Society Review*, Vol. **81**, pp. 39.

12. Mintzberg, H. (1983), *Power in and around Organizations*, Englewood Cliffs: NJ: Prentice Hall.

13. Sreekumar, Hari (2008), Power, Politics and Organization Development: A Review, *International Journal of Knowledge, Culture and Change Management*, Vol. **8**(7), pp. 55–60.

14. Salancik, Gerald and Pfeffer, Jeffery (1977), Who Gets Power—and How They Hold on to It: A Strategic-Contingency Model of power, *Organizational Dynamics*, No. 5.

15. McClelland, David (1970), The Two Faces of Power, Journal of International affairs, Vol. **24**(1), pp. 29–47.

16. Mintzberg, Henry (1983), *Power in and around Organizations*, Englewood Cliffs: NJ: Prentice Hall.

17. French, John R.P. and Bertram Raven (1959), The Bases of Social Power, in Dorwin Cartwright (Ed.), *Studies in Social Power*, Institute for Social research of the University of Michigan, Ann Harbor, pp. 159–67.

18. Broom, Michael F. (2013), Organization Development is A Paradox of Clashing of Paradigms: A Double-Loop Exploration of The Field practitioners available at www.chumans.com/.../practicing-organization-development.html.

19. Greiner, Larry and Schein, Virginia (1988), A Revisionist Look at Power and OD, *The Industrial and Organizational Psychologist*, Vol. **25**(2), pp. 59–61.

20. Cobb and Margulies (1981), Organizational Development: A Political Perspective, *Academy of Management Review*, No. 6, pp. 50–59.

21. French and Bell (2000), *Organization Development*, Pearson Education, New Delhi; Michael Beer and Anna E. Walton (1980), *Organisational Change and Development, Annual Review of Psychology*, 38, pp. 39–67; Porter, Elisabeth, Politics, change and reflective practitioners, findarticles.com/p/articles/mi_qa5427/is.../ai_n21317366/-

22. McLean, et al. (1982), *Organization Development Transition: Evidence of an Evolving Profession*. England: John Wiley & Sons.

23. Gellermann, William, Frankel, Mark S. and Landenson, Robert F. (1990), *Values and Ethics in Organization and Human Systems Development*, New York: Jossey-Bass.

24. DeVogel, S.H. (1992), Ethical decision-making in an organizational development: current theory and practice, Unpublished doctorate dissertation, University of Minnesota.

25. The ethics of organizational development and intervention, www.Toolpack.com/a/ethics.html; "Field Guide to Consulting and Organizational Development"—to obtain the entire book, select "Publications" at http://www.authenticityconsulting.com; Snell,

R. (1980), Questioning the ethics of management development: A critical review. Management Education and Development, **17**(1), 43–46; Frankel, Mark S. (1987), *Values and Ethics in Organization and Human Systems Development: An Annotated Bibliography*, AAAS Publication, October; and White, Louis P. and Wooten, Kevin C. (1986), *Professional Ethics and Practice in Organization Development*, New York: Praeger Publishers.

26. Craemer, Mark (2010), Combining Best Practices of Expert Consulting and OD Consulting, craemerconsulting.wordpress.com/.../combining- ... best-practices-of-expert-consulting-and-od-consulting/-

27. Yeager, T.F., Head, T.C., & Sorensen, P.F. (2006), *Global Organization Development: Managing Unprecedented Change*, Greenwich, CT: Information Age Publishing Inc.

28. Hofstede, G. (2001), *Culture's Consequences* (2nd ed.), London: Sage.

Chapter **3**

Organizational Design

Learning Objectives

After studying this chapter, you will be able to:

- Know the concept, scope and nature of organizational design
- Discuss the steps in organizational design
- Recognize the influence size, environment and technology on organizational designs
- Examine how organizational effectiveness can be achieved

Vignette: Reorganizations

Reliance Communications, India's second-largest mobile phone carrier by subscribers, is restructuring its wireless business to increase its competitiveness. The current structure with three regional heads, will be discontinued to create a leaner and flatter structure. There will be a single Chief Operating Officer to oversee its three zonal units—North, South and East. The move will make around 10 per cent of its 7,000 executives redundant, and also result in redeployment of another 2,000 employees to field functions.

Reorganizations are taking place at Infosys for every two or three years, since 1998. The latest one is stimulated by the intensifying competition with the likes of TCS and Cognizant. It is a move that will make the company more agile and to create measurable business value for clients through a combination of transformation, innovation and operation services. The name to Infosys from Infosys Technologies is expected would accurately reflect the company's evolution over the last 30 years from technology services to business-led consulting and solutions. Infosys is now organized into four Industry Sector Units: (i) Financial Services and Insurances, (ii) Energy, Utilities, Communications and Services, (iii) Manufacturing, and (iv) Retail, Consumer Packaged Goods, Logistics and Life Sciences. The three service and innovation groups: (i) Consulting and

Systems Integration, (ii) Business Operations Services and (iii) Products, Platforms and Solutions, to complement the four industry sector units to ensure the over-arching strategy and capability for their offerings is kept best-in-class. Finance, BPO and Product Engineering remain as they were. A new subsidiary Infosys Public Services is chartered to address US government entities. The healthcare provider portfolio is integrated with Infosys Public Services. India continues to be the global headquarters and domestic market will be served through a self-contained regional structure.

B.G. Srinivas, Member of the Board, Head of Europe said "The number one challenge in business today is finding innovative paths for additional growth. Our endeavour has been to future proof the businesses of our clients as we address key market challenges in the European region". In its bid to consolidate industry verticals and select service lines, the company may align its sales force geography-wise based on countries, rather than verticals in Europe and the delivery manpower. These changes may also turn out somewhat painful as some middle and senior management may have to exit.

The above two cases[1] are only limited examples of the structural changes, taking place in Indian industry. They suggest the need for knowing organizational design types and factors that determine their choices.

INTRODUCTION

Organizations are contrived socio-technical systems designed by matching people, information, and technology. They are evolved to direct, or pattern, the activities of a group of people towards a predetermined vision, purpose and strategy. As organizations are dynamic, they are periodically redesigned in response to changes in the environment. Obviously, learning how to design is a team life skill. Managers, therefore, should be aware of the principles and tools of organizational design to maintain and enhance organizational effectiveness.

CONCEPT

Organizational design is an important exercise to create new capabilities to compete in the present and future markets. However, some managers employ it to make cosmetic changes while others use it for concrete purposes. Accordingly, organization design is defined differently by different authors.

In the narrow sense, it is the process of reshaping organization structure and roles to make it more effective in meeting the requirements of an organization. Firms that do not understand its significance go for repeated cosmetic changes in its organization structure. They do likewise because changes in structure are relatively easy to execute and help create an impression that something substantial is happening. However, such attempts often result in little benefit to the business. They may in fact cause more harm by creating cynicism and confusion within the organization. Effective change occurs when managers undertake the design exercise following a systematic approach with clear design objectives driven by a new business strategy or forces in the market.

Taking a broader view, organization design can be defined as the alignment of structure, process, rewards, metrics and talent with the strategy of the business[2].

Roy H. Autry provides the following definition.

More specifically, Organization Design is a formal, guided process for integrating the people, information and technology of an organization. It is used to match the form of the organization as closely as possible to the purpose(s) the organization seeks to achieve[3].

SCOPE

Organization design has become a field of knowledge with a strong theoretical base and a variety of tools. Peter Drucker and other key thinkers like Lawrence & Lorsch, Galbraith and Nadler, have contributed significantly to it[4]. However, it is viewed as a part of organization effectiveness and organization development. Many organizational experts argue that structural design cannot be an isolated theme, and it requires integration with behaviors, such as leadership behaviors and team effectiveness.

According to Banner and Gagné organizational design involves study of the following: how an organization is put together; who reports to whom; the degree of centralization or decision-making power concentrated at the top; and the extent of the rules, policies, regulations, and procedures in an organization[5].

NATURE

The process of organizational design has the following features.

Evolutionary

Entrepreneurs or founders pay little attention to organizational design for two reasons: (i) the size is small and functions are limited, and (ii) environment is narrowly interpreted. As a result, the organization takes shape of a charismatic, line type organization employing a functional structure with centralized decision-making. Over time, as the organization grows, expanding and diversifying activities, a divisional structure becomes necessary and coordination problems crop up. Pressure builds for changing the organization. Thus, every organizational design has a chronological history.

Burton and Thakur trace the evolution through five stages of a life cycle: birth stage, youth stage, middle stage, maturity stage and decay stage[6].

1. *Birth stage:* In this stage the organization is informal. A sort of line organization forms with highly centralized decision-making. There are usually few rules and regulations, no professional staff and no internal system for planning.

2. *Youth stage:* As sales for the company's products and services increases in this stage, a few professionals and administrative personnel are employed. Though authority is centralized, there is emergence of consultative leadership as a few trusted employees are involved in decision-making process. With increase in activity some formal rules and procedures will be formulated.

3. *Middle stage:*   By this stage, organization is successful and grown in size. There is an attempt at formalising organization. The structure is loaded with departments, supporting staff departments and professional groups and clerical staffs. With large set of rules and regulations it becomes a bureaucratic set-up.

4. *Maturity stage:*   In maturity stage organization has become very large. Managers capable of driving its growth will attempt to make it innovative and flexible. They decentralise authority, create project and matrix structures and flatten the organizations. The lateral structures are filled with a variety of liaison personnel, task forces, and project teams.

5. *Decay stage:*   Some organizations become inflexible with bureaucratic rules and regulations, and centralized authority. As a result of the rigid virtual hierarchy, they move towards stagnation and decay.

Socio-technical

Organizational design is a socio-technical activity. A design is a solution to problems and requires learning new attitudes, skills and knowledge by people associated with it. It cannot, as such, adopt a mechanistic approach. It requires human touch and be guided by social values. It must meet the job expectations of people for variation and meaning in work. It has to consider the needs for continuous learning, team work, and meaningful relationship with outside society.

Continuous

Organizational design is a continuous process. Managers operating in a dynamic environment have to learn how to periodically re-fashion their organizational arrangements. With changes either inside or outside of the organization existing design falls out of balance, warranting a new exercise. High performance seeking managers have to appreciate that organization design is a continuous process.

Flexible

Organizational design needs to be compatible with goals and strategies of the organization. The process of design must be complementary with the changes in the environment. As such, a fair degree of flexibility is important in design process and outcomes. Variations during the design process are to be incorporated and resulting organization has to be flexible, interactive and participatory.

DESIGN PROCESS

The organization design process can be divided into the following steps and explained:

Step 1:   Identify Need for Organizational Design

Organizational design process is necessary in two situations: (i) At the time of setting up a new enterprise, and (ii) when existing organization has become ineffective in delivering results. The failure to perform can be due to internal or external factors as illustrated in Table 3.1.

TABLE 3.1 Causal Factors for Organization Design

Factor	Suggested changes in organization
Overstaffing	Downsizing
Excessive diversification	Focus on power brands. Simplification
Inefficiency in processes	Lean organization
Lack of innovation	Learning organization
Global expansion	Geographical dispersion
Information technology	Virtual organization
Rise in standards of processes and products	High tech organizations with team work
Rise of services	Flat, team based organizations

Step 2: Create Strategy

Organization design begins with the creation of a strategy, derived from clear, concise statements of purpose, and vision, and mission of organization. Organizations strive to achieve some explicit long range goals, in accordance with their mission, vision and values. Mission defines the overall purpose to which organization is basically committed both philosophically and functionally. Vision refers to the image that people have in their minds about how the organization should be in future. Values are the norms shared among organizational members to make choices consistent with the society standards adopted by the organization.

Strategies are made at the top and handed down to the chief executive officer for implementation. Strategy unifies the intent of the organization and provides unity of direction for members to accomplish desired outcomes. Develop Key Performance Indicators (KPIs) to guide the decisions and actions in the organization.

Step 3: Design Structure

Develop a structure that defines the formal relationships among people and specifies both their roles and their responsibilities. Different types of structures are experimented by different organizations. One can use them with necessary modifications to serve the designed purposes.

Step 4: Establish Systems

To connect people with each other in meaningful and purposeful ways employ necessary information and technology. The various methods through which systems can be established are:

1. *Decision-making:*   Conduct decisions analysis and specify the decision-making process and decision-making roles. Establish relationships for proper reporting by each decision maker to the concerned superiors.

2. *Administrative system:*   Design administrative systems that govern the organization through guidelines, procedures and policies.

3. *Information system:* Setup information flow to provide inputs to decisions, design information processing methods for decision-making, and streamline information sharing approaches among members. Also, establish procedures to store and capture information.

4. *Technical system:* Conduct activities analysis. Integrate activities for high performance by linking tasks with technologies required and placing them in the right layout of buildings/facilities.

Design people system

Establish proper systems for people to cooperate and achieve excellence in their assignments.

1. *Staffing systems:* Create right kind of employment and engagement practices to attract and retain competent people.

2. *Skill harnessing system:* Put in place a talent management system. Develop high performance orientation through proper leadership practices (developing, coaching, mentoring, appraising, counseling and rewarding).

3. *Culture:* Identify the kind of characteristics, skills and work place behaviors desirable in the organization along with the guiding principles that govern their work and achievement. Establish and reinforce them through education, training and reward systems.

Step 5: Implementation

It is important to create a team of people who are responsible for implementation. Set up time-lines, provide resources required, and evolve contingency plans taking into cognizance potential bottlenecks. To make implementation effective the implementation team should be involved in the whole design process. Then they will develop commitment to the change, and be capable of explaining the rationale behind the change process to others. As a result, the implementation takes place much more easily and seamlessly.

Step 6: Review and Renewal

Organization design is not a one time process. There is a need for periodical reviews for deciding on changes needed to ensure continuing optimum performance. Develop a review calendar. Based on reviews take renewal decisions. An organization redesign process may take anywhere between one and five years. It all depends on the culture of the organization, nature of environment and the commitment of top management to the process.

Robert Simons outlined the steps involved in organization design[7]. Table 3.2 shows them.

TABLE 3.2   Steps in Organization Design

Steps	Variables	Description
Examine the 4Cs	Customer definition	Identify customer segments and their characteristics
	Critical performance variables	Establish strategic intentions, milestones and tactics
	Creative tension	Decide on degree of innovativeness and scope for experimentation
	Commitment to others	Know the importance of shared responsibility in achieving goals
Apply the tools at hand	Resources	Identify availability of resources used in the organization
	Measures and awards	Examine the system of goals, whether they are challenging but achievable, and design incentives
	Out-of-the-box pressure	Ascertain the need for creative ideas and novel behaviors
	Leadership	Identify style of leadership-participatory or bureaucratic
Design the four levers	Unit structure	Decide whether it is individual or group
	Diagnostic control systems	Establish measures used to monitor organizational outcomes and correct deviations from standards
	Interactive networks	Decide on the extent of manager's involvement regularly and personally in the decision of subordinates
	Shared responsibilities	Define responsibility to the mission, customers, team, and other constituents
Align the four spans	Control	Specify the range of resources under control of a manager for which he is accountable
	Accountability	Establish the range of trade-offs that affect the performance measures in performance evaluation of managers
	Influence	Define the width of the influence-scope to shape behavior of others
	Support	Establish the range of support that a manager can expect from people in other units

TYPES OF ORGANIZATIONAL DESIGNS

Internal organization structures or departments can be designed in the following forms:

1. Simple organizational design
2. Functional design
3. Bureaucratic design

4. Divisional design
5. Matrix design
6. Team structure design
7. Network design
8. Virtual structure design
9. Adhocracy design

Simple Organizational Design

This is employed in case of small business or service organizations, which have fewer employees, limited branches and small turnover. A sole trading firm or a primary school can be good examples of the same.

Features

The features of the simple organization are:

1. *Flat structure:* It consists of 2–3 levels of authority.

2. *Centralized authority:* The decision-making power resides at the top in the hands of owner or his representative. The span of control will be wide.

3. *Low formalization:* Activities are not structured. Work is structured through direct supervision and control.

4. *Limited specialization:* Most of the employees will be able to perform variety of tasks as there is no emphasis on specialization. However, some functions like legal affairs, production, accounting and sales may be specialized.

Merits

The merits of the simple organization are:

1. *Simplicity:* The structure is simple with less number of levels and functions.

2. *Centralization:* Decisions are taken at the top. Quick decision-making is possible as subordinates are not involved.

3. *Communication:* Mostly top-down and oral.

4. *Economical:* It is inexpensive at it employs people who are less qualified.

Demerits

Following are the demerits of the simple organization:

1. *Overburdened top:* Top manager is over burdened as all authority is centralized.

2. *Poor morale:* People who like freedom and participation will feel dissatisfied.

Functional Design

Most of the organizations today employ functional structures at one level or other. Frederick Winslow Taylor advocated functional specialization at shop floor level. He advocated functional foremanship by separating planning and execution functions. In all, he suggested a system of 8 bosses—four in planning and four in executions[8].

- *Bosses in planning:* Instruction card clerk, time and cost clerk, route clerk and shop disciplinarian.
- *Bosses in execution:* Gang boss, Speed boss, Repair boss and Inspector.

Today, the concept is applied at the top level to put the specialists in the top position throughout the enterprise. Firms having limited product lines, operating in a stable environment and limited market segments will adopt this type of structure.

Features

The features of the functional organization are:

1. *Specialization:* Organizational activities are divided into specific functions, such as operations, finance, marketing and human resources.

2. *Varied authorities:* Three type of authorities exist—line, staff and function. Line authority is concerned with decision-making and execution. Staff authority is limited to providing assistance or advice to line managers. Functional authority is limited to the specific function to facilitate decision-making by functional experts.

3. *Expert leadership:* Each functional area is put under the charge of functional specialists with requisite functional authority.

4. *Standardization:* Procedures and repetitive tasks are standardized to make them routine as far as possible.

Merits

The merits of functional structure are given as follows:

1. *Functional specialization:* Employees working in a functional area become experts by learning more by observation, study and experience. There are opportunities to learn more by way of interaction with other employees.

2. *Efficiency:* As people perform same tasks repetitively, they will be able to perform them more efficiently. Further, standardization of activities will help improve efficiency of employees.

3. *Sound decision-making:* As there is functional centralization, the decisions will be sound and quick. The assistance as well as expert advice provided by staff departments help improve decisions of line managers.

4. *Supervision and control:* Well-trained supervisors monitor the performance of subordinates and ensure attainment of desired results. Management by exception that focuses on deviations (gaps, mistakes and overlaps) can be practiced.

5. *Operational economy:* Standardization of work eliminates unnecessary expenditure of effort and time and minimizes costs.

Demerits

Some of the demerits of this type of organization are as follows:

1. *Narrow outlook:* Too narrow division of work leads to loss of general perspective. Cross-functional skills cannot be developed.

2. *Conflicts:* Inter-functional rivalry and conflicts arise. Functional managers may resort to empire building and pursue goals that may come into conflict with those of other functions or organization.

3. *Boredom and monotony:* Employees performing routine tasks in a narrow domain may experience boredom and monotony.

4. *Problem in horizontal integration:* Horizontal integration across functional departments becomes difficult when organizations become large with multiple products and operates at multiple locations.

Bureaucratic Design

Max Weber, a German sociologist, identified and described bureaucratic organization[9]. He called them rational-legal structures as they follow rules and function within the bounds of authority given by organization.

Features

According to Weber, following characteristics are found in bureaucratic organizations:

1. *Division of work and specialization:* There is a division of work leading to each office functioning with a defined sphere of competence.

2. *Hierarchy:* A structure with many levels is formed by the division of power and ranking of offices.

3. *Formalization:* A written description of rules and guidelines defining clearly authority and responsibility of each job and department is provided. Selection and appointments, salaries, promotion and other manpower decisions are guided by rules of organization.

4. *Discipline:* Every employee should follow the rules and regulations and never overstep the bounds of the authority, entrusted to him or her by the organization.

5. *Procedures and records:* Officers deal with clients according to rules and procedures.

Merits

The merits of the structure are given as under:

1. *Decision-making:* As decisions are based on well-established rules and procedures decision-making will be quick and unbiased.

2. *Equality:* Decisions and procedures are standardized to provide equity, to bring uniformity in decisions and actions as well as to enhance effectiveness and efficiency of offices.

Demerits

The merits of the structure are given as under:

1. *Impersonal:* Going by rules and regulations (controls), organizations ignore human needs of employees and clients. Job dissatisfaction, absenteeism and employee turnover are observed.

2. *Rigidity:* Organizations are slow in adaptation to changing situations.

3. *Red-tape:* With too many levels, there will be inordinate delays in decision-making and implementation.

4. *Stifles creativity:* Rigidity and bossism stifles creativity and initiative of employees at subordinate levels.

Divisional Design

Organizations start with functional design. As they expand and serve markets in different places they incorporate place design features and become multilocation and multinational firms. When new opportunities for further growth are found in diversification, they seek diversification add new product lines and become multi-product firms. As business expands and customer segmentation becomes necessary, organizations resort to customer divisions or departments. Large organizations which have become complex with multiple products, multiple markets, and multiple locations have two options.

1. Spin-off into a free-standing subsidiaries.
2. Design divisional structures to cater to products, customers or locations and make each division a Strategic Business Unit (SBU).

Smaller organizations can employ cross-functional work teams as follows:

1. Establish project teams/task forces on ad hoc basis
2. Set up dedicated departments

Three different types of divisional structures are found in practice. They are as given in Table 3.3.

TABLE 3.3   Types of Divisional Structures

Design	Description	Suitability
Geographic/place	Establishing branches or divisions at different places with in a country or in other countries	When a company decides to take advantage of demand for products and services in different geographic areas
Product	Setting up divisions for different products or product lines of an organization	When a company adopts product/service diversification strategy
Customer	Creating units or branches or divisions to serve different customer groups	When a company finds focusing on different customer segments is profitable

Features

It has its own resources such as finance, marketing, equipments, maintenance, etc. These divisions work independently, taking strategic directives from the top management.

1. There will be several parallel teams focusing on a single product or service line.
2. They are semi-autonomous and mostly self-managed groups. Each division manages its own HR, marketing and production functions. However, each division will act according to the strategic directives provided from top management (headquarters).
3. Each division will have its own top executive—often a Vice President.
4. Each division focuses on a product or customer or market.

Merits

The advantages of creating divisions are many.

1. Focus: Divisions can focus upon a single product or service or market, and develop sound business.

2. Tailor-made strategies: Strategies can be developed to promote a product or serve a customer or a specific market.

3. Effective controls: With decentralization, the responsibility for results like profit/loss is placed on divisional manager.

4. Right culture: Culture can be built in the division appropriate to the place and function. However, uniform culture in all divisions may not be possible.

5. Right decisions: As decisions are close to the scene of action, they will be quick and meet local needs effectively.

6. Innovation: Functional specialization fosters creation and sharing of knowledge and encourages innovation.

7. Training: It offers an excellent training ground for higher-level general managers.

Demerits

The disadvantages of this arrangement are:

1. *Inter division rivalry:*   Divisions may compete for resources with self interest. Sometimes it can be detrimental to the organization.

2. *Uneconomical:*   Duplication of equipment and resources may increase costs.

Challenges

However, it poses the following challenges to top management in establishing relationships between head office and divisions.

1. *Uniformity vs diversity:*   Among divisions, how much uniformity should be imposed and how much diversity should be allowed? Top management has to examine this issue carefully.

2. *Division vs company image:*   With different divisions operating in different cultures, the onus of creating and maintaining the company image becomes a challenge. Top management has to coordinate the efforts of different divisional managers.

3. *Service needs vs economy:*   The provision of adequate services at different divisions may result in duplication and create cost disadvantages. As such, top management has to make staffing decisions carefully.

Matrix Design

Matrix organization structures were introduced in the airspace industry in the 50's to cope with complex projects. Matrix organization is also called project organization or grid organization. The adoption of matrix organisation becomes necessary when functional needs and product or place concerns are significant.

Evolutionary approach

Ford and Randolph observed that companies respond in a gradual way to growing demands like new product development or cultivation of new markets[10]. The response will move from ad hoc arrangements to permanent structures as follows:

Stage **1:** *Temporary task force:*   When new opportunities are identified organization responds by forming a temporary task force consisting of representatives from different functional departments to respond appropriately.

Stage **2:** *Permanent committee:*   To consolidate response to the new found opportunities, and to find for new opportunities, the temporary task force is replaced by a permanent committee.

Stage **3:** *Project organization:*   When an action oriented team of people are essential to achieve an accepted goal, project managers are appointed and provided staff drawn from the permanent functional structure. This results in the formation of a matrix organization.

Features

It is formed using two variables—functional and another one product/project.

1. It uses teams of cross-functional employees.
2. Employees report to their boss in the parent department (functional head) as well as to the project manager.
3. Each project represents a potential profit center. Each project manager reports directly to the Vice President and the General Manager.

For example, a project organization may be organized in different technical departments, such as mechanical engineering, electrical engineering, and civil engineering. In addition, project teams or departments are formed drawing required people from the technical departments. Typically, the employees may move from one project team to another as new projects are started, but their parent technical department remains the same.

Types

Three variants of matrix structure are: weak, balanced and strong ones. Table 3.4 shows the role of managers in the three types of structures.

TABLE 3.4 Roles of Managers in Matrix Structures

Type	Functional manger	Project manager
Weak/functional	Full control over the resources and project areas	With limited authority oversee the cross-functional aspects of the project
Balanced/functional	Shares authority with project manager	Oversees project
Strong/project	Provides technical expertise and assign resources as needed	Responsible fully for the project

Merits

The merits of this structure are given as under:

1. *Specialization:* Employees specialize under the guidance of functional manager.

2. *Skill development:* With the experience gained in different projects, employees develop a wider set of skills.

3. *Motivation:* Teams will have high degree of commitment and motivation.

4. *Communication:* There will be good sharing of information among employees working in a team.

5. *Resource coordination:* Resources are allocated efficiently and managed for different projects based on a priority basis.

6. *Flexibility:* Teams can be changed and utilized as per changing needs.

7. *Economy:* As key people can be shared, the project cost is minimized.

Demerits

The demerits of this structure are as follows:

1. Conflict: Dual reporting relationships may sometimes lead to stress and conflict.

2. Need for high level of skills: Project managers need good interpersonal skills, to resolve problems arising between functional and project orientations and complaints of functional managers.

3. Power struggle: Struggle for power is found as boundaries of authority and responsibility overlap.

4. Difficulty in controlling: Difficulties in monitoring performance of employees may arise. There will be a tendency of passing the blame on others.

5. Employee attitudinal problems: Employees used to unity of command, and working in a permanent set up have to adopt to the dual authority relationships and temporary nature of the organization.

Team Structure Design

Team-based lateral organizational structure emerged during the 1990s, and was implemented by corporations such as Ford, Proctor and Gamble and General Motors.

Features

The distinguishing features of this organization type are:

1. It is built with self-managed teams.
2. The teams are formed with employees on the same level to make a specific product and offer a service to a specific client group.
3. It is flat in structure with less number of levels.
4. It relies on extensive lateral communication.

Merits

The merits of this structure are:

1. Team work: There will be good cooperation and sound decision-making among self-managed teams.

2. No delays no overheads: There will be less reliance on managerial hierarchy. Decisions will be collective and implementation will be fast.

3. Empowerment: Employees are empowered and trained to perform well in teams assuming responsibility for goal achievement.

Demerits

The demerits of this arrangement are:

1. *Stress:* Employees experience stress due to pressure to perform better, and desire to gain recognition. Team leaders experience stress in the early stages of team development as there will be resistance to take up responsibilities.

2. *Lack of clarity in career path:* Career paths are not as clear as we find in hierarchical structures.

3. *Loss of power:* Managers desirous of power, experience loss of functional power.

Network Design

A network structure is also called modular, cluster or spider web arrangement. It is a collaborative structure formed by alliance of several organizations for producing a product or providing a service.

Features

The features of this arrangement are:

1. *Network:* A firm forming network is the core or hub of the structure. It networks with several satellite organizations. The satellite organizations may be located anywhere in the world.

2. *Distinctive competence:* The core firm provides one or two core competencies, which it considers critical for maintaining its competitive advantage.

3. *Competent partners:* It unbundles the non-critical tasks to satellite organizations, which have the required core competencies to perform the assigned tasks, and specifies what result is expected.

4. *Customer-oriented:* The core firm will be in contact with the customers. In fact, the organization is more outward oriented with focus on customers and less internally driven.

5. *Communication:* The core firm will maintain communication with firms on the network through information and communication technology.

 This type of structure becomes necessary under the following conditions:

 1. When a firm finds it difficult to perform its operations which have become varied and complex.
 2. When it fails to keep up with the changing technology.

Merits

The merits of this structure are:

1. *Competitive advantage:* Facilitates distributing work to units that have appropriate competencies.

2. *Flexibility:* Outsourcing involves contractual relationships. As such, one can add or reduce them as per changing needs.

3. *Cost effective:* Satellite firms operating at their maximum efficiency will be cost-effective in supplying outputs.

Demerits

Following are the demerits of this structure:

1. *Threat of copying:* Information sharing for the purpose of coordination may pose a threat of infringement of intellectual property rights.

2. *Coordination problems:* Difficult to exercise control on operations of satellite firms—to ensure right supply and right quality. There is a danger of failure when member units fail to deliver products or services as expected. There is a need for integration managers.

Virtual Structure Design

Virtual organization is a special form of boundary less organization. It is evolved to face challenges arising from global operations and critical issues related to resources, personnel and logistics. Today, more and more organizations are looking at virtual organizations. Lipnack & Stamps define a virtual team as follows.[11]

A group of people who interact through interdependent tasks guided by common purpose, that works across space, time, and organizational boundaries, with links strengthened by webs of communication technologies.

Features

The important features of this organization are:

1. *Network:* It represents a geographically dispersed network of companies, institutions and/ or individuals.

2. *Reciprocal relationship:* The members function with a common business understanding and deliver a product or service. They are provided with authority and responsibility along with a statement of mission, vision and goals. They function to meet customer demands.

3. *Technology enabled:* Telecommunications and computing technologies help overcome barriers of distance and time.

4. *Informal communication:* Owing to a lack of formal rules, procedures, clear reporting relationships, informal communication dominates.

Merits

Given below are the merits of the organization structure:

1. *Competitive advantage:* Facilitates teamwork and enhances competitive advantage.

2. *Flexibility:* Responds readily to dynamic changes in the environment and adopts quickly.

Demerits

The following demerits are identified with the structure:

1. *Wastage of time:*   Due to absence of supervisor, employee my focus on non-work activities

2. *Communication problems:*   Problems of accent and slang in oral communication and confusion over teleconferencing protocols are common.

3. *Stress:*   Traditional managers feel insecure particularly in a crisis.

4. *Insecurity:*   Threat from hackers who may steal or destroy databases.

5. *Absence of human touch:*   Employees miss the face-to-face interaction.

6. *Integration problems:*   Organization setting up virtual network has to take steps to integrate partners to achieve teamwork and success.

Adhocracy Design

Adhocratic structures refer to free form or organic organization structures. They are employed in high technology and high growth organizations.

Features

1. There is no formal structure.
2. It is usually small.
3. Managerial styles tend to be more informal and situational.

Merits

1. They are flexible and adaptive.
2. They bring together people with diverse professional skills to solve a problem.
3. They are well-suited for complex and non-standard work and rely on informal structures.

Demerits

1. Network problems, power outages and poor connectivity of cell phones paralyse their functioning.
2. Lack of clear communication lines.
3. Lack of formalised procedures may lead to in consistent decision making.

DESIGN DETERMINANTS

Richard Daft has divided dimensions of the organization into structural and contextual categories[12].

1. **Structural dimensions** are centralization, formalization, hierarchy, rountinization specialization and training.
2. **Contextual dimensions** are culture, environment, goals, size and technology.

According to Robert Simon, managers must design organizations that can adapt over time[13]. Organizations have to learn to reconcile the tensions between: (i) strategy and structure, (ii) accountability and adaptability, (iii) ladders and rings, and (iv) self interest and mission success.

1. *Strategy and structure:* Strategic decisions are dependent on structure as it is the structure that determines the speed and quantity of information processing. As such, in an entrepreneurial organization, structure design decisions are based on the requirements of strategy. In simple terms, structure follows strategy.

2. *Accountability and adaptability:* Authority without responsibility is detrimental to organizational interests. Employees are to be made answerable for performance on some measured dimension. Accountability, should not limit freedom to experiment and innovate. It should foster a spirit of adaptability and creativity.

3. *Ladders and rings:* Effective organizations need hierarchical structure (ladders) as well as networks (rings). When the emphasis is more on ladders, organizations tend to be bureaucratic.

4. *Self-interest and mission success:* Organization should promote employee interests while promoting organizational purposes.

Managers have to examine four issues before undertaking organizational design:

1. Customer definition—who is the primary customer?
2. Critical performance variables—strategic intensions, tactics, milestones
3. Creative tension—need to encourage experimentation and new ideas
4. Commitment to others—importance of shared responsibility in achieving organizational goals.

STRUCTURAL COMPONENTS

Organizational design is a challenging task of evolving a structure that provides role clarity and proper opportunity for people to contribute to the effectiveness of organizations. An effective organizational design, as such, has to consider the elements given in Table 3.5.

TABLE 3.5 Structural Components of Organizations

S.No.	Component	Description
1	Specialization	The degree to which activities are divided into separate jobs
2	Departmentalization	The degree to which specialized and common jobs are grouped together or cross-functional teams encouraged?
3	Centralization	The degree to which authority is concentrated at the top level
4	Formalization	The degree which activities and decisions are governed by policies, procedures, standards and rules
5	Span of control	The degree to which span of control is made wide
6	Hierarchy of authority	The degree to which the levels are created
7	Coordination	The degree to which people and groups are integrated to perform effectively together

Specialization

Specialization refers to focusing on learning and doing a limited work. It is achieved by division of work and training. Classical theorists advocated division of work, which refers to dividing work into separate, manageable jobs and assigning them to employees, and training them to gain expertise. As a result of work specialization, are able to get benefits in terms of efficiency and productivity. Specialization at operating level has resulted in problems like fatigue, boredom, low quality and employee absenteeism. To remedy this, organizations have adopted techniques, like job enlargement and job enrichment. At functional level, specialization resulted in departmentalization.

Departmentalization

While specialization provided division of work, departmentalization provided basis for grouping of jobs to facilitate performance and coordination of common tasks. Traditional approaches to departmentalization used bases, like function, product, location and customer. They proved to be successful in stable environments. As environment has become dynamic, modern approaches required new bases for design. As a result, we have today, matrix, team, network and virtual organizations which allow the functioning of cross-functional teams.

Centralization

According to Fayol "Everything which goes to increase the importance of the subordinate's role is decentralization and everything which goes to reduce it is centralization[14]." Two types of centralization measures are described.

1. *Vertical centralization:* It is high when decision making power resides in a small group of people at the top. It is low when employees at lower levels of hierarchy are allowed to take independent decisions.

2. *Horizontal centralization:* It is high when central authority makes all decisions. It is low when different organizational units are permitted to take decisions.

The optimal level of centralization depends on situations. Centralization is desirable when organizations are small, and environments are hostile. Larger organizations tend to decentralize to become market responsive. When environment is dynamic offering growth opportunities, decentralization is preferred.

Formalization

Formalization refers to the extent to which work, authority and responsibility are codified and followed. Work is formalized by standardization of time and methods. Decisions are formalized by policies and procedures. Behaviors are formalized by establishing formal relationships, rules and code of conduct. Formalization is influenced by factors like technology, size and organizational traditions.

1. Organizations having routine technologies are more formalized, than those using non-routine technology.
2. Large organization formalize more to achieve standardization, coordination and uniformity than small ones.
3. Tradition refers to the way people are used to do things in organizations. If an organization has codified organization procedure manuals, it continues to follow it and remain more formalized over time.

Research has shown that professional management has favored less formalization to give scope to individual initiatives and team performance.

Span of Control

It refers to the number of employees that a supervisor can handle effectively. There are two types of span of control—narrow and wide. In narrow span, a manager supervises a limited number of employees at one time, whereas in wide span, a manager is required to supervise a large group of persons at one time. Span decisions are influenced by several factors. Narrow span is preferred when work requires tight control and subordinate employees are less mature. Wide span is possible when work is standardized, or when self-directed teams with informal communication and specialized knowledge are to be supervised.

Hierarchy of Authority

A hierarchy represents the chain of authority relationships or levels of authority in an organization. The hierarchy of authority in an organization can be neatly presented by drawing an organization chart. Hierarchy of authority is related to two key concepts of organization-chain of command and unity of command.

1. *Chain of command:* It is referred to as the scalar chain. It is a vertical, clear unbroken line of authority and responsibility relationships from top to lowest level positions in organizations.

2. *Unity of command:* It holds that a subordinate has to take order from only one boss.

In today's competitive environment, chain of command has become short and unity of command is less emphasized.

Coordination

Coordination refers to synchronization and harmonization of the work of individuals, teams and units in the organization. Synchronization refers to bringing together in respect of time factor, whereas harmonization refers to the mutual understanding and cooperation. The coordination problem arises due to four main differences—in goal-orientation, in time-orientation, in interpersonal orientation and formality of structure.

Coordination is achieved by different mechanisms, like informal communication, formal hierarchy and standardization.

1. Large organizations create integrator roles that use informal communication to coordinate activities. For example, brand managers seeks to coordinate the activities of marketing, production, design and warehousing.
2. Formal hierarchy provides superior positions of authority to achieve coordination in the work of subordinates.
3. Standardization of work and procedures reduce uncertainty, and help create routine behaviors. As such, they facilitate better understanding and timely performance among work groups.

ORGANIZATIONAL DESIGN AND SIZE

Size is measured by number of employees, volume of outputs, volume of sales/turnover, number of customers, size of assets, or operational capacity. Structural characteristics differ with size.

Large is Complex and Tall

As organizations grow, complexity increases. There will be problems of handling large volumes of inputs and outputs, operating processes and managing people. There is a tendency of formalization with division of labor with emphasis on specialization and formation functional structures with line and staff departments. The differentiation increases complexity, and to achieve greater coordination, layers of management will be added. As hierarchy increases organizations grow tall. Concentration of power at the top becomes difficult and decentralization with controls will be introduced. Control is retained through standard written policies and procedures.

Small is Simple and Flat

Typically, small organizations have flat structures with 2 or 3 levels of hierarchy. They look like team structures with narrow spans of control and informal relationships. There is little specialization. In fact, small organization could be paralyzed by too much specialization.

Tall vs Flat Organizations

Tall structures are found in case of organizations having number of products and locations.

Advantages
Some of the advantages of tall organizations are:

1. *Close supervision:* Due to narrow span of controls, each manager can supervise his employees closely and get desired results.

2. *Clarity:* The structure provides clear understanding of relationships and paths of progression in career.

Disadvantages

Some of the disadvantages of tall organizations are:

1. *Slow decision-making:* The process of decision-making will be slow as approval process is lengthy. Approvals are necessary at different layers of authority.

2. *Poor communication:* Communication flows tend to be slow and there is the danger of distortion as communication is filtered through different levels.

3. *High costs:* The supervision costs are high as there are more supervisors due to more levels.
Flat structure is limited to small organizations such as partnerships, co-operatives and some private limited companies.

Advantages

The advantages of flat organizations are:

1. *Communication:* Information flows in many directions and reaches all the people in less time. Networks, self managed teams, and wide span of controls, permit better communication among employees.

2. *Sound decision-making:* Decision can be taken based on collective opinion of participants and good communication. As such, decisions as well as decision processes will be sound.

3. *High morale:* Employees tend to be more satisfied and willing to commit to organization.

Disadvantages

The disadvantages of flat organizations are:

1. *Violation of unity of command:* Flat organization structures in case of large organization tend to make use of matrix structures. In these organizations dual command is common.

2. *Multiple roles:* Employees play different roles and get involved in different tasks or projects. As such, there is no clarity in career progression paths.

Recent Trends

Many large organizations especially the public sector enterprises in mid twentieth century were founded on linear, segmented, hierarchical design principles suggested by classical theorists. Mabey, Salaman and Storey[15] maintained that tall structures with 20 plus levels between the chief executive and shop floor operative were created and the governing principles were— hierarchy and command control. A trend away from tall structures began in the beginning of twentieth century. The major drivers were changes in environment like advancement of technology, globalization, and intensifying competition. There were mergers and demergers and experiments with different design approaches. New approaches, like downsizing, reengineering, delayering, and outsourcing gave way to flat organizational designs. Organizations slimmed down to become flexible and effective.

ORGANIZATION DESIGN AND CULTURE

Organizational design has to take into cognizance the cultural factor. While the structure establishes the positions of CEO, GM, etc., it's the culture that decides how people actually work and take decisions. In fact, good managers must work from a more anthropological model. Culture refers to the values and norms. Values indicate preferences for certain behaviors and outcomes, and norms specify the acceptable ways of pursuing goals. Culture creates a set of shared understanding of solving problems relating to internal integration and external adaptation. Cameron and Quinn's provided a categorization[16] of organizational effectiveness perspectives and associated types of organizations, as shown in Table 3.6.

TABLE 3.6   Types of Cultures

Focus	Task	Stability/Control	Change/Flexibility
Internal	Integration	Hierarchy	Clan
External	Differentiation	Market	Adhocracy

We will now find out the structures that arise from these cultures.

1. *Hierarchy or control culture:*   The prefer controls. They value well-defined structure for authority and decision-making, standardization in work, and control.

2. *Clan or collaborate culture:*   Though similar to hierarchy is inward focus they emphasize on flexibility and discretion to facilitate collaboration of employees in facing external environment.

3. *Market or compete culture:*   Organizations value competitiveness and productivity. For this, they emphasize on external partnerships and internal stability through hierarchical control.

4. *Adhocracy or create culture:*   They emphasize on flexibility and discretion like the clan culture, and seek differentiation like market culture through external partnerships. High-tech companies adopt this culture to get innovative ideas from external sources through media networks.

Handy identified organization structures suitable for four types of culture[17] as shown in Table 3.7.

TABLE 3.7   Culture Types and Organization Structures

Culture type	Description	Structure
Power	Power and control radiate from the center like a web	Bureaucracy
Role	Role descriptions with authority and responsibility as well as rules and procedures	Hierarchical bureaucracies
Task	Team approach for task performance	Matrix structure
Person	Individuals believe themselves superior to the organization	Charismatic

ORGANIZATION DESIGN AND TECHNOLOGY

Technology is defined as the application of knowledge to create products, processes, equipment and tools/techniques. In other words, it refers to the process by which an organization converts the inputs (people, materials, equipment, money, plant, and facility, etc.).

Woodward Study

Joan Woodward[18] conducted research to find linkage between technology and structure by studying 100 manufacturing firms in the southern part of England. She found that organizations were more effective when their technology matched the organization's structure. She described the technical complexity of a manufacturing process as the degree of its mechanization—unit technology as the least complex and the continuous process production as the most complex. She identified three types of technology and found organizations structures suitable to them. Table 3.8 shows the technology classification and organization structures.

TABLE 3.8 Production Systems and Organization Structure

Production/ technology	Technology	Description	Example	Organization structure
Small batch production	Unit technology	Identical products Small volumes Customized to market Flexible processes	Furniture, bakeries, and packaging	Organic structure
Mass production	Mass technology	Standard products in different models Large volumes Assembly line Automation for standard and repetitive tasks	Automobiles, Refrigerators.	Mechanistic structure
Continuous production	Complex technology	Standard product with some variety Large volume Series of processes, often automated	Oil refinery, Nuclear power plant	Organic structure

Small Batch Production/Craft Production

This is employed to produce identical products in small numbers. Products are literally custom made. Production process and methods are flexible. As such, machines and work patterns will frequently change. Craft production process depends mostly on people's skills and knowledge. The work processes are flexible and unpredictable, as such, it is not amenable to automation or programming. The organization structure is simple and organic with the following features:

1. Wide supervisory span of control (23 members)
2. Less formalized and less centralized
3. A few levels of hierarchy (3 levels) leading to flat organization
4. Staff mix is comprises more workers and less number of managers

5. There is close interaction among workers through heavy oral communication and less written communication

Mass Production

This is employed to carry out large scale production of standardized, identical products. Through routine tasks and standard procedures number individual components are assembled through many stages of a production line. Automation of tasks enables small number of workers to achieve large volumes of output. Some degree of customization is possible. Different models are created through variations of basically similar products to customize products to different market segments.

The organization structure is complex and mechanistic with the following features:

1. Wide supervisory span of control (48 members)
2. More formalized and highly centralized
3. More number of levels of hierarchy (4 levels) leading to tall organization
4. More number of managers
5. Workers are interdependent but socially isolated. Less oral communication and more written communication

Continuous Process Production

Production is carried out through a series of standard processes without interruption–running 24 hours a day, seven days a week to maximize production. Often automated, it requires a few workers. The organization structure is organic with the following features:

1. Relatively narrow supervisory span of control (15 members). The workers are skilled and less in number due to automation
2. Less formalized and less centralized
3. More number of levels of hierarchy (6 levels) leading to tall organization
4. More number of managers
5. Close interaction among employees; more oral communication and less written communication

Charles Perrow's Models

Charles Perrow[19] focused on exceptions (novel, unexpected events) that affected structure. He developed a classification of technology based on two dimensions:

1. *Task variability:* The number of exceptions (unexpected, novel events) that occur in the process. Exceptions are few in routine technology, like assembly line and more in non-routine technology like R&D.

2. *Problem analyzability:* This refers to methods to respond to variability—ranging from analyzable to unanalyzable.

He identified two approaches to problem-solving. They are:

1. ***Standard, Analytical approach:*** Exceptions which can be solved by adopting an orderly, analytic search process (like mechanic fixing car).

2. ***Novel, Intuitive approach:*** Exceptions which can be solved by relying on intuition or guesswork (like advertising, and film-making).

Table 3.9 shows the Perrow's framework of technology. Table 3.10 presents the structures suitable to the four types of technology.

TABLE 3.9 Technology and Structures

Category	Few exceptions	Many exceptions
Unanalyzable	Craft technology Intuitive approach can be used (Pottery, specialty glass, artwork, plumbing, computer services)	Non-routine Intuitive approach can be used (Film making; aerospace)
Analyzable	Routine technology Standard procedures can be used (Assembly line, screws, daily sales reports)	Engineering Standard design procedures can be used. (Custom machinery, constructing bridges, and dams).

TABLE 3.10 Organization Design Options

Factors	Routine	Engineering	Craft	Non-routine
Structure	Mechanistic	Mostly mechanistic	Mostly organic	Organic
Formalization	High	Moderate	Moderate	Low
Span of control	Wide	Moderate	Moderate to wide	Moderate to narrow
Centralization	High	Moderate	Moderate	Low
Power and discretion	More for Supervisor and relatively less to subordinate	More for Supervisor and relatively less to subordinate	Less for Supervisor and relatively more to subordinate	Maximum to decision maker and implementer
Interdependence	Low between decision maker and implementer	Low between decision maker and implementer	Low between decision maker and implementer	High between decision maker and implementer
Coordination	Planning and feedback from customers	Feedback from implementer key for decision maker	Planning and feedback from customers	Feedback from implementer key for decision maker
Communication	Vertical and written communication	Written and verbal communication	Horizontal, verbal	Horizontal communication, meetings
Staff qualifications	Little training and experience	Formal training	Work experience	Training and experience

Thompson's Technology Classifications

James Thompson[20] has identified three different technologies as explained here.

1. *Mediating technology:* It links the service provider and clients. For example, a customer makes payments to a retailer through a bank credit card.

2. *Long-linked technology:* It links different stages of production to convert raw materials into finished product. Example: Assembly line.

3. *Intensive technology:* It refers to application of a variety of technologies to a process. For example, Hospitals use different technologies to diagnose and cure diseases.

He further identified three types of interdependence of units in the organizations.

1. Pooled interdependence
2. Sequential interdependence
3. Reciprocal interdependence

Table 3.11 shows how coordination is achieved by organizations adopting different technologies.

TABLE 3.11 Thompson's Organizational Types

Form of interdependence	Communi-cation	Coordination	Need to locate close	Type of technology	Example
Pooled	Low	Standardization, rules and procedures	Low	Mediating	Bank
Sequential	Medium	Plans, schedules and feedback	Medium	Long linked	Assembly line
Reciprocal	High	Mutual adjustment and meetings	High	Intensive	Hospital

Pooled interdependence—Mediating technology

The major features are:

1. *Differentiation:* There are several subunits—each one different in nature of tasks and purposes.

2. *Standardization:* The tasks in each subunit are standardized. Different standards are adopted by different units to meet the expectations of different clients.

3. *Uncertainty reduction:* By integration of units, uncertainty in performance is reduced.

Sequential interdependence—Long-linked technology

The major features are:

1. *Serial design of processes:* The processes is sequentially arranged.

2. *Standardization:* The tasks in each subunit are standardized. The standards conform to the standards expected of the final output.

3. *Uncertainty reduction:* This is achieved through planning and scheduling and by ensuring adequate supply of inputs and outputs.

Reciprocal interdependence—Reciprocal technology

The major features are:

1. *Reciprocal relationships:* There is an exchange of outputs among units. Output of one unit becomes input to another unit.

2. *Differentiation:* There are several subunits—each one different in nature of tasks and techniques.

3. *Standardization:* The tasks in each subunit are standardized to achieve efficiency and excellence.

4. *Uncertainty reduction:* By developing a variety of techniques and coordination, uncertainty is reduced. Coordination is achieved by selection, mix and sequencing of techniques.

Impact of Information Technology

Information technology has impacted greatly organization design and the nature of jobs. It has led to the creation of flatter organizations, knowledge work, network structures and self-managed teams.

ORGANIZATIONAL DESIGN AND ENVIRONMENT

Environment refers to factors outside the organization which influence the functioning of organization. Considerable research was conducted on how organization designs vary with nature of environment. The environment-structure linkage is explained by different theories as follows:

Open Systems Theory/Biological Model

The emergence of dynamic and complex environment that influenced behaviors of organizations led to the inception of a new generation of theories, which were based on the open systems model, during the 1960s and through the 1970s. Open systems have following characteristics:

1. *Holistic view:* Systems view provides a big picture. It sees organization as an interrelated subsystem within the supra-environmental system (environment).

2. *Sub-systems:* Systems comprise interdependent and interacting subsystems.

3. *Goals:* Systems have defined goals. Each subsystem will have its own goal and it seeks to optimise its performance due to interlinkages with other subsystems. Their effectiveness is measured by the goal accomplishment and participant satisfaction.

4. *Boundaries:* Open systems have permeable boundaries, which allow exchange of flows and information with environment.

5. *Symbiotic relationship:* The open system approach views organizations as having a symbiotic relationship with the environment. Viable organization needs a constant inflow of resources for planning, and coordination and outflows of outputs acceptable to customers, society and government.

6. *Dynamic steady state:* Systems are dynamic and keep pace with the environment to maintain equilibrium. They engage in maintenance and corrective processes like socialization and control as well as change processes, like learning, growth and differentiation.

7. *Negentropy:* Systems receive continuous feedback (energy) that helps them to recreate and survive for a long period of time.

Kast and Rosenzweig[21] maintained organizational design should focus on creating structural subsystem in relation to goals and value subsystem, psychosocial subsystem, technical subsystem and the coordinating managerial subsystem.

Natural Selection or Ecology Theory

Ecology theories draw on Darwin's theory of natural selection and survival of the fittest. Freeman and Hannan postulated that environment selects organizations that have characteristics that find 'best fit' with its own characteristics[22]. Such of those organizations which could not change to fit to the environment will die-out. This view suggests the need for having dynamic and flexible structures.

Resource Dependency Theory

Pfeffer and Salancik developed resource dependency theory[23]. Organizations are dependent on environment for resources, which are finite. According to Pfeffer and Salancik three factors: (i) overall importance of the resource to the firm, (ii) scarcity of the resource, and (iii) competition between organizations for control of that resource, influence the level of dependence of organizations on particular resources. The lack of control over these critical resources, gives rise to environmental uncertainty. To reduce environmental uncertainty, organizations develop strategies. For example, in hostile environments characterised by scarcity and competition, organizations resort to tight controls on resources utilization through measures like centralization, and formalization.

Strategic Choice Theory

According to Resource dependence theory a firm's strategic options were determined to a large extent by the environment. As such, firms have little strategic choice. However, the finding that some organizations were more effective than others in the same environments, led to the theory of strategic choice. Child[24] observed that organizations adopt bridging strategies like: cooptation, merger, acquisition, etc.

Contingency Theory

Burns and Stalker explained how organizational design is influenced by environment types and explained the characteristics of Mechanistic and Organic structures[25].

1. *Stable environment:* The environment is fairly constant over the time and characterized by certainty. Use mechanistic structures.

2. *Unstable environment:* The environment changes quickly and characterized by uncertainty. Adopt organic structures.

The research of Paul Laurence and Joy Lorsch indicated that managers perceive environment differently by segmenting it[26]. The greater the complexity of environment, the greater the differentiation of internal environment and need for integration. The coordination mechanisms include liaison managers, task forces and teams.

A Summary View

The varying relationships between environment and organizations are identified by McShane and Travaglione[27] as given in Table 3.12.

TABLE 3.12 Environment and Organization Structures

Environment	Situation	Type of structure
Dynamic	High rate of environmental change and uncertainty; Needs continual adaptation	Organic. Networks and team-based structures are needed
Stable	Regular cycles of activity, steady changes in supply of inputs, predictable. Requires Standardization and specialization	Mechanistic. Functional and divisional structures
Complex	Many environmental elements to monitor. Decisions should be close to the scene of action	Decentralized structures
Simple	Few environmental elements to monitor	Centralized structures
Hostile	Resource scarcity and competition create environmental uncertainty.	Organic
Hostile-extreme	Acute shortage of resources may call for tight controls of supply chain	Centralized
Munificent	Plentiful resources and limited competition. Effectiveness is achieved by standardization and formalization	Mechanistic

Mechanistic vs Organic Models

As the Gibson, Ivancevich, and Donnelly stated:

"While the mechanistic model seeks to maximize efficiency and product, the organic model seeks to maximize satisfaction, flexibility and development[28]".

The principal characteristics of these organizations are shown in Table 3.13.

TABLE 3.13   Mechanistics Organic (M–O) Structures

Characteristic	Mechanistic	Organic
Environment	Stable and certain	Dynamic and uncertain
Task differentiation	Low; Tasks are stable and rigidly defined	High; Changed according to environment.
Jobs	Each person corresponds to one task	People play different roles simultaneously over time
Standardization	Extensive use of rules and procedures	Tasks are changed and mutually adjusted
Formalization	High. Well defined hierarchical relationships of authority and responsibility	Low; Network structure of control, authority, and communication
Centralization	Decision-making kept as high as possible	Decentralized, Authority to control tasks is delegated
Integrating mechanisms	Simple, well-defined hierarchy of authority	Complex, Integration by task forces and teams through rapid sharing of information
Specialization	Individual, Employees work and specialize in one task	Joint Specialization, Employees work together and coordinate tasks
Communication	Vertical. Mostly downward much written communication	Lateral, upward, and downward. Much verbal communication

Since organizations are growing entities, continual adaptation to environment is necessary. Rarely companies operate at either end of the M-O spectrum. They employ a blended approach incorporating some mechanistic and some organic traits.

ORGANIZATION DESIGN AND STRATEGY

The relation between structure and strategy is complementary. Without an appropriate structure, it is difficult to develop and implement strategies.

1. *Strategy development:* An organization structure that does not allow creative thinking and cross fertilization of ideas may hinder and weaken the processes of innovative strategy creation.

2. *Strategy implementation:* A sound strategy fails to deliver results if the structure of organization does not facilitate implementation. Effective implementation requires proper alignment of organizational structure with strategic goals and tasks.

In view of this, strategy-structure alignment has become necessary, and there are two approaches to guide designers. Managers have to choose the appropriate approach in view of the challenges faced by the organizations.

1. *Structuralist's approach:* A company's strategic options are bounded by the environment. In other words, structure shapes strategy.

2. *Reconstructionist approach:* This is based on the paradigm of blue ocean strategy, which posits that, the ideas and actions of individual players can shape the economic and industrial landscape. In other words, strategy shapes the structure.

Table 3.14 shows the structural options that best match the strategy.

TABLE 3.14 Strategy and Structural Options

Strategy	Structural options
Cost leadership	Mechanistic functional structure with specialization standardization and formalization
Differentiation	Matrix structure or team based structure with less centralization
Innovation	Organic structure with networks and decentralization. Learning organization

DESIGN INTERVENTIONS AND TEAMS

Organizational design interventions may vary from evolutionary, soft interventions to revolutionary, hard interventions.

1. *Soft intervention:* A soft intervention does not aim at radical structural changes. The focus is on changing the way of functioning within the organization by redefining and clarifying authority relationships, creating interactive networks, such as task-forces, cross-functional teams and dotted line relationships.

2. *Hard intervention:* A hard intervention, focuses on bringing about changes in the units related to operations and interactions with market. It may results in a new structural configuration or realignment of spans of control.

The design process can be outsourced or executed internally as well.

1. *Outsourcing:* Organizational design is a specialized area and there are many large and small consulting firms offering design assistance to companies. Consultants are hired for the following purposes:

- Diagnose organization and recommend a new model.
- Teach the design model and the use of tools and methodology.
- Guide design process and conduct periodical reviews to ensure the design effort stays on track.

2. *Internal:* Some companies entrust the task to internal staff resources, especially when the change is not substantial.

3. *Mixed:* When external assistance is considered important, an internal management team is set up to support consultants in organization design initiatives.

The drivers of the organization redesign process may be as follows:

1. *Organization leader:* The person in the organization who champions and sets the direction for the change process. He or she appoints the Steering Committee.

2. *Steering committee:* The responsibility of organisation design is entrusted to this committee. The committee consists of key leaders from within the organization and union officials.

3. *Design team:* The team consists of 6–12 employees drawn from a diversity of functions. The team is responsible for regularly reporting on design choices being recommended and getting the input of the Implementation.

4. *Implementation team:* Either the whole or part of the organization will be involved in implementation. Accordingly the leaders of organisational parts involved in implementation will be included in the team as members.

5. *Renewal team:* A team is set up to examine post-implementation situation. The team monitors and assess the effectiveness of design and identifies needs for changes in future.

SUMMARY

Organizational design is an important exercise to create new capabilities for competing in the present and future markets. The process of organizational design is evolutionary, socio-technical, continuous and flexible. The design process comprises the following steps—identification of the need for organizational design, creation of strategy, designing structure, establishing systems, designing people system, implementing the design and making reviews and renewals. Internal organization structures or departments can be designed in the following forms: simple organizational design, functional design, bureaucratic design, divisional design, matrix design, team structure design, virtual structure design and adhocracy design. The design decisions are influenced by: (i) structural dimensions, like centralization, formalization, hierarchy, routinization, specialization and training, and (ii) contextual dimensions like culture, environment, goals, size and technology. Organizations have to learn to reconcile the tensions between strategy and structure, accountability and adaptability, ladders and rings, self-interest and mission success. Size is another consideration. Typically, small organizations have flat, team structures with 2 or 3 levels of hierarchy.

Organizational design that arise from four different cultures (hierarchy or control culture, clan or collaborate culture, market or compete culture and adhocracy) are bureaucracy, hierarchical bureaucracies, matrix structure and charismatic. Research found a linkage between technology and structure. Small batch production and complex technology require organic structures, whereas mass production employs mechanistic structure. Environment also influences organization structure. Dynamic environment forces organic design and network structures, whereas stable one permits the use of functional and divisional structures. Strategy is another determinant. Cost leadership focus needs mechanistic, functional design, whereas differentiation and innovation require matrix and organic designs. Design implementation is essentially a team work.

EXERCISES

I. Review Questions

1. Explain the organizational design process.
2. Make a classification of organizational designs.
3. Discuss the factors that influence organizational design.
4. What are the components of an organization structure?
5. Examine the relationship between organization design and size.
6. Examine the influence of culture on organization design.
7. How does technology influence design decisions?
8. Explain the types of designs suitable to different environments.
9. Is structure determined by strategy? If yes, how? If no, why?
10. How is design activity undertaken in organizations?

II. Discussion Questions

1. Discuss the merits and demerits of different forms of internal organization structures.
2. What are the major determinants of organizational design? Identify the organizational components that require design consideration.
3. Examine the influence of culture and technology on organizational design.
4. Discuss the influence of environment on organizational design.
5. Write notes on:
   (i) Large vs small organizations
   (ii) Flat vs vertical structures

📖 MINI-PROJECT

Visit a local hospital, educational institution and a manufacturing unit and study their organization structures. Interview employees, to identify the structure of authority and problems faced by them, in getting approvals or sanctions from superiors. Prepare a SWOT for each organization. Based on the data, write a report giving your views on the appropriateness of the existing structures.

🖱 WEB ASSIGNMENT

Visit the website of Center for Organization Development (Organizational Design Consulting, www.centerod.com/consulting/) and find their approach to organizational design. Write a paper for presentation.

CASE STUDY

TCS Makes Structural Changes

Tata Consultancy Services, India's largest outsourcing company has drawn plans for expansion into fast-growing emerging markets. Presently, its largest revenue streams come from North America and Europe. Along with global business the competitors, TCS is looking for opportunities in high-growth regions, including Asia, the Middle-East and Latin America.

In the long-term, it is expected that these markets contribute "upwards of 20% for TCS" in terms of overall revenues, compared with 7% two years ago. However, TCS is struggling to crack opportunities in China, as it was in Japan due to cultural barriers and high turnover of employees.

Leading the Pack

According to Jaypee Capital's IT analysts, TCS has consolidated its position as the new leader of the IT sector, outperforming Infosys and regarded. It has emerged as the new information technology bellwether by a gap of 38% between it and Infosys in terms of absolute profits. The impact of recession was less in case of TCS. It held ground, with a fall of just 1.5% as against Infosys's fall of 21% during the same period.

Restructuring Decision

After taking over the reins of TCS, CEO, has made some significant structural changes. He created a small group of seven leaders to take charge of businesses with sizes ranging from a few hundred millions of dollars to over a billion. They will report directly to him.

Drivers of Reorganization

As a company grows larger, one cannot continue to rely on the same organization structure. Voicing this view, one strategy analyst observed: "The earlier structure worked well for TCS all these years. They are being pro-active and preparing for the future." The last major re-organization was made in 2008. At that time, company moved from a geography-based structure to a customer and vertical-led structure. The company formed 23 verticals reporting to the COO. Since the COO position was vacant, the 23 leaders were reporting directly to the CEO. The move is also considered necessary in view of growing need for customer engagement.

Customer engagement has become more critical for two obvious reasons: (i) the top outsourcing clients such as Daimler and banks like JP Morgan and Citi are looking for vendors who can help develop their next iPad solutions as well advice them in identifying the next big business opportunities, and (ii) competition is intensifying with markets becoming dormant.

Govind Iyer, partner at executive search and strategy firm, Egon Zehnder International opined that firms are now building up to better serve the customer at a global level, to get the next $5 billion. Their success depends on how they can structure themselves better to be more globally attuned.

Perceived Benefits

An important benefit will be the organization will become customer-centric. It is claimed that the new structure will provide more management bandwidth and allows leaders to engage with customers closely. This structural intervention of adding a new layer saves CEO's time, and helps him pay more attention for strategy issues and customer calls.

The company will continue to have 23 vertical heads. However, the span of management is reduced now as these heads report to one of the seven group leaders. It means that 2–3 verticals will have the same boss. It will offer better scope for verticals to work closely with each other. It gives scope for people talk across verticals, rather than function in silos. An analyst with a domestic brokerage house observed: "I see this structure as being similar to Infosys' executive council but without some of the disadvantages. In Infosys, the members of the executive council are overloaded".

More importantly, the leadership layer offers a new career path to managers. It will help motivate existing pool of leaders to compete for the new roles with more responsibility. The vertical-led structure is effective in generating business and profits even during the recession. It is evident from the revenue growth from ₹ 18,685 crore in FY07 to ₹ 37,325 crore in FY11. It is successful in increasing the business from clients. The top ten clients of TCS contribute around 30% of its revenues.

Questions for Discussion

1. Analyze the organizational structural changes at TCS.
2. Are the changes consistent with the goals and expected outcomes?
3. Suggest changes keeping in mind, the structures adopted by competitors and the changes expected in the next five years.

Source: N. Shivapriya, TCS CEO N. Chandrasekaran creates new layer to oversee verticals...articles. economictimes.indiatimes.com › Collections › Clients, 25 May 2011—and TCS to Expand Its Business | TopNews.org, topnews.org/content/2670-tcs-expand-its-business,2 Jul 2011.

REFERENCES

1. RCom to *reorganise* wireless business | Firstpost, *www.firstpost.com/.../rcom-to-reorganise-wireless-business-76496.ht...5* Sep 2011—*Infosys reorganisation* sees industry sector units, established *www.finextra.com/news/announcement.aspx? pressreleaseid=40143* 12 Jul 2011.

2. Organization design–Wikipedia, the free encyclopedia en.wikipedia.org/wiki/Organization_design

3. Roy H., Autry (1996), What is Organization design? www.inovus.com/organiza.htm, 19 November, 1996.

4. Drucker, P.F. (1973), "*Management: Tasks, Responsibilities, Practices*", New York; Harper&Row, Galbraith, J.R. (1995), *Designing Organizations: An Executive Briefing*

on Strategy, Structure and Process. San Francisco: Jossey-Bass, and Nadler, D.A., Gerstein, M.S., Shaw, R.B. (1992), *Organizational Architecture: Designs for Changing Organizations*, San Francisco: Jossey-Bass.

5. Banner, David K. and Elaine Gagné, T. (1995), *Designing Effective Organisations: Traditional and Transformational Views*, Thousand Oaks, California: Sage Publications.

6. Gene Burton and Manab Thakur (1995), *Management Today: Principles and Practice,* New Delhi: Tata McGraw-Hill Publishing Company Limited.

7. Simons, Robert (2005), *Levers of Organization Design*, Boston: HBS Press.

8. Taylor, Frederick W. (1911), *Principles of Scientific Management*, New York: Harper & Bros.

9. Weber, Max (1947), *The Theory of Social and Economic Organization*. London: Collier Macmillan Publishers.

10. Ford and Randolph (1992), Cross functional structures: A review and integration of matrix organization and project management, *Journal of Management*, Vol. **18**, pp. 267–94.

11. Lipnack & Stamps (1997), *Virtual Teams: Researching Across Space, Time, and Organizations with Technology*, New York: John Wiley and Sons.

12. Daft, Richard (1992), *Organizational Theory and Design*, St. Paul, Minnesota: West Publishing.

13. Simons, Robert (2005), *Levers of Organisation Design*, Boston: HBS Press.

14. Quoted in Koontz, H. and C. O'Donnell (1972), *Principles of Management*, New York: McGraw-Hill.

15. Mabey C., Salaman, G. and Storey J. (2001), Organizational Structuring and Restructuring, in Salaman, G. (Ed.), Understanding Business Organizations: London: Routledge.

16. Cameron, Kim S., and Robert E. Quinn (1999), Diagnosing and Changing Organizational Culture: Based on the Competing Values Framework, Reading, MA: Addison-Wesley Publishing Co.

17. Handy, C.B. (1985), *Understanding Organizations*, Harmondsworth: Penguin Books.

18. Organizational Effectiveness, Structure, and Technology apps.business.ualberta.ca › Home › Archive

19. Organization Theory and Design—Google Books Result books.google.co.in/books?isbn=0324598890...Richard L. Daft–2009.

20. Thompson, James D. (1967), *Organizations in Action: Social Science Bases of Administrative Theory,* New Jersey: Transaction Publishers. and ProvenModels_technology typology—James David Thompson, www.provenmodels.com/40.

21. Kast, F.E. and Rsoenzweig, J.E. (1986), Organisation and Management: A Systems and Contingency Approach, New York: McGraw-Hill.

22. Freeman, J.H., Carroll, Glenn and Hannan, M.T. (1977), The population ecology of organizations: *American Journal of Sociology*, Vol. **82**(5).

23. Pfeffer, J. and Salancik, G.R. (1978), *The External Control of Organizations: A Resource Dependence Perspective,* New York: Harper and Row.

24. Child. J. (1972), Organization structure, environment and performance: The role of strategic choice, *Sociology*, January, Vol. 6, No. 1, pp. 1–22.

25. Burns and Stalker (1961), *Management of Innovation*, London: Tavistock.

26. Laurence P. and Lorsch, J. (1967), *Organization and environment: Managing differentiation and integration,* Boston Division of Research, Boston: Harvard Business School.

27. McShane and Travaglione (2003), *Organisational Behaviour on the Pacific Rim*, Australia: McGraw-Hill Australia.

28. Gibson, J.L., Ivancevich, J.M., and Donnelly, J.H., Jr. (1994), *Organizations: Behavior, Structure, Processes* (8th ed.), Boston, MA: Irwin.

Chapter 4

Organizational Climate

Vignette: Safety and Health Climate

A top priority in HUL is safety and health of the employees. The organization has initiated a wide spectrum of activities that vary from communication to well-designed programs that address physical, emotional and mental health issues. The company-wide periodical activities include one-to-one discussions, vitality workshops, direct mailer campaigns and onsite poster campaigns. The company arranges annual medical checks and practical advice is dispensed on identified health concerns. Follow up actions are a norm rather than an exception.

HUL has a policy on HIV/AIDS. The company has initiated several measures to improve awareness and prevention of its transmission. A non-discriminatory working environment for those afflicted with HIV is provided. Counseling and recreation facilities are set up to provide advice and promote physical fitness.

HUL has a vision of being an "injury free organization." The drive for safety is top-down; there is direct involvement of the board. The top management supports safety of employees by demonstrating their leadership and concern. The company has evolved a safety and health policy with prevention at the core. The policy is implemented organization-wide. The company has spelt safety parameters and integrated them into their business processes spanning people, processes, systems, technology and facilities. Safety is incorporated as a condition of employment. It has been included as a key responsibility in line management and business performance.

Employee involvement is encouraged through ongoing education and training, and counseling. An important benefit of employee involvement is swift reporting of problems for immediate correction. Periodical audits both internal and external are conducted. In addition, reality checks surveys and scorecard are employed to upgrade services.

Company goes beyond workplace to address safety issues of the employees and their families. HUL has launched a Value Life Value Safety (VLVS) campaign that laid emphasis on diverse safety aspects, such as road safety, home safety, pedestrian safety, cooking safety, etc. It has got tremendous response. HUL provided safety checklists to its vendors and asked its employees to monitor the vendor behavior on safety, while using their services. To encourage and reinforce safety practices, suitable rewards and penalties are instituted. Through these measures, the company has succeeded in increasing awareness, and thereby employee engagement on safety[1].

The case showcases the effort of a leading organization, in creating climate that not only offers protection but also provides inspiration for people to work. In this chapter, we explore the concept and measurement of organizational climate.

INTRODUCTION

Organizations operating in a dynamic, competitive, global environment face the tough challenge of achieving and sustaining superior performance over a long period. Today, managers are meeting this challenge by creating high performance organizations. High performance organizations require talented people, and the talented persons prefer great places to work. As such, it has become necessary for managers to develop and maintain right organizational climate.

CONCEPT

The concept of organizational climate has become popular in the industrial organizations with the writings of Litwin and Stringer[2] and others. Climate refers to typical atmosphere and it varies from region to region and time-to-time. Climate is measured in terms of temperature or humidity. Climate can be categorized into hot, warm and cool. Some people prefer warm climate whereas some others prefer cool ones. In a similar way, organizational climate refers to the ambience or environment within the organization or the perceived comfort employees have in working in the environment. Researchers have adopted the later point of view of measuring perceptions of employees about climate.

Forehand and Gilmer defined OC in the following terms:

A set of characteristics that (a) describe the organization and distinguish it from other organizations, (b) are relatively enduring over time and (c) influence the behavior of people in the organization[3].

Campbell, et al. described OC as:

A set of attributes specific to a particular organization that may be induced from the way the organization deals with its members and its environment. For the individual member within the organization, OC takes the form of a set of attributes and expectancies which describe the organization in terms of both static characteristics (such as degree of autonomy) and dynamic characteristics (such as behavior outcomes)[4].

Moran and Volkwein explained Organizational Climate as:

"a relatively enduring characteristic of an organization which distinguishes it from other organization, hence,

    (a) *embodies members' collective perceptions about their organization with respect to such dimensions as autonomy, trust, cohesiveness, support, recognition, innovation and fairness;*

    (b) *produced by member interaction;*

    (c) *serves as a basis for interpreting the situation;*

    (d) *reflects the prevalent norms and attitudes of the organization's culture; and*

    (e) *acts as a source of influence for shaping behavior[5]."*

From the given definitions, the following salient features can be highlighted:

1. OC refers to set of characteristics—both static (such as degree of autonomy) and dynamic characteristics (such as behavior outcomes)
2. Reflects the way the organization deals with its members and the culture in organization
3. Influences behavior of people and provides employee job satisfaction and organizational goal achievement
4. An enduring one
5. Helps understand the way people think about the organization

CLIMATE VS CULTURE

The organizational context is characterized by numerous features (e.g., leadership, structure, rewards, communication) which can categorize as determinants of organizational climate and culture. Accordingly, researchers have identified two sources of climate perceptions: (i) structure and (ii) culture.

The structural approach suggests that employee perceptions on climate are influenced by the characteristics of the organization's structure. According to it, the influence of individual is limited to perceptions of structural variables and their influences on employee behavior. Climate is an outcome of culture. Culture describes values and norms that determine the behavior of the organization. Climate is a description of the work setting by the employees working in the organization. It is behaviorally oriented, and it describes what is happening to organizational members. On the other hand, organizational culture provides the reasons for what is happening in terms of shared values and common beliefs held by organizational members.

Burke and Litwin draw the difference in simple terms. They contend that organizational climate is in the foreground of organizational members' perception, but organizational culture is in the background[6]. A similar distinction is drawn by Schneider. According to him organizational climate can be seen as a surface manifestation of organizational culture[7]. For example, structured leadership and limited participation in decision-making signify a type of culture common to all employees, the interpretation of it (perceived climate) may vary. Some may view it negatively, whereas some others may view it positively. The variations are due to social influences and individual attitudes.

In practice, researchers employ quantitatively based questionnaire measures to measure organizational climate and qualitative measures to measure organization culture. When it comes to change, changing the culture is not easy. "You cannot just tell people; From now on it's going to be done this way." For instance, women in corporate face discrimination because, men can not change their preference to men. On the other hand, climate is the feeling the employees have on practices of organizations. These feelings can be changed within a few hours, days or weeks. Communication by the supervisors, peers and other employees can create positive or negative perceptions.[8]

MEASUREMENT

The concept of organizational climate is nebulous and controversial with different approaches to define and measure it. There are three issues to be resolved before measuring organizational climate. They are:

1. Which climate? General or specific (aspect like safety, motivation, etc.)
2. Whose climate? Individual or group (departmental) or organizational climate.
3. What dimensions? What dimensions or factors are to be taken to measure?

General Versus Domain-Specific

The dimensions and content of climate measures should differ depending on the organizational outcome taken into consideration. We find, different researchers have measured different climate concepts, like political climate, motivational climate and innovation climate.

1. *Political climate:* Political climate is the environment surrounding power and decision-making. Recognizing political climate sets the stage for bargaining support for collaboration. Studies have shown that political climate caused negative job attitudes among employees of lower status than those of a higher status[9].

2. *Achievement climate:* In the achievement-oriented climate, emphasis will be placed on goal-attainment, The achievement climate leads to innovative behavior and high job satisfaction[10].

3. *Motivational climate:* It has been documented that employees' attain high performance when they are made to feel welcomed at work. A study measured motivational climate by measuring perceived competence, preference for challenge, interest in the lesson, and perceived importance of the work.[11]

4. *Innovation climate:* Goran Ekvall identified 10 dimensions of organizational creativity-challenge, freedom, idea time, dynamism, idea support, trust and openness, playfulness and humor, conflicts, debates and risk taking.[12]

Some researchers have attempted at categorizing the climate into different types. For instance, Ginsberg described three basic climates—inception, post-entrepreneurial and bureaucratic[13], whereas Halpin and Croft categorized climate into six types, open, autonomous, controlled, familiar, paternal or closed[14].

Individual or Group

Organizational climate is perceived at three levels, further complicating the measurement effort.

1. Individual (or psychological) climate is the individual's perception of the work environment;
2. Group climate is the perception of work groups or subgroups; and
3. Organizational climate is the collective perception of all employees within a unit.

Psychological vs Organization climate

James and Jones distinguished psychological climate with organizational climate[15]. Psychological climate is measured by individual's perceptions; whereas organizational climate is measured by aggregating many individuals' perceptions. Organizational climate should be taken into consideration when there is less difference in the many psychological climates. In a similar way, Sharma has pointed out that when organizational climate is studied within a particular organization (i.e. individual is used as a unit of analysis) we may use the term psychological climate, but when cross-organizational comparisons are made by averaging the responses of the members of a particular organization, (i.e. the unit of analysis is the organization) then we can use the term organizational climate[16].

Payne has argued that the concept of organizational climate is invalid. One can measure only departmental climate but not organizational climate. The reasons is people in different parts of the organization maintain radically different perceptions of the organization. Where perceptions are consensually shared in small groups, what they represent is departmental, but not organizational climate[17].

How to Measure?

To facilitate measurement of organizational climate, researchers have dissected it's characteristics into dimensions. However, selecting the right dimensions and items is a difficult task, since there is no agreement on what items represent climate. Box 4.1 shows the different measures.

BOX 4.1 Different Dimensions of Organizational Climate[18]

D.C. Hall and Benjmin Schnieder (1973)
1. Work challenge, 2. Autonomy, 3. Valued work activities, 4. Support in achieving his work goals.

P.M. Muchinsky (1977)
1. Quality of leadership, 2. Amount of trust, 3. Communication: Upward and Downward, 4. Feeling of Useful work, 5. Responsibility, 6. Fair rewards, 7. Responsible job pressures, 8. Opportunity, 9. Responsibility controls, Structure and Bureaucracy, 10. Employee involvement.

J.E. Newman (1977)
1. Supervisory style, 2. Task characteristics, 3. Performance-reward relationship, 4. Co-worker relations, 5. Employee work motivation, 6. Equipment and arrangement of people, 7. Employee competence, 8. Decision-making policy, 9. Work space, 10. Job responsibility/importance.

B.R. Sharma (1987)
1. Scope for advancement, 2. Grievance handling, 3. Monetary benefits, 4. Participative management, 5. Objectivity and reality, 6. Recognition and appreciation, 7. Safety and security, 8. Training and education, 9. Welfare facilities.

Causal Variable or Outcome Variable

Climate is seen as an independent variable causing certain positive and negative outcomes in organisation. It is also seen as a dependent variable—an outcome of organizational practices.

Independent variable

Climate is seen a factor that influences various work outcomes both positive like productivity, satisfaction, and motivation, and negative like absenteeism, turnover and accidents.

Pritchard and Karasick have found that OC is more closely related to employees' job satisfaction than to their performance. They have also found that a higher job satisfaction is more likely to be associated with supportive climate regardless of personality characteristics[19]. S.K. Srivastava took 150 textile employees from private textile industry in Kanpur to examine the relationship of OC and need satisfaction with job involvement among the employees of the private textile industry. He found that favourable OC leads to higher involvement. Higher order needs (self-esteem, autonomy and self-actualization) are positively and significantly related with job involvement[20]. The study of Pooja Garg and Renu Rastogi revealed that the teachers working in public schools exhibit higher levels of Organizational Citizenship Behaviors (OCBs) and that public schools offer a more positive working climate than private schools. Teachers above 36 years exhibit higher levels of OCBs. Female teachers contribute more to the development of climate than male teachers[21].

Dependent variable

Climate can also be seen as an outcome of organizational structure and management practices. In this sense, climate may be a useful index of organization's safety, health, human resource development, etc.

Pooja Purang compared the perceptions of 247 middle level managers from five organizations; two from public sector, two from private sector and one from multinational company. Participation, organizational development, training, appraisal and reward and welfare climatic factors are more positively perceived by private and multinational organization than public sector organizations.[22] Akhilesh and Pandey selected 140 executives from nationalized banks (100) and private sector banks (40) to measure organizational climate. Nationalized bank was inclined to 'Affiliation orientation' and Private Sector slightly to 'Task orientation'[23]. Patel made comparative study of HRD climate in high and low performing branches of District Central Cooperative Bank (DCCB). High performing branches were found better than low performing branches in various items of HRD climate[24].

Moderating variable

It can be seen as a moderating variable—caused by organizational processes (leadership function) and causing some organizational outcomes (productivity). Litwin and Stringer through their experimental studies, found that a given leadership style produced a characteristic climate which, in turn, aroused a particular motive[25]. Sinha studied relationship among OC, leadership styles, motivation and organizational performance. It was found that the nurturing task created a more favourable climate for his subordinates[26].

What dimensions?

The first issue question relates to the concept taken for measurement. The choice is to be made between objective (physical or structural) features of the organization and the subjective (perceptual) reactions of employees to the organization. Richard M. Hodgetts has given an analogy with an iceberg where there is a part of the iceberg that can be seen from the surface and another part that is under water and is not visible[27]. The visible part that can be observed or measured include the structure of hierarchy, goals and objectives of the organization, performance standards and evaluations, technological state of the operations, and so on. The second category contains factors that are not visible and quantifiable and include such subjective areas as supportiveness, employee's feelings and attitudes, values, morale, personal and social interaction with peers, subordinates and superiors and a sense of satisfaction with the job. Both of these categories are shown in Figure 4.1.

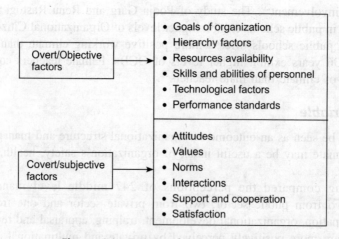

Figure 4.1 Factors of Organizational Climate.

SIGNIFICANCE

Organizational climate is important at it stimulates employees to shape their behaviors and facilitates team work for success.

1. *Basic task of management:* As organizational climate has significant influence on the success of an organization. Managers have to pay attention to the design and maintenance of organizational climate. In fact, Harold Koontz and Heinz Weihrich[28] define management as "the process of designing and maintaining an environment in which individuals, working together in groups, efficiently accomplish selected aims."

2. *Signifies organizational personality:* First, the climate of an organization is grounded in the relatively stable conditions that and they give the organization a distinct identity or atmosphere. As early as 1967, Halpin characterized organizational climate as the personality of an organization[29]. Hoy and Miskel wrote "[The] climate of a school may roughly be conceived as the personality of a school, i.e., personality is to the individual as climate is to the organization"[30].

3. *Stimulates behaviors:* A new employee often learns about the behavioral norms of his organization by observing his superior, behavior and interaction with subordinates. Subsequently, he constructs a reality about the organization environment and adapts his behavior accordingly.

4. *Facilitates success:* Researchers have found that organizational climate is an important determinant and predictor of organizational success. Organizational climate encourages employee involvement and empowerment in decision-making. The organizational climate facilitates the firm to identify the deficiencies in organizational structure, HR related practices, physical atmosphere, and organizational culture. Thus it helps improve the climate and secure desired effectiveness. Table 4.1 shows how good and bad climates influence behaviors and outcomes.

TABLE 4.1 Climate-behaviors and Outcomes

Climate	Behaviors	Outcomes
Bad	Stressful, sabotage, go-slow, and bullying	Poor performance, wastage, accidents, and turnover
Good	Risk-taking, open communication, employee development, trust, team and work	Job satisfaction, loyalty, affective commitment, and morale

5. *Great place to work:* The individual selection follows the selection-attraction-attrition route. It states that individuals and organization, both seek to find a certain match between the individual and the organization. If there is incongruence, people quit or seek transfer, whereas organization may terminate or transfer an employee.

DESIGNING CLIMATE

Many organizations, struggle to cultivate the climate they need to succeed and sustain their competitive advantage. According to Pareek, organizational climate results from interaction among organizational components (structure, systems, culture, leader behavior and employees' psychological needs)[31].

As such, organizations can take steps to build a more positive and employee-centered climate by considering the following factors:

1. **Personal factors**

    Expectations: Types of expectations regarding how managers behave and take decisions.

2. **Cultural factors**

    Values: The guiding principles of the organization and whether they are modeled by all employees, including leaders or not.

    Norms: The normal, routine ways of behaving and treating one another in the organization.

3. **Structural factors**

    Structure: It provides for authority distribution and participation of people.

    Policies and rules: These convey the degree of flexibility and restriction in the organization.

    Programs: Programs and formal initiatives help support and emphasize a workplace climate.

4. **Management factor**

    Leadership: Leaders that consistently support the climate desired.

    Communication: How often and the types of means by which information is communicated in the organization.

CREATING A CLIMATE FOR INNOVATION

Sustained innovation depends on the right climate, which is inextricably linked to leadership, culture, and organizational design. Box 4.2 presents a questionnaire which help assess the innovation climate in an organization[32].

The factors that help create innovation climate can be explained as follows[33]:

Personal factors

Employees in innovative organizations play the role of intrapreneurs and generate ideas for creating new products or processes. They expect to have the following:

1. Freedom and authority to explore new ideas
2. Chance to decide projects on which they serve
3. Opportunity to select members of the teams

S.No.	BOX 4.2 Innovation Climate Questionnaire					
S.No.	**Statements**		**Scale***			
Personal factors						
1	People feel a strong desire to make contributions to this company and to the people in it	5	4	3	2	1
2	Most people leading innovation projects are self-selected intrapreneurs	5	4	3	2	1
Cultural factors						
3	There is tolerance of risk, mistakes, and failures	5	4	3	2	1
4	Effective intrapreneurs are generally rewarded	5	4	3	2	1
5	Vision and strategic intent is communicated among all employees	5	4	3	2	1
6	Organization encourages people thinking well into the future ahead	5	4	3	2	1
7	There is a written commitment to ethical priorities beyond what is required by law	5	4	3	2	1
Structural factors						
8	Project teams in our organization have considerable freedom to make decisions and act on them without needing to ask for permission	5	4	3	2	1
9	Less time is spent getting or waiting for permission to act rather than taking action or gathering information	5	4	3	2	1
10	There is freedom to employees to use some of their time to explore new ideas and hunches without having to ask permission	5	4	3	2	1
11	Intrapreneurial leaders and at least half the core team frequently stay with the project from near the beginning to full implementation	5	4	3	2	1
12	Employees cross boundaries to get help and support for innovation	5	4	3	2	1
13	There is focus on how to better serve customers that drives organization toward productive innovation	5	4	3	2	1
14	Teams often have a choice among several internal suppliers of services such as IS, training, sales, manufacturing, and software engineering	5	4	3	2	1
15	Specific measurements that encourage innovation are developed and communicated	5	4	3	2	1
Management factors						
16	Information flows freely, both horizontally and vertically	5	4	3	2	1
	Managers have the skills, power, commitment, and courage to be effective sponsors of intrapreneurial initiatives	5	4	3	2	1
17	There is genuine concern for employees, backed up by supportive actions	5	4	3	2	1
18	The firm is good at managing many small businesses in a decentralized way, so there are many small beginnings in many different places	5	4	3	2	1

*5–Strongly agree 4–Agree 3–Neutral 2–Disagree 1–Strongly disagree.

Cultural factors

Cultural factors that predominantly influence the innovation climate are:

1. *Values:* Innovation climate needs emphasis on values than on capabilities. Values like risk taking, change and freedom of expression are to be instilled. The values should lead to a new mind set within organization. Leaders as well as the doers, movers, and shakers should think as follows:

- 'Within my realm, how can I do things differently?'
- 'What is the customer asking for?'
- 'Can I do something that more effectively addresses their needs?'
- 'Can I exceed their expectations?'

2. *Tolerance:* Tolerance of mistakes and failures is another important virtue of innovative organizations. If people trying new ideas are punished for mistakes, people stop experimenting and cover up failures.

3. *Cooperation:* Cooperation and collaboration are next significant values. Politics and rivalry are discouraged. Focus on internal politics tends toward conservatism, wrong prioritization, and failure to exploit genuine ideas.

Structural factors

Structural factors like authority and role design merit consideration. The different organizational designs that promote innovation are:

1. *Separate units:* The creation of an R&D department or a central research laboratory is one of the common forms of promoting innovations.

2. *Project organization:* Projects require team efforts, because they need to bring together technical talent from diverse disciplines (as in the case of building the space shuttle) or functions (as in the case of the cross-disciplinary teams in new product development processes). There are two forms of permanent project organizations utilized by firms: matrix organizations and quasi-structure.

3. *Matrix organization:* It is a combination of the project organization with functional organization. Quasi structures are built with formal authority systems, but make an extensive use of committees, task forces, teams, and dotted-line relationships. High-tech firms prefer quasi-structure, as they have to continuously innovate for survival.

New venture division (NVD): NVDs are staffed and managed differently from the regular operating organization. NVDs allow more entrepreneurship and attract more risk-takers; the rewards are based on the success of the venture, not on predictable milestones as in an operating division.

Systems

Ideas do not create innovations. The system that converts them into profitable outcomes is necessary. The components of a fully-developed idea pipeline are as follows:

1. *Supporting top:* A senior-level committee to systematically select new ideas and allocate resources among the best ideas.

2. *Policies and rules:* Firms keen on innovations should be transparent in processing ideas and show tolerance to failures. They need performance methods that assess leaders not only on outcomes but also on effort. For instance, short-term business results may suffer, when pursuing a challenging innovation.

3. *Discretionary time:* New ideas and hunches require time for exploration. Innovative organizations give people the freedom to use some of their time without having to ask permission.

4. *Programs:* Programs that offer training and motivation as well as develop new ideas for processes and products.

Management factor

Two important factors that determine innovation support of managers are leadership style and communication.

Leadership style: Leaders have to possess broad competencies for leading innovation. They have to be open to new ideas and change. Pradip Khandwalla identified four management styles, that can promote innovativeness.[34] Table 4.2 shows them.

TABLE 4.2 Creativogenic Management Styles

S.No.	Style	Description
1	Entrepreneurial	Search for big new opportunities, risky decisions, forceful leadership with rapid growth as goal.
2	Organic	Openness, participation, unrestricted flow of information, sharing of resources for innovation and adaptability.
3	Participative	Democratic procedures, team work, trust and collaboration.
4	Altruistic	Leaders as trustees, commitment to ethics and corporate social responsibility.

Types of competencies

Three types of competencies are identified:

1. *Head:* Leaders need to make a personal commitment to innovation and communicate the same to all members. They should lead by example, emphasizing innovation in their day-to-day decisions.

2. *Heart:* Leaders need to build trust and mutual respect with employees. They should foster open airing of problems and disagreements. Conflict resolution should be creative.

3. *Guts:* Leaders should challenge people to find novel approaches. They should be willing to take risks in allocating resources and experimenting innovative ideas.

Communication

Communicating is critical to instilling corporate values and encouraging ideas. The key communication needs are given as follows:

1. Instilling corporate values that encourage innovation among all employees in the organization.
2. Focusing idea generation in areas given priority status by organization.
3. Maintaining transparency in the idea processing and rewarding processes.
4. Providing systematic feedback to the originators of ideas to encourage engagement in idea generation.

An open communication system such as an innovation portal on the corporate intranet will help facilitate developing and critically evaluating new ideas, with participation from external partners.

DEVELOPING HRD CLIMATE

Most researchers agree that an optimal level of development climate is essential for achieving organizational goals. Human Resource Development (HRD) is a process by which the employees of an organization are provided opportunities to sharpen and enhance competencies required to perform their present and expected future roles, and develop a synergetic culture in which teamwork and collaboration among sub-units are strengthened leading to the professional well being, motivation, and pride of employees[35].

HRD climate is characterized by supportive personnel policies, and supportive HRD practices that focus on individual development and empowerment for achieving excellent results with good job satisfaction. It involves the following values and practices:

Personal factors

Employees prefer to work in an organization that offers the following:

1. *Challenging jobs:*   Jobs provide autonomy, variety and opportunities for good performance.

2. *Job satisfaction:*   Jobs provide satisfaction and promise career advancement.

Cultural factors

HRD climate emphasises on values that promote development, cooperation and achievement.

1. *Work ethic:*   The work culture is synergetic making environment conducive for working hard. There exists a strong normative pressure for working and hard work is rewarded.

2. *Empowerment:*   There is an understanding that employees form the most important resources and developing employees is the job of every manager.

3. *Cooperation:*   The focus is on integrating employees with the organisation. Values like equity, and equality guide interactions and decisions in organization.

Structural factors

The structural factors should consider the following:

1. *Organic structures:* Organic structures facilitate decentralization, team work that goes beyond functional boundaries.

2. *Job design:* Jobs are made challenging by job enrichment that provides for autonomy and variety.

HRM and development policies

The policies that need to be supportive to people development and performance are:

1. *Career planning:* There is a clear design of career path and the progression opportunities are well-communicated in the organization.

2. *Succession planning:* The succession line is established to avoid uncertainty and politicking in the organization.

3. *Human resource information:* The information regarding human assets of the enterprise are publicised through in house journals, newsletters, circulars, pamphlets, posters, etc. It serves two purposes: (i) helps the firm to know the talent available, and (ii) helps the employee gain recognition.

4. *Training:* Training helps employees acquire new knowledge and skills and improve attitudes toward work, achievement and organization.

5. *Counseling:* Counseling offers an opportunity to employees to have advice and guidance to lead better life and perform better.

6. *Appraisal:* Appraisal helps obtain evaluation of employee performance and potential. Performance appraisals form the basis for training and reward decisions. Potential appraisal helps take decisions on future assignments to be given to employees.

7. *Reward and welfare:* Satisfaction and commitment are important outcomes of HRD climate. Besides other practices, motivation through reward and welfare measures are important to create them. It is important that the benefits are equitable and desirable.

8. *Organization development:* Using different types of interventions, organizations solve problems and rebuild organization, for meeting challenges of growth. The development projects stimulate employee development and motivation and help them to attain high performance levels in the present jobs and accept new jobs that are more challenging.

Management factors

Two important variables that influence HRD climate are leadership and communication.

1. *Leadership:* Managers adopt participative style to develop the competencies in the employees by updating and sharing their expertise and experience with employees. They motivate employees to contribute more and take measures to promote their well-being.

2. *Communication:* Managers share relevant information with employees to increase their awareness about organizational processes and strategies, and the role to be played by them. Also information necessary to facilitate team work and decision-making is made available to all employees.

ESTABLISHING MOTIVATIONAL CLIMATE

Motivational climate is one which makes employees to work on their own, and enjoy high level of job satisfaction. Two types of environments that contribute to motivation are identified by researchers[36].

- First, autonomy-supportive environment that facilitates decision-making by employees.
- Second, the task involved climate. Two types of climate, the task-involved and ego-involved are observed by researchers. The task-involved climate emphasizes personal growth and team effort, whereas the ego-involved climates focus on winning and establishing superiority.

The motivation climate is more a result of management style than organizational structures. Though organic structures provide greater opportunities for self-motivation and self-determined behaviors, high level of motivation can be created by sound HR policies and concern for people in mechanistic structures.

Motivational Analysis of Organizational-Climate (MAO-C)

The level and type of motivation prevalent in organization is measured by different frameworks. The widely used one by researchers is the Motivational Analysis of Organizational Climate (MAO-C) instrument developed by Pareek. It identified following six motives in relation to 12 dimensions of organization[37].

1. *Achievement:* Emphasis on achievement of goals and attaining quality and excellence.

2. *Expert influence:* Emphasis on use of expertise for the benefit of the organization.

3. *Extension:* Emphasis laid by organizational members in making themselves relevant and useful to others.

4. *Control:* Emphasis laid by organizational members on consolidation of personal power.

5. *Dependency:* Practice of deferring decisions/actions and seeking seniors'/others' approval for everything.

6. *Affiliation:* Emphasis on building and maintaining friendly personal relationships, even when it may impair organizational performance.

The 12 dimensions of organizational working are:

1. Orientation
2. Interpersonal relationships
3. Supervision

4. Problem management
5. Management of mistakes
6. Conflict management
7. Communication
8. Decision-making
9. Trust
10. Management of rewards
11. Risk taking
12. Innovation and change

For each dimension, MAO-C defines representative behaviors corresponding to each one of the six climate motives. Two highest scores are taken into consideration to identify the dominant climate and the next highest the secondary climate. The overall motivation climate is interpreted in terms of the two dominant ones. Based on the findings, steps are taken to build right motivational climate.

SUMMARY

Today, managers face the challenge of creating right climate to ensure high performance levels. Organizational climate refers to the perceived comfort employees have in the work environment. It reflects the way the organization deals with its members and the culture in organization. The perceptions on climate are determined by organizational features, like leadership, structure, rewards, and communication and cultural factors, like values, assumptions norms and beliefs. When it comes to measurement, there are three nagging questions—Whether general climate or specific climate? Whether the perception of individuals or groups? What dimensions are to be considered? Is it to be considered as a causal variable or mediating variable or outcome variable? Organizational climate is considered significant as it is a basic task of management. In fact it denotes organizational personality, stimulates behaviors and facilitates success. When climate has warmth, the company will be rated as great place to work.

According to Pareek (1989), organizational climate results from interaction among organizational components (structure, systems, culture, leader behavior and employees' psychological needs) By taking the factors into consideration, one can build positive climate. Climates can be built with different emphasis. You can build one for innovation by encouraging employee creative behaviors and experimentation, HRD climate by encouraging development through initiatives like coaching, mentoring and empowerment. A motivational climate can be established by autonomy-supportive environment and task involved climate.

EXERCISES

I. Review Questions

1. Explain the concept and significance of organization climate.
2. Discuss the types of climate and their implications to managers.
3. Identify the factors that determine climate.
4. How do you design a motivational climate?

II. Discussion Questions

1. Explain the concept and problems in measurement of organizational climate.
2. What factors do you consider in designing an organizational climate?
3. Explain how you would go about when asked to design HRD climate?
4. How can a manager establish a climate that fosters innovation?

📖 **MINI-PROJECT**

Conduct interviews with about 20 students pursuing different course in your institute. Elicit their perceptions on the climate in your institute. Based on this preliminary information, develop an organizational climate questionnaire and administer to teachers and students. Compare their perceptions on the climate. Discuss in class the implications of your study findings.

 WEB ASSIGNMENT

Refer the following and similar papers and prepare a PowerPoint presentation for 10 minutes on relationship between organizational climate and intent to leave.

Ruvarashe Saungweme and Calvin Gwandure, Organisational Climate and Intent to Leave among Recruitment available at *Organisational Climate* and Intent to Leave among Recruitment ...*www.krepublishers.com/.../JHE-34-3-145-11-2183-Saungwem-R-Tt...*

CASE STUDY

Focusing on People

The 75 year old Rane Group, one of India's leading auto component manufacturers, is known for its focus on TQM and operational excellence. It has evolved a people philosophy of aligning aspirations, inspiring to take on challenges and partnering in healthy and profitable growth. Chairman L. Ganesh asserts, 2011–20 will be a decade of accelerated growth for the $500 million Rane group. L. Lakshman, Chairman of Rane Holdings, said "TQM helped us with total employee engagement." He opined that the real challenge is to generate intellectual properties, and it requires retaining right talent. Accordingly, its focus has been on innovative culture and continuous learning.

Competency Focus

The focus on competency is seen right from selection. Selections are competency-based across levels to meet both the current and future requirements. A centralized hiring process is in place for entry level jobs to ensure better control and consistency. The selection process rigoros with a combination of aptitude tests, psychometric profiling, and group discussion and personal interview.

There is senior management commitment to the recruitment process. The Chairman takes part in senior level recruitments. A pool of senior HR and line leaders is extensively trained in selection skills. The interviewing process is structured to make it unbiased and effective. Induction program is intensive for all new entrants, and it consists of "Know Your Group" and "TQM for new recruits". It has a right blend of classroom and on-the-job exposure.

Exciting Work Place

The HR vision of Rane is "To stimulate and nurture the intrinsic desire in people to learn, grow and enhance performance to achieve business success and growth". The group strives to live up to the employer brand promise of creating an exciting workplace. The promise is guided by the principles of values, fairness and transparency and seeks to offer a career to each employee. Addressing a press conference chairman said, "brand Rane always stood for trust and reliability. Integrity has been one of the core values of our group".

The group, has a two-pronged approach to achieve growth through competence. They are:

- Creating an environment that encourages innovation and offers opportunities to employees.
- Creating an exciting workplace which provided everybody a good learning experience.

A major finding of internal and external employee perception surveys is employee pride in the company. They reported favourably on three aspects—management credibility, meaningful job and opportunity to learn and grow. The group has high performance culture, through updated Performance Assessment and Development System (PADS) and Individual Development Plans (IDP).

Development Focus

At Rane, the focus is on development of next generation leaders. The 3P Initiative (People, Performance and Potential) across levels focuses on retaining individuals with good performance and high potential with an objective promoting to the top. Accordingly, development opportunities are provided to employees at all levels. A four-level Professional Development Architecture (PDA), which focuses on identifying and grooming talented people for future roles is designed. The focus is on developing conceptual skills followed by experiential learning and customised coaching. The development initiatives include:

- Rane Advanced Management Program (RAMP) that builds a robust leadership pipeline for future senior management positions.
- Coaching for Leadership development for senior managers.
- Customised Strategic Leadership Program (SLP), like the one at IIM Bangalore for senior managers.
- Learning updates series provide for interactions with professionals from diverse backgrounds.

- Talent Review meetings to review current talent status and future succession needs. The Annual Corporate Talent Review meetings take stock of the 'talent readiness' of the organization to meet emergent challenges.

The outcome of the development initiatives is encouraging—over 30% of the senior management talent in the organization has multiple business/geography experience, and retention levels are in excess of 90%. Rane group is recognized for excellence in training by the Employer Branding Institute as part of Asia's Best Employer Awards. The structuring of training is relation to strategic business plans and individual competency development plans, involvement of both HR and line managers and tracking for future improvements have contributed to the success.

Equality and Diversity

There is presence of women in workforce and in new projects. As part of the affirmative action initiatives, they partner with NGOs, CII, etc., in skill building initiatives and extend training to students from less privileged backgrounds in the neighborhood of their plant.

HR Agenda for the Future

The agenda for future according to R.Venkatanarayanan, President-Corp Services, Rane Group focuses on intensifying employee engagement, sustaining a stable employee relations climate, nurturing a culture of innovation, developing leadership talent, building a succession pipeline for all key and critical positions, leveraging the multi-generational workforce for pursuing opportunities on a global scale and increasing the use of technology and tools like social media.

Questions for Discussion

1. What, in your view, kind of organizational climate exists at Rane group?
2. What are the missing ingredients of the climate in view of changing environment, growing competition and attrition problems?
3. What future steps do you suggest to Rane for improving its climate?

Source: Gopalakrishnan, Hema, We have an array of growth and development initiatives, *The Hindu*, August 29, 2012, Opportunities, p. 2 and Special Correspondent, Rane group trains efforts on accelerating growth, *The Hindu*, December 13, 2011.

REFERENCES

1. Ensure Health and Safety | Our People | Hindustan Unilever www.hul.co.in/sustainability/OurPeople/Ensurehealthnsafety.aspx and Unilever exposed workers to chemicals | Health and Safety at Work ... www.healthandsafetyatwork.com/.../unilever-exposed-workers-chemi...., Sept. 2008.
2. Litwin, George H. and Robert A. Stringer (1968), *Motivation and Organizational Climate*, Boston: Harvard University Press.

3. Forehand G.A. and Von H. Gilmer (1964), "Environmental Variations in Studies of Organizational Behavior", *Psychological Bulletin*, Vol. **62**, pp. 361–382.

4. Campbell, J.P., Dunnette, M.D., Lawler, E.E. and Weick K.E. Jr. (1970), *Managerial Behavior, Performance and Effectiveness*, New York: McGraw-Hill.

5. Moran, E.T. and Volkwein, J.F. (1992), The cultural approach to the formation of organizational climate, *Human Relations*, Vol. **45**, pp. 19–47.

6. Burke W.W., and Litwin, G.H. (1992), A causal model of organisational performance and change. *Journal of Management*, Vol. **18**(3), pp. 523–545; Svyantek, D.J., & Bott, J.P. (2004), Organizational culture and organizational climate measures: An integrative review in J.C. Thomas (Ed.), *Comprehensive Handbook of Psychological Assessment: Industrial and Organizational Assessment*, Vol. **4**, pp. 507–524, N.J.: Wiley: Hoboken.

7. Schneider, B. (1990), The climate for service: An application of the climate construct. In B. Schneider (Ed.), *Organizational Climate and Culture*: Jossey-Bass: San Francisco, 383–412, CA, and Schneider, B. (2000). The psychological life in organisations. In N.M. Ashkanasy, C.P.M. Wilderon and M.F. Peterson (Eds.), *Handbook of Organizational Culture and Climate* (xvii–xxi). Thousand Oaks, CA: Sage Publications.

8. Hellriegel, D., and Slocum, J.W. Jr. (1974), Organizational climate: Measures, research and contingencies, *Academy of Management Journal*, **17**(2), pp. 255–280.

9. Drory, Amos, Perceived Political Climate and Job Attitudes, available at oss.sagepub.com/content/14/1/59.abstract, 1993.

10. Orpen, Christopher (1994), Organizational level as a moderator of the relationship between perceived political climate and employees' work attitudes, *Psychological Reports*, Vol. **75**, Issue, pp. 769–770.

11. Litwin, George H. and Robert A. Stringer (1968), *Motivation and Organizational Climate,* Boston: Harvard University Press, pp. 199–207.

12. Patterson, M.G., West, M.A., Shackleton, V.J., Dawson, J.F., Lawthom, R., Maitlis, S., Robinson, D.L., and Wallace, A.M. (2005), Validating the Organizational Climate Measure: Links to managerial practices, productivity and innovation. *Journal of Organizational Behaviour*, Vol. **26**(4), pp. 379–408.

13. Quoted in Adrian Furnham, Corporate climate questionnaire: A new multi-dimensional and international instrument to audit employee perceptions, available at Climate and Culture Questionnaire by cymeon, www.cymeon.com/climate/climate_on_net.asp, 5 Apr 2011.

14. Halpin, Andrew W. and don. B. Craft (1962), The Organisational climate of schools, Report submitted to US office of Education, quoted in John W. Hall (1972) *Administrative Science Quarterly*, Vol. **7**(4), p. 586.

15. James, L.R., & Jones, A.P. (1974), Organizational climate: A review of theory and research. *Psychological Bulletin*, 81, pp. 1096–1112.

16. Sharma, B.R. (1989), "Organizational Climate: A Property of the Individual or the Organization?", *Indian Journal of Industrial Relations*, Vol. **25**(1), July, pp. 23–34.

17. Payne, R.L. (1971), *OC: The Concept and Some Research Findings*, Prakseologia, NR/39/40/ROK.

18. Hall D.T. and Schneider, B. (1973), *"OC and Careers: The Lives of Priests"*, New York: Seminar Press; Muchinsky, Paul M. (1977), "Organizational Communication: Relationship to OC and Job Satisfaction", *Academy of Management Journal*, December, pp. 592–609, Newman, John, E. (1977), "Development of measure of perceived Work Environment (PWE)", *Academy of Management Journal,* Vol. **20**(4), pp. 520–534; and Sharma, Baldev R. (1987), *"Not by bread Alone: A Study of Organizational Climate and Employer-Employee Relations in India"*, New Delhi: Shri Ram Centre for Industrial Relations & Human Resources, pp. 42–50.

19. Pritchard, R.D. and Karasick B.W. (1973), "The Effects of OC on Managerial Job Performance and Job Satisfaction", *Organizational Behavior and Human Performance*, Vol. **9**, pp. 126–146.

20. Srivastava, S.K. (1999), "Correlation Study of Organizational Climate and Need Satisfaction with Job Involvement", *Abhigyan,* Vol. **17**(3), January–March, pp. 37–41.

21. Garg, Pooja and Renu Rastogi (2006), "Climate Profile and Organizational Citizenship Behaviors: A Comparative Analysis of Teachers Working in Public and Private Schools", *The ICFAI Journal of Organizational Behavior,* Vol. **5**(4), October, pp. 7–17.

22. Purang, Pooja (2006), "HRD Climate: A Comparative Analysis of Public, Private and Multinational Organizations", *Indian Journal of Industrial Relations*, Vol. **41**(3), January, pp. 407–419.

23. Akhilesh, K.B. and S. Pandey (1986), "A Comparative Study of Organizational Climate in Two Banks", *Indian Journal of Industrial Relations*, Vol. **21**(4), April, pp. 456–461.

24. Patel, M.K. (1999), "HRD Climate: A Comparative Study among Two Ends of Performance", *JIIMS 8M*, Vol. **4**(3), July-September, pp. 24–27.

25. Litwin, George H. and Robert A. Stringer (1968), *Motivation and Organizational Climate,* Boston: Harvard University Press, pp. 199–207.

26. Sinha, J.B.P. (1973), "OC and Problem of Management in India", *International Review of Applied Psychology,* Vol. **2**, pp. 55–64.

27. Hodgetts, Richard M. (1991), *"Organizational Behavior: Theory and Practice"*, New York: Macmillan Publishing, pp. 428–430.

28. Koontz, H. and Weihrich (1972), *Principles of Management*, New York: McGraw-Hill.

29. Halpin, A.W. (1967), *Theory and Research in Administration,* New York: Macmillan.

30. Hoy, W.K. and Miskel, C.G. (2008), *Educational Administration: Theory, Research and Practice,* New York: McGraw-Hill.

31. Pareek, U. "Motivational Analysis of Organizations—Climate (MAO-C)." in J.W. Pfeiffer (Ed.), The 1989 Annual: Developing Human Resources University Associates, San Diego, California, USA, pp. 161–180.

32. Purang, Pooja (2006), HRD Climate, A Comparative Analysis of Public, Private and Multinational Organizations, *Indian Journal of Industrial Relations*, **41**(3), January. Paula Jorde Bloom, Ann Hentschel and Jill Bella (2010), A Great Place to Work: Creating a Healthy Organizational Climate, New Horizons: Illinois.

33. Based on form built with Infopoll Designer. Available at *Innovation Climate* Questionnaire, infopoll.net/live/surveys/s27054.htm. France, Carole, Christina Mott and David Wagner, The innovation imperative, How leaders can build an innovation engine, available at The Innovation Imperative; How Leaders Can Build an Innovation ... www.mmc.com/knowledgecenter/.../The_Innovation_Imperative.php *and Climate* for *creativity* and Innovation, www.m1creativity.co.uk/innovationclimate.htm.

34. Khandwalla, Pradip (2003), *Corporate Creativity*, New Delhi: Tata McGraw-Hill, pp. 177–196.

35. Pareek, Udai, Osman-Gani, Aahad M., Ramnarayan S. and Rao T.V. (Eds.) (2002), *Human Resource Development in Asia: Trends and Challenges*, New Delhi: Oxford & IBH Publishing Co., Rodrigues, Lewlyn L.R., (2004), Correlates of Human Resource Development Climate Dimensions: An Empirical Study in Engineering Institutes in India, *South Asian Journal of Management,* April 1, Srimannarayana, M. (2008), Human resources development climate in India, *Indian Journal of Industrial Relations,* October.

36. Research update: creating motivational climates: how to make the most out of your recreation environment. goliath.ecnext.com/.../Research-update-creating-motivational-climate... 1 Jan. 2007 and Papaioannou A. (1997), Perceptions of motivational climate, perceived competence, and motivation of students of varying age and sport experience. *Percept Mot Skills,* October, **85**(2): pp. 419–30.

37. Pareek, U. "Motivational Analysis of Organizations—Climate (MAO-C)." in J.W. Pfeiffer (Ed.), The 1989 Annual: Developing Human Resources University Associates, San Diego, California, USA, pp. 161–180.

Chapter 5

Organization Culture

Vignette: Doing Well by Doing Right

ING Life has taken initiatives for fostering a performance culture. The belief at ING Life is success comes by 'Doing Well by Doing Right'. At ING, the idea of 'can-do' is promoted. For this, employees are recruited placing emphasis on matching people's personality with the culture. They are encouraged to set challenging goals, and take responsibility to make things happen. The environment fosters mutual respect, personal freedom and self-responsibility. Professional development is considered as co-responsibility. Employees work with line managers to identify suitable training programs and projects. The company strives to create learning framework, and fosters a culture of self-paced learning. Training aims at bridging competency gaps and matching priorities of organization. The focus is on systematic building of Organizational core capability, Individual role-based capability and leadership capability.

Tata Steel Group Vision 2012 is "We aspire to be the global steel industry benchmark for Value Creation and Corporate Citizenship". They seek to make difference through people (team work, talent, leadership capability and pace, pride and passion in action), offer (supplier of choice delivering premium and value products), innovation (providing leading edge solutions) and conduct (safety, care, ethics and environmental concerns). A new performance culture that applies to all employees at all levels across the Group has four pillars: (i) Safety and social responsibility, (ii) Continuous improvement (iii) Aspirational target setting, and (iv) Openness and transparency is envisaged to achieve its sustainability aims.

Hindustan Unilever is a family, not merely a company or an organization. The values for which HUL stands for are honesty, integrity, truth, courage, concern and care, which according to them culminate in just one – character. According to former Chairman Prakash Tandon, the word that captured HUL leadership qualities is character. Character is the overall umbrella under which their value system is nourished, takes root and thrives. HUL has a long tradition of rich rituals and storytelling that helps the team bond better, and communicates the hopes, aspirations and values of the organization. Whatever the company does as a family is shared with one and all. The greatest value nourished by company is professionalism in anything they do. "Be fair to all stakeholders". Indeed, this has actually been the core of the company from the very beginning[1].

The cases indicate that concern for culture building is common for all the enterprises. In this chapter, we will explore the diverse cultural aspects, and gain understanding of different types of organization culture.

INTRODUCTION

It is important for managers to understand how to integrate people with the organization, and make them work as teams to achieve the goals of the organizations effectively and efficiently. During 1980s, organization culture gained significance as an important concept and tool for understanding how people work and what drives them to work in a specific way. Each organization is a social system, with a specific social structure, behaviors and outcomes. Different cultural patterns can be observed not only among different organizations but also in different units of same organization. As such, understanding, maintenance and innovation of culture have become a challenge to the managers.

CONCEPT, CHARACTERISTICS AND SIGNIFICANCE

Different researchers have viewed culture differently and studied it from different perspectives. It is seen as a concept with two faces and many levels.

Two Faces of Culture

Rice defines culture as values, attitudes, beliefs, artifacts, and other meaningful symbols represented in the pattern of life adopted by individuals. He further states that culture helps individuals interpret, evaluate and communicate as members of society. It affects and describes behaviors of individuals[2].

According to Herskovitz, (culture is conceived as the human-made part of environment (it consists of physical elements (e.g. educational system, institutions and rituals) as well as subjective elements (e.g. beliefs, attitudes, norms and values)[3].

From the definitions, culture can be seen as a complex phenomenon with two concepts—descriptive and explicative[4].

- Descriptive concept focuses on what is observable, be it material artifacts (e.g. clothing, architecture and literature) or immaterial ones (e.g. language and social manner). It describes everything at the surface of the society. It can be labeled as—surface culture.

- Explicative concept focuses on the subjective, causal factors, the invisible behaviors like attitudes, norms and approaches. It can be termed as deep culture.

Levels of Explicative Culture

From the explicative view, culture is defined as influential hidden factors aimed to influence and develop a structure for behaviors. Schutte and Ciarlante described explicative culture as an iceberg with three distinct levels[5]:

1. Behavioral practices
2. Values, beliefs, preferences and norms
3. Basic assumptions and customs

He observed that the manifest behaviors are only the tip of iceberg, it is necessary for managers to gain a firm understanding of values and other lower level influencers that are critical to understanding and shaping individual behaviors.

ORGANIZATIONAL CULTURE

Organizational culture refers to the culture in a company or organization. Gareth Morgan[6] defined organizational culture as a character of a company.

"The set of beliefs, values, and norms, together with symbols like dramatized events and personalities that represents the unique character of an organization, and provides the context for action in it and by it."

Schein provided a simple view of organization culture with focus on group and individual behaviors. He stated that culture is what a group learns over a period of time; how it tries to solve its problems of survival in an external environment, and its problems of internal integration. It is defined as a complex of three processes: cognitive, behavioral, and emotional process that occurs simultaneously as given in Table 5.1.

TABLE 5.1   Organizational Culture and Its Processes

Dimension	Activity
Cognitive	Group learns how to solve problems and how to integrate
Behavior	Group solves problems and integrates
Emotional	Group experience feelings of achievement and affiliation

According to Schein, a culture, that has worked well and proved valid will endure. It will be taught to new members as the correct way to respond to the problems[7].

From the two definitions, the elements, processes and benefits of organization culture can be stated as given under.

- **Elements:**   Symbols, behaviors and norms, values and shared assumptions
- **Processes:**   Cognitive (learning and rational), behavior (functional or dysfunctional) and emotional (feelings and sentiments) processes
- **Benefits:**   Solving problems for survival, external adaptation and internal integration

Organizational Culture vs Corporate Culture

The two terms are often used interchangeably. However, they are different concepts[8]. While all corporations are organizations, all organizations are not corporations. Organizations include a wide range of institutions, like government, hospitals, schools, temples, non-governmental organizations, and service agencies.

Corporate culture is typically characterised by profit ethic. It is often determined by the founder and senior management and modified later by organizational members. Sometimes, cultural change may take place when a new culture is imported, through employees or mergers. For example, when a computer professional joins an organization, his language and behaviors can influence the culture of the organization as a whole.

Characteristics

Organization culture is characterised by the following features.

1. *Evolutionary:* The organization culture forms in a gradual manner over period of time. It is not something that is created over night. It takes long time for the formation of assumptions, values and beliefs, and sharing them among the organization members.

2. *Created by people:* The creation of culture, in general, is initiated by the founder of the organization. However, it is not just possible for him or a single individual to create the culture of an organization. It is enunciated, evaluated, and established by experiences of all the people working in the organization. Every person, worker to manager has a marginal or significant role in shaping the culture.

3. *Existence of subcultures:* Organization culture is like a system that has subsystems. In large organizations, subcultures present within the organizational culture, formed by distinct groups or departments. In other words, organization is a cluster of groups having different needs, activities, norms and sentiments. As a result, each group may have its own culture that guides, and rewards their behavior.

4. *Transmitted:* Cultures are hereditary. A culture which has got recognition of majority of the people in the organization will be passed on to the new employees through the process of socialization. The new employees learn by interacting with the peers the way things are done in the organization.

5. *Durable:* Culture is durable. Once formed, it is not an easy task to change the culture, because change requires unlearning existing assumptions, values and beliefs. Many find it difficult to change their old ways of thinking and doing things and learn doing new things. As such, change has to be gradual and exciting with a promise of better rewards.

6. *Unique:* Often we find different cultures in different organizations like factory, university, bank and hospital. This is because the observable, material artifacts, like architecture, furniture, uniforms and photographs, and immaterial ones, like language and social manners differ significantly. A further investigation reveals clearly that values, beliefs and assumptions differ from one organization to another. Another variable that causes difference between two similar cultures is the strength of the culture; some organizations have weak cultures while some have strong cultures. Thus, each organization has its own culture that is different from others.

Significance

Organizational culture has become more important today, as firms have to respond to a changing, competitive environment. Culture is recognized as one of the competitive advantages of firms, and is moved from the original operational level, to the strategic level, Culture performs a number of functions within an organization as:

1. *Identity:* It plays a boundary-defining role, and creates distinctions between one organization and another. It provides a sense of identity for members of the organization.

2. *Commitment:* It facilitates the generation of commitment to the larger, common goals subordinating one's self interest.

3. *Stability:* It enhances social system stability. Culture is the social glue that bonds the organization together.

4. *Coordination:* It serves as a control mechanism. It controls speech and behavior of employees through values, norms and standards. It aligns individual goals with organizational goals.

5. *Development:* It acts a sense making mechanism for self control and development. It guides and shapes the attitudes and behavior of employees.

6. *Ethical conduct:* It influences ethical conduct of employees. Ethics at work place evolves from the collection of values and behavior, which people feel are moral. Ethical values at work place include integrity, loyalty, fairness, caring and citizenship.

7. *Learning:* It fosters, information sharing and continuous learning among organization members.

8. *Performance:* The contribution of organization culture to organizational performance is significant and quantifiable. Researchers have found that an effective culture can account for 20–30% of the differential in performance compared with culturally unremarkable competitors.

9. *Innovation:* It provides an atmosphere of inquiry and research for creating new ideas profitable to individuals and organizations.

Harvard Business School's Professor, James Heskett, studied the adaptive cultures of Southwest Airlines, Wal-Mart, IBM, ING, 3M, and Proctor and Gamble and summarized the benefits of culture under a Four R framework given under[9].

1. *Referrals:* Current or former employees create a big pool of potential employees.

2. *Retention:* Effective engagement leads to lower costs of recruiting, hiring and training, minimizes productivity costs because of greater employee loyalty.

3. *Returns to labor:* Greater productivity per rupee of compensation.

4. *Relationships:* Larger benefits of customer relationship management like loyalty, lower customer acquisition costs, and more sales.

TYPES OF ORGANIZATION CULTURE

Organization cultures can be categorized into different types. What is the benefit of categorization of culture? Categorization of cultures helps managers in an understanding of the pros and cons of a particular culture, and helps determine what cultural changes are necessary. Such an understanding forms the basis for designing appropriate people related policies. Here we shall take a look at different categorizations of culture.

Based on Nature of Organizations

Researcher Jeffrey Sonnenfeld[10] identified the following four types of cultures as shown in Table 5.2.

TABLE 5.2 Types of Organization Culture

Types	Employees	Organization	Example
Academy culture	Competent people seeking rise in hierarchy	Provides a stable environment for work and development of people	Universities, hospitals, large corporations, etc.
Baseball team culture	Specialists in a particular field	Fast-paced, high risk organizations	Investment banking, advertising, etc.
Club culture	Employees stay longer with the organization to reach high positions	Values seniority and promotes within. It provides job security and encourages efficiency	Military, Consultancy firms, etc.
Fortress culture	Employees are 'stars' with specialized skills. They hold insecure positions, but can move from one firm to another.	Frequent reorganization. It seeks to shift power from employees to top level management. It shifts workers camaraderie into workers competitiveness as relationships become less stable and more situational	Large car companies

Strong and Weak Cultures

Culture is classified into strong and weak cultures based on the degree of alignment members have with organizational values. A strong culture indicates a high alignment, whereas weak culture indicates little alignment. Strong and dominant culture refers to the system of shared meaning held by organizational members. Perrow[11] observed that a strong culture is said to exist when:

- beliefs, values, assumptions, and practices are pervasive
- there is a high degree of consistency of beliefs, values, assumptions
- practices across organizational members, and
- members respond to situations with the shared meaning

Weak and dissonant culture is said to exist when:

- beliefs, values, assumptions, and practices are held differently by different groups
- members act guided by the parochial values and self-centered beliefs

A strong culture is considered beneficial to all organizations for the following reasons:

- It encourages solidarity and integrates people with the organization
- It fosters motivation, and commitment
- It provides unique identity by showing coordinated functional behaviors
- It replaces formalization and thrives on voluntary participation, and involvement of people.

However, strong cultures may develop certain dysfunctional tendencies, like groupthink. People in strong cultures develop groupthink, which reduces capacity for innovative thoughts. They strive for unanimity; they do not show motivation to realistically appraise alternatives of action avoid conflict. They seek to establish a friendly climate. They do not challenge status–quo. As a result, decisions may be less effective and innovation will be limited.

Peters and Waterman, observed that excellent organizations have shared common values and strong cultures[12].

Healthy and Unhealthy Cultures

A simple way of distinguishing the healthy and unhealthy organizational cultures is provided by Gerald Caiden's definition of bureaupathology[13] which is characterized by the following:

- Process is more importance than purpose
- Authority is more important than service
- Form is more important than reality
- Precedence is more important than adaptability

On the contrary, the hallmarks of healthy organizations are: purpose, service, reality and adaptability.

Herbert Shepard provided another way of identifying healthy and unhealthy organizational cultures[14]. He categorized them based on two types of mentality assumptions:

- *Primary mentality assumptions:* They refer to coercion, cut-throat competition, and compromise of principles.
- *Secondary mentality assumptions:* They refer to cooperation, collaboration, and consensus-seeking behavior.

In healthy organization cultures, secondary mentality assumption are the norm. In contrast, the primary mentality assumptions are associated with unhealthy organizations.

Yet another way of viewing healthy and unhealthy organizational cultures is suggested by Ruth Benedict. His classification is based on the concept of synergy groups and societies[15].

- A low synergy group or society is one in which the interests of individuals and the interests of the group are divergent.
- A high synergy group or society is one in which the interests of individuals and the interests of the group are in harmony.

Unhealthy organizational cultures are those characterized by low synergy and healthy organizational cultures are those characterized by high synergy.

The characteristics of healthy organizations are described in the following way[16]:

1. *Facilitative leadership:* Managers in leadership positions play a facilitative role in carrying out the mission of the organization. They employ non-threatening, non-coercive, and educational approaches which are ethical and goal-oriented.

2. *Energizing interactions:* The actions are driven by positive motivators, such as pride, confidence, enthusiasm, and affection and not by negative motivators, such as shame, fear, guilt, anxiety, distrust, or hatred.

3. *Participative and self-determined behaviors:* Managers are not inclined to act in controlling, manipulative, and stress-inducing ways. Employees take initiative and participate in decision-making.

4. *Continuous learning:* Learning is encouraged based on experience gained in tackling normal and crisis situations. Support to people for finding novel solutions and risk taking is made available.

5. *No scapegoats or passing the blame:* Mistakes are tolerated and there is support and forgiveness. When things go wrong, neither blame is passed on to others nor are innocent ones victimized.

Cultures Associated with Gods

Charles Handy classified organization cultures into four types and associated them with Gods[17]. The four elements of an organization—process (role), power, task and people form the basis for his classification.

Role Culture (Apollo)

A strong role culture is found in bureaucratic organizations which encourage formalization, functional specialization and role descriptions. Role playing by rules, procedures and systems is valued than personal initiatives and excellence. Performance beyond role is not encouraged. An apollonian ignores changes in the environment, and places heavy reliance on the existing set of routines. This type of organization is compared to a Greek temple. The apex of the temple is top administrative area where decision-making takes place. The functional units of the organization which implement the decisions are like pillars of the temple.

This type of culture is appropriate in organizations which are operating in a stable environment. Public sector companies are found having this type of culture.

Power or Club Culture (ZEUS)

Handy described power culture as web. Power is concentrated at the centre of the web, and radiates out from the centre. In a family organization, usually a key personality in the family will hold power and sends orders down to departments or units. Those away from the centre are at the receiving end, and cannot influence decisions and events. However, one way of gaining significance is by staying close to the power center. The boss maintains a network of friendships and old boys, which can be referred to as power club. By getting close to such people, one can exercise considerable influence.

In a changing environment, the power culture may adapt to changes very rapidly as authority is centralized or fail to see the need for change, and die. This kind of culture is prevalent in small organizations like brokerage firms and private educational institutions.

Task culture (Athens)

Task culture is represented by a net or lattice work. People are task-oriented, and power is derived from expertise. There is close liaison between departments, and specialized functions. In fact, the work is the best integrator. Employees move from one project or group to another. Team work, adaptation to change and innovation are predominant features of this culture. Consultant firms, ad agencies and start-up high tech firms will be working in this kind of culture.

Existential or Person culture (Dionysius)

The culture is characterized by individual freedom, value for expertise and achievement orientation among individuals. Decision-making is influenced by professionals. This culture works well as long as individuals work positively to make meaningful contribution. However, when they take a negative stand, it leads to ideological wars among the professionals. Architects or doctors who share space will develop this kind of culture.

Evolving Culture Types

Carmazzi posited a symbiotic relationship between psychology and culture, and proposed five levels of culture[18]. Based on the assumption that "Every Individual in the organization wants to do a good job", he stated that behind every culture there is psychology. People strive to create right culture for doing a good job. If behaviors that result in poor performance are found, the fault lies with the group or organization and the policies, leadership and communication adopted by them. Therefore, managers have to understand their role in the psychological dynamics behind the culture, and make changes to move the culture to the next higher level. Table 5.3 shows the five levels of culture described by him.

TABLE 5.3   Five Levels of Culture

S.No.	Culture level	Description
1	Blame culture	People play safe; avoid risk taking. Pass blame on others to avoid being reprimanded
2	Multi-directional culture	Each department becomes a clique. Cross-department communication and cooperation are less. Loyalty is to the department to which an employee belongs. Lack of cooperation and inefficiency are common
3	Live and let live culture	It is characterized by dominance of personal relationships and complacency. There is no vision and passion for achievement. Cooperation and communication lead to average performance

(Contd.)

S.No.	Culture level	Description
4	Brand congruent culture	Employees take pride in working for the organization. They feel good about product of company and work with passion. They even step out of their roles to solve problems. They work in groups. However, they may not always agree with management
5	Leadership enriched culture	This culture encourages development of employees as leaders. Individual goals are aligned with the goals of the organization. Employees work in wellknit groups and contribute as a team. Organization is like a family and individual fulfilment often transcends ego

Cultures Based on Risk and Feedback

Decisions taken in organizations can be analyzed based on two factors—risk and time taken to get the outcomes. The risk can be high or low and time taken for implementation can be short or long. In case of long-term decisions or projects, the feedback on realization will be slow. Based on this understanding, Deal and Kennedy classified cultures taking the two parameters—feedback (monetary, praise, reward) and risk (uncertainty)[19]. Figure 5.1 shows the classification.

Quick feedback	Slow Feedback	
Tough guy Macho culture	Bet your company culture	**High risk**
Work hard/play hard culture	Process culture	**Low risk**

Figure 5.1 Types of cultures based on feedback and risk.

1. *Tough-guy macho culture:* This type of culture results in when risks are high and feedback is quick. Though rewards are high, it can be very stressful in practice. Fast moving financial activities and competitive team sports, such as professional football operate in this type of culture.

2. *Work hard/play hard culture:* This is characterized by low risks and rapid feedback. It is exciting to work in this type of culture, though sustaining the excitement may be difficult. Usually, large organizations oriented to high quality customer service establish this type of culture.

3. *Bet your company culture:* High risk decisions are taken, but the feedback will be slow. It may take years to know the results. R&D organizations and Oil prospecting firms operate in this type of culture.

4. *Process culture:* In this culture, bureaucratic tendencies will be dominant. Due to operational focus, efficiency will be high and due to this narrow vision, people may lose focus on the bigger picture of what is to be achieved. This culture is suitable to public service institutions.

Cultures Based on Action Orientation

People respond to situations in four ways: constructive, passive, aggressive and defensive. Based on this observation, Robert A. Cooke classified organizational culture into three types as follows[20]:

1. *Constructive culture:* Employees work with achievement orientation and seek to attain self-actualization. Organization will be humanistic and foster team work. Concepts like empowerment, total quality management, continuous improvement, transformational leadership and reengineering are appreciated and implemented.

2. *Passive-defensive culture:* Employees interact with each other in ways that do not threaten their own security. Organization emphasizes on formalization. Employees are expected to obey their superiors and avoid interpersonal conflict. Rules and procedures are emphasized. As a result, there may be lower level of motivation and satisfaction.

3. *Aggressive-defensive culture:* Employees try to look competent and compete with each other to establish their superiority and power of controls. However, they will be careful not to threaten their own security or status. Not to look weak, they do not admit mistakes Those who admit to shortcomings are considered weak. In this culture, short-term gains outweigh long-term growth.

Cultures Based on Competing Values Framework

Quinn and Rorbaugh evolved Competing Values Framework[21] for cultural assessment with two dimensions as shown in Figure 5.2.

Internal focus and integration	Flexibility and discretion		External focus and differentiation
	Clan	Adhocracy	
	Hierarchy	Market	
	Stability and control		

Figure 5.2 The competing values map and cultures.

The four hierarchies are to some extent historical in their development and are presented in the order as follows:

Cultures that Encourage Internal Focus and Integration

1. *Hierarchy culture:* The emphasis is on stability and control. As such, it depends on a vertical, formalized, bureaucratic organization to achieve them. There is respect for position and power. Managers in the hierarchy facilitate coordination and exercise controls. Employee behavior is guided by well-defined policies, processes and procedure.

2. *Clan culture:* The emphasis is on flexibility and discretion. Accordingly, organizations are created with less emphasis on structure and controls. People are given considerable freedom; they are not driven by rules. They are required to decide and act in accordance with vision, shared goals, and desired outputs.

3. *Clans often have flat organizations:* Clan leaders act as facilitators and provide support to people working in teams to act more autonomously. People are related by the sense of family that develops a shared cause among the members and loyalty to one another.

Cultures that encourage external focus and differentiation

1. *Market culture:* The emphasis is on stability and control, but with focus on market. There is market orientation in all transactions of the enterprise. Decisions are driven by results. In all actions and decisions, gaining competitive advantage will be given importance.

2. *Adhocracy culture:* The emphasis is on flexibility and discretion with focus on market. This kind of culture becomes necessary when market success requires greatest speed and adaptability. There is encouragement to risk taking, innovation and quick results. Accordingly, there is more preference to prototyping and modifications, rather than long, big-bang projects and development. There will be rapid formation of teams to face new challenges and greater independence to makes innovative decisions.

Cultures Based on Sociability and Solidarity

Goffee, R. and G. Jones, developed a classification of cultures based on two factors: (i) degree of sociability, and (ii) degree of solidarity[22]. Sociability is a measure of friendliness amongst members of an organization, inside or outside of work. Solidarity is a measure of unity among people in achievement of tasks. Figure 5.3 depicts the four generic types of cultures.

Low solidarity	High solidarity	
Networked culture	Communal culture	High sociability
Fragmented culture	Mercenary culture	Low sociability

Figure 5.3   Types of cultures based on sociability and solidarity.

Networked culture

People are related by concern, friendship and kindness. They feel like family and socialize. They show empathy and develop mutual trust. They interact frequently and discuss a wide range of topics. The office is designed accordingly with open spaces. However, privacy is respected. Open door policy is followed. Time is taken to socialize both within work, and outside of it.

Mercenary culture

Mercenary cultures encourage both individual ambition and organizational success. As such it creates a powerful drive to get things done with swift communication, rapid thinking, and quick action. Goals are set for the organization or team, and members are given individual targets. Winning is very important to the organization and to the members. In this culture, personal ambition is dominant and loyalty is weak. People, may leave the organization when they find good opportunities. We observe sportsmen abandoning their teams when they find a better opportunity. Similarly, we find employees in IT companies changing jobs frequently to get better pay and benefits.

Communal culture

The communal culture is characterized by a strong sense of community and shared responsibility. The friendship of networked culture and the drive and ambition of the mercenary culture are found in this culture. People work for the mission of the organization with a passion. Office space will be shared. Communication flows freely binding people together. A sort of family atmosphere can be found. This kind of culture can be found in social service organizations and small business organizations.

Fragmented culture

An organization which fails to motivate people as well as integrate them with organization will have this kind of culture. People prefer working in isolation without interruptions. They work in offices that are well equipped and follow closed door policy. They pursue professional goals and do not interact much with other members. Whatever communication takes place it will be work related. For transacting with clients they may conduct work away from office. A multi-speciality hospital having consultant doctors on contractual basis will display this kind of culture.

Other Cultural Models

Different writes have attempted to classify cultures differently and analysed them. In addition to the above, the following four culture types are worth considering.

1. *Entrepreneurial culture:* Stephen McGuire defined entrepreneurial organizational culture[23]. This is similar to the Adhocracy.

- *Values:* Creativity and tolerance of creative people
- *Belief:* Innovating and seizing market opportunities are appropriate behaviors to deal with problems of survival and prosperity, environmental uncertainty and competitors' threats
- *Behaviors:* Expects organizational members to behave accordingly

2. *Empowerment culture:* Empowerment is a process for unleashing the potential and power in people by transfer and acceptance of power to the lowest appropriate level. Opportunity for individual imitativeness, risk taking, responsibility and commitment is provided.

3. *High performance culture:* John Case found that many companies could accomplish a high performance culture by adopting the system and philosophy of open book management[24]. In this, information available is not used to intimidate, control or manipulate people. Rather it is used to gain control over their lives through teaching how to work and achieve common goals.

4. *Soft and synergetic cultures:* Two distinct work cultures soft and synergetic work cultures are identified by Sinha, (1990) in Indian organizations[25]. These represent the two broad extremes of a continuum of work-culture. The public sector organizations have a soft work-culture while the private sector organizations have a synergetic work-culture.

- In a soft work-culture, work seems to have been displaced from its central place in the organization by non-work activities and interests, like social obligations, etc. Employees in such organizations do not feel positive affect to work, do not derive satisfaction from their job and work is not at a central place in their lives. These employees take work easily and maximize personal gains.
- The synergetic work culture is the complete opposite. In a synergetic work culture the organization has an environment conducive for working hard and the employees have a positive effect to work. This is also because hard work is rewarded, and there exists a strong normative pressure for working hard. Those managers who realize, anticipate, or strive to realize their important values through work experience, are seen to give work a central place in their lives.

Which Culture is Right?

There is nothing like right culture for any organization. Right organizational culture must fit with the environment to meet the goals. For instance, strong culture may prove wrong when innovation and quick adaptation to environment are necessary. Strong culture creates traditions and habits and shuns change and creativity. On the other hand, weak culture encourages individual ideas and contributions. When operational efficiency is important strong culture is appropriate.

FACTORS INFLUENCING CULTURE

Based on the organizational and environmental characteristics, suitable organization culture can be evolved. It is noted that formation of culture will depend on a whole host of factors including company history, ownership, organization structure, technology, critical business incidents and environment, etc. The culture of an organization will be subjected to examination when certain changes take place. The different factors that have influence on organization culture are enumerated here.

Environmental Factors

Today, the environment is in a constant state of flux. Destabilising forces, like competition, globalization, mergers and acquisitions, are threatening the survival of firms. In view of this, firms need better coordination across organizational units to generate, quick and efficient response to environmental forces. They need either a dominant, strong culture or well integrated sub-cultures. The different drivers of culture change are:

1. *Innovation needs:* Firms have to be creative to continuously innovate new products, processes and strategies. Innovation requires a culture of risk taking, experimentation and dislike for tradition. The culture that fosters learning and sharing of knowledge, and encourages new ideas is necessary for modern organizations.

2. *Diversity management:* The twenty first century firms are facing new challenge of workforce diversity due to geographical expansion and cross cultural operations. It has become necessary employ people of different nations, castes, races and genders. We find organizations trying to construct of meta- or hybrid-cultures that merge aspects of different cultures to facilitate teamwork and fulfillment of individual needs.

3. *Knowledge work:* Today, organizations have become tech-savvy. By adopting new technologies, they have become structurally elegant and functionally efficient. The work force of these organizations constitutes mainly, intellectuals as opposed to material assets. Maximizing the value of employees as intellectual assets requires a learning and knowledge sharing culture.

Country Cultural Factors

Companies planning to become multinational have to look at cultural differences among nations. Hofstede looked for national differences between over 100,000 of IBM's employees in different parts of the world, and identified five dimensions on which differences can be drawn[26]. Table 5.4 shows the how the five dimensions differentiate cultures.

TABLE 5.4   Dimensions of Culture

S.No.	Dimension	High score countries	Low score countries
1	Power distance	East European, Latin, Asian and African countries	Germanic and English-speaking Western countries
2	Uncertainty	East and Central European countries, Latin countries, Japan and German speaking countries	English speaking, Nordic and Chinese culture countries
3	Individualism	Developed and western countries	Less developed and eastern countries
4	Maculinity	Japan, German speaking countries, and some Latin countries like Italy and Mexico	Masculinity low in Nordic countries and Netherlands
5	Long-term orientation	Long-term orientation high in East Asian countries, like China, Hong Kong, Taiwan, Japan, and South Korea	USA and Britain

1. *Power distance:* The degree to which differences in the levels of power is acceptable. Low score means willingness to treat others as equals.

2. *Uncertainty avoidance:* The extent to which uncertainty and risk is acceptable. Low score indicates ability to deal with unstructured situations.

3. *Individualism:* The extent to which people are to stand up for themselves or for the group to which they belong. High score on collectivism indicates affiliation orientation.

4. *Masculinity:* The extent to which value is placed on traditional male or female values. High score on masculinity shows less power to women.

5. *Long-term orientation:* The extent to which choice of focus for people's efforts is laid on the future. High score on long-term shows emphasis on steady progress.

IT Factor and Cyber Culture

Escobar conceives cyber culture as a cultural mode that involves the realisation that we increasingly live and make ourselves in techno-biocultural environments structured indelibly by novel forms of science and technology. Jakub Macek describes cyber culture in the following words:

Cyber culture can be described as a heterogeneous, continuously growing set of more or less cohesive subcultures, communities and individuals sharing (in the role of inventors or first users) access to Information and Communication Technologies (ICT) and an interest in their development and impact on society and culture[27].

The cybercultural discourses and cybercultural narratives are using new technological jargon focussing on the issue of technologically determined social and cultural change. Virtual worlds are adding a new dimension to the social, economic, cultural and educational environments. They are creating new contexts and new modes of socialization and new identities to individuals. A new horizon has opened up in organizations for socialization and formalization of functions and performance[28].

1. *Work-culture:* The 24/7 work patterns, video-conferencing, work-from home and flexible working systems have redefined working styles. The new work-culture is thus characterized by freedom as well as high levels of stress.

2. *Socialization:* Internet as an instant communication media along with new social media have enriched workplace communication, and provided new opportunities for conversation with employees, customers and general public. However, the loss of common workplace, workplace personal relationships and gossips, and community relationships is a demotivator to some employees.

3. *New problems:* Issues like privacy and security, and dysfunctional tendencies, like Internet addiction and misuse of office resources for personal gains are posing challenges.

4. *Strategy factors:* Strategy decisions like mergers and acquisitions, technology absorption and globalization pose challenge to organization culture.

MANAGING CULTURE

The development of culture in an organization focuses on two important aspects: (i) external adaptation, and (ii) internal integration. For managing culture, Schein suggested that modern organizations must embrace external connectivity, as well as promote internal integration[29].

1. Dealing with external environment
   - Be future-oriented, not predominantly present/past-oriented
   - Be proactive, not just reactive
   - Be capable of influencing and managing the environment, not just adapt

2. Dealing with internal integration
   • Be pragmatic, not idealistic
   • Embrace diversity, not uniformity
   • Be relationship-oriented, not just task-oriented

External Adaptation

External adaptation can be achieved by defining mission, values, goals and strategies.

1. *Establish the mission and values:* Establish the mission of the organization. It is the responsibility of the founders to make it clear the basic purpose for which organization is started, and the values they would like to follows in both decisions and actions.

2. *Develop vision statement:* Looking into the future, develop a vision statement that portrays the status and function of organization in society at a point of time in future.

3. *Specify the goals of the organization:* Make clear the long range goals of the organization, and the criteria for measurement of goal-directed performance within the organization.

4. *Formulate strategies:* Design strategies to take advantage of the opportunities and achieve the goals of the organization. Thus ensure a fit between founder aspirations, organization and environment.

Internal Integration

Internal integration process involves designing organization structure and employing right leadership styles and communication methods for establishing shared values and norms for acceptable behaviors.

Structure and Systems

The design of organization structure and systems that promote the behaviors acceptable to management from organizational success point of view is the next important step.

1. *Design right structures:* The choice of structure depends on the desired style of functioning by superiors and subordinates in the hierarchy. Tall structures facilitate superior directed behaviors and promote either power cultures or role cultures. On the other hand, flat structures facilitate self-directed or team behaviors and result in clan culture or entrepreneur culture.

2. *Establish appropriate systems:* The formalization of processes results in systems. For creating role cultures, you have to establish rules, disciplinary procedures, limited information flows and tight controls. On the other hand, to encourage high performance or innovation cultures, create open systems, participative decision procedures, fair compensation system with non-monetary rewards, development mechanisms and free information flows.

Leadership

The role of people management in establishing right culture need not be overemphasized. A leader is not only a creature of the culture but also its creator. Care is to be taken in hiring suitable persons with right skills and attitudes. Further, they should be led by adopting right kind of style.

1. *Hire right staff and skills:* People are asset to the organization when they are right people who fit organization culture. The fit employees are those who have the required qualifications, work experience and skills but also possess values that match with those of the existing culture. Only when there is a right match, the newcomers could integrate with his functional groups and contribute to the whole operation of the company. When there is a mismatch, he or she would become a liability to the organization.

2. *Employ right style:* A leader has to be a mentor, coach and role model for others in the organization. The way the leader pays attention to people, prioritizes alternative courses of action, makes statements and acts in different situations will be watched, evaluated and emulated by followers. In fine, it can be said that, his style manifests in organization and becomes institutionalized. As such leaders have to match their deed to words. For instance, a leader who announces customer service as their priority, a customer service team is to be set up with clear goals and direction and provided required resources and facilities. Further, as a representative and champion of the culture, leader has to bring changes in the existing culture when required.

Box 5.1 presents how the problem of culture fit is resolved in case of mergers and alliances.

BOX 5.1 Culture Fit Solutions

A substantive body of theory and research on the role of culture in Mergers and Acquisitions (M&A) has concluded that cultural differences are major obstacles to achieving the benefits. The research by Accenture revealed that less than 1% of all proposed alliances are killed for purely cultural reasons. KPMG revealed that 83% of all Mergers and Acquisitions (M&A) failed to produce any benefit for the shareholders and over half actually destroyed value. The issues such as identity, ego clashes, communication problems, and inter-group conflicts, arise due to cultural differences.

The solution lies in creating a new culture for all the employees. It involves cultural innovation followed by cultural maintenance. Two techniques for cultural conciliation are: cultural learning audit (to review cultural compatibility) and culture work out (to integrate cultures). A wide range of structural and operational approaches, to resolve cultural issues are found.

Structural solution: One global chemical company uses a 50–50 independent-joint venture structure when large cultural differences exist. Such structures—characterized by limited resource flows and no staff exchanges between the joint venture and its corporate parents—insulate the alliance from the parents' cultures, and thus, encourage it to develop a culture of its own.

(Contd.)

| |
BOX 5.1   Culture Fit Solutions (*Contd.*)

Operational solution: One computer hardware maker with a consensus-driven style and a workforce proud of its friendliness was forming an alliance with a software company known for being highly individualistic, combative and blunt. To manage this difference in operating style, the hardware maker agreed to appoint as its alliance manager one of its more plainspoken employees. In return, the software company chose a particularly team-focused and conciliatory manager to run the alliance from its side. The partners took a similar "move toward the middle" approach to differences in communications processes. While the software company used e-mail and the hardware company favoured the telephone or face-to-face meetings, both made an effort to balance the use of these channels in the alliance.

Source: Walker, Pippa, After the alliance: Managing cultural differences, available at Point of View, www.accenture.com/.../PDF/managing_alliance_cultures_pov_rev.pd... Bing, Ed.D., and Lionel Laroche, (2001). The Impact of Culture on Mergers & Acquisitions, *CMA Management, March. Available at* The Impact of Culture on Mergers & Acquisitions, www.itapintl.com/.../the-impact-of-culture-on-mergers-a-acquisitions...and Stahl, Günter K. and Andreas Voigt (2008), Do Cultural Differences Matter in Mergers and Acquisitions? A Tentative Model and Examination, *Organization science*, available at orgsci.journal. informs.org/content/19/1/160.abstract.

Principles

Denison (1990) suggested the following four principles for managing culture, which represent its characteristics and ability to affect behaviors of employees[30]. To them, one more principle—principle of continuity is added.

1. *Principle of consistency:*   The more the common perspective, shared beliefs and communal values among the organizational participants the more will be internal coordination and a sense of identification on the part of its members.

2. *Principle of mission:*   The stronger the shared sense of purpose, direction, and strategy the more organizational members can be galvanised toward collective goals.

3. *Principle of involvement/participation:*   Involvement and participation contribute to a sense of responsibility and ownership and thereby to organizational commitment and loyalty.

4. *Principle of adaptability:*   Norms and beliefs that enhance an organization's ability to respond to the signals of environment will promote its survival, growth, and development.

5. *Principle of continuity:*   It is suggested that managers must maintain some sense of continuity with the past, while evolving a new culture. Collins and Porras (1994) found that companies with long-term success had a limited but strong set of timeless core values preserved them while stimulating progress.[31]

MAINTAINING CULTURE

Edgar Schein opined that one of the important decisive functions of leaders is the creation the management, and—if and when that may become necessary—the destruction of organizational culture. The maintenance of an established culture is not an easy task[32].

Problems

The following problems may arise in the context of preserving and continuing the culture:

1. *Lack of awareness among new hires:* New hires entering the organization will be naturally unaware of the culture of the organization. For some individuals, the new organizational culture may produce culture shock if there is a significant difference between the organization he worked and the organization he has joined. It takes time to unlearn old practices and attitudes and learn the new ones.

2. *Conflicts:* The positive effects of culture on the performance of an organization can me negated by the existence of conflict in organizations. When conflicts in terms of resources and personal egos arise among employees, there will be unhealthy competition and dysfunctional performance. A leader interested in maintaining high performance culture has to educate employees to learn values like collaboration, team spirit and achievement.

Solutions

The maintenance of culture is an ongoing process and whatever efforts were made earlier to develop a specific culture are to be carried out with necessary improvements.

- *Creating an understanding:* Organizational culture is created when the schematas (schematic structures) of differing individuals across and within an organization come to resemble each other. Schemata (plural of schema) are knowledge structures in a person. They are formed from past experiences, current events and interaction with others. Stanley G. Harris argues that five categories of in-organization schemata are essential for creating and maintaining organizational culture[33].
- *Self-in-organization schemata:* This refers to one's view of themselves as a member of the organization. It consists of an understanding of personality, position, role and behavior in the organization.
- *Person-in-organization schemata:* This consists of a person's impressions and expectations of other individuals and memories of events and relationships.
- *Organization schemata:* This comprises a person's generalized perspective on others as a whole in the organization.
- *Object/concept-in-organization schemata:* This refers to the knowledge an individual has of organization structure, systems, etc.
- *Event-in-organization schemata:* This is related to a person's knowledge of social events within an organization.

Employ Communication

Communication plays a major role of educating organization members and shaping their behavior. It explains the rationale of strategies, structures and systems in the context of the defined mission, vision and values of the enterprise. It facilitates sharing of norms, values and beliefs. It makes clear what is expected of the members in terms of contribution and behaviors.

It helps create strong, congruent cultures supportive of organizational structures, systems and strategies.

1. *Symbols*: Symbols are noticed through the sensory organs. They include physical ones like organizational building, layout, landscape, office décor, furniture, status or power indicators, such as parking spaces and executive washrooms and socialization tools, like etiquette, reception, and organizational dress, and identity creators, like organizational logos, brochures and slogans.

2. *Routines*: They refer to day-to-day activity which is repetitive in nature. For example, the way employee attendance problems are dealt with, the manner of answering telephone calls, the method of dealing with customers, etc., are routine activities, which exemplify values of organization.

3. *Rituals*: Rituals are situation-specific, repetitive actions with a specific meaning.

- *Rites of passage:* They refer to actions that facilitate transition to new roles like training programs.
- *Rites of enhancement:* Actions that help rise power and status or improve behavior like awards, and felicitations.
- *Rites of degradation:* Actions that reduce or remove identity, status and power like disciplinary actions, demotion and termination.
- *Rites of integration:* Actions that promote socialization, and create social networks like meetings, office parties, picnics, etc.
- *Rites of renewal:* Actions that improve existing social structures by changing composition of group members to revive or establish certain interests and practices.
- *Rites of conflict reduction:* Actions that resolve arguments between certain members or groups like meetings, discussions, negotiations, etc.
- *Rites of integration:* Actions that reinforce feelings of membership in the organization.

4. *Ceremonies and celebrations*: They include foundation day, founder's birthday, national holidays especially May day, Independence day and Republic day and festivals.

5. *Conversations*: According to Edgar Schein, leaders through their daily conversations created and changed culture[34]. The arrival of social media and e-communications has expanded the scope of communication in modern organizations. Culture can be embedded and transmitted through metaphors, stories, jokes and history. Use of metaphors is the simple way of creating identity. By comparing organization to a family, quite often leaders create an impression of emotional togetherness, responsibility and loyalty Stories often focus on the life and achievements of founder, a legend or a role model or in the industry. They may also be weaved around successful firms. They may deal with a bad guy who was vanquished by a good guy or firms that failed to succeed due to own mistakes. Stories can be true or mythological. Stories from epics presenting heroes like Rama and Krishna may be used to inculcate certain values. Cartoons in newsletters and house journals can be effective in communicating cultural values.

Facilitate Socialization

Organizational socialization or on boarding, refers to the process of imparting necessary knowledge, skills, values and behaviors to new employees to make them effective members of an organization. Daniel Feldman defined organizational socialization as the process through which individuals are transformed from outsiders to participating, effective members of an organization[35]. Taylor and Francis describes the 3 stages of socialization process as follows[36]:

1. *Pre arrival stage/anticipatory stage:* It take place during the recruitment process. Potential employee gets a glimpse of the organizational culture, image and values from the recruiting personnel. The individual makes a decision on whether to join the organization or not.

2. *Encounter/entry/breaking-in period:* Employee joins the organization, and receives orientation to the organizational practices. Information about the functional aspects, the duties and responsibilities of the new job and the role he/she is going to play in the organization. The employee gains an understanding of work ethics and code of conduct.

3. *Metamorphosis stage:* Employee learns to become part of organization and a supporter and promoter of the organization's philosophies. Employee appreciates the values, image and culture of the organization, and adopts his personality to fit in to the organization. Socialization becomes a tough challenge when it comes to shifting an employee from one culture into a new organizational culture. First, help should be provided to overcome the culture shock. Then the new cultural values and norms are transmitted. Managers can makes use of two means of socialization—informal and formal.

- Formal means of communication include training, company meetings, mentoring, and orientation by experienced workers, employee hand books, company literature and jargon. Inspirational office stories that are legendary are told in a spirit of camaraderie.
- Informal approaches include exchanges during coffee or lunch breaks and gossips, stories and jokes.

CHANGING CULTURE

Changing an organization's culture is a major challenge for the reason; culture comprises an interlocking set of values, systems and styles. For this reason, single-fix changes, such as the introduction of teams, or knowledge management, or some new process eventually fail to make desired impact due to passive response from related units. An effective culture change should be an organization-wide initiative, embracing all the subsystems and employees of the enterprise.

In general, an effective culture change strategy makes use of three types of tools:

- *Leadership tools:* Mission, Vision or story of the future, and value statements.
- *Management tools:* Role definitions, measurement and control systems, code of conduct, etc.
- *Power tools:* Position descriptions, coercion and punishments, and disciplinary procedures.

The process of changing culture involves the following steps[37].

- *Understanding current culture:* Before deciding on a culture change, one has to first understand the current culture and its effectiveness with internal focus. When it is recognized that the current organizational culture is deficient and is not able to support the organization's success and progress, change can be contemplated. As a consultant or manager, how do you analyse and assess the culture? Table 5.5 shows the four levels of analysis.

TABLE 5.5   Four Levels of Analysis

Level	Description	Tools
Symbols and artefacts	Slogans, mission, creeds, facilities, offices, furnishings, visible awards and recognition dress, and socialization	Observation
Values and beliefs	Local and personal values held by members and resultant behaviors	Questionnaires and interviews
Assumptions	Unspoken rules and tacit understanding of organizational systems and behaviors known to experienced people in the organization	In-depth interviews
Overall	Different components of cultures and their influence on working of organization	Culture audit

- *A word of caution:* Analyst may sometimes come across paradoxical organizational behaviors. For instance, an organization which professed highly aesthetic and moral standards may not hesitate to bribe government officials to get a license. An organization which states that they value customers, may not respond to the customer complaints as expected.
- *Decide the strategic direction:* Analyze the culture with reference to the future strategies and vision of the company with external focus. Decide what the organizational culture should look like to support the game plan of the organization. Identify ways to achieve strategy—culture fit. Prepare the culture road map.
- *Model organizational culture:* Depending on the needs for external adaptation and internal integration; leaders have to choose a model of culture. Wide varieties of culture models are found in practice. Leaders can adopt one of them or innovate a new culture type.
- *Select change agents:* Appoint a team of change agents under the leadership of a highly respected insider, who supports the change and devise strategies for change.
- *Top management commitment:* Top management in the organization must support the cultural change. The support should be explicit, going beyond verbal support. They should be at the forefront of the change. They should change their own behaviors and provide consistent support to the change agents.
- *Training:* Culture change requires a clear understanding of future expectations and roles. Members of the organization should be given training to help them in acquiring knowledge and skills necessary to transform their behaviors.

- *Create value and belief statements:* Form employee focus groups, by department and ask them to describe the mission, vision, and identify their impact on their job. This exercise involves employees in appreciating the emerging culture.
- *Practice effective communication:* Develop good communication channels and tools to keep all employees informed about the organizational culture change process. Today, social media can be gainfully employed as it has become an effective tool for conversations.
- *Review organizational structure:* Make changes in the structure of the company to align it with the desired organizational culture.
- *Redesign your approach to rewards and recognition:* Change the reward system to encourage the behaviors vital to the desired organizational culture.
- *Review all work systems:* Evaluate the different systems, such as motivation and reward system, communication system and performance appraisal system and align them with the desired culture.
- *Clarify and strengthen culture:* To successfully establish culture, leaders often engage their teams by telling the story of their shared vision, and publicly celebrating the achievement of milestones. To ensure that employees appreciate the culture, they should be given opportunities to test, voice opinions and suggest alternatives without fear of reprimand.

DEVIANT CULTURE

A deviant organization culture occurs when leadership permits immoral and illegal behaviors and rationalizes them to achieve goals and targets[38]. Culture at any time, is the creation of leadership. When a charismatic leader endowed with a narcissistic personality takes over the organization, he disregards company's reputation, ethics and goals to achieve personal needs and self-interest. He chooses members of low self esteem and rewards them in financial terms for being "yes-men". He shows blatant disregard for the social norms and tends to develop a corporate cult of blindfolded followers. The culture survives by the following factors:

- *Group think:* Members relinquish responsibility for their own actions and seek group consensus, endorsement and support.
- *Passive submission:* They find safety in following group norms. Members disagreeing with some aspects do not voice it.
- *Closed system:* External information, which is contrary to the group's direction and objectives, is discouraged.
- *Coercion:* People raising voices against the leader or group norms are punished. As Aristotle said, "Evil gets men together."

How to change the deviant culture?

To change the culture the following initiatives are essential:

1. *Change in leadership:* A new leader known for integrity and character has to be chosen to lead the organization and monitor the cultural change. As E. Bruke said, "The only thing necessary for evil to triumph is for good men to do nothing." As such, to build a healthy culture the power should be with the strong, good men.

2. *Cognitive therapy:* A formal training process should be established to deal with abrasive managers,

3. *Open system:* Open book management is to be set up to encourage new ideas, and propagating ideals.

4. *New direction:* The culture should be re-established with a vision and mission statement, followed with a code of business ethics, policies and procedures.

5. *People with integrity and character:* The bad apples need to be removed as a signal to the others that deviant behavior is unacceptable to the organization.

6. *Whistle blowing:* Employee feedback on malpractices should be encouraged by opening multiple channels for reporting. Mechanisms to take action based on the reports should be set up and made effective to prevent employee releasing such information to public and mass media. The employees reporting malpractices should be given protection and rewards for their commitment to right conduct.

Changing a culture is a time-consuming task. It may take years to build and activate new culture. However, it is worth the effort as rewards are high.

CONTINUOUS LEARNING CULTURE

A learning organization will have at its heart the concept of continuous learning and development. It invests effort, time and money in creating a learning culture. Employees would make learning a habit. They would learn something new everyday from different sources. Leading management thinker, Peter Senge has identified five disciplines of a learning culture that contribute to building a learning organization[39].

1. *Personal mastery:* Create an environment that encourages personal and organizational goals to be developed and realized in partnership. Encourage open and honest dialogue among organizational members. Ensure free flow of information throughout the organization.

2. *Mental models:* A person's internal picture of their environment will shape their decisions and behavior. Create right environment for people to work intelligently. Encourage challenges at work, reducing the fear of failure and removing stessors and frustration.

3. *Shared vision:* Top management commitment becomes clear when there is a shared vision. Provide a clear statement of the organization's mission, and vision along with the concerns for human resource development needs. It will establish right spirit for development, and build a sense of group commitment by developing shared images of the future.

4. *Team learning:* Develop team thinking through conversational and collective thinking skills. A group's capacity to reliably develop intelligence and ability is greater than the sum of its individual member's talents. Reduce conflict among members and encouraging team-based assignments and achievements. Facilitate the sharing of successes and failures and best practices across organizational members.

5. *System thinking:* Develop holistic thinking—the ability to see the 'big picture' within an organization. Also help understand how changes in one area affect the whole system.

IMPORTANCE OF LEADERSHIP

Many top executives give lip service to the organization's culture, and walk away from the task of shaping it. They concentrate on the development of new strategies, systems, processes, products, and facilities. Of late, however, there is considerable change in the attitudes. The need for focusing attention on culture is well recognized and leaders are playing a crucial role in maintaining and changing culture. In the context of organization culture, leadership roles are critical and diverse.

- *Creator:* Leaders have to play a crucial role in codifying and maintaining an organization's purpose, values, and vision.
- *Initiator:* An organization's norms and values are not formed through speeches, but through actions. Leaders must set the example by living the elements of culture: values, behaviors, measures and actions.
- *Trainer:* Leaders have to track which values and objectives are less understood by every employee and target these areas of low recognition for additional training or reinforcement.
- *Innovator:* Cultures cannot endure for a long time. When an organization embraces changes by introducing growth strategies like diversification or quality improvement efforts like TQM, it requires new culture. Leaders have to play a visionary role and prepare employees for the change and add value to the change effort by modeling new ways to think and act.

Research studies have suggested that upto 80% of an organization's culture is created by the words, and deeds of people at the top. Highlighting the importance of culture management to leaders, Edgar Schein wrote[40]:

"The bottom line for leaders is that if they do not become conscious of the cultures in which they are embedded, those cultures will manage them. Cultural understanding is desirable for all of us, but it is essential if leaders are to lead."

SUMMARY

Each organization is a social system, with a distinct cultural pattern that significantly influences employee behaviors. Culture helps individuals interpret, evaluate and communicate as members of society. It affects and also describes behaviors of individuals. It is visible at three distinct levels behavioral practices, values, beliefs, preferences and norms and basic assumptions and customs. Organization culture is evolutionary and transmitted by one generation to another. It is created by people and is made up of sub-cultures. It is durable and unique. Organizational culture is recognized as one of the competitive advantages of firms, as it provides identity, facilitates commitment, stability and coordination. There are many ways of classifying culture. The culture of an organization' is developed based on external and internal challenges as well as principles distilled by research. The important principles are: Principle of consistency, Principle of mission, Principle of involvement/participation, Principle of adaptability and Principle of continuity.

The process of developing a culture can be evolved based on McKinsey's 7-s framework of strategy, structure, systems, staff, skills, style and shared values. Organizational culture is created when the schemata (schematic structures) of differing individuals across and within an organization come to resemble each other. Other problems include—lack of awareness among new hires, and conflicts. Communication plays a major role of educating organization members and shaping their behavior. Symbols, routines, rituals, ceremonies and celebrations, conversations, and socialization help create culture.

An effective culture change strategy makes use of three types of tools—leadership tools (Mission, Vision or story of the future, and value statements), management tools (Role definitions, measurement and control systems, code of conduct) and power tools (Position descriptions, Coercion and punishments, and disciplinary procedures). Change in culture is a process that involves steps like: (i) understanding current culture (ii) decide the strategic direction, and (iii) model organizational culture. The question of deviant culture and the challenge of creating continuous culture are common concerns for managers. It is leadership that can make difference, and hence, it is valued in the context of developing and managing culture.

EXERCISES

I. Review Questions

1. Explain the concept and levels of culture.
2. Describe the nature and significance of organization culture.
3. What are the different types of culture?
4. Identify the factors that influence culture of an organization.
5. How is culture created in an organizations?
6. What kind of measures do you suggest to maintain desired culture?
7. Why culture change becomes necessary? How is cultural change effected?
8. How is deviant culture corrected?

II. Discussion Questions

1. Explain the concept and significance of organization culture.
2. Discuss the types of culture and their implications to managers.
3. Describe the methods of creating, maintaining and changing culture.

📖 MINI-PROJECT

Describe the culture of your organization by asking 10 organizational members to respond to the following questions:

1. If your organization is an animal it would be a .... because ....
2. If your organization is a body part of a human being what organ would it be? Why?
3. Your organization has just won an award. What was it for? Who received it? What difference did it make?
4. List three norms or rules that govern behavior of people in your organization.
5. Complete the sentence given under:

Statements	
Our organization always	
Our organization never	
Our organization loves	
Our organization fears...	
Our organization desires...	
Our organization hates	

🖱 WEB ASSIGNMENT

Look at the research article; *The assessment of organizational culture*, available at *vtt.fi/inf/pdf/ tiedotteet/2002/T2140.pdf*. Prepare a short paper for presentation in your class.

CASE STUDY

Motivation Culture at Tata Telecom

Tata Communications Limited (TCL), a leading global communications and enterprise IT service provider is a part of the $83.3 billion Tata Companies. It owns and operates the world's most advanced subsea cable network, delivering first class infrastructure, enterprise solutions and partnerships to carriers and businesses worldwide. It has offices in more than 80 cities across 31 countries. It strives to ensure a happy and motivated work culture for its employees.

Values

Tata Communications is guided by a commitment to ethical and responsible conduct exemplified by the following values:

- *Integrity*: Do business fairly, with honesty and transparency
- *Understanding*: Show caring, show respect, compassion and humanity for our colleagues and customers

- *Flexibility:* Support customers and people with adaptive thinking and action
- *Excellence:* Achieve the highest possible standards in day-to-day work and in the quality of the goods and services
- *Unity:* Build strong relationships based on tolerance, understanding and mutual cooperation
- *Responsibility:* Continue to be responsible, sensitive to the countries, communities and environments in which we work.

Talent Management

At TCL, the manpower acquisition goal is to hire people for various positions from within or with the reference of employees.

- *Internal job postings program:* At TCL, employees can apply for any position open in any of the 40 countries. They can apply either before or concurrent with the consideration of external candidates for employment. The program aims at employees' career growth as well as an increase in their engagement levels.
- *Employee Referral Program:* The company believes that its employees can aid in helping find the right new talent. Because they are well aware of the work culture, ethics and roles, they shall consider them while referring candidates.

Welfare Image

As a member of Tata Group, the company is viewed as a welfare company. It is the Tatas, who were the first to introduce employee welfare rules, ahead of the laws. Some of the provisions are:

- Free annual health check-up to those who are 40 years and above.
- Family in the health insurance program that covers employees and their parents and/ or parents-in-law.
- APEX (Achieving Personal Excellence) program for alleviating stress, maintaining work-life balance and learning self-management and leadership skills.

Employee Development

TCL strives to create a culture where people are encouraged to learn, develop new skills and grow.

- *Learning Management System:* Through this program employees can choose more than 1000 programs to participate in.
- *Career Action Plan:* For each top performer, a unique and customized career action plan is developed to develop him or her for one or more future roles.
- *Leadership development programs:* Employees can also participate in this program offered by Tata Management and Training Centre.
- *Training calendar:* When it comes to employee development, TCL has a quarterly training calendar. It focuses on development of management, career and different type of skills.

Employee Recognition and Rewards

The senior management of TCL has an open door policy. Employees requiring help or advice can always approach their seniors for guidance. Several programs, such as, 'Rewards and Recognition program' for recognizing good performers and 'Pro Club' to celebrate achievers are set up. The top 1% performers receive the most coveted ProClub award. They are taken on an all-expense paid trip to an exotic location along with other winners and the team of senior executives.

Gender Equality and Diversity

Tata Communications is an equal opportunity employer. Everyone irrespective of their gender, language, nationality, religion, belief, caste or creed is given an opportunity for employment in the company. A heartening feature is more women are joining the global workforce, and have reached senior positions and became the highest achievers. The HR policies are lined up to integrate diverse employees. For instance, a 'Cross-cultural training program' will soon be rolled out.

People Strategy Integrated with Business Strategy

TCL is building people strategy as a part of business strategy. Employee Engagement program is used to demonstrate company strategy, drive the leadership programs and facilitate performance management. Informal approaches are used to establish openness and a sense of working towards common company goal and objectives, together, as a team.

Questions for Discussion

1. Examine the steps taken by TCL to create a motivating culture.
2. Evaluate the effectiveness of the measures taken and suggest measures for creating right culture of motivation.

Source: Gopalakrishnan, Hema, We strive to ensure a happy and motivated work culture, *The Hindu*, June 13, 2012, Opportunities, p. 3. and Our Culture—Tata Communications. *www.tatacommunications.com/about/culture.asp.*

REFERENCES

1. Adopted from :ING Life Insurance: Careers–Winning *Performance Culture*, *www.inglife. co.in/careers/waywework/wpc.shtml*PUBLIC COMPANY LTD CORPORATE ... –Tata Steel India,
   www.tatasteelindia.com/corporate-citizen/pdf/csr-2007-08.pdf
   Doing Well by Doing Good—*Hindustan Unilever*
   www.hul.co.in/.../HUL_75Years_Special_Issue_tcm114-194253.pdf

2. Rice, C. (1993), *Consumer Behavior: Behavioral Aspects of Marketing*, Oxford: Butterworth Heinemann.

3. Herskovits, M. (1955), *Cultural Anthropology: An Abridged Revision of Man and His Works*, New York: Knopf.

4. Osgood, C. (1951), The Koreans and their culture, Ronald, New York, and Kluckhohn, C. (1951), "Values and value orientations in the theory of action, toward a general theory of action", in: Parsons, T./Shils, E.A. (Eds.), Toward a general theory of action, Harvard University Press, Cambridge, MA, pp. 388–433.

5. Schutte, H. and Ciarlante, D. (1998), *Consumer Behavior in Asia*, London: Macmillan.

6. Quoted in *Definition of Organizational Culture*, www.organizationalculture101.com/definition-of-organizational-cult...

7. Schein, Edgar H. (1992), *Organizational Culture and Leadership*. San Francisco Jossey-Bass Publishers.

8. Montana, P., and Charnov, B. (2008), *Management*, Barrons Educational Series, New York: Hauppauge.

9. Heskett, James T. (2011), *The Culture Cycle: How to Shape the Unseen Force That Transforms Performance*, New Jersey: FT Press.

10. Sonnenfeld, Jeffrey, quoted in *Understanding Organisational Culture* | Articles, www.thestairway.co.uk/.../understanding-organisational-culture.html.

11. Perrow, Charles (1979), *Complex Organizations: A Critical Essay*: Glencoe, IL.:Scott, Foresman.

12. Peters, Tom, and Robert Waterman (1982), *In Search of Excellence: Lessons from America's Best Run Companies*, New York: Harper and Row.

13. Caiden, Gerald E. (1971), *The Dynamics of Public Administration*, New York: Holt, Reinhart, and Winston.

14. Quoted in *Changing Organizational Culture: Unleashing Creative Energy* users.rcn.com/pgordon/homeland/change_culture.pdf.

15. Quoted in. Maslow A.H. (1964), "Synergy in the Society and in the Individual". *Journal of Individual Psychology*, 20 (November): pp. 153–164.

16. J.K. Fordyce and R. Weil, Managing with People. Reading, MA.: Addison-Wesley, 1971, pp 11–16, and Ron Edmondosn, 10 *Characteristics* of a *Healthy Organization* or Team | Ron ...*www.ronedmondson.com* > *Leadership* > *Business*.

17. Handy, Charles (1996), *Gods of Management: The Changing Work of Organizations*, New York: Oxford University Press.

18. Carmazzi, A.F. (2007), *The Psychology of Creating the Right Corporate Culture*, Gilsdorf, J: Veritas Publishing.

19. Deal T.E. and Kennedy, A.A. (1982), *Corporate Cultures: The Rites and Rituals of Corporate Life*, Harmondsworth: Penguin Books.

20. Cooke, R.A. (1987), *The Organizational Culture Inventory*. Plymouth, MI: Human Synergistics Inc.

21. Quinn, R.E., & Rohrbaugh, J. (1983), A spatial model of effectiveness criteria: Towards a competing values approach to organizational analysis. *Management Science*, **29**, pp. 363–377.

22. Goffee, R. and Jones, G. (1998), The Character of the Corporation. Harper Collins, and Organisational *Culture, www.al-consulting.co.uk/.../ ORGANISATIONAL%20 CULTURE.pdf.*

23. McGuire, Stephen J.J. (2003), Entrepreneurial Organizational Culture: Construct Definition and Instrument Development and Validation, Ph.D. Dissertation, The George Washington University, Washington, DC.

24. Case, John (1998), "The Open-Book Experience: Lessons From Over 100 Companies Who Successfully Transformed Themselves". NewYork: Basic Books.

25. Sinha, J.B.P. (1990), *Work culture in the Indian Context*, New Delhi: Sage Publications.

26. Hofstede, G. (1991), *Cultures and Organizations: Software of the Mind*, London: McGraw-Hill.

27. Escobar, Arturo (1996), Welcome to Cyberia: Notes on the Anthropology of Cyberculture, pp. 111–137 in Cyberfutures: Culture and Politics on the Information Superhihgway. Ed. Sardar, Ziauddin; Ravetz, Jerome R. London: Pluto Press and Antonio Bernal Guerrero and José María Fernández Batanero. New Ways to Build the Identity in Cybercultural Contexts, *The International Journal of Diversity in Organisations, Communities and Nations*, Vol. **8**(2), pp. 113–120.

28. Macek, Jakub (2004), Defining Cyberculture *Média a realita* (Binková, P. Volek, J.), Masaryk University Press, pp. 35–65.

29. Schein, Edgar H. (1992), *Organizational Culture and Leadership*. San Francisco: Jossey-Bass Publishers.

30. Denison, Daniel R. (1990), *Corporate Culture and Organizational Effectiveness*, New York: John Wiley & Sons.

31. Collins, James C. and Jerry I. Porras (1994), Built to Last: Successful Habits of Visionary Companies. New York: Harper Business.

32. Schein, Edgar H. (1992), *Organizational Culture and Leadership* (2nd ed.). San Francisco: Jossey-Bass, and Johnson, G. (1988), "Rethinking Incrementalism", *Strategic Management Journal,* Vol. 9, Issue 1, pp. 75–91. Manage the Culture Cycle, *The World Financial Review, www.worldfinancialreview.com/?p=690.*

33. Harris, Stanley, G. (1994), "Organizational Culture and Individual Sense making: A Schema-Based Perspective", *Organization Science*, Vol. **5**(3), pp. 309–32.

34. How Leaders Can Optimize Organizational Culture, *managementcraft.typepad.com/ Culture%20Whitepaper%204-09.pdf* and How Leaders Can Optimize Organizational Culture, *pdffinder.net/How-Leaders-Can-Optimize-Organization...*—United States.

35. Feldman, Daniel C. (1981), "The Multiple Socialization of Organization Members". *The Academy of Management Review,* Vol. **6**(2), pp. 309–318.

36. Taylor and Francis (2010), *Your Socialization Experiences: Stages of Socialization,* retrieved from *Http://mgtclass.mgt.unm.edu/.../06.Your%20Socialization%20 Experiences_Stages%20of%20Soc.*

37. Susan M. Heathfield, How to Change Your Culture: Organizational Culture Change, available at *humanresources.about.com/.../organizationalculture/.../culture_chang* and Employee *Cultural* & Performance Survey, *Corporate ... www.culturestrategysurvey. com/.*

38. Deviant Organization Culture << *Sonia Jaspal's RiskBoard, soniajaspal.wordpress. com/2010/08/01/deviant-organization-culture/*

39. Senge, P.M. (1990), *The Fifth Discipline. The art and practice of the learning organization,* London: Random House.

40. Schein, Edgar (2010), Organizational culture and Leadership, San Francisco: Jossey-Bass, available at organizational Culture and Leadership, Fourth Edition > THE ..., *my.safaribooksonline.com/book/leadership/9780470190609/.../22.*

Chapter 6

Organizational Change

Vignette: Coping with Change

L&T Infotech implemented a change program for a USD 50 million food processing company engaged in catering, private labeling and industrial products. It sought to establish a highly integrated system with good business security sensitivity. It was proposed to undertake SAP R/3 full life cycle implementation. The change team addressed the dual nature of change—process and people. A Change Management Program was conducted for the Executives and the Top Management, and another customized program for executives and leaders. A communication charter was prepared with the mission of providing consistent information tailored to the specific needs of the stakeholder groups. The roles for important functions, like Demand Planner and MRP Controller were defined and necessary training was imparted. The change team effected change without much resistance, minimized project risks, and optimized current and future processes and structures.

In another case, L&T Infotech assisted a multi-dimensional diversified organization with Global Head Quarter at Dubai, UAE. They selected SAP to map all the current supply-chain business processes throughout the enterprise. The change management team identified certain problems, like low change readiness, and technological gap between legacy and SAP resulting in process reengineering at many places. They also identified the need for working in an integrated environment with new roles and responsibilities. Accordingly, communication and training were used to provide adequate preparedness to the executives and the senior management for process/ practice change. Process reengineering was done involving process champions, end users and external stakeholders of the project like customers, vendors and other business partners. The implementation was completed with least resistance.

Robert Senior of Saatchi & Saatchi opined that the greatest risk in today's world is to carry on as you were before—to believe that if we don't change anything, and keep doing things as we did, we'll all be fine in the end. Supporting this view, the Executive Vice-Chairman of Ashok Leyland, R. Seshasayee observed that volatility and unpredictability are forcing organizations to change. A good leader, according to him must be able to destroy what he has created. For instance, ICICI Bank, transformed from a financial institution to a bank. When regulatory changes allowed private players to come in, ICICI Bank brought in K.V. Kamath, and he triggered a major change which had involved lot of learning and unlearning[1]. In this chapter, we will address issues related to change management.

INTRODUCTION

Change is the law of life for individuals as well as organizations. It can be caused by a variety of factors—threats and opportunities—at different times in the life of the organization. Change management requires multiple levels of analysis and multi-pronged approaches. It has to take into cognizance the abilities and apprehensions of people, flexibility in organization and vagaries of the environment. The decision-making involves complex trade-offs and dilemmas. Managers, therefore, have to acquire good understanding of change management to be able to model change in such a way that, the organization is benefited from the change with less perturbation.

CONCEPT AND TYPES

Change means to alter; to make different; to cause to pass from one state to another. In the context of organization, it signifies alterations which occur in the overall work environment of an organization. Looking from the way it occurs, change can be defined as an effect caused by a disturbing force, either internal or external to an organization. Since change is continuous without any stop, it is defined as a process, with series of alterations in one or more directions. Hempel & Martinsons[2] defined. Organizational change as the process of transforming an organization from an existing state to a desired state of being.

Classification of Changes

Organizational changes can be classified in different ways based on sources, degree of impact, degree of certainty, management style and expectation as shown in Table 6.1. The most common and oft referred classification is first order and second order changes.

- *First order change:* It is incremental and continuous. It involves adjustments in systems, processes, and structure but does not affect strategy and core values.

- *Second order change:* It is radical and discontinuous. It involves substantial transformation of organization in nature and style.

However, the two types of change present two polar points. In reality, organizations take two different approaches.

- *Tectonic change:* Middle of the road approach, also called as tectonic change is suitable to today's dynamic environments. Companies go for radical transformation in a planned way without adversely affecting employee relationships and loyalty.
- *Punctuated equilibrium:* Organizations seek to maintain equilibrium by fostering stability over a long period. However, disequilibrium is created by short bursts of radical changes. Equilibrium is again restored and continued by stabilizing operations.

TABLE 6.1 Types of Changes

Base	Types	Description
Source	Internal	Change introduced by pressures from inside like the decision to automate a firm's operations
	External	Change caused by external forces like competition, which required improvement in quality of products and customer services
Degree of impact	Evolutionary, continuous or incremental	Change introduced in a creeping manner. For instance, introduction of new training programs to provide new skills to employees
	Revolutionary, discontinuous and radical	Change that destroys old patterns and paves way for the emergence of new ways of working. For example, internet has provided a new opportunity of e-commerce, social media, etc.
Degree of certainty	Predictable	When environment is stable, changes will be more internal and incremental. Hence they can be predicted
	Unpredictable	When environment is turbulent change can arise unexpectedly. There can be surprises or shocks in a changing environment
Management style	Planned	Planned change occurs when management develops a plan of action for design and implementation of change
	Adhoc	Adhoc responses refer to management style that prefers temporary responses to changes that arise from time-to-time
Expectation	Anticipated change	Changes planned ahead of time and occur as intended
	Opportunity-based change	Intentionally introduced during the ongoing change process in response to an unexpected opportunity
	Emergent change	Changes that arise spontaneously from innovation in way of doing things by employees

Source: Based on Orlikowski, W.J. and Hofman J.D. (1997). An Improvisational Model for Change Management: The Case of Groupware Technologies, *Sloan Management Review*, Winter, pp. 11–21 and Planner, I., Dunford R. and Akin, G. (2008), Managing Organizational Change, (New Delhi: Tata McGraw-Hill).

NATURE AND LEVELS

What are the characteristics of change? Here are some features of organizational change from management point of view:

1. *Process as well as a tool:* Change is a process of altering the organization. It is described as a series of sequential steps that leads to a predictable outcome. Change is also a tool for managing as it helps managers to improve organization-environment fit and employee-organization fit. It is a technique of organization development.

2. *Positive or negative:* Change can throw an opportunity or pose a threat. The decision of Indian government to invite Foreign Direct Investment (FDI) in retailing is seen as a threat to the existence by small retailers, while it is described as a progressive step and viewed as an opportunity for business development by corporate enterprises.

3. *Surprise or shock:* Changes are associated with rational logic as well as emotional feelings. The declaration of fraud by Ramalinga Raju of Satyam computers left everyone shocked. On the other hand, the appointment of Mistry as chairman Tata companies gave pleasant surprise to shareholders and employees.

4. *Steady or abrupt:* Change can be described as an event that can occur in a slow and steady manner. Increasing the capacity of an organization, by adding additional capacities in a phased manner is visible and traceable. If a firm decides to expand capacity by taking over another company, it will be an abrupt and sudden change.

5. *Domino effect:* Change can cause domino effect. A row of dominoes stood on end will fall in succession if the first one is knocked over. Likewise, change in one element or subsystem may cause more or less same degree of change in other elements or subsystems. As one change sets off a chain of similar, it results in a cumulative effect.

6. *Creative-destructive:* As Pablo Picasso observed: "Every act of creation is first of all an act of destruction." Every change breaks the connection—to some degree—with traditional patterns of operation and establishes a new pattern of thinking and action in organizations.

Changes can occur at two different levels.

1. *Macro level:* Changes that affect people and organizations universally. For example, globalization has impact on all the industries in the country.

2. *Micro level:* Changes within organization that impact life of people as a group and as single individual. For instance, decisions like downsizing will impact the whole organization.

Organizations as such require a holistic, systems approach. As different subsystems are interrelated, change in a subsystem may trigger changes in another and can produce a domino effect. Hence, proper attention is to be given to all levels of the system including macro-level variable, such as culture, technology and the environment, and micro level variables like employees, tasks, and structure. Within an organization, change can take place at four different levels as given in Table 6.2.

TABLE 6.2   Levels of Change

Level	Focus of change	Change initiatives
Vision	Shaping the future	New mission and vision statements, new culture and new strategies
Strategy	Building core competencies	New hiring and training policies and practices, New work assignments, and appraisal systems, New technology and equipment.
System	Overhaul or engineering	Business process reengineering, TQM, JIT, etc.
Operations	Efficiency and response	Customer service improvements, new operational procedures, etc.

Levels one through three, focus on big picture elements, such as analysis of the marketplace, outsourcing, mergers and bring substantial change in the management and support systems of the company. Companies that use these methods should have a high need for change, risk-tolerance and entrepreneurial culture. Organizations engaged in electronics, information systems and telecommunication industries will be focusing on these changes. Military, government offices and healthcare organizations mostly use incremental tools (level 4) as their need for change is modest. They are risk-avoidant, and only have limited awareness among themselves on what to do.

PRESSURES FOR CHANGE

The factors that cause organizations change can be internal or external or both.

Internal Factors

Internal factors include the following:

1. *Changes in ownership:* Enterprises may gradually grow from small to large sized ones, from sole proprietary firms to joint stock companies, by reinvesting the ploughed back profits and external funding. When such changes take place, there will be changes not only in structure, but also in other components of organization.

2. *Poor performance:* When employee performance is dismal and requires action, managers initiate change process by diagnosing the organization to find reasons and introduce appropriate changes in systems, leadership styles, work environment, etc.

3. *Change in leadership:* When there is a change in leadership, there may be changes in the goals and values of organizations. An entrepreneurial leader may look for establishing innovative mechanisms and risk taking culture. A principled leader may try to bring changes in shared values, systems and structure to encourage ethical decision-making and behaviors.

4. *Overcome stagnation:* Change is important to offer challenging jobs and opportunities to progress in their careers. To keep going, with a team of spirited and skilled employees, organizations question the status quo and explore new ways of creating great workplaces.

External Factors

External environmental factors that propel change in the organizations can be discussed using the SLEPT (social, legal, economic, political, technological) framework.

1. *Social factors:* The social factors like age, gender, caste and occupational distribution lead to change in the organizations. Consider the following: Rise in the number of women employees has resulted in introduction of flexi work systems and gender mainstreaming policies. The emergence of youth as leaders of organizations has led to creation of innovative cultures.

2. *Legal factors:* Changes in government regulations may create pressures for compliance. Environment protection may require investment in anti-pollution equipment, appointment of committees, establishing procedures to change the way of treating processes and environment in and around the factory.

3. *Economic factors:* Economic factors, like recession, competition, shifts in demand, etc., can change the organizational strategies and styles of functioning. For instance, competition may drive an organization to set-up customer-based structures, to develop Customer Relationship Management policies and programs and to strengthen R&D and creativity in organization.

4. *Political factors:* The government policies and investment priorities make significant impact on organizational growth plans. For example, a policy of government that is biased to small firms, may lead large firms to opt for outsourcing. They may network with small firms, by putting in place proper quality control mechanisms.

5. *Technological factors:* Technological changes cause incremental or radical changes in the organizations. Evidently, ICT has brought revolutionary changes in the way people work and communicate. The lower level jobs disappeared and organizations are now employing knowledge workers. There are flat organizations, virtual offices, project teams, and 24/7 work systems.

RESPONSES TO CHANGE

Response to change depends on the ability to recognize, interpret and convert it into an opportunity. Some leaders give importance to change and foresee them. Others ignore and remain blind to their occurrence. Depending on the response patterns, two types of strategic postures are given as follows:

1. *Proactive:* Proactive or revolutionaries, they seek to create change, which is radically different, and is capable of creating a new order. Change sensitive organizations will take cognizance of changes and the course of their development from embryonic stage to the current one and create change readiness and change coping strategies. Having decided to be proactive, a firm does not limit itself by what seems easy or comfortable—or even necessarily possible. It sets out by describing its dream for the future—even if it looks very different and crazy from the stand point of present life. Firms which have visionary leadership or strong R&D focus can be proactive.

2. *Reactive:* Reactionaries are those who adapt to change. They can be aggressive or passive. The aggressive ones are the first to sense the change and embrace it to gain competitive advantage. The passive ones are at first sceptical; they look at change with suspicion, and treat it with caution. They view it as a destabilizing force and observe how others respond to it.

Take, for instance, changes in technology. A passive reactionary would voice concerns about employees loosing jobs, shortage of skilled persons, and resistance from employees. An aggressive one would speak about opportunities created–improvements in productivity, removal of drudgery and new products.

The reactionary approach values the established practices and prefers to celebrate the achievements of the past. It helps to keep things on track, ensures stability for long term goals and projects. It is good for those organizations which have established routines. For them, sticking with what worked yesterday is the best way to reach towards its goals. Transactional leadership prefers to be passive, whereas transformation leadership likes to be aggressive.

Besides these two strategic postures, two interesting concepts relevant to modern managers are Red queen effect and organization renewal.

Red Queen Effect

Whatever posture managers may adopt, the response should be competitive as well as innovative. In today's competitive world, managers have to keep moving and they have an advice from biologists, who coined the term Red Queen Effect. It describes the evolutionary necessity to evolve faster than one's predators or prey. It is picked up from Lewis Carroll's 'Through the Looking Glass' (the sequel to 'Alice in Wonderland'), where the Red Queen points out to Alice:

It takes all the running you can do to stay in the same place. If you want to get somewhere else, you must run at least twice as fast as that[3].

To be ahead of competitors, companies research or study the competition and implement counter strategies. Competition becomes the set-point or an internal mental model of "how things should be around here." With reference to the set point, everyone makes all kinds of adjustments and corrections to deviations or deficits, to return to the set-point.

However, this kind of controlling effort, aimed at surpassing the competition, does not help the company to move forward or grow. Growth requires innovation and not competitive operations and quick adjustments. The Red Queen Effect is a metaphor used to describe the unsuccessful efforts of a company to get ahead of its competition.

Organization Inertia

Inertia refers to an organization's inability to respond to change. Organizational inertia is caused by years of successful experiences—experiences that make them believe that their path is best. Organizations exhibit inertia by laying mainly on perpetuating the operational habits which proved to be efficient. They rely more on controls and disciplinary procedures. In this process, they tend to ignore the signals of change. They remain blind to the fact that they are stagnating and decaying. It requires a massive effort to put them on the track of change.

Organization Renewal

Along with ongoing changes in customers and markets, organizations must continually sow fresh seeds of change, if they are to remain a viable force in tomorrow's markets. However, the Peter Principle that, "In a hierarchy, every employee tends to rise to his level of incompetence[4]." Seems to apply to organizations as well. Caught in the whirlpool of change, managers may experience a sense of helplessness and fail to find a way out. The goal for managers, then, is twofold: to sustain current success and to simultaneously build new products, services, or processes for the future. To be capable of doing this, they have to make their organizations productive and innovative.

Operational vs strategic approach

Renewing organization requires vision and long-term goals. The operational measures, like freezing all hiring, reducing salaries by X%, cutting all budgets by X%, eliminating all training, eliminating employee overtime, freezing capital spending by X%, cutting back on marketing events, micro-managing travel and so on, which help gain cost advantage are just remedial. They can never reinvigorate organizations. The good aspects of these initiatives are, they are simple, well-understood in most organizations and historically-recognized as acceptable business acumen. Most managers and employees are familiar with them. As such, there will be quick results without much conflict. These measures may not have adverse effects on organizations which employ traditional organization structures. Most modern integrated business models suffer severe consequences, when the cut measures interrupt carefully constructed cross-functional and cross-enterprise links.

Using a strategic approach to renewal requires the following:

- Engaging in the problem-solving process with a clear set of tools and techniques, for achieving greater success in the future.
- Employing a multi-disciplinary team of highly experienced specialists.
- Developing a data-driven understanding of the key issues like specific opportunities and potential threat.

Organizational renewal requires strategic approach that involves evolving the following subsystems:

- Customer strategy
- Operational effectiveness
- Technology optimization
- People performance

Continuous organization renewal integrates three distinct and desirable types of organizations to create a HALO (High Performing, Agile, Learning, Organization): a High performing organization [H] that strives for continuous improvement, an Agile organization [A] that strives for continuous adaptation, and a Learning Organization [LO] that focuses on competency development [5].

DILEMMAS IN CHANGE

The hunter who chases two rabbits catches neither one. Establishing a single, clear, goal is the first and most important element in engineering a change in organizations. Managers seeking to cope with organizational change face certain dilemmas. Dunphy and Stace (1996)[6] broadly categorize them into 'soft' and 'hard' approaches to managing change as given in Table 6.3.

TABLE 6.3   Dilemmas in change: Hard vs. Soft Options

Dimension	Hard option	Soft option
Strategy	Rational strategy development	Adaptive strategy
Impact type	Radical transformation	Continuous improvement
Authority	Leadership and command	Empowerment
Change focus	Structural change	Cultural change

Adaptive vs strategic

Whether to keep a pace with changes by adaptation or wait for finding a way to bring about radical transformation? Continuous changes may create role ambiguity and confusion among employees. Shareholders may be apprehensive about the moves unable to connect them properly. Too many changes, though incrementally taken, may raise questions on credibility of management. On the other hand, waiting long for making a transformation after change is consolidated and its impact is observed in other organizations may place the organization, competitively in a disadvantageous position.

Structure vs culture

Structure is framework within which culture grows. Structural changes envisage changes in levels of hierarchy, networks, span of management, authority distribution and positions. Every structural change will have some degree of influence on the mind and behavior of people. While minor changes may not warrant significant modifications in culture, high leverage changes will have a profound impact on the culture. Similarly, attempts at culture change often warrant structural modifications. Organizations may distribute new mission statements, beautiful posters with new values on them to create new enthusiasm and different work styles. However, they doom to disappear, when the existing structure of the workplace does not support the new ways of doing things.

Organizations thus show a close relationship between culture and structure. In view of this, a manager seeking structural change faces the dilemma to preserve or change the present culture. Similarly, a manager seeking culture change faces the dilemma—whether to tinker with existing organization or transform it into a new one.

Empowerment vs Command

The source of change can be top-down or bottom-up and internal or external. Participative management approaches like quality circles, ross functional teams and involvement of enthusiastic people in idea generation through social networks has shown that the source of change ideas need not be top management. The experience in change process in the recent past has proved that change is effective only when people are involved and educated to participate.

The dilemma of a traditional manager is whether to make changes by command or by empowerment of people. Even when the later option is chosen, there is another question pertaining to the degree of empowerment. Should it be—less or more?

Consultant led vs. management team led

This is another dilemma faced by organizations interested in making changes. Consultants bring experience and wisdom and can suggest better ways of change. However, the implementation process may not be effective as their understanding of culture is limited. On the other hand, internal team can monitor change process better but they cannot bring in fresh perspectives to decision-making.

CHANGE MANAGEMENT: NATURE AND APPROACHES

Change management is a process, a science, an art and a profession.

1. *Process:* Moran and Brightman defined change management as the process of continually renewing an organization's direction, structure, and capabilities to serve the ever changing needs of external and internal customers[7]. Change management is described as a process of n-steps. It involves conceptualization, design and implementation of change for the benefit of organization. Different researchers have come up with different models of change to reduce uncertainty and mystery associated with it.

2. *Science:* Researchers have found that around 80% of all change efforts, whatever their name and purpose, failed. The main reason is there was a significant lack of science and focus on the long-term. They are more cosmetic and superficial. In the process, they wasted millions of rupees and more importantly they lost the trust of the employees and customers. Change management is supported by theory. In fact, there are different theories that explain causes, process and outcomes of change.

3. *Art:* Change management needs skills and techniques. It requires conceptual, design, technical and social skills. As resistance is an integral part of every change, there is a need to attach more importance to social skills. Change managers make use of a wide variety of techniques that employ social skills and create a win-win situation for all the members.

4. *Profession:* Change management has become a professional task. The availability of consultants has helped organizations to undertake change management projects relatively in more effective and ethical ways.

The various dilemmas relating to ethics are resolved with the help of the expertise and experience of consultants. How does manager's approach change management tasks? Which one is more appropriate? The different approaches to change management are discussed in the following sections.

Top-down vs Bottom-up

Is change driven by internal stimuli generated by top management or external environment forces? It can be either.

Top-down approach or trickle down model assumes that change takes place with the initiative of top management, who are aware of the organizational needs for change. This is usually referred to as classic approach as it is based on the assumption that environment is either stable or controllable by management. As such, change is anticipated and planned. There is a strong assurance that intended outcomes will be achieved.

Bottom-up approach, on the other hand, postulates that change is a continuous phenomenon in organizations as they are impacted by external environment which changes continually. This view is based on systems approach to management, and suggests that organizations are essentially open systems and learning organization. This approach is also called as identity search model as it seeks to establish the identity of organization, which is under constant threat by ever-changing environment. By adapting, organizations seek to regain the organization-environment fit, of course progressively at a higher level. As such, the change is emergent and unanticipated. Outcomes can be unintended. Managers have to follow flexible plans to get intended outcomes.

The classical paradigm has relevance from change management point-of-view, whereas system paradigm has significance from organizational change diagnosis perspective. All the change management process models assume that management can plan, organize, lead and control change programs. However, to find the change needs, one has to take holistic view and determine the substance and direction of change. We can say the two approaches are complimentary in nature.

Individual vs Group vs Systems

Change can be approached from individual or group or system.

1. *Individual:* Behaviorists see individuals as rational and focus on modifying behaviors either by increasing self-awareness or modifying the external stimuli. They believe that behavior is caused by an individual's interaction with the environment and interpretation of the stimuli.

2. *Group:* Group dynamics theorists, such as Lewin[8] and Schein[9] advocate effecting change through group behavior rather than individual behavior. Since people try to associate with either formal or informal groups, effecting individual behavior requires change in group norms, values and work patterns. As such, change should begin at group level and go down to the level of an individual.

3. *System:* Proponents of the systems approach argue that it is the organization that is in continuous interaction with the environment. As the organization seeks to find fit with environment by adapting, the change goals should be set up at organization level. The goals should be passed on to the relevant divisions/departments and change effort should be made to achieve overall synergy rather than on optimizing any one individual sub-system.[10]

Planned vs Contingency Approaches

Change can be planned and implemented in a predetermined manner. OD practitioners have helped managers understand the complexity of change. They assisted them in designing and implementing change in a systematic way, neutralizing the restraining forces. Lewin, Kotter and others offered process models in support of this perspective.

The emergent approach was popularized in the 1980s. Theorists like Burnes proposed it as an alternative to the planned approach to the management of change.[11] It includes what other theorists have described as processual or contextualist perspectives.[12] It suggests that change should not be frozen or viewed as a linear sequence of events, but that it should be viewed as an ongoing process. It is based on the premise that if environment creates and fosters a readiness for change, it is not only easily accepted, but is actually embraced by the organization.

The contingency theorists proposed dependent relationship between an organization and its environment. They believed that there is no one best way to change, because organizations are impacted by multiple environmental variables. The decision on the scale and substance of change is to be determined through organizational analysis and implemented. The implementation can be corrective and progressive. It can be collaborative or consultative.[13]

THEORIES OF CHANGE

Change management is a science and it has sound theoretical base. From a brief survey of literature, you can find different theories presenting different perspectives on organizational change. The major theories are briefly presented here[14].

Theories on first order change

These theories explain incremental change behavior of organizations. In essence, they state that change decisions are founded on deterministic laws that have governed the past adaptations.

1. *Life cycle theory:* Organizations, like individuals are viewed as living organisms. Like humans, the organizations pass through different stages, say start up, growth, harvest and termination. They exhibit progressive changes in a linear and sequential manner. As such, change can be anticipated, and response can be designed.

2. *Evolutionary theory:* Based on Darwinism, organization's life is seen as a series of events relating to competitive survival. Organizations compete for limited natural resources and markets, for survival and growth. The moves are governed by the principles of differentiation, natural selection and retention.

Theories on second order change

They explain causes for revolutionary change behavior of organizations. They are in essence constructive of novel changes, caused by new goals of organization or by the pressures to resolve conflicts.

1. *Teleological theory:* Change is shaped and implemented through a goal setting mechanism and collaborative and consensus building approaches.

2. *Dialectic theory:* Change is outcomes of conflict and its resolution mechanisms and processes. There is conflict with a state and resolution requires moving to a new state. The conflict resolution passes through three stages: thesis-antithesis-synthesis.

Theories based environment perspective

At least four theories can be found in literature which explain environment as a source of change.

1. *Contingency theory:* The theory focuses on stability and complexity of environment. Stability refers to rate of change occurring in the industry and complexity refers to the number of factors influencing organization. When environment is stable, mechanistic organizations will be designed to deal with environment. The need for change in such an environment is incremental, in relation to slow changes in environment. When environment is unstable or turbulent, changes can be revolutionary and organizations adopt organic structures to facilitate transformation.

2. *Resource-dependence theory:* The theory proposes that organizations which are dependent on environment for resources, may exhibit powerlessness characterized by vulnerability and uncertainty. To reduce this, they take political decisions that cause change in organizations. They evolve internal strategies to change organization to fit the environment and external strategies to change environment to fit the organization. Pfeffer and Salancik identified eight such strategies shown in Table 6.4.

TABLE 6.4 Power Gaining Change Strategies

Focus	Strategy	Description
Internal change	Domain choice	Venturing into new markets
	Recruitment	Appointing people who can exercise required power
	Environment scanning	Studying environment for creating change readiness
	Buffering	Having extra suppliers, inventory etc., to reduce risk of shortages
External change	Lobbying	Influencing regulatory bodies
	Contracting	Entering into long-term contracts to ensure certainty in services or supplies
	Co-opting	Nominating influential people in governing bodies
	Coalescing	Gaining resources through alliances, mergers and acquisitions

Source: Based on Pfeffer J and Salancik G.R., (1978), The external control of organizations: A Resource Dependency Perspective, New York: Harper & Row.

3. *Population-ecology theory:* It deals with the change decision affected by competition for resources—the dependence of population (firms which require same resources in environment) on environment (supplier of the required resource). When population is large and resources are limited, competition results in struggle for survival in case of small organizations and dominance in case of larger ones. Organizations evolve change strategies that aim either at reducing the demand for a resource in short supply or innovating to shift to new resources.

4. *Institutionalization theory:* The theory explains how organizations try to have legitimacy by conforming to norms, values, regulations and laws in a given socio-political environment. Legitimacy provides them access to resources required for their operations. The tendency to conform makes organizations look similar, and even resemble each other in respect of structures and styles of behavior. In essence, the theory says that adaptive change for conforming is the result of three isomorphism strategies—imitation, compliance or influence. Table 6.5 summarizes them.

TABLE 6.5 Institutionalization by Isomorphism

S.No.	Strategy	Description
1	Imitation	Copying the organizations that have legitimacy and social sanction
2	Compliance	Adhering to rules and regulations of regulatory bodies
3	Influence	Based on guidance and learning provided by professional managers and consultants

Theories Based on Implementation Perspective

They explain how change goals can be achieved. Theory E and Theory O presented Beer and Nohria[15] are from this perspective.

1. *Theory E:* It pursues the goal of shareholder wealth maximization. It takes hard approach to change. It focuses on maximizing profitable performance and results. In the operational context, change is focused on incentive structures and mechanisms. At the strategy level, change initiatives include downsizing, lay-off, restructuring, etc.

2. *Theory O:* It focuses on maximizing organizational capacity. It follows soft approach to change. At operational level, measures like job enrichment, participative decision-making, team work and good communication flows are adopted. At strategy level, the change initiatives may include creation of high performance culture, organization learning, and organization development.

CHANGE MODELS

The models of change can be categorized into process and content models.

Process Models

There are many models on change process. These models provide a conceptual understanding of change process for you to prepare a change road map. However, they can neither prescribe nor predict the change process that you can adopt or experience.

Content Models

The content models are developed by researchers to provide a systems framework to help managers understand the change sequence in terms of cause—transformation-outcome. Thus, they have utility as organization diagnostic tools as well as change design tools. They provide answers to the three questions.

1. *Rationale for change:* What internal and external factors are causing concern and necessitating change initiative?

2. *Substance of change:* What kind of change is desirable? What should be the interventions?

3. *Outcome of change:* What will be the organization after the completion of the change process?

　　Some of the popular models like Nadler-Tushman congruence model and Burke-Litwin Performance and change model fall under this category. They are discussed in Chapter 8.

PROCESS MODELS

In reality, change process is not only shaped by your design but also by situations that arise in course of its progress. As such, knowledge of different models will help you to take bits and pieces from each model and evolve your own unique model. We will now discuss some of the important process based models.

Lewin's Freeze Change Model

Kurt Lewin[16] developed a three phase model, known as Lewin's Freeze Phases in the early 20th century. Even today it is a widely known and discussed. He observed that managing change involved three stages which are characterized by different physical and psychological states as shown in Figure 6.1.

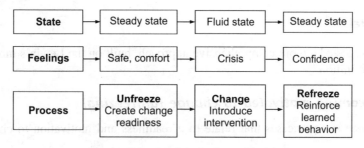

Figure 6.1 Lewin's 3-phase model.

Unfreeze

According to Lewin, change involves a move from a static state. Using force-field analysis, he observes that systems are held in a steady state by equal and opposing forces. In other words, equilibrium—a cosy state from which people do not want to move—occurs when restraining forces are equal to driving forces.

He recognized that people find safety, comfort and sense of control as well as derive a strong sense of identity from their environment. As such, they lend support to create a frozen state. Any move that threatens the status-quo will cause them discomfort. As such, it is perceived as a threat and opposed.

The task of change agents is to create awareness of employees about incongruity between the desired and current behaviors and attune them to the need for change. The phase ends when change readiness is spread among the concerned employees.

Change

Given this understanding, Lewin suggested some form of intervention is necessary to unfreeze them and to get them moving. It may be an exercise of restructuring, or the creation of a perception of a real crisis or presenting the cold hard logic of irrefutable facts or any form of intervention that can destabilize people. It should be rational and emotional in appeal and be capable of overcoming restraining forces. It should move organization in the desired direction. The intervention may cause changes at the following levels:

- *Individual:*   Change in attitudes, beliefs, values, skills and behaviors
- *Structure:*   Change in roles, structures and systems
- *Process:*   Change in processes, styles, relationships and climate within the organization

Refreeze

In the final phase, new patterns of behavior are established as the norm. The emergent structures, cultures, and policies are stabilized for developing routines. The new state of equilibrium and desired behaviors are preserved by employing reinforcing mechanisms like appreciation, recognition, rewards, and publicizing benefits through different communication vehicles, like website, newsletter, brochures and social networks. People regain their cozy state and feel more confident than before.

Schein's Model

Edgar Schein suggested a more comprehensive approach, built on the Lewin's model. He called it cognitive redefinition.[17]

Stage 1:   Becoming motivated to change (unfreezing)

He identified three sub-processes that relate to a readiness and motivation to change.

1. Disconfirmation: The present behaviors are disconfirmed. The identified gap between personal goals and goal accomplishment due to present conditions lead to dissatisfaction. It creates a belief for change to occur. The belief is strong when the gap is narrow. If it is wide, the information on gap will be ignored.

2. *Induction of guilt or survival anxiety:* It refers to the feeling that change is necessary for one's needs and goals to be met. However, the survival anxiety may be countered by the fears relating to incompetence and identity.

- *Fear of temporary incompetence:* This is based on the apprehension that new situation exposes inability to deal with the new tasks and punishment will be given when this incompetence is discovered or assessed.
- *Fear of loss of individual identity:* The fear that identity established in relation to a role or group affiliations will be lost when change affects roles and relationships.

3. *Learning anxiety:* The compulsive need to learn triggers defensiveness and resistance. The pain of having to unlearn generates anxiety and the response to this occurs in three stages: (i) denial; (ii) scapegoating and passing the buck; and (ii) maneuvering and bargaining. To move past this stage, the preconditions are:

(i) The survival anxiety is greater than the learning anxiety.

(ii) The situation is favorable to reduction in learning anxiety or creation of psychological safety.

Stage 2: Learning new concepts (moving to a new state)

Moving from existing state to a new state involves learning. Learning may involve imitation of role models and finding solutions through trial-and-error learning. The new information will result in three things.

- *Semantic redefinition:* Words take on new or expanded meaning
- *Cognitive broadening:* Concepts are interpreted within a broader context
- *New standards of judgment or evaluation:* Adjustments in the scale used in evaluating new input

Stage 3: Making the change permanent (refreezing)

In the final refreezing stage, new concepts and meanings are internalized and new behaviors are habituated. There will be development of a new self-concept and identity and establishment of new interpersonal relationships.

Galpin Wheel

Galpin[18] proposed a change process wheel that consists of nine wedges as steps. Table 6.6 presents the steps. He made a classification of the steps based on how change is planned and implemented. In his view, organizations must target two levels:

1. *Strategic level:* This refers to the upfront, initial effort to bring about a change and involves two primary goals: (i) technical or analytical goal of conceptualization and recommendation of change, and (ii) soft side goal of gaining momentum for change. At this level the key players include top management and consultants.

2. *Grass root level:* This effort at this level is directed to implantation of the planned change.

TABLE 6.6 Galpin's Model

Level	Step	Description	Duration
Strategic	1	Establish the need for change	1–2 months
	2	Develop and disseminate the vision of the change	
	3	Diagnose the current situation	4–6 months
	4	Generate recommendations	
	5	Detail recommendations	4–6 months
Grass root	6	Pilot test recommendations	
	7	Prepare recommendations for roll out	4–6 months
	8	Roll out changes	
	9	Measure, reinforce and refine changes	On going

Kotter's 8-step Model

Kotter introduced his eight-step change process[19]. The steps and the desirable actions in each step are given as follows:

1. Create urgency
2. Form a powerful coalition
3. Create a vision for change
4. Communicate the vision
5. Remove obstacles
6. Create short-term wins
7. Build on the change
8. Anchor the changes in corporate culture

Step 1: Create urgency

To spark-off motivation to change and ignite thoughts on necessity of change. Initiate the following actions:

1. Open an honest and convincing dialogue about developments in market place.
2. Make sure that many people talk about the developments and inherent challenges to the firm.
3. Publicize stories of companies that are responsive to environment.
4. Request support from stakeholders concerned.

Step 2: Form a powerful coalition

To demonstrate the need for change and gain momentum for it, effective change leaders have to work as a team.

1. Identify competent people in your organization.
2. Form a coalition of people drawn from different departments and different levels within your company.

3. Work on team building.
4. Motivate them to float ideas on change to create change readiness and motivation.

Step 3: *Create a vision for change*

The views on change differ among people. To bring about a smooth change, common understanding about the direction and substance of change is essential. One should take the following measures:

1. Identify and describe the values that are central to the change.
2. Develop a vision statement that describes what you see as the future of the organization.
3. For realizing the vision, develop a strategy.

Step 4: *Communicate the vision*

Develop a shared meaning of vision by communicating it to all your employees. To make the communication effective, one has to take the following actions:

1. Create a special identity for the communication by communicating it through special media.
2. To embed it in the minds of people, make the communications powerful and frequent.
3. Walk the talk. Deeds are more powerful than words. Tie every significant activity to the vision.

Step 5: *Remove obstacles*

After the change idea has gained significant acceptance, put in place the structure for change. The change process may be hindered by both expected and unexpected obstacles. For successful execution of change, the following initiatives should be considered.

1. Identify from within or hire from outside change leaders, and assign them the task of delivering the change.
2. Make necessary structural changes to ensure that systems are compatible to change.
3. Generate enthusiasm by rewarding people who facilitated change process.
4. Locate the people resisting the change, and remove their apprehensions.

Step 6: *Create short-term wins*

People cannot wait patiently for a long time to get results. Delay in getting results will cause impatience and builds up suspicion in the intent and process of change. To avoid this, following precautions should be taken:

1. Aim at a series of short-term targets and not just one long-term goal.
2. Implement sure-fire projects which showcase the benefits of change.
3. Don't choose expensive projects though they may yield quick results. Sometimes, their benefit may not be justifiable from investment point-of-view.

Step 7: Build on the change

There is the danger of change projects failing when victory is declared too early. Real change takes time and it may take different turns. Quick wins are only the beginning and are to be taken as indicators and not as final results. As such, one has observe the following:

1. After every win, encourage teams to analyze what went wrong and what needs improvement.
2. Set goals for continuous improvements.
3. Keep door open for fresh ideas as well as constructive criticism.

Step 8: Anchor the changes in corporate culture

Finally, integrate change with the organization culture, to make it visible and durable. The following measures should be initiated to achieve this:

1. Elicit support from key employees and leaders to talk favourably about the change.
2. Tell success stories of the change in different forums.
3. Find new leaders to champion the change stabilization process.

LEADERSHIP ROLES IN CHANGE

Palmer, Dunford and Akin[20] identified two dominant images of manager—one management as controlling and two management as shaping—which are similar to the reactive and proactive stances described in the previous section[20]. While controlling (function) adopts mechanistic approach, that focuses on activities, efficiency, and employee satisfaction. Shaping adopts organic approach that focuses on capabilities, excellence and employee delights. They identified three possible types of change: (i) intended (ii) partially intended and (iii) unintended.

Intended change outcomes

This is referred to as planned change. It can be categorized into three types based on how intentions are developed in the organization.

1. Empirical-rational strategies: People are rational and entrepreneurial. When the cases of the positive outcomes of change are presented to them, they decide to change. They cooperate to secure the intended outcomes.

2. Normative-re-educative strategies: People are receptive and empathetic. When information about change and its desirable outcomes are provided to them, they change their attitudes and values. They provide support to realize the intended outcomes.

3. Power-coercive strategies: People are dormant or apathetic. Legitimate authority is exercised to coerce them to neutralize their negative intentions to change. Their support is obtained by rules and threats of punishment to achieve intended outcomes.

Partially intended change outcomes

Though management is an effective governing organ of an enterprise, it may not always be possible to obtain intended outcomes. There can be forces within and without enterprise, which subvert the course of change. Management may have to find the middle ground and accept modifications to change.

Unintended change outcomes

For a variety of reasons which are non-controllable, intended outcomes may not be achieved. Such compelling factors can be imposition of restrictions by government, agitations by political parties, introduction of new technology by competitor, hostility of trade unions and the like.

Roles of Managers

Based on the two approaches—controlling and shaping, and three outcomes—intended, partially intended and unintended, Palmer, Dunford and Akin identified six roles of manager as given in Table 6.7.

TABLE 6.7   Classification of Managerial Roles in Change

Outcomes	Images	
	Controlling	Shaping
Intended	Director	Coach
Partially intended	Navigator	Interpreter
Unintended	Caretaker	Nurturer

Now, we will briefly discuss, when and how these roles are played by managers in the change contexts.

Director

The role is assumed by a change manager when situation is stable and certain.

1. Manager can control and get desired outcomes.
2. There are n-step models to carry out the change.
3. Using a process model, manager can effect change in a particular style of his choice.
4. There are many different styles to manage change.

The applicability of this role is limited by uncertainties in the change situation. The architect of 8-step model, Kotter, opined that successful change efforts are messy and full of enterprises.

Navigator

The role is suitable when organizations face less certain environment.

1. Manager can only partly control the change process. As such, intended outcomes are partly realized.

2. The change process requires use of cross-functional teams and effective interactions and collaboration.
3. The people factor causes variations due to differences in attitude, behavior and values.
4. Manager responds to the problems as and when they arise and steers enterprise in the right direction.

Caretaker

This role will be played when situation is characterized by internal stability and external fluidity.

1. Manager can exercise control, but are less effective.
2. Organizations are bureaucratic, with formal controls.
3. Organizations seek to be entrepreneurial and innovative to meet challenges imposed by external pressures.

Coach

This role is found appropriate when employees engaged in change lack required skills to manage change.

1. Manager or consultant acts as a coach providing training to employees.
2. Employees structure their activities and manage themselves.

Interpreter

This role will be played when change creates conflicting views among affected people. Examples of this kind of change decisions are downsizing, lean organizations and business process reengineering.

1. Managers have to sell change, as it has mixed benefits.
2. Organizations make change decisions that are less pleasant.
3. Adversely affected people criticize change.
4. The need for change and the long run benefits of it are to be explained to employees.

Nurturer

This role is similar to the role of parent bringing up a child.

1. Managers nurture organizations by encouraging self-organizing capabilities.
2. Organizations have to cope with less stable and more chaotic situations.
3. Organizations continuously learn and adapt. Periodically, they regenerate.

UNDERSTANDING RESISTANCE TO CHANGE

Resistance to change is found in almost all change management projects. Leaders must develop proper attitude toward resistance and develop plans to overcome it.

Definition

Resistance refers to disagreement, manifest in unwillingness to act in the expected way. Resistance to change is reaction of individuals and groups to a proposed change when they perceive the change as a threat to them. Ansoff defined it as follows:

Resistance is a phenomenon that affects change process, delaying and slowing down its beginning, obstructing or hindering its implementation, and increasing its costs[21].

Nature

What is the right way of looking at and treating resistance? The different views on resistance to change are examined here.

1. *Legitimate:* Resistance is a perfectly legitimate response of a worker. It is a natural survival mechanism within organizations that tests, adapts and sometimes stops decisions by fallible and often ill informed senor management.

2. *Is it symptom or problem?* Judson opined that resistance to change is not a problem but a symptom[22]. It is manifestation of a hidden problem, and its discovery requires a systematic exploration and diagnosis of the change in a holistic way.

3. *Is it negative?* Is resistance unhealthy and undesirable? The answer is not always. Negative resistance is an outcome of psychological factors, like fear, rational factors, like loss of income or position, and social factors like conflicts between groups. It may sometimes be threatening. However, resistance supported by constructive criticism will help managers examine the rationale of change and clarify the goals and actions. It helps identify and remove the weak spots in the proposed projects.

Reactions to Change

How do people react to change? People in any organization will pass through different cognitive and affective phases. The process of knowing about change starts from unawareness and ends with an understanding. During the phases of learning about change, through information, interaction, observation and experience, employees undergo feelings of anger, fear, denial, sadness, grief, frustration and low self-esteem.

Phases of reaction

A six phase model of reaction to change is given in Table 6.8. It is important to note that different people move at different rates of speed. One person may require two months, whereas other persons require relatively more time. Further, the movement need not be linear and phase by phase. One can simultaneously have feelings of two phases at a time. Also some persons may skip some phases.

TABLE 6.8 Six Phases of Personal Change

S.No.	Phase	Cognitive response	Affective response
1	Anticipation	Unaware of the change, employees make their guesses about it.	Feelings of unrest. Is it necessary?
2	Confrontation	Change plans are announced. Employees become curious and start suspecting its intentions.	Fear of losing identity and power. What is it? What are the potential benefits and hidden threats?
3	Realization	Understandings that change is imminent and things are going to be different hereafter.	Suspicion about the intents of change. Doubts on issues of change. How can I face it? What kind of difficulties are ahead of us?
4	Depression.	A sunken feeling, loss of hope and sense of powerlessness.	Upset with anger and tension. Who will help me? What kind of help can I get in this struggle?
5	Acceptance	Change is accepted.	Confident and ready to face change. What kind of training is necessary? How to play the new roles effectively?
6	Enlightenment	Appreciation of the change and acceptance of new status quo.	Happy about the change. How to sustain good performance?

Source: Adapted from Managing the Resistance to Change, www.managingchange.biz/manage_change_resistance.html.

Types of resistors

O' Connor analysed reactions of people based on two dimensions—overt and covet expression of resistance and conscious and unconscious motivation to resist[23]. They identified four extremes of behavior as shown in Table 6.9.

TABLE 6.9 Types of Resistors

Reaction	Resistor	Description
Conscious and covert	Saboteur	Sabotage change plans for personal gains
Unconscious and covert	Survivor	Opposes but fails. Remains disappointed
Conscious, overt	Protester	Protests rationally and resolves issues
Unconscious, overt	Zombie	Though agrees to change, cannot easily change behavior

Types of reactions

Bovey and Hede (2001) analyzed reactions by considering behavioral and affective dimensions[24]. The reaction is shown by two types of behaviors—active and passive and emotions are expressed in two ways: overt (open) and covet (concealed). The combination of these types yield four types of reactions as shown in Table 6.10.

TABLE 6.10 Types of Response to Changes

Reaction	Support	Resistance
Active and overt	Initiate, embrace	Oppose, argue, obstruct
Passive and overt	Agree, accept	Observerefrain, wait
Active, covert	Support, cooperate	Stall, dismantle, undermine
Passive, covert	Give-in, comply	Ignore, withdraw, avoid

Another way of classifying reactions to resistance is given as follows:

1. *Rational:* This is manifest in terms of disagreement with the nature, scope and goals of change.

2. *Emotional:* This is observed in the feelings of insecurity, loss of control, fear of unknown and loss of esteem, etc.

3. *Social:* This can be observed by group protests, dharnas, agitations, etc.

Researchers have found that people develop defensive mechanisms to safeguard their interests. The adaptive mechanisms include humor and anticipation; maladaptive mechanisms include denial, dissociation, projection and acting out. Those who strongly resist change will adopt maladaptive mechanisms.

SOURCES OF RESISTANCE

Resistance can arise from two sources: cognitive (understanding) and affective (emotional feelings).

Cognitive Factors

These are objective factors and can be identified and measured easily. They include economic and job-related aspects.

1. *Misunderstanding:* Due to selective processing of information, people hear what they want to hear. They ignore information that challenges the status quo, when they are comfortable with the existing situation. This may lead to misunderstanding of the proposed change.

2. *Perception of risks:* Change involves anticipation of something unknown. As such, individuals may perceive threat to job, income, relationships and expertise.

- *Income risks:* Either partial or total loss of income and benefits
- *Job risks:* Loss of present job, status, position, and power. In case of transfer, shift to a new job that demands new routines, new skills and additional responsibilities. In case of termination, the need to search for a job in other organizations.

Inertia of organization

Sometimes, lack of response from individuals may be due to external factors, such as inertia of systems, groups and managers.

1. *Structural inertia:* Systems are established in organizations to ensure stability and achieve efficiency in operations tend to change slowly. A system involving a set of procedures, rules and processes may not change as quickly as expected. Though an individual is ready for change, his progress is restrained by the inertia of organizational systems.

2. *Group inertia:* Employees in organizations are members of some formal groups (trade union) as well informal groups. When the groups oppose, bound by group norms and affiliation ties, an individual may oppose change.

3. *Managerial decision-making:* Individuals resist performing in new roles, when they are not provided with adequate resources. When resource allocations, lag behind the change, change may become less effective.

Affective Factors

Depending on the nature and degree of understanding, people will develop a variety of emotions, both positive (happiness, confidence, surprise) and negative (fear, anxiety, tension, depression, guilt, shock, etc.).

1. *Fear of the unknown:* Changes may not be properly understood when (i) the person communicating is not trustworthy, and (ii) change information is inadequate or complex to comprehend. Unaware of the change and its impact, people develop fear psychosis and resist the change.

2. *Anxiety due to insecurity:* People, who feel secured in their jobs and long to continue in such cosy situation, may become anxious about their future position. They may feel change as a threat to their present secure position.

OVERCOMING RESISTANCE

To manage reactions to change, enterprises have to develop countervailing forces that can mitigate resistance to change and commit people to change process. The resistance reduction measures include: (i) structural arrangements and (iii) strategies.

Structural Arrangements

In organizations that are experiencing change, every manager is responsible for it. However, for effective management of resistance, a person or group may be specifically chosen to be the change managers. Described below are two formal ways in which change managers can be identified: transition management teams and change agents.

Transition management teams

It is a specific group of eight to twelve managers whose full-time responsibilities are to manage and facilitate the change process in the organization.

1. *Areas of concern:* They are concerned not only with structural and procedural changes but also with managing emotions and resistance to change. The teams are engaged after the change decisions are taken and change is planned. They are as such not a planning committee; they are concerned with effective execution of change plans.

2. *Reporting:* These teams monitor and facilitate change and regularly report to the chief executive officer of the company. Necessary corrective measures are planned immediately to keep change process on track.

3. *Existence:* Transition teams represent temporary structural mechanisms. They owe their existence to change in progress and once the company has successfully changed, they are dissolved.

Change agents

A change agent may be an employee or an outside consultant. He or she is appointed to formally guide a change effort from planning to execution. The difference between this arrangement and transition teams is in terms of responsibility for change. The transition management team is concerned with transition or execution part of change; the change agent is involved in all steps of organizational change.

Who can be a better change agent—employee or consultant? The choice is dependent on the perceived benefits of hiring an outside consultant.

What are the benefits of hiring an outside consultant?

1. Consultants take unbiased view of the organization and its problems.
2. They bring more innovative or creative ideas to the company.
3. They may be used as a scapegoat when change has failed to yield expected results or when negative emotions of organizational members become irresistible.

Against the benefits, one has to take into cognizance the following demerits:

1. They can be more costly.
2. They may leak trade secrets to competitors.
3. Being outsiders, their ability to understand internal dynamics of organization is limited.
4. They face problems of distrust. As much employees trust insider, they may not trust an outside consultant.

Strategies to Overcome Resistance

Change management is essentially a people-driven process. People at different levels of organization are to be understood and their cooperation is to be enlisted. For this the following approach is necessary:

Situation analysis

Having an understanding of people and their possible reactions is the first steep in design of strategies. Two types of assessment are necessary:

1. *Impact assessment:* Before and during change process, change manager has to make an assessment of the state of the organization, to gauge the impact of the change on people. The important questions will be: who are affected? Is the impact emotional or functional? What is the degree of impact?

2. *Readiness assessment:* Given the information on change what is the reaction of people? Is their reaction open or concealed? Are they showing empathy or apathy?

Measures

The following measures will be helpful to make change process smooth and effective.

1. *Sponsorship:* Winning cooperation should start from the top. Secure active sponsorship for the change at a senior executive level. Without top management commitment change can never be successful.

2. *Buy-in:* Gaining buy-in for the changes from those involved and affected is the next difficult task. Inform, convince and persuade people through educative measures and, directly or indirectly.

3. *Collaboration:* To strengthen cooperation, collaborate with people by involving them in the design and implementation of changes.

4. *Communication:* Keep informing people. It helps remove hidden fears and apprehensions. It shows transparency in change and builds trust in the persons and processes.

ENCOUNTER STRATEGIES

Change managers face the challenge of designing strategies to overcome resistance. Resistance to change can be managed proactively by creating change readiness in organizations. Alternatively, it can be actively overcome by taking appropriate measures.

Proactive Strategy

Managers of successful companies, manage resistance by taking proactive measures like developing change readiness and agility. Change readiness is the ability of firm to continuously initiate and respond to change in ways beneficial to firms. Change agility represents a company's ability to engage people and deliver the changes envisioned by the decision makers. It indicates a firm's capacity to stretch when necessary and quickly shift resources to the place, where they will make the most difference.

Reactive Strategies

The reactive strategies can be designed differently to face different situations and different types of protestors. Table 6.11 shows the manifestations of resistance to change at different levels in organizations.

TABLE 6.11 Manifestations of Resistance

Level	Dysfunctional tendencies
Individual	Demotivation, underperformance and lack of commitment Displacement, sabotage, other dysfunctional behavior
Group	Direct group resistance, projected group resistance and declared underperformance Inter-group conflict, extreme in-group conformity pressures for and groups actively pursuing their agendas
Organization	Industrial disputes, work—to rule, etc.

Resistance may move from passive disagreement to aggressive conflict. Passive disagreement may lead to gossiping against organization, discourteous behaviors, and adoption of play safe tactics. These resistive symptoms can be identified by careful observation and feedback. Consider the following examples of mild and concealed opposition.

1. At a staff meeting, it is unanimously agreed to implement a new procedure. After some time, in the review meeting it is found that the procedure was not implemented. People offer excuses for their failure.
2. A boss asks his subordinate to prepare a report in a new format. He obeys saying: It is ready in the old format. But if you say, I should change, I will". The boss insists on changing it. Later the subordinate makes some change to appear cooperative, but retains most of the old format.

Active resistance is easy to find, as it is manifested and many-a-time publicized. It takes the form of open arguments and dysfunctional behavior. Kotter and Schlensinger suggested six strategies[25] which can be categorized into development-oriented and conflict resolution-oriented ones.

Development-oriented strategies

Three strategies which are development in nature are: education, participation and facilitation.

1. *Education:* Awareness of change and its potential benefits as well as threats is the cornerstone of successful change management. Change managers have to go beyond announcements of change. They have to furnish details of change and explain the rationale behind it. They should provide opportunities for discussion and exchange of views on change process and outcomes. Education process can involve one-on-one discussions, presentations to groups, or memos and reports. As managers communicate future scenarios, employees can visualise their own role in the future.

2. *Participation:* If change process is to be effective, commitment of people is necessary. Research has showed that participation leads to commitment. Positively, participation through cross-functional teams will not only make people involved but also provide an opportunity to get creative ideas for better change management. However, participation has its own weak points. It is not easy to enlist the cooperation of people without any conflicts. Further, participation may be time consuming, if not properly managed. However, problems like conflict and delays can be minimised by proper training of employees and well-planned schedules and targets.

3. *Facilitation:* The active employees involved in change process can do better if they are supported in different ways. Support measures include—listening and clarifying, offering emotional support, training in new skills, coaching and giving employees time-off after a demanding period. Coaching is a more personalized one to one process, that offers significant learning opportunities. Like participation, facilitation is time-consuming and requires patience.

Conflict resolution-oriented strategies

Three strategies which aim at securing cooperation through resolving differences and exercising power are: negotiation, manipulation and coercion[26].

1. *Negotiation:* When employees recognize that they are going to lose by the proposed change, they oppose it by voicing demands for justice. If management does not respond properly, they resort to different forms of protest like demonstrations and strike. As such, change managers should, in right spirit, respond to the demands. Through negotiation, management can amicably settle the demands and enlist cooperation.

2. *Manipulation:* Management adopts this approach, when the other methods prove time consuming and expensive. Two types of manipulation are observed—(i) manipulation of information and (ii) manipulation of individual or group.

When positive approaches fail, managers resort to manipulating information channels. They try to scare people into thinking there is a crisis coming which they can avoid only by changing. Another approach is co-opting an individual or group whose support is critical. Sometimes, co-optation may be detrimental to the interests of the organization. The co-opted may distort the changes and manager may develop a bad image of a manipulator.

3. *Coercion:* When other methods fail, management may force people to accept a change by explicitly or implicitly threatening them. They portray unfavourable picture of the present situation by pointing out the loss of jobs, job stagnation, transfers, lay off and termination. They enforce rules and regulations, remind people of their obligations, and monitor behaviors with tight controls.

SUMMARY

Change management requires multiple levels of analysis and multi-pronged approaches. Organizational change is the process of transforming an organization from an existing state to a desired state of being. Different classifications of change are found in literature. The factors changes in ownership, poor performance, change in leadership, and overcome stagnation and external environmental factors occur in SLEPT framework (Social, Legal, and Economic, Political and Technological factors).

Depending on the response patterns, we can identify two types of strategic postures: proactive and reactive. Red Queen Effect describes the evolutionary necessity to evolve faster than one's predators or prey. Organizational inertia refers to an organization's inability to respond to change. Organization renewal refers to continual change to remain a viable force in tomorrow's markets. Organizational renewal requires strategic approach that involves evolving the following subsystems: Customer Strategy, Operational effectiveness, Technology optimization and People performance.

Managers seeking to cope with organizational change face certain dilemmas. Dunphy and Stace (1996) broadly categorize them into soft and hard approaches to managing change. The theories of change are: Life cycle theory, Evolutionary theory, Teleological theory, Dialectic theory, Contingency theory, Resource dependence theory, Population ecology theory, and Institutionalization theory. Based on implementation perspective, Beer and Nohria (2000) presented Theory E and Theory O.

The important change process based models are Lewin's freeze change model Schein's model, Galpin wheel and Kotter's 8-step model. The content models explain rationale, substance and outcome of change. Further, three types of change are observed: (i) intended, (ii) partially intended and (iii) unintended. Accordingly, the roles are played by managers are: Director, Navigator, Caretaker, Coach, Interpreter, and Nurturer. A six phase model of reaction to change are: anticipation, confrontation, realization, depression, acceptance and enlightenment. The Change Curve model describes the four stages in change process—Status quo, Disruption, Exploration and Rebuilding. O' Connor (1993) analyzed reactions of people based on two dimensions-overt and covert expression of resistance and conscious and unconscious motivation to resist. Bovey and Hede (2001) analyzed reactions by considering behavioral and affective dimensions. The reaction is shown by two types of behaviors—active and passive and emotions are expressed in two ways: overt (open) and covet (concealed). Resistance can arise from two sources: cognitive (understanding) and affective (emotional feelings). The resistance reduction measures include: (i) structural arrangements and (ii) strategies to reduce the change. Resistance to change can be managed proactively by creating change readiness in organizations. Alternatively, it can be actively overcome by taking appropriate measures.

EXERCISES

I. Review Questions

1. Explain the concept of change.
2. What are the types of change?
3. Explain the features of organizational change.
4. Describe the macro and micro level changes.
5. What the drivers of change in modern organizations?
6. How do organizations respond to change?

7. What dilemmas managers face with respect to change?

8. Explain the roles in change management.

II. Discussion Questions

1. Explain the concept, levels and nature of change in organizations.
2. Identify the significance and drivers of change in organizations.
3. Explain the change process based on the models of Lewin and Schein.
4. Explain change process as described by Kotter.
5. Discuss the reasons for resistance to change in organizations.
6. Elaborate the strategies to overcome resistance to change.

 MINI-PROJECT

Visit any two local organizations and inquire about changes that have taken place, and develop case studies of change with a description of: (i) antecedents to change (ii) change process and (iii) after change situation and benefits obtained.

WEB ASSIGNMENT

Attitudes towards organizational change: validation ...2005
www.psychologyinspain.com/content/full/2005/full.asp?id=9010

CASE STUDY

Maharaja in Chains

In the early 1970s, Air India was one of the top five airlines in the world under the leadership of JRD Tata. The India's biggest carrier, with 158 aircraft is now saddled with a debt of ₹ 43,000 crore, and has not been able to pay its 33,000 employees for the past three months. Accenture, in its report on national carriers, suggested the merger of Air India and Indian Airlines and replacement of the ageing fleet would result in a profit of ₹ 1,000 crore in the first year itself. However, following the merger in 2007 losses escalated from ₹ 1,200 crore in the first to ₹ 2,600 crore in the second to ₹ 5,500 crore in the third and today the accumulated losses are to the tune of ₹ 16,000 crore. Its market share is going down as shown below:

2007–08	2008–09	2009–10	2010–11
18.4%	15.9%	17.7%	17.1%

The Comptroller and Auditor General (CAG) in its report on Air India, found fault with Air India for making pay revision and offering Performance Linked Incentives (PLI) without following any set procedures and violating the norms of Department of Public Enterprises (DPE).

Half-baked Merger

The merger was not carried out in a systematic manner. Key areas, such as integration of IT and migration to the so-called single code (a unified passenger service system) took nearly four years after the merger. Integration at higher levels of management and common fuel distribution and accounting was done, but the mapping of HR and salary issues were neglected. The pilots of the erstwhile Indian Airlines were promised parity with Air India pilot, but nothing was done about it. Criticizing management for side tracking employee problems, a union leader said, "When the airline is not even in a position to pay our salaries, talking about safety and security is meaningless".

Search for Solutions

Justice D.M. Dharmadhikari chairman of the committee set up for resolving staff integration issues in Air India, opined that the biggest challenge lies in the fact that Air India and Indian Airlines are working as separate entities even after merger in 2007. The pay structure and promotion opportunities vary greatly in both airlines.

While employees of Indian Airlines seek parity with Air India, the employees of Air India are against any cuts in their salaries. Pilots of the domestic operations of the erstwhile Indian Airlines had resorted to a 10-day strike, whereas several pilots have quit Air India due to delayed payment of salaries. The merger agreement provides scope for level mapping, promotion chances to be at par without denting the present arrangement.

The committee has met 5 of the 29 associations. The pilots of Indian Airlines' want a fixed flying allowances, as is the case with Air India. There are three stakeholders in this process: passengers, employees and management—and in that order. There are department of public enterprise guidelines, budgetary constraint and company's capability to bring about changes. The committee is looking at how mergers have taken place in other airlines across the world like Delta and British Airways.

Plans are on the anvil to cut salaries of about 5,000 employees, including pilots and engineers. A senior member of a pilots union observed that pilots would cooperate if there is a sound rationale, and the proposed salary cuts are marginal.

Views and Suggestions

Dr. Karan Singh, the country's first Aviation Minister, opined that the merger of Air India and Indian Airlines was very bad idea. He maintained: "To my mind, the merger was a very bad idea. The two airlines—one based in Delhi and the other in Mumbai—had different ethos, different philosophy".

An analyst opined that the objective should be to save airline. It requires employees to make sacrifices. The employee salaries and perks were devised when competition was less, fuel prices were low and ticket prices were high. Wage cuts and cost controls are imperative at the moment.

Another observer opined that employees are heading towards 'what's in it for me' concept. The company needs good corporate governance to influence, mindset of people. In fact, there is a need to professionalize the management of Air India.

Clear Authority

Civil Aviation Minister Praful Patel told press that merger is not a single day process, it can be three to five year process, and management was given full freedom to take any step to deal with disruptions. Arvind Jadhav, the managing director has his own way of doing things. He seems to be inclined to 'teach the pilots a lesson'. He did not carry negotiations when pilots went on strike. Prime Minster announced the government resolve to sort out issues surrounding Air India. Pranab Mukherjee (who heads the Group of Ministers on AI's turnaround) is asked to take expeditious decisions on this matter.

Questions for Discussion

1. In your view, what are the critical issues confronting Air India?

2. What steps do you suggest to make the human side of Air India, more effective in its turn around?

Source: 'Air India-Indian Airlines merger is only on paper'—Indian Express
www.indianexpress.com/.../air-indiaindian-airlines-merger-is.../8207...
22 July, 2011 and Rajiv Pratap Rudy Maharaja in chains: Merger of Air India, Indian Airlines behind airline's money troubles, *Business Today*, May 29, 2011.

REFERENCES

1. *change management* | consulting—L&T Infotech
   www.lntinfotech.com/.../change-management/change-management.as...
   Bureau (2011), Companies need to constantly evolve to cope with ... —*The Hindu Business Line*, November 29, and Gokul Krishnamurthy (2011), The greatest risk in today's world is to carry on as you were before' *The Hindu Business Line*, November 17, Brand line.

2. Hempel, P.S. and Martinsons, M.G. (2009), "Developing international organizational change theory using cases from China", *Human Relations*, Vol. **62**(4), pp. 459–480.

3. Quoted in Tom Kelley—The Red Queen and the Race for Innovation,
   www.leighbureau.com/speakers/tkelley/essays/redqueen.pdf.

4. Peter, Laurence J. and Hull, Raymond (1968), *The Peter Principle: Why Things Always Go Wrong,* New York: William Morrow Company.

5. Renewal Paradigm, www.capsnap.com/dialogue1.asp.

6. Dunphy, D. and Stace, D. (1996), The Strategic Management of Corporate Change. *Human Relations*, Vol. **46**(8), pp. 905–18.

7. Moran and Brightman, (2001), Leading Organization Change, *Career Development International,* Vol. **6**(2), pp. 111–118.

8. Lewin, K. (1958), Group Decisions and Social Change. In *Readings in Social Psychology.* Swanson, G.E., Newcomb, T.M. and Hartley, E.L. (Eds.), New York: Holt, Rhinehart and Winston.

9. Schein, E.H. (1969), *Process Consultation,* New York: Addison-Wesley.

10. Mullins, L. (1989), *Management and Organisational Behaviour,* London: Pitman.

11. Burnes, B. (1996), *Managing Change: A Strategic Approach to Organisational Dynamics*, London: Pitman.

12. Dawson, P. (1994), *Organisational Change: A Processual Approach, London:* Paul Chapman Publishing.

13. Palmer, I., Dunford, R. & Akin G. (2009), *Managing Organizational Change—A Multiple Perspectives Approach*, New York: McGraw-Hill.

14. Van de ven A.H. and Poole M.S. (1995), Explaining development and change in organizations, *Academy of Management Review*, Vol. **20**(3), pp. 510–540.

15. Beer M., and Nohria, N. (2000), Cracking the code of change, *Harvard Business Review*, Vol. **78**(3), May-June, pp. 133–141.

16. Kurt Lewin's Change Theory in the Field and in the Classroom... forteza.sis.ucm.es/apto/alum0203/scheinlewin.pdf.

17. Lewin/Schein's Change Theory, www.entarga.com/orgchange/lewinschein.pdf

18. Galpin Timothy (1996), *The Human Side of Change: A Practical Guide to Organization Redesign*, San Francisco: Jossey-Bass.

19. Kotter, John and Rathgeber, Holger, (2005), *Our Iceberg is Melting: Changing and Succeeding Under any Conditions,* New York: First St. Martin's Press.

20. Palmer, Ian, Dunford, Richard and Akin, Gib (2008), *Managing Organizational Change*, New Delhi: Tata McGraw Hill, pp. 23–33.

21. Ansoff I.H. (1990), *Implanting Strategic Management*, London: Prentice-Hall International.

22. Judson A. (1966), *A Manager's Guide to Making Changes*, London: John Wiley & Sons.

23. O'Connor, C.A. (1993), Resistance: the repercussions of change, *Leadership and Organization Development Journal*, Vol. **14**(6), pp. 30–36.

24. Bovey, W.H. & Hede, A. (2001), Resistance to organizational change: The role of defence mechanisms, *Journal of Managerial Psychology*, Vol. **6**(7), September, pp. 534–547.

25. Kotter, John P. and Shlensinger, Leonard A. (1979), Choosing strategies for change, Harvard Business Review, March-April, Vol. **57**(2), pp. 106–114.

26. Choosing strategies for change, https://www.ihm.org.uk/.../ certificate_managing_ people_choosing_st...

Part Three: Processes

Chapter 7

Action Research

Learning Objectives

After studying this chapter, you will be able to:

- Explain the concept, and types of action research
- Describe the evolution of action research
- Understand action research models for OD
- Appreciate appreciative inquiry and process consultation as variants of OD

Vignette: Research and Action at Wipro

Wipro Applying Thought in Schools, which began in schools in 2001, has evolved in respect of philosophy, strategy and action through application of scientific approaches, benchmarking learning objectives, and integrating syllabus. They supported an action research experiment for creating an effective ICT curriculum, which can influence overall pedagogical and classroom practices.

When the management of Wipro Technologies found it necessary to institutionalize the solution-centric approach of conducting business amongst the teams, they decided to deploy appreciative inquiry to enable teams to move from problem-centric to solution-centric approach. According to Rajesh Sharma, Manager-Talent engagement and development and Head HR (Finance Solutions) the program was deployed to create a win-win dynamics for one of the project teams in the establishment.

A facilitator inquired the selected team to go back in time, and openly share some of the high's and low's that the team had encountered in their lives (personal or professional). To enable participants think in right direction, facilitator raised some key questions: What have I done better and how can I do things to drive relevant results? 'What can I do further so as to be able to deliver a more positive action at the work place? The members were asked to focus on some of their experiential involvements in projects, generic experiences, critical incidents or stories for their exploration and explanation. After the positive inquiry and deliberations generated a new interest and enthusiasm, the members were asked to reflect on how to evolve action plans that can collectively and pro-actively impact the business.

Were there benefits from this exercise? The company claims that AI has actualized a couple of deliverables. In the words of Rajesh Sharma, "For one, the process of (open and complete experience sharing) enabled the teams to resolve any issues that might normally pace down the functioning of a normal team." Further, the collective awareness of the positive experiences helped in changing the perspectives. It was expected that the intervention would in course of time create a culture that encourages and enforces openness in approach and good communication amongst the teams[1].

Different types of OD approaches and interventions are found in practice. The process-focused and action-oriented approaches that help participants improve attitudes, enhance competences and adapt to changes are examined in this chapter.

INTRODUCTION

Action research has become a useful research methodology for solving business and management problems in recent years. There is a spate of research papers explaining how action research has been effective in solving a variety of business problems related to product development, manufacturing, engineering and operations management, organizational change and transformation, Information systems and E-commerce, Accounting, small business and management development[2]. However, action research is not an easy process to implement due to its multi-dimensional nature. It requires a good understanding of the theory, process, people and organization concerned with change. In this chapter, we will first discuss action research process, and then examine the two related processes appreciative inquiry and process consulting.

CONCEPT OF ACTION RESEARCH

Today, for corporate enterprises, action research is a means of coming to grips with their dynamic and turbulent environments. It is referred to as participatory research, collaborative inquiry, and action learning. In simple terms, action research is learning by doing. It is based on the premise that knowledge is always gained through action and for action. Drinan cautions that "in defining the concept of action research, one must be careful to include aspects of both action and research. There is a risk otherwise that action research can become a tool rather than a means of genuine critical reflection and social action[3]".

In everyday inquiry, humans learn from their actions and use that learning to improve their actions. However, action research is different from it in that it is relatively a systematic and deliberate process. As Kemmis and McTaggart opined, one must plan, act, observe, and reflect more carefully, more systematically, and more rigorously than one usually does in everyday life and also use the relationships between these moments in the process as a source of both improvement and knowledge[4].

Some of the definitions of action research are given as follows:

McCutcheon and Jung (1990) observed: It is a "systemic inquiry that is collective, collaborative, self-reflective, critical and undertaken by participants in the inquiry[5]".

Kemmis and McTaggert maintained that action research is "a form of collective self-reflective inquiry undertaken by participants in social situations in order to improve the rationality and justice of their own social or educational practices, as well as their understanding of these practices and the situations in which these practices are carried out[6]".

Rapoport opined that, "action research aims to contribute both to the practical concerns of people in an immediate problematic situation and to the goals of social science by joint collaboration within a mutually acceptable ethical framework[7]."

CHARACTERISTICS

From the above definitions, the following features of action research can be identified:

1. *Focused:*   Action research is client-centered, problem-centered and action-oriented.

2. *Used in real situations:*   Action research is applied in real situations, rather than in contrived, experimental studies. It is chosen when circumstances require flexibility and the involvement of the people in the research.

3. *Quick and holistic:*   Social scientists make use of this approach when change must take place quickly or holistically.

4. *Multi-level approach:*   At the personal level, it interprets and evaluates one's actions with the goal of improving practice. At the organizational level, it helps understand the system of interactions that define a social context and guides change. At the scholarly level, it facilitates sharing of the knowledge gained with the larger research community, through written research papers or oral presentations at conferences.

5. *Twin goals:*   Gilmore and others opined that action research aims to study a system and concurrently to collaborate with members of the system in changing it in a desirable direction. It combines investigation with action[8].

6. *Cyclical process:*   Lewin introduced this scientific process and explained it as a spiral of steps, each of which is composed of a circle of planning, action, and fact-finding about the result of the action[9].

7. *Collaborative:*   Action research emphasizes on active collaboration of researcher and client. It involves the client system in a diagnostic, active-learning, problem-finding, and problem-solving process.

8. *Less scientific in research:*   In diagnostic phase, the scientific methods employed in data gathering and quantitative analyses can be less rigorous as it relies on qualitative research to gain insights.

9. *Self correcting and self-renewal:*   Action research makes client organization a self-correcting mechanism for enhancing the effectiveness. As such it can sustain the ability to carry out self-analysis and self-renewal.

10. *Ethical:* Action research is carried out in real-world circumstances, with the knowledge and participation of people in problem finding, goal setting, and task design and implementation. As such, it is based on ethical principles that emphasize on equality, equity, honesty and transparency.

TYPES

Action research is classified in many ways based on the inquiry approach, people involved and method employed.

Based on Nature of Research

Grundy identified three modes of action research: technical, practical and emancipatory[10]. Holter and Schwartz-Barcott have identified in a similar way three approaches: technical collaborative approach, a mutual collaborative approach and an enhancement approach[11]. Hart and Bond described four types of action research; experimental, organizational, professionalizing and empowering[12]. An observation of them reveals that the action research types can be placed upon a continuum as shown in Figure 7.1. A comparative analysis of the three methods is presented in Table 7.1.

Consensus model of society ⟷		Conflict model of society
Research based ⟷		Action focused
Technical	Practical	Emancipatory
Experimental	Organizational	Professionalizing	Empowering

Figure 7.1 Action research typology.

TABLE 7.1 Comparative Analysis of Action Research Types

Aspects	Technical	Practical	Emancipatory
Problem definition	Defined in advance	Defined in situation	Defined in the situation based on values clarification
Focus on theory	Validation, refinement, deduction	New theory, inductive	Validation, refinement, new theory, inductive and deductive
Knowledge produced	Predictive	Descriptive	Predictive and descriptive
Change duration	Short-lived	Long lasting, dependent on individuals	Social change, emancipation
Relationship between consultant and manager	Separate	Interrelated, dialogic	Interrelated, embedded in society

Technical

It is scientific method of problem-solving with the objective of testing a particular intervention based on a chosen theoretical framework. The researcher identifies the problem and a specific intervention. He will collaborate with the practitioner to facilitate communication to the group. Projects in this category of research are taken up on the request of a particular person or group of people, who have technical authority. The researcher encourages participation of people in the process improvement. He also seeks to validate and refine existing theories based on deductive logic. The research results in two things: (i) enhancement of effectiveness and efficiency in practice, and (ii) the accumulation of predictive knowledge.

Practical

In this type, the researcher and the managers collaborate to design interventions. The problem is defined after dialogue with the researcher and the practitioner. Together, they explore the underlying causes and identify possible interventions. This type of research, as such, is more flexible, by accommodating interactive and phenomenological perspectives. However, the interventions tend to be short-lived. The changes tend to be connected to the individuals directly involved in the change process, and when they leave the system the change process will stop abruptly.

Emancipatory

This is an action-oriented approach with three distinct phases: theory, enlightenment and action". However, the emancipator research does not begin with theory and end with practice. It is informed by theory and often it is in confrontation with the theory that provides the initiative to undertake the practice. The researcher seeks to test and validate new ideas or tacit knowledge acquired through the process of reflection driven by critical intent. The reflection will give rise to enlightenment in the form of authentic insights. The researcher, rather than thrusting enlightenment on the participants, allows symmetrical communication to occur from which enlightenment will flow to them. The process of enlightenment results in action, which is freed from the dominating constraints of the environment.

Based on Research Persons

Action research can be carried out at individual or group/organizational level.

1. *Individual research:* Research is conducted by one organizational member with the aim of analyzing and improving a specific task. In education, a teacher may decide to test a hypothesis that seminar method will help improve learning. The teacher alone performs research by conducting seminars for a certain length of time and finds out from the results whether the hypothesis is right.

2. *Group research:* It refers to research that involves a group of people. In the education setting, collaborative research involves teachers teaching one subject and the principal, leads the team of teachers in verifying the efficacy of the teaching method.

Based on Method

Based on the method employed, action research can be classified by Chein, Cook and Harding as follows[13]:

Diagnostic vs participatory

In diagnostic type, the consultant diagnoses the problem situation and makes recommendations to the client. The recommendations are intuitive, and are not pretested. They are drawn from the experience and knowledge of the consultant. As this method does not involve client organization members actively in the process, the recommendations may or may not be implemented. The second type of research, the participatory one, involves organization members in all stages of research—diagnosis and problem definition, action planning and implementation. Hence, it is more effective in brining about improvements in practice.

Empirical vs experimental

Empirical research is case based. The consultant collects data relating to the issue under consideration and keeps a record of it for analyzing the problems and finding solutions. The method has certain limitations like: (i) the data collected may not be adequate, due to observation of less number cases; (ii) the cases observed may be too divergent to make a coherent explanation of the issue. In view of this, some researchers prefer experimental method of research. Observation of real-life experiences in controlled situations will help locate the deficiencies in the system. Also an intervention can be tested for its efficacy by introducing it in the real-life situation. Thus it is action oriented in case of both problem finding and testing interventions.

HISTORY OF ACTION RESEARCH

Action research can be seen as an off-shoot of the scientific method. John Dewey is credited for influencing researchers with his Interpretive research, which is a form of field research methodology. His views have led to the emergence of action research. However, it is Kurt Lewin who coined the term action research, in 1946. He takes credit for not only coining the term but also for suggesting its methodology. He is generally considered the father of action research. He forwarded action research concept with his famous statement, "No research without action; no action without research[14]".

Kurt Lewin, Trist and their associates applied their research to systemic change in and between organizations. They affirmed the principle of participative decision-making, and argued that decisions are best implemented by those who help make them. Accordingly, they emphasized on collaboration between professionals and clients and gave importance to group relations.

However, action research failed to sustain the interest of researchers for long. In the next two decades, it was relegated to background for two reasons. Its critics labeled it as an unscientific, amateur, little more than common sense approach. The rise of experimental methodology with research designs and quantitative data collection was another factor for the waning interest in action research.

By the 1970s, action research staged a comeback. Thanks to education practitioners. They questioned the efficacy of scientific research methods in solving education issues, and preferred the use of action research. By the mid-1970s, four streams of research became popular-traditional, contextual (action learning), radical, and educational action research[15].

1. _Traditional action research:_ It stemmed from Lewin's work within organizations and encompasses the concepts and practices of field theory, group dynamics, T-Groups, and the clinical model. It was applied to bring improvements in areas like 'Quality of Work Life (QWL) and Organizational Democracy'.

2. _Contextural action research:_ It is also known as Action Learning and is derived from Trist's work on relations between organizations. It seeks to bring in social transformation through consensus and normative incrementalism. It attempts at reconstituting the structural relations among actors in a social environment. It requires participants to act as project designers and co-researchers. New concepts like organizational ecology, and search conferences became popular with this type of research.

3. _Radical action research:_ This is emancipatory, participatory type of action research. It helps participants overcome power imbalances and strives for social transformation via an advocacy process.

4. _Educational action research:_ This fourth stream, had its foundations in the writings of John Dewey, who believed that professional educators should become involved in community problem-solving. The practice of action research continued to gain visibility and by 1980, according to Abraham Shani there were 100 published reports of action research projects linked to organization development[16]. Action research continued to gain popularity, due to its applicability to different situations as well as its ability to solve problems and develop people. It is now being used in various social, community and organizational settings.[17]

MERITS OF ACTION RESEARCH

Action research as a method of developing right solutions for improvement of practices has the following merits[18]:

1. _Universality:_ Action research is a practical approach to professional inquiry in any social situation. Though it became popular in the field of education in the beginning, it has found application in various settings—industry, medicine, public administration, social work, community health, etc. The context for inquiry may change, but the principles and processes are the same.

2. _Supports future inquiry:_ The findings of an action researcher can produce an understanding which he or she can pass onto others to try. Since they cannot be applicable directly to organizations facing similar situations, the benefit is limited to knowing the intricacies and experiences of research. This awareness helps improve the research process.

3. _Improves theory:_ Action research helps validate and build theory. Carr and Kemmis (1986) argued that the twin assumptions that all theory is non-practical, and all practice is non-theoretical are, entirely misguided. Knowledge cannot be generated out of a practical vacuum[19]. Since action research combines both research and practice, it leads to simultaneous improvement in practice and theory.

4. *Fosters spirit of democracy:* The most important feature of action research is it fosters the spirit of democracy and individual capability as knowledge makers. It can make participants feel responsible. It can help them feel in control of their own situation and enhance their professional development.

ROLE OF CONSULTANT

The consultant role is to implement the method in such a manner as to produce a mutually agreeable outcome for all participants. The consultant is an expert when analyzing the data and a facilitator when helping the client in developing an action plan. He has to find a delicate balance between the changing responsibilities of being an expert and facilitator[20].

- *Expert:* Consultants conducts research, and develops action plans.
- *Nurturer:* Consultants nurture leaders in organization for having effective collaboration and to sustain the change.
- *Facilitator:* Consultants facilitate dialogue and foster reflective analysis among the participants.
- *Communicator:* Consultants provide the organizational members, with periodic reports and final report, at the end of research.

MODELS OF ACTION RESEARCH

Action research is a collaborative process of problem solving for improving practices in organizations. It is depicted differently by different researchers; some of them are brief and some others are elaborate.

Systems Model

Lewin describes action research as a cyclical process of planned change. A systems model is shown in Figure 7.2. It has three distinct stages corresponding to three phases of change described by Lewin[21].

Stage **1:** *Planning:* The client and consultant work together and initiate a series of planning actions. This process involves various steps like preliminary diagnosis, data gathering, feedback of results, and joint action planning.

Stage **2:** *Action:* This stage includes learning about roles and organization through reflective processes and feedback from planning Based on this learning, action-planning is done jointly by the consultant and members of the client system and action steps are carried out on the job.

Stage **3:** *Results:* Desired changes in behavior are the primary outcome. Feedback helps to make necessary adjustments in learning activities and initiate corrective actions necessary.

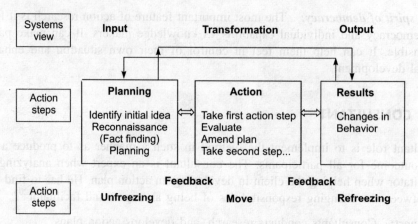

Figure 7.2 Systems Model of Action Research.

Source: Adapted from en.wikipedia.org/wiki/Action_research and kurt lewin: groups, experiential learning and action research, www.infed.org/thinkers/et-lewin.htm.

LIMITATIONS

Action research may fail to deliver the expected results due to some weaknesses in the process. They can be categorized into: (i) consultant related, and (ii) method related problem.

Consultant Related Problems

The problems arise due to factors like time, values, bias and unawareness.

1. *Lack of time:* Action research demands time and attention of consultants. The professional consultants may work in the hurly burly of their own business. At times, they may not be able to justify their roles.

2. *Ignorance of values:* Action research requires working with client or practitioner. The practitioner may not be fully aware of his or her values when suggesting a solution.

3. *Researcher bias:* As action research involves people who belong to the system, there may be bias in investigation, interpretation and intervention choices.

4. *Unfamiliarity with the methods:* Some researchers may be less familiar with the methods. Since there is no way to judge the rigour of the analysis, whatever methods action researcher chooses will be accepted by the practitioner.

Method Related Problems

The problems arise due to the nature of findings and method of presentation.

1. *Findings are not generalizable:* The results of action research lead to development of new knowledge. However, it can be added to the existing theory at best as a case example, and not as a new theory applicable to many organizations.

2. *Inhibiting approach:* Action researchers make use of different diagrams and maps to make tight, orderly presentations which trap participants within a narrow framework and they continue to think in those lines. Thus there is a danger of inhibiting independent action by participating members.

APPRECIATIVE INQUIRY

Appreciate Inquiry (AI) is first developed by David Cooperrider in the 1980s. It is considered as an important advance in action research in the past decade (Bushe, 1995); as a powerful second generation OD practice (French and Bell, 1995) and as model of a much-needed participatory science, a "new yoga of inquiry" (Harman, 1991)[22].

Progress

In 1980, Cooperrider was involved in the study of Cleveland Clinic, and found that employees were depressed by criticism. With the approval of the clinic, he focused his analysis on positive factors that led to success at the clinic. Participants were asked to focus only on the factors that contributed to success when the organization was most efficient. The approach was so successful that the clinic asked him to apply it to the whole group. With this success, AI progressed, and in 1987, a Canadian firm employed it on a large scale in its organization. When working with Romania's health care system, in 1990, Cooperrider created the 4-D model and improved it when working with the US Agency for International Development (USAID)[23]. In 1996, GTE won an award for the "Best Organization Change Program". Since it was based on AI, the method became globally popular. In 2002, Nokia conducted an appreciative inquiry summit for their employees. In its June 2004 issue, Training Magazine, reported that corporations ranging from British Airways, McDonald's, NASA, and British Petroleum have all used appreciative inquiry as an approach to change[24].

Concept and Characteristics

Kolb states, "Appreciation is a process of affirmation. Unlike criticism, which is based on skepticism and doubts, appreciation is based on belief, trust, and conviction[25]. "Appreciative Inquiry is a co-evolutionary search for the best in people, their organizations, and the relevant world around them. It can be applied to a variety of purposes, like organizational redesign, mergers and strategic planning. The philosophy of AI is based on the view that organization is a miracle to be embraced rather than a problem to be solved, and the process has the following characteristics:

- *Appreciative:* It looks for the positive in individuals and organizations.
- *Applicable:* It is a practical one, grounded in reality, keeping in mind the constraints and limitations.

- *Provocative:* It encourages risk taking and demands the use of design capabilities.
- *Collaborative:* It involves everyone, to act as a team to explore and evolve future plans.

Process

In AI, what the researcher looks for is not the problem, but rather, its gifts the building blocks of the organization. The method asks: "What is working well around here and how do we build on it?" David Cooperrider and Diana Whitney suggested a 4-D model: Discovery, Dreaming, Design and Delivery (Destiny).

Assumptions

Appreciative Inquiry is grounded in an "organizational theory of affirmation" (Cooperrider 1990). It is based on the following assumptions[26].

1. *Vision:* The guiding images of the future (its vision of itself and the world) is a better clue to the organization's overall well being.

2. *Openness:* Any pattern of organizational action is open to alteration and reconfiguration.

3. *Imaginativeness:* Organization's imaginative projections are the key to their current conduct.

4. *Growth:* Organizations are heliotropic in character, that is, they grow toward the light, toward a positive vision of the future.

5. *Positive imagery:* The more an organization focuses on positive imagery, the better it will become.

6. *Reaffirmation:* Affirmative competence is the key to the self-organizing system. Every organization needs constant reaffirmation. Through appreciation of organizational life, members of an organization learn to value not only the life-enhancing organization itself, but also learn to affirm themselves.

4-D model

The four stages of the model are briefly described here. It starts with an appreciation of strengths and moves to dreaming a desirable future state. The next two steps are critical; they translate the dream goals into achievements. Without them exercise will end as a feel good experience. Table 7.2 summarises the focus, and principle of the model. It also indicates who the participants are in different stages. Box 7.1 presents how Institutional Learning and Change (ILAC) put in practice AI method.

Anne Acosta and Boru Douthwaite described a five step model adding Definition as the first step. We will now elaborate the 5 step process.

1. *Definition:* This phase defines the scope of the inquiry—the focus of inquiry and concerned stakeholders. The phase includes building awareness among key stakeholders by involving them in discussions on what holds back the system from what it wants to become. An examination

TABLE 7.2   Key Aspects in 4-D Model

Discovery	Dream	Design	Delivery /Destiny
Strengths	Goals	Plans	Achievements
What is it? What has worked?	What might be?	What should be? What is the idea?	How to make it happen?
Individuals and groups	Large and small groups	Small groups	Small groups
Constructionist, positive and poetic principles	Anticipatory and novelty principles	Simultaneity principle	Continuity principle

of resources available (people, time and money) is important to know whether they are acting as constraints. AI holds that it is important to get the questions right, as it heightens desired awareness of a particular aspect of the system.

2. *Discovery:*   The focus is on recognizing excellence and achievements of individuals and groups.

1. Participants are asked about their individual positives—high points in career, experience that stands out as exceptional and truly memorable. For this, structured interviews may be used.
2. As a next step, participants will be asked to work individually to map out their stories and share them with others, in pairs.
3. Finally, they are asked to form groups to identify the common themes behind their examples of excellence. These could be anything from core practices, values, customer service, or capacities, such as leadership.

3. *Dream:*   The goal is developing a future picture.
1. A large group conference is convened. Participants are asked to develop a future vision based on the common themes that were evolved in the first stage. They can be guided by asking:
   Imagine a leap of 5 or 10 years in the future, and discovering that your organization has made its highpoint experiences the norm. Your organization has become so successful that a journalist is about to interview you on how your organization is working. What do you say?
2. Small groups are formed and encouraged to develop a picture of the ideal future, which is applicable to the organization.

4. *Design:*   The goal of this phase is mapping the steps that will turn the dream into reality. Small groups are asked to develop short- and long-term goals through consensus, to achieve the dream. This is inspired by a provocative proposition. Example of provocative proposition is "Our organization will do whatever is necessary to achieve superior customer service within two years". Whitney and Trosten-Bloom (2003) propose the following organizational dimensions that might be considered when developing provocative propositions:[27]

- Vision and purpose
- Strategy

- Structure
- Leadership
- Decision-making processes
- Communication
- Systems
- Roles and relationships
- Knowledge management
- Policies and procedures
- Products and services

5. *Delivery/Destiny:* The idea is to develop an implementable plan for accomplishing goals. Implementation is accomplished most effectively by implementation teams, comprising committed individuals and groups. The team develops strategies and action plans to meet the stated goals. This is supported by identification and definition of roles and responsibilities for organizing, monitoring, evaluation and feedback. The team drives the change continually seeking and sharing success stories.

BOX 7.1   AI to Strengthen a Community of Practice

The researchers at the International Center for Tropical Agriculture (CIAT) formed Learning to Innovate (LTI) Group. The Group took part in a one-day Appreciative Inquiry (AI) workshop.

Definition: An AI workshop would normally take three days. Since it was planned for one day, the inquiry focus was defined before the workshop started in terms of two objectives: (i) creating a vision and evolving a process for its implementation, and (ii) learning about AI.

Discovery: The participants interviewed each other one-on-one. They formed groups of six to eight and shared interview highlights and identified three themes. The interview questions relating to the three themes were as follows:

1. *Fostering innovation*
   - Reflect on your time at CIAT or other experiences.
   - What were the highpoints for you working to foster innovation?
   - Select one highpoint, at a time when you felt happiest and most alive, when you felt you were doing creative, useful, meaningful work that really made a difference.
   - What were you doing, what felt good, who else was involved and what did you feel you achieved?

2. *Cooperative relations*
   - Identify and describe a scenario that demonstrates the positive aspects of working together, cooperating to get something done.
   - Who and what was involved, why did it work, what were you doing and what were other people doing?

(Contd.)

3. *Effective communication and knowledge sharing*
- What different types of communication occur between CIAT's different geographic locations?
- What do you value most about effective communication?
- When does this happen for you?
- Who and what is involved in the best types of communication?
- Why is effective communication good for you and for work on fostering innovation?

Dream: Participants were asked to imagine they had woken up 5 years ahead into the future, when the LTI Group had become famous. They were asked to describe this success under the three themes. These descriptions were in the form of provocative propositions. The facilitator suggested that the propositions should stretch, challenge and interrupt the status quo; be grounded in the group's collective history; describe something we want—our preferred future; and be stated in bold affirmative terms in the present tense. The provocative propositions were later combined through discussion on their LISTSERVE.

Source: Adapted with permission from Acosta, A., and Douthwaite, B. (2005), Appreciative Inquiry: An approach for learning and change based on our own best practices. *ILAC Brief No. 6.* Rome, Italy: Institutional Learning and Change (ILAC) initiative. http://www.cgiar-ilac.org/files/ILAC_Brief06_inquiry_0.pdf.

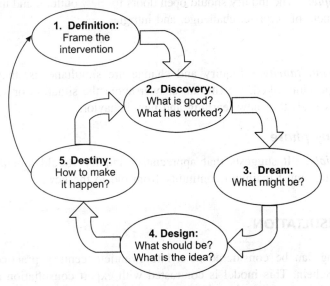

Figure 7.3 Appreciative inquiry, 5-D Model.

Principles

Here are some guiding principles that are central to theory of AI, that correspond to the 4-D models.

Discovery phase

1. *Constructionist principle.* Knowing (organizations) stands at the center of any and every attempt at change. To be effective one must be adept in the art of understanding, and analyzing organizations as living, human constructions.

2. *Positive principle.* Building and sustaining momentum for change requires positive things like hope, excitement, inspiration, and sheer joy in creating something meaningful together.

3. *Poetic principle.* Human organizations are more like an open book than, a machine. An organization's story comprises past, present and future, and is constantly being coauthored.

Dream phase

1. *Anticipatory principle:* The image of the future, guides the current behavior of any organization. Humans project ahead of themselves a horizon of expectation as a mobilizing agent.

2. *Novelty principle:* The inquiry should open doors for new outlook and understanding. There should be an element of surprise, challenge, and intrigue.

Design phase

1. *Principle of simultaneity:* Inquiry and change are simultaneous, they are not separate moments, To a question asked, we find an answer about the situation or self, or discover the unknown and this leads to a new learning and new behavior.

Delivery/Destiny phase

Continuity principle: It suggests that appreciative inquiry should aim at a change that is planned. The change must maintain continuity from old to the new.

PROCESS CONSULTATION

Process consulting can be considered as a late twentieth century practice espoused in the works of Edgar Schein. This model is contrasted with expert consultation as it is not merely problem-centered, but also client-centered. It focuses on helping relationship and the consultant works with and not for the client. In this process, consultants combine subject expertise with process helpfulness, to enhance client's problem-solving ability to find solutions to the client's problems. Consultations in Organization Development (OD) are mostly process consultations as the aim of OD is to build self-renewing organizations capable of adapting to changes.

Definitions

Process consultation is defined in different terms by different authors. However, conceptually they are not different.

Edgar Schein defined it as follows:

Process consultation is the creation of a relationship with the client that permits the client to perceive, understand, and act on the process events that occur in the client's internal and external environment in order to improve the situation as defined by the client[28].

Reddy provides a similar definition. According to him,

Process consultation is the reasoned and intentional interventions by the consultant, into the ongoing events and dynamics of a group with the purpose of helping that group effectively attain its agreed-upon objectives[29].

Characteristics

Process consultation is characterized by the following features.

1. *Partnership:* The consultant and the client act as equals in process consultation. They share knowledge and work for solution. The client provides information about the goals, operations and issues of organization and the consultant provides information on methods of thinking and problem-solving techniques.

2. *Mutual responsibility:* In process consultation, the consultant helps the client see the issues and find what needs to be done. The client plays the operative role and consultant plays the supportive role. In short, they complement each other.

3. *Emphasis on ability:* The focus of consultation is, not on solving the problem, but on building problem solving ability of the client organization. The role of consultant is positive, instructive and constructive. He develops positive attitudes in client to open up and freely discuss issues. He provides instruction to client to develop problem-solving skills. Working with the client, he enables the client to design durable solutions.

4. *Emphasis on learning:* As everyone becomes involved in all phases of the organization and everyone becomes responsible for the organization's development, there will be a need for more people to know and to use more principles and more practices in more situations. For example, dialogue is a staple of the process consultation effort. It will be used not simply in special situations or just for team-building purposes; it will be treated as a part of the organizational culture. It will be a tool of organization and not just of the consultant.

Assumptions

The process consultant works with the following assumptions to help client discover solutions and develop problem-solving capabilities.

1. People often fail to perceive their problems on their own. They need the help of a third party to identify and diagnose them.
2. Most people have a constructive intent and inherent capability to improve things, but they remain dormant.
3. Most organizations can be more effective if they are equipped with their own problem-solving ability.
4. No organization form is perfect. Compensatory mechanisms are hence needed to make them effective.

Role of Process Consultant

The role of process consultant is quite different from the expert type consultant[30]. Here is a brief description of what the consultant does.

1. He tries to understand the processes rather than the work.
2. He seeks to know what clients know and think about the process rather than exhibit what he knows and thinks.
3. He stays silent to enable clients to speak and open up.
4. He refrains from making value judgments to help clients explore alternative solutions.
5. He will not offer advice; he offers additional insights and alternatives to the clients.
6. He plays the role of coach and counselor rather than a problem-solver.

Obviously, process consultants need some additional skills for playing the roles counseling and coaching.

Benefits

Process consultation offers the following benefits to client organization[31]:

1. *Better solution:* The sharing of knowledge for problem-solving provides a shared understanding of mission, values and vision of the organization and the toolkit of best practices. Mutually the consultant and client will find solution that fits the organization's needs and interests.

2. *Developed people:* The expert consultant is compared to masked rider who provides a silver bullet and rides-off into the sunset. But too commonly the ammunition does not last, and SOS (save our souls) is raised. The process consultant however, is different. He will involve employees and builds up facilitation and consultation skills in the organization. There will be internal consultants and capable teams, at all levels of the organization.

3. *Learning organization:* In the process consultation model, learning organization is the second outcome. The goal of the consultant here is not only to fix a situation, but also the creation of a better organization.

Principles

Edgar Schein said, "I measure my success in every contact by whether or not I feel the relationship has been helpful and whether or not the client feels helped" and suggested from this point of view ten principles for consultants to follow[32]:

1. *Always try to be careful:* Sustain the intention to be helpful. It is rewarding and leads to mutual learning.

2. *Always stay in touch with the current reality:* Pragmatic outlook helps place the issues in right perspective.

3. *Access your ignorance:* Learn to distinguish 'what I know' from 'what I assume I know', from 'what I truly do not know'.

4. *Everything you do is an intervention:* Every interaction is in essence diagnosis; it reveals some useful information. In the same way, every action is an intervention as it will have consequences both for the client and the consultant.

5. *It is the client who owns the problem and the solution:* The consultant's role is to show the problem and not to take it onto his shoulders. Further his role is not to find solutions but help client find solutions.

6. *Go with the flow:* Move along with people and processes at their own natural rhythm and pace. Do not impose your own sense of flow on an unknown situation. As the relationship reaches a certain level of trust, flow itself becomes a shared process.

7. *Timing is crucial:* Be aware that there is a right time for every action and word. The same remark uttered at two different tines can give entirely different results.

8. *Be constructively opportunistic with confrontive interventions:* When working with people, knowing their openness and readiness is important. When the client signals a moment of openness, seize those moments and try to make the most of them.

9. *Everything is a source of data; errors are inevitable-learn from them:* One cannot know enough of the client's situation to avoid errors. Learn from mistakes and avoid defensiveness, shame, or guilt.

10. *When in doubt share the problem:* Occasionally one may run out of gas. The ego centered, expert consultant may feel frustrated and get paralyzed. In such situations as a process consultant, your outlook is different. You should not assume that you always know what to do next. You can share your problem with the client.

SUMMARY

Action research has become a useful research methodology for solving business and management problems in recent years. It is referred to as participatory research, collaborative inquiry, and action learning. In simple terms, action research is learning by doing. McCutcheon and Jung

(1990) defined it as a "systemic inquiry that is collective, collaborative, self-reflective, critical and undertaken by participants in the inquiry".

The features of action research are: it is a multi-level approach, with twin goals of investigation and action, a process which is cyclical, collaborative, less scientific, but focused, holistic, quick, self correcting and self renewal, ethical and useful in real situations. Action research is classified in many ways like: (i) technical, practical and emancipator; and (ii) experimental, organizational, professionalizing and empowering; (iii) individual research and group research; (iv) diagnostic vs participatory; and empirical vs experimental.

Kurt Lewin is generally considered the father of action research. He forwarded action research concept with his famous statement, "No research without action; no action without research". By the mid-1970s, four streams of research became popular—traditional, contextural (action learning), radical, and educational action research. Universal application, support to future inquiry, improvement in theory, and fostering spirit of democracy are the virtues of action research. The consultant role is finding a delicate balance between the changing responsibilities of being an expert and facilitator.

Lewin describes action research as a cyclical process of planned change with three distinct stages of change process. According to Wilson and Streatfield, it involves diagnosis, problem definition, action planning and implementation. Action research may fail to deliver the expected results due to some weaknesses in the process. On the consultant side, problems include: lack of time, ignorance of values of organization, bias, and unfamiliarity with methods. The method provides less scope for creative thinking by participants, and its findings being situation specific, are not generalisable.

Appreciative Inquiry (AI) is first developed by David Cooperrider in the 1980s. Kolb (1984) states, "Appreciation is a process of affirmation. Unlike criticism, which is based on skepticism and doubts, appreciation is based on belief, trust, and conviction. "The process is appreciative, applicable to situations, provocative and collaborative. It is based on the following assumptions: (i) vision is a good clue to future, (ii) organizational action is open, (iii) current conduct is based on imagination, (iv) organizations grow positively, (v) positive thinking helps grow positively, and (vi) reaffirmation gives strength. The principles that guide the process are: (i) Constructionist Principle, (ii) Principle of Simultaneity, (iii) Poetic Principle, (iv) Anticipatory Principle, (v) Positive Principle, (vi) Novelty principle, and (vii) Continuity principle.

Process consulting can be considered as a late 20th century practice espoused in the works of Edgar Schein, who defined it as reasoned and intentional interventions by the consultant, into the ongoing events and dynamics of a group with the purpose of helping that group effectively attain its agreed-upon objectives. Process consultation is characterized by partnership, mutual responsibility, and emphasis on ability and learning. The process consultant works with the assumption that people need support to find problem and they have ability to solve it and plays the roles of counseling and coaching. Process consultation offers better solution, develops people, and creates learning organization.

EXERCISES

I. Discussion Questions

1. Explain the concept, characteristics and types of action research.
2. Describe the evolution and merits of action research.
3. Explain action research models for OD.
4. Describe the process and principles of appreciative inquiry.
5. Discuss process consultation as a variant of OD.

II. Review Questions

1. Explain the concept of action research.
2. What are the different types of action research.
3. Identify the merits of action research.
4. What is the role of consultant in action research?
5. Identify the limitations of action research.
6. Explain 4-D model of appreciative inquiry.
7. What are the principles of appreciative inquiry?
8. What is process consulting? What are its benefits?
9. What are the principles of process consulting?

MINI-PROJECT

How does Appreciative Inquiry (AI) work?

(a) Forming groups: Select 20 students as participants in the exercise.

(b) Exercise:

1. Form students into groups of five and ask them to sit in a circle.
2. Discuss the value of feedback about strengths.
3. Provide a sheet of A4 paper, to all of them.
4. Ask them to write their own name on the bottom of the paper and pass it to the person on the left.
5. Ask each person to write a phrase or few words about the person whose name is at the bottom of the page and fold it so that the comments are covered.
6. Pass it to the next person and he or she does same things of writing, folding and passing it to the next person. At the end of this process, everyone has his or her own paper.
7. Ask everyone to read out the comments quietly. No discussion.
8. Ask each person which comment(s) he or she likes the best.
9. Ask each person to say what comments about him or her, the members have missed to write.
10. Ask each person to say loudly the strength she or he liked (I am... or I have....)

(c) Feedback: Now ask each member how he or she was feeling at the end of the session. Is there a greater understanding of self and a new resolve to develop?

(d) Report: Make a report and submit to your instructor.

WEB ASSIGNMENT

Write a paper on efficacy of appreciative inquiry, as a team intervention.

Refer Bushe, G.R. (1998), Appreciative inquiry in teams. *The Organization Development Journal,* **16**(3), pp. 41–50 available at www.gervasebushe.ca/aiteams.htm.

CASE STUDY

Courage To Lead

Wipro Applying Thought in Schools is a social initiative of Wipro. Their strategy is driven by the many concerns and questions on school education and their endeavor is to seek answers to these questions in specific contexts by working with schools. It partnered with DISHA, a voluntary organization to launch in 2008 the 'Courage to Lead' program, with a vision to develop a community of schools and school leaders. The programs aimed at bringing about desired change in the school education system,

Principles of DISHA

Some of the principles, which guide the thoughts and practices of the DISHA can be classified as given under.

  (i) Learning capacity
- All children are different
- Capacity to learn and create is infinite

 (ii) Learning medium
- Children learn by doing
- Learning about life through life
- Productive and creative work as the medium of teaching and learning

(iii) Context of learning
- Learning in the context of the child's social, political and economical environment.
- Integrated learning

(iv) Teacher as facilitator
- Children learn from each other
- Children as active partners in the learning
- Teachers as designers, facilitators and co-creators
- Real freedom, empowerment and confidence

 (v) Role of school
- Education as the process of social transformation.
- Schools as part of the community

An Intervention

A 30 year school required change to update its processes and systems to provide meaningful education to children. The courage to lead intervention was undertaken to develop teachers as change agents for initiating, managing and sustaining change in schools. The idea is to equip teachers with an understanding of the current reality of school education, and the trends in process of learning, especially the experiential one. It also sought to help teachers discover self as a leader and mentor and empower them. It is a 12 day leadership empowerment program with three modules of 4 days each, spread over six months. After each module one-on-one coaching sessions and project work are arranged, to help participants apply learning from each module in their own context and devise an action plan for school improvement.

Begins with Knowing What

The change process began with the following measures for introducing appraisal process.

1. The change team met a group of teachers and inquired them about the culture in the school and tried to know whether it is ready for changes and the appraisal process.
2. They met a group of core teachers and did an appreciative inquiry with them. The inquiry helped to identify the positive aspects of the schools and figure out expectations.
3. They met all the leaders (principal vice-principal and class teachers). The discussion was focused on—understanding how teachers and leaders perceive the school and also to figure out what is going right and what is not in the school.
4. The findings of this inquiry are as given under.
   • The system is too dependent on the founder
   • The teachers are not ready for a formal appraisal process
   • Teachers are less clear about what kind of change is necessary to take the school forward

In Search of Solution

The following sessions were conducted one at a time in weekend spread over four weeks.

1. How can I make the teaching learning process more effective?
2. How can I capture evidence of learning in my classroom?
3. How to shift from telling to asking and engage children in activities?
4. How to become more open to learning and feedback for improvement?

Suggestions

The following components of an action plan for improvements in working of the school emerged:

• Working on academic plan before the beginning of the new academic year
• More focus on structured observation and assessment to be conducted during sessions
• Refresher course for teachers to get better clarity on classroom management
• Communication skills and public speaking to build confidence in the classroom
• Regular meetings to discuss improvements in functioning of school

Questions for Discussion

1. Critically evaluate the effectiveness of the intervention in the case, keeping in mind principles of DISHA and changing context of education?

2. Do you think further interventions are necessary? If yes, what are they and how do you structure them? If no, why?

Source: Adapted from Courage to Lead—Disha-India| Wipro Applying Thought in Schools, www. wiproapplyingthoughtinschools.com/?q=node/66, projects update—Wipro Applying Thought in Schools, wiproeducation.com/reports/files/assets/downloads/publication.pdf and Disha India, dishaindiaeducation.org/ program.html.

REFERENCES

1. Assessment of our Education work | *Wipro* Applying Thought in ......
www.wiproapplyingthoughtinschools.com/? q=node/45
January 2001, Wipro Inducts 'Appreciative Inquiry' For Better Team Work The financial express: Monday, Dec. 02, 2002 available at www.financialexpress.com/ news/...appreciative-inquiry-for.../63961/2 December 2002.

2. Abraham, S. (1994), Exploratory Action Research for Manager Development, ALARPM, Brisbane; Anders, D. and Agnar, G. (2003), Exploring the Concept of Multiple Product Development via an Action Research Project, *Integrated Manufacturing Systems*, Vol. **14**(3), p. 208; Boon, S. and Ram, M. (1997), Implementing Quality in a Small Firm—An Action Research Approach, *Personnel Review*, Vol. **27**(1), pp. 20–39; Kaplan, R.S., (1998). Innovation Action Research: Creating a New Management Theory and Practice, *Journal of Management Accounting Research*, American Accounting Association, USA. Vol. **10**, pp. 89–118. Kock, N.F. and McQueen, R.J. (1995), Integrating Groupware Technology in *Business Process Improvement Network, Information Technology and People,* Vol. **88**(4), pp. 19–34; Kotnour, T. (2001), Building Knowledge for and about Large-scale Organisational Transformations, *International Journal of Operations and Production Management,* Vol. **21**(8), pp. 1053–1075; and Westbrook, R. (1995), Action Research, a New Paradigm for Research in Production and Operations Management, *International Journal of Operations and Production Management*, Vol. **15**(2), pp. 6–20.

3. Drinan, J. (1991), Reflections on the first days proceedings: values and action research. In O, Zuber-Skerritt (Ed.) Action Learning for Improved Performance: Key Contributions to the First World Conference on Action Research and Process Management.

4. S. Kemmis and R., McTaggart (Eds.), (1988), *The Action Research Reader*, Geelong: Deakin University Press.

5. McCutcheon, G., and Jurg, B. (1990), *Alternative Perspectives on Action Research*: *Theory into Practice*, Vol. **24**(3), Summer.

6. Kemmis, S., and McTaggert, R. (1990), *The Action Research Planner*, Geelong: Deakin University Press.

7. Rapoport, R.N. (1970). Three Dilemmas in Action Research. *Human Relations,* Vol. **23**(6), pp. 499.

8. Gilmore, Thomas Jim Krantz and Rafael Ramirez (1986), "Action Based Modes of Inquiry and the Host-Researcher Relationship," *Consultation*, Vol. **5**(3) (Fall) pp. 161.

9. Lewin, K. (1946), Action Research and Minority Problems, *Journal of Social Sciences*, Vol. **2**, pp. 34–46.

10. Grundy, S. (1982), *Three Modes of Action Research*, as cited in Kemmis, S. and McTaggert, R. (Eds.), (1988), The Action Research Reader (3rd ed). Geelong: Deakin University Press.

11. Holter, I.M. and Schwartz-Barcott, D. (1993), Action Research: What is It? How has it been used and how can it be used in nursing? *Journal of Advanced Nursing,* Vol. **128**, pp. 298–304.

12. Hart, E. and Bond, M. (1995), *Action Research for Health and Social Care: A Guide to Practice*, Buckingham: Open University Press.

13. Isadore, Chein, Stuart Cook and John Harding (1948), "The Field of Action Research", *American Psychologist*, No. 3, Februrary, pp. 43–50.

14. J. Masters, The History of *Action Research*— SCU*www.scu.edu.au/schools/gcm/ar/arr/arow/rmasters.html*

15. McFarland, K.P. & Stansell, J.C. (1993), Historical perspectives. In L. Patterson, C.M. Santa, C.G. Short, & K. Smith (Eds.), *Teachers are Researchers: Reflection and Action*. International Reading Association. New York: DE.

16. *Action Research*, www.lab.brown.edu/pubs/themes_ed/act_research.pdf.

17. Noffke, S.E. & Stevenson, R.B. (Eds.), (1995), *Educational Action Research: Becoming Practically Critical,* New York: Teachers College Press.

18. Action Research in Education, www.edu.plymouth.ac.uk/*resined/actionresearch/ arhome.htm*

19. Carr, W. & Kemmis, S. (1986), *Becoming Critical Education, Knowledge and Action Research* Lewes, Falmer.

20. Rory O'Brien, An Overview of the Methodological Approach of Action Research, available at Overview of *Action Research* Methodology. www.web.ca/~robrien/papers/arfinal.html

21. Lewin, K. (1948), *Resolving Social Conflicts*, New York: Harper and Action Research– Wikipedia, the free encyclopedia, en.wikipedia.org/wiki/Action_research

22. Bushe, G.R. (1995), Advances in Appreciative Inquiry as an Organization Development Intervention, *Organization Development Journal*, Vol. **13**(3), 14–22; Harman,

W.W. (1990), Shifting Context for Executive Behavior: Signs of Change and Revaluation. in S. Srivastva, D.L. Cooperrider, & Associates (Eds.), *Appreciative Management and Leadership: The Power of Positive Thought and Action in Organizations* San Francisco, CA: Jossey-Bass Inc. pp. 37–54; French, W.L. and Bell Jr., C.H. (1999), *Organization Development: Behavioral Science Interventions for Organization Improvement*, New Jersey: Prentice Hall.

23. Cooperrider David L. and Whitney, Diana (2005), Appreciative Inquiry: A Positive Revolution in Change, Berett-Koehelr publishing Inc. available at Action Research & Appreciative Inquiry. www.Primary goals net/Leadership/Action research. html. and Cooperrider, David Diana Whitney, and Jacqueline Stavros (2007), *Appreciative Inquiry Handbook* Berrett-Koehler. Appreciative Inquiry Commons. San Francisco Available at: http://appreciativeinquiry.case.edu/

24. Caryn Vanstone (2004), "Affirmative Action," *Training Magazine*, p. 22, ABI/Inform Trade and Industry Database.

25. Kolb, David A. (1984), *Experiential Learning*, Englewood Cliffs, NJ: Prentice-Hall.

26. Cooperrider, David L. (1990), "Positive Image, Positive Action: The Affirmative Basis of Organizing". in *Appreciative Management and Leadership*, Srivastva, Suresh (Ed.) Cooperrider, David L. and Associates. San Francisco: Jossey-Bass Publishers.

27. Whitney, D., and Trosten-Bloom, A. (2003), *The Power of Appreciative Inquiry: A Practical Guide to Positive Change,* San Francisco, USA: Berrett-Koehler.

28. Edgar Schein (1969), *Process Consultation: Its Role in Organization Development*, New York: Addison-Wesley.

29. Reddy, Q. Brendan (1994), *Intervention Skills: Process Consultation for Small Groups and Teams*, California: Pieffer.

30. Process Consultation–Taylor Nelson, taylor-nelson.com/page12.html

31. Process Consultation, www.manage2001.com/pc.htm

32. Schein, Edgar H., Process Consultation and the Helping Relationship in Perspective available at andewal.com/archive/process_consultation.pdf.

Chapter 8

Organizational Diagnosis

Learning Objectives

After studying this chapter, you will be able to:

- Explain the concept, nature and approaches to organizational diagnosis
- Identify the methods of inquiring the state of affairs at individual, group and organizational levels
- Discuss different models of organizational diagnosis
- Know how feedback can be given to client

Vignette: Diagnosis for Solutions

PsyAsia is an organization of professional and experienced consultant organizational psychologists who can give a thorough and professional audit on areas, like organizational culture, morale, work design, and many other areas. Also they design and use effectively survey and statistical analysis tools to achieve the goals of diagnosis.

Capelle Consulting an integrated Organization Development (OD) and Human Resources (HR) consulting firm uses a six-dimensional Organizational Capability Survey to determine how well an organization aligns its people to the business objectives and engages their hearts and minds. The six dimensions are—common destiny, leadership, competencies, people management, processes and interfaces as well as employee satisfaction. They also conduct Organizational Capability Audit that encompasses corporate strategy, organizational capability as well as employee capability, mindset and governance. As a part of audit, they use Organizational Capabilities Questionnaire, focus groups and interviews.

Roxanne Ray, Senior Performance Consultant for Advocate Health Care, presenting a paper at the OD Network Conference in San Francisco (2006) discussed how assessments can be used to set baselines and benchmarks for individuals, groups and organizations. For effecting cultural change in Advocate Health care, a Human Synergistics' Organizational Culture Inventory® (OCI) that includes 120 statements describing behaviors that might be expected or implicitly required of members of an organization was employed.

Dutta Roy of Indian Statistical Institute reported that a public sector organization interested in improving organizational health and job satisfaction of its employees at different levels administered organizational health and job satisfaction questionnaires to a random samples managers, supervisors and staff and analyzed the data using hierarchical multiple regression analysis.

Potentia, a HR and OD consultant offers tools to measure the level of personal emotional capital and provide an Emotional Capital Report (ECR). The ECR delivers a report of your scores on the ten leadership competencies that research has identified as characteristic of outstanding leaders.

Human dimension uses assessments to provide an assessment of self-awareness or the current reality for clients to affirm their strengths, and determine goals for growth and self-improvement. Some of the self-report and 360 degree assessments they utilize are: Myers-Briggs Type Indicator® (MBTI®), Hay-McBer® Emotional Competency Inventory (ECI™), Human Patterns® Personality Inventory, Denison® Leadership Development Survey and video[1].

As no one size fits all, consultants develop a variety of tools to assess and understand individual, group and organizational aspects and facilitate the discovery of solutions to problems. In this chapter, we shall examine the organization diagnosis approaches and tools.

INTRODUCTION

OD consultants should adopt professional approach in working with the client organizations. In the OD process (Entry → Diagnosis → Action Planning → Implementation → Termination), organizational diagnosis plays a key role. It involves knowing how individuals and groups are working within organization and understanding the relations of organizations with outside groups and environment. The consultant should be possessing knowledge of behavioral science to maintain working relationships with people and overcome their resistance to participate. Also, she should have ability to apply appropriate diagnostic tools.

MEANING

Organizatioanl diagnosis is the process of examining an organization to understand how it is currently functioning and suggesting the need for change interventions. There is a false notion that diagnosis is data collection. Weisbord draws distinctions by saying that data refers to bits and pieces of information from which a diagnosis may be built[2]. Data means assembling facts and it is means to clues, not hypotheses. It is diagnosis that assigns meaning, weight, priority, and relationship to the facts and leads to the development of conclusions.

Dr. Noolan[3] defined organizational diagnosis as:

A collaborative process between organization members and the OD practitioner to (1) collect relevant information, (2) organize it, and (3) feed the data back to the client system in such as a way to build commitment, energy and direction for action planning.

Alderfer[4] provides a similar definition in the following words:

Organizational diagnosis is a process of entering a human system, collecting valid data about human experiences with that system, and feeding that information back to the system to promote increased understanding of the system by its members.

Misty River Consulting[5] explained with an emphasis on ultimate outcomes as follows:

Organizational Diagnosis and Assessment is a comprehensive analysis of every critical aspect of an organization's behavior and infrastructure, and its causal relationship to the effectiveness and efficiency of the organizations performance.

Another definition from Wikipractice[6] has process and performance emphasis as given under.

The organizational diagnosis is a method which aims at identifying the forces and the weakness of a company and at exploiting the potential of improvement of its performance factors. The result of this diagnosis can lead to an optimization of the processes, a process reengineering or the other types of intervention to improve the organizational performance.

NATURE

Like the diagnosis of physician, organizational diagnosis is professional, and possesses the following characteristics:

1. *Holistic:* It is similar and holistic like that of a physician's clinical diagnosis. Holistic medicine refers to examining the whole body system. In case of organization, open systems view requires examining the whole organization in its environment. The diagnosis, hence, would not only focus on systems and subsystems but also on organizational processes, such as goal setting, decision-making, communication patterns and styles, intra and inter-group relationships, work-flow patterns, and so on.[7]

2. *Scientific process:* Like the patient suspecting or experiencing a problem based on certain symptoms, approaches a physician, a client experiencing failure will meet a OD consultant. The process of examination is scientific in both cases. Both the physician and diagnostician depend on instruments and methods. The results of diagnosis in both cases are shared with the clients and remedial actions are advised.

3. *Recursive:* It is a recursive process. In each phase consultant works with a definite objective and clear understanding of what is to be done. However, some activity relating to other phases would be necessary. For instance, there is some data collection and some feedback during entry, some entry and some feedback in data collection, and some entry and some data collection at feedback. Thus, the process repeats itself several times before its completion.

4. *Narrow or broad:* The scope of a diagnosis may be either narrow and symptomatic or broad and systematic. When client is looking for quick fixes, consultant will focus on rapid diagnoses. It involves a very quick scan of the organization, focusing on trouble spots. Too often, the problem crops up again and again. On the other hand, systematic examination of the entire system using organizational models facilitates finding permanent solutions.

5. *Enabling process:* Diagnosis is a cyclical process with built-in enabling effect. It increases the ability and interest of the managers in analyzing organization on a continuous basis. The interaction between consultant and client can have this lasting impact.

APPROACHES

In practice, one may find consultant taking different stances in conducting diagnosis. The role of an organizational diagnostician is to diagnose an organization to the point of finding the present ailment; and presenting them with his prognosis estimates of the likely consequences over a period of time) and recommending prescriptions of active interventions.

Prospective vs Prescriptive

Diagnostician may take prospective or prescriptive stance. When asked to examine the present state of affairs of the organization as well as the effectiveness of current strategies in relation to the future goals of the organization, she takes prospective stance. Alternatively, the diagnostician may assume a prescriptive or normative stance, when asked to find out where the deviations exist in the organizational units and suggest corrective actions. Diagnosticians who take up such cases are referred to as business healers.

Selling vs Relating

Bhattacharyya, Chattopadhyay and Sengupta[8] found that only in case of 43% of the surveyed clients, consultant involved them in jointly arriving at a diagnosis. About 12% of the clients reported that the consultant made his own diagnosis and announced it to them. The remaining 45% used consultative approach by seeking opinions of organizational members.

PROCESS

Organizational diagnosis consists of three distinct phases—entry, research and feedback.

Entry

The phase begins with the meeting of consultant and client. The meeting results in a decision leading to an understanding to work together to undertake organizational diagnosis. The objective in this phase is to arrive at an understanding on two issues:

(i) Organizational units (individual, group, and organization) to be focused, and
(ii) Roles of client and consultant during data collection and feedback

The interaction between client and consultant is facilitated through conversations, observation and documents. At the end of the phase, four things occur:

1. The client will have the consultant point of view of the organization.
2. The consultant will be relieved of the anxiety related to potential acceptance or rejection by the client.
3. Consultant will establish some type of liaison system to manage the process. The liaison system may be an individual, a series of individuals, or a group.
4. The data collected during this phase helps formulate working hypotheses for testing in the next phases.

Research

Research process consist of the following steps: (i) Formulating research objectives, (ii) Formulating data collection and analysis procedures, and (iii) Interpretation of findings.

The objective of data collection is to gather valid information on the systems chosen for diagnosis and deliver it to the client during the next phase, i.e. feedback.

The data collection process involves both entry and feedback phases in its different stages. Since problems are not always easily identifiable, data collection cannot be specific and well-defined in the beginning. Consultants keep revising hypotheses by making several attempts to go deep and wide for studying multiple facets of the system. Box 8.1 describes how in-depth analysis can help realize the real problems. Each attempt is like an entry and the resulting outcome is a feedback to the client. Based on the outcome, consultant becomes more specific and focused in his search for precise information.

BOX 8.1 In-depth Analysis

A company experienced poor sales performance. It was to be attributed either to incompetence of sales people or their lack of motivation. The company, confident of its selection and training processes viewed it as a motivation problem, and designed a motivational plan and implemented it immediately. Even after its implementation, sales did not increase significantly.

The Sales Vice-president decided to look into the problem. He interviewed the people related to the situation—sales representatives and supervisors. He found that the product line is competitively inferior, and technical service department is failing to meet their expectations. Questions like the following surfaced:

- Why sales people or supervisors did not give feedback to management on these issues?
- Why is production defective?
- Is quality control ineffective?
- Is there problem in production process?

A joint meeting of the heads of production, design, quality control, technical service and sales departments was held. Numerous problems in staffing, training, responsiveness, and quality control had surfaced. Also it was found that there was little meaningful communication between sales, product engineering, manufacturing and support services.

(Contd.)

BOX 8.1   In-depth Analysis (*Contd.*)
Bureaucratic procedures and cultural barriers restricted the flow of communication to and from middle-managers and first-line supervisors. The company now shifted its focus on team work, and inter-departmental coordination for promoting team work and technology up gradation for better quality controls.

The choice of data collection instruments varies with the situation. Consultants should choose less-structured methods in the early stages of the investigation and more-structured methods in the later phases. The different methods of data collection can be as given under:

- Unstructured observation
- Individual interviews
- Group interviews
- Questionnaires

The liaison system established in the entry phase will help the consultant in planning for data collection. Decisions like what data to collect, from whom to collect it, when to collect it, and how to collect can be made with the support of the members. Further, the liaison system can be a source of advice about the content and design of feedback.

Feedback

Feedback indicates the completion of the diagnosis and preparation for a transition to planned change. The objective of feedback is to promote good understanding of the system by the liaison system and client. The feedback phase involves entry and data collection. Consultant will be away from the client organization for some period to carry out data analysis. To deliver feedback he will re-enter the system. The feedback process provides an opportunity to get some more useful data to validate and utilize the findings. The reactions and behavior of people and their arguments during the meetings provide another source of data.

BENEFITS

The primary purpose of organizational diagnosis is to know how good or how healthy the organization is to survive and succeed in the changing environment. In addition, there can be other benefits. The benefits from diagnosis can be threefold mentioned as follows:

1. To take decisions for removing weaknesses and surmounting obstacles hindering growth and performance.
2. To create an environment of change and innovation, through sharing of diagnostic data and questioning the appropriateness of the current practices
3. To strengthen human component of organization by engaging them in diagnostic, reflective and strategy making processes.

INQUIRY METHODS

Some important consideration in use of inquiry methods are given as follows:

1. *Validity and reliability:*   Consultants should use standard and rigorous methods of enquiry (need not be quantitative). They may use fixed-choice questionnaires or observations using a standard coding, which are consonant with accepted standards of scientific inquiry.

2. *Structured inquiry:*   The existence of plurality of interests and conflicting opinions, pose a problem to investigators. The plurality has to be treated as a significant organizational feature in its own right and make efforts to get an independent view point.

3. *Methodological overkill:*   Investigators should avoid methodological overkill. For example, if the intent is to find whether employees are either satisfied or dissatisfied with regard to a practice, there is no need to use a 5-point scale.

4. *Support of other methods:*   To strengthen the inquiry and interpretation processes, investigators may use other methods. Besides a questionnaire, a consultant might prefer to use non-rigorous methods, such as discussions and observations.

5. *Cultural fit:*   The methods chosen need to fit the culture of the client organization. In a high technology firm, quantitative techniques are viewed scientific. On the other hand, in other firms especially small ones prefer observation and interview methods.

Types of Methods

OD consultants make use a variety of methods for collecting data for organizational diagnosis. For example, Russel Professional Group[9] claims that its psychologists use a wide range of tools listed below:

- Document analysis
- Environmental scan
- Behavioral observation
- Individual interviews
- Exit interviews
- Employee opinion survey
- Focus groups
- Organizational audit

We will briefly explain some of the methods.

1. *Observation:*   In unstructured observation, consultants will collect relevant documents from the client organization. They may include newsletters, chairman reports, and brochures. He may walk around in selected places, conversing with individuals or groups.

2. *Case history:*   A brief description of the organization covering its major aspects will provide a broader understanding of the contextual and operational issues of the organization. The case narrative may contain the following information: (i) identification data, like name, location and type of organization; (ii) historical data of achievements and problems faced, the crises and the solutions, the organization folklore, etc.; (iii) structural data-organizational chart, formal job descriptions, ecology of the organization (spatial distribution of individuals, activities), rules and regulations, etc.; (iv) organizational functioning-employee perceptions, learning, culture, climate, collaboration, conflicts, etc. and (v) achievements and ailments—The current success information, the future projections, the perceived problems and weak spots.

Questionnaires

Behavioral scientists have developed a number of standardized questionnaires for organizational diagnosis. Choice of a questionnaire depends on the purposes of diagnosis. Questionnaires are used for measuring dimensions like—organization health, organizational climate, HRD climate, motivational climate, leadership and supervisory styles, etc. Such readily available questionnaires have some limitations:

(i) They are standardized for other organizations (a questionnaire prepared for educational institution may not be applicable to business settings)

(ii) They focus on a few specific aspects

In such cases, it is useful to construct separate questionnaire exclusively for a given organization/situation. The following are some considerations that could be kept in mind while preparing the questionnaire:

- Identify the areas of concern through interviews, complaints, observed symptoms or general opinions voiced by the top management and other key persons
- Develop variables in the chosen areas of concern, for example, if communication is perceived as an issue, variables relating to communication are to be developed
- After conducting pilot test, improve the questionnaire and administer to a representative sample of employees
- Compute organization-wide scores on each item
- Identify the items that show low scores and design interventions for them

Interviews

Interview is used as a first as well as the last stage of diagnosis. They can be used to sense and identify trouble spots, or for probing for details and getting deeper insights into a given problem or getting ideas for improvements.

Interviews can be categorized based on purpose of inquiry, such as exploratory interviews, hypotheses testing interviews, and change inducing interviews. They can be categorized based on people involved, such as individual or group interviews. Another classification is based on the degree of structuring as structured or semi-structured. If interviews are to be effective the following precautions are to be taken by the interviewer.

- Request top management to legitimize the study by informing all those employees who have to take part in it.

- In the beginning of interview, clarify once again the purposes and assure the confidentiality of responses.
- Be receptive and inquisitive to know. Boasting about self, lecturing, criticizing, etc., work negatively and hinder the communication process. Avoid them.
- Use questions that are open-ended, information seeking and suggestive. They are effective in creating positive exchanges of communication.
- Conduct diagnostic interviews in settings which are free from noise and other disturbances.
- Be patient in developing hypothesis. After interviewing a few, do not rush to develop a hypothesis.

Psychometric Tests

Psychometric tests are structured questionnaires with some scales to measure. They aim usually at assessing numerical and reasoning abilities, leadership styles, team building skills, etc. The tests are objective and produce fairly hard numerical outputs.

Focus Groups

Focus groups are an excellent tool for identifying problems as well as solutions. Focus groups require effective moderators. The moderator has to be objective in retaining focus in the discussion and allowing ample opportunities for participants to express their views. To be successful, moderator has to form the groups keeping in mind the following points:

1. *Optimum size:* Focus groups are composed of 30 people, better 5–15 people.
2. *Right people:* Focus groups provide an opportunity for disclosure among people who have common workplace interests and experiences. For example, in case of workplace harassment, the employees who experienced or observed it can effectively voice the issues related to it.

They are used when tools like questionnaire fail to give proper understanding of the issues. Focus group discussion can produce data and insights that other techniques cannot provide. It can create a kind of chaining or cascading effect in the group discussion. The group members speak linking their ideas with those of others and try to further refine them in the process. However, focus groups are not without limitations. The participants may not reveal full information or may provide answers that are acceptable to others.

Workshops

Workshops solicit active participation of organizational members in problem-finding and problem solving exercises. For instance, a participative organization design workshop is a highly structured participative process in which participating employees engage in conversation, discussion and inquiry to identify weaknesses in the existing organization and design a new reflective and adaptive organization resilient to change as well as an efficient socio-economic engine to survive and succeed. Box 8.2 shows the design of workshop. A brief description of a workshop employed for details of workshop as used by Management Sciences for Health (MSH)[10] are given as follows:

> MSH developed the Management and Organizational Sustainability Tool (MOST) for use by public organizations and NGOs. It is a structured, participatory process and the cornerstone of the process is a 3-day workshop. During the workshop, the organizational leadership and selected staff come together to build consensus about the stages of development of their organization's management practices, the improvements needed, and an action plan for making those improvements.

BOX 8.2   Design of the Workshop

The workshop follows the design process involving three stages as given as follows:

Analysis phase: The day begins with general introductions and a run through of the plan of action. Everybody gets the same message at the same time and, can see how the work is progressing relative to time constraints. The first briefing deals with explanations of Design Principle 1 and its limitations in meeting their psychological needs, which are labeled as 6 criteria (adequate elbow room, continuous learning, an optimum level of variety, mutual support and respect, meaningfulness, and a desirable future.) Presentation is made simple, brief and visual to reach every one.

Change: The second briefing deals with Design Principle 2 and organizational redesign. The effects of Design principle 2 and its effects in terms of the 6 criteria, skills and communication are discussed. It also deals with alternative models and organizational designs and ends with instructions for drawing up the workflow and structure and redesign challenges. Groups draw up the workflow and formal legal structure and redesign the structure.

Practicalities: The groups redesign their section of the structure and submit it for evaluation. When the workshop managers can sign off as workable, the third briefing is presented. It deals with the practicalities—the implementation problems like resistance, resources needs, new skills, etc.

Source: Based on the approach of Merrelyn Emery discussed in Democratizing work through participative design << NewUnionism's ...
newunionism.wordpress.com/2011/11/20/participative-design/

Diagnostic Audits

Diagnostic audits using selected criteria can systematically throw light on structures, process and systems to gain an objective picture of the current state of health of an organization, its individual areas of activity and groups and indicate need for interventions for improving its health. In simple terms, auditing is a systematic, disciplined approach to evaluate and improve the effectiveness of an organization. A typical audit involves the following steps:

1. Defining the scope and objectives for the audit.

2. Develop an understanding of the business segment under review in terms of objectives, transactions and measurements. Data may be gathered through review of documents and interviews and presented in the form of flowcharts and narratives.
3. Develop methodology for eliciting the data on organizational aspects under review based on a model. (If 7-s framework is adopted inquiry will be in the areas of strategy, structure, systems, shared values, staff, skills and styles).
4. Feedback periodically the findings at appropriate intervals to concerned groups or departments and add new information based on feedback.
5. Report problems identified and work out action plans with management to address the problems. The length of the report is based on the size and complexity of the organization. The findings of the report may contain five elements, of the 5 C's framework as given in Table 8.1.

TABLE 8.1 5 Cs Framework of Diagnostic Audit

Condition	Problems identified and the degree of seriousness of the problems
Criteria	The standards relating to the area like a company policy or a benchmark and the extent to which the standard is not met
Cause	The causal factors for the failure to meet standards
Consequence	The risk/negative outcome (or opportunity foregone) because of the problem
Corrective action	Action decided by management, steps taken and proposed to be taken in future

Source: Based on *Internal audit*—Wikipedia, the free encyclopedia, *en.wikipedia.org/wiki/Internal_audit*

NEED FOR MODELS

OD consultants and researchers have developed a wide variety of models. A survey of the models reveals the following:

- Each model identifies some important organizational elements and their interrelationships
- Each model has a theoretical base to explain its rationale.
- The number of variables vary from one model to another. Leavitt's model contains fewest number of variables (four) and Burke-Litwin model has the greatest number (12 variables).
- Same variables are found in more than one model but not necessarily in the same way or with the same emphasis.

Benefit of Models

The use of models offers the following benefits:

1. *Provide a systematic approach:* A conscious diagnostic model improves the efficiency of the data collection and analysis process. It provides structure and discipline in the process. In doing so, it ensures that data on all the relevant aspects of the system is collected, that too in a systematic manner.

2. *Minimize bias of researcher:* The temptation to collect data that the consultant feels comfortable is eliminated by models. Models help managers look at organizations through proper frames to appreciate the depth and complexity of organizational life.

3. *Provide a mechanism for research:* Successful managers or consultants are those who are benefited by their intuition. However, not all managers or consultants are endowed with the power of visualizing the entire system and understanding effectively the complicated and ambiguous world of an organization. An explicit introduction of various variables and their blending into a coherent, pragmatic model can enrich any manager's native intuition.

4. *Provide a common language:* The vocabulary for people to use in interactions will be made explicit by the models. Visual models create better and quick understanding.

DIAGNOSTIC MODELS

We will discuss in the following points, some of the popular models of diagnosis:

1. Four frames model
2. GRPI model
3. Six box model
4. 7'S framework
5. Five/eight track model
6. Nadler-Tushman congruence model

Four Frames Model

Every manager develops a personal frame and gets locked into a single path of thinking. This produces error in understanding and judgement. Managers need integrated view to understand and manage the complex world of organizations. Bolman and Deal[11] had integrated four different schools of thought in their model, to have the advantage of conceptual pluralism. The model provides four theoretical perspectives through its four frames or windows on the world and helps to order the world and decide what actions to take. The four frames are as follows:

1. *Structural frame:* This represents the rational, tough-minded side of organizations. It provides the framework within which employees cooperate for accomplishment of common goals.

2. *Human resource frame:* This is the human side of enterprise that examines strengths and weaknesses of current approaches in creating congenial environment to maximize employee performance and satisfaction.

3. *Political frame:* This is the darker side of organizations. Organizations are viewed as arenas of scarce resources and the desire to posses them leads to conflict, coalitions and struggles for power and positions.

4. *Symbolic frame:* This is the emotional side of an organization. It shows the cultural aspects like symbols, stories and rituals that reside with rational aspects like policies and procedures. Table 8.2 provides diagnostic view of the four frames.

TABLE 8.2 Diagnostic Questions in Four Frame Model

Frames	Sample diagnostic questions
Structural	To what extent there is formalization of roles in organization? Is there standardization of practices? Is there role clarity in the organization at different levels? Are the roles and performance in congruence with goals? Is there coordination among people, departments and divisions? Is there proper organization-technology fit? Is there appropriate organization-environment fit?
Human resource	Is job design capable of providing good experience and satisfaction to employees? Are employee engagement practices effective? Does the organization have enablers for people to perform and achieve goals?
Political	What are the current and potential conflict areas? How are conflicts resolved in the organization? Are conflict resolution methods and systems effective? What steps would reduce conflicts?
Symbolic	What are the shared values and are they properly communicated? What are the myths, symbols, rituals and ceremonies prevalent in the organization? Is there story telling practice in organization? If yes, what are the favorite stories in circulation? Who are admired as heroes in the organization?

Choice of framework

As a change agent, one has to find which framework applies to a given situation.

1. When individual commitment and motivation are essential—the right frameworks are Human Resource and symbolic.
2. When technical quality of the decision is important—structural framework is right choice.
3. When there is ambiguity and uncertainty in organizational roles—political and symbolic frames are appropriate choices.

Application of frameworks

How do the frameworks assist in change processes? Table 8.3 provides an explanation of the role to be played by senior management, the likely barriers to change and the appropriate strategies to be employed in different frameworks. It also indicates the what motivates employees and how communication is to be facilitated.

TABLE 8.3 Four Frame Approach for Diagnosis

Aspect	Structural	Human resource	Political	Symbolic
Effective leader	Analyst architect	Catalyst, servant	Advocate, negotiator	Prophet, poet
Barriers to change	Confusion and lack of stability	Anxiety and feeling of incompetence	Powerlessness and conflicts	Loss of identity and purpose
Strategies	Communication, negotiation and alignment	Training and development	New coalitions and power groups	Celebrating change like mourning the past and welcoming change
Motivation	Economic incentives	Growth and self-actualization	Coercion, manipulation, and seduction	Symbols and celebrations
Communication	Transmission of facts and information	Exchange of information and feelings	Manipulation of attitudes and values	Story telling

GRPI Model

The model developed by Beckhard[12] helps conduct diagnosis, in terms of goals, roles, practices and interactions.

1. *Goals:* An understanding of long-term, strategic goals in relation to the mission is the first step in this model.

2. *Roles:* In view of the priorities and performance expectations, the roles people have to play are to be designed.

3. *Practices:* For the roles to be effective, the organization should design performance environment by way of formal facilitators (policies, procedures and rules) which may find support from informal facilitators (norms and communication).

4. *Interactions:* Role effectiveness is dependent on communication that takes place between the role player and other interdependent roles.

Beckhard advises to work from the top down. For instance, when a group is in conflict, a consultant may focus on inter-personal or inter-group dysfunctionality. But Beckhard argues that it makes more sense to start at the top, from the mission and vision.

Mission or Purpose

It is important to have clarity in the purpose of the organization. Consider the questions and sample answers in Table 8.4 that help state mission.

TABLE 8.4 Mission Statement

Who you are?	We are a management institute
What is your business?	devoted to developing future managers
Who are your customers?	young men and women across the globe
Why do you do this business?	To improve the life of people in society
What do you do?	We deliver management courses
What is your image?	World class in quality
What roles do your people and technology play?	Provide on-line and off-line learning through competent and committed staff

A series of diagnostic questions, that help identify the problems in the four areas of inquiry are given in Table 8.5.

TABLE 8.5 Diagnostic Questions in GRPI Model

Inquiry focus	Sample diagnostic questions
Goals	What are the long-term goals of the company-strategically? What are the operational goals? What are the milestones and success criteria, for short-term and long-term?
Roles	How is the work sequenced? How is the work divided in the team/group? How are the individual responsibilities and authority structured? How is the role interfaces designed? How do they work in practice? How does leadership emerge in the group?
Practices	What are the policies that guide employees in organization? Are they relevant, clear and implementable? Are the procedures adequately defined and properly established? Are they being followed? What are the rules in force? Are they appropriate and adequate? Are they being enforced properly? What are the group norms that are facilitative and restrictive of individual and group performance? Are the practices of communication, both formal and informal, facilitative in the organization?
Interactions	Which roles are mutually supportive? For what needs and expectations are they mutually dependent? What kind of trust and support did they develop and foster? How do they exchange feedback?

Though the model developed by Beckhard was originally addressed for teambuilding, consultants have found it equally useful in dealing with a wide range of groups and companies.

Six Box Model

Weisbord[13] proposed a model with six broad categories in his model of organizational life, including purposes, structures, relationships, leadership, rewards and helpful mechanisms. It can be seen as a radar screen and problems appear as blips of varying intensity indicating gaps between, 'What is' and 'what ought to be', or 'what is produced', and 'what should be produced.' The gaps or missing pieces in each box may be due to dysfunctionality of formal or informal processes. Leadership is responsible for the corrective mechanisms. In each of the six areas Weisbord rises diagnostic questions for each category.

Box 1: *Purposes:*   Based on mission and environmental demands organization sets up its priorities (purposes) in terms of short-term and long-term goals. They should be communicated to gain agreement and support from employees.

Box 2: *Structure:*   It refers to authority relationships that provide a framework for performance of people to achieve the established purposes. It can be functional, product, project or matrix based one for developing special competence required.

Box 3: *Relationships:*   It includes the ways in which people and units interact formally and informally. Also it refers to conflict management and coordination of a unit.

Box 4: *Rewards:*   This category includes the intrinsic and extrinsic rewards in relation to work. The way rewards are given may help or inhibit the fit between individuals and organizational goals.

Box 5: *Leadership:*   It refers to typical leadership styles and tasks, that strikes a balance between the other categories. It is the leadership that can scan the entire environment and act on behalf of the whole. It keeps the entire organization in balance, continually creating mechanisms to communicate purposes, modify structure and define appropriate relationships and rewards.

Box 6: *Helping mechanisms*:   These are the planning, controlling, and information systems that facilitate achievement of organizational goals. They contribute to accomplishment of purposes. An effective organization continually revises its mechanisms, for removing gaps between what is and what ought to be. Hence, the creation of improved mechanisms is key to the identification and closing of gaps.

Supra environment

The external environment is also depicted in Weisbord's model as a factor influencing purposes. Weisbord identifies money, people, ideas, and machinery as inputs and products and services as outputs.

The questions that require answers in the six box model are given in Table 8.6.

TABLE 8.6 Diagnostic Questions in Six Box Model

Box no.	Box name	Diagnostic questions
1	Purposes	What business are we in? What does the organization need to do to fit with the environment? Do organizational members agree with and support the organization's mission and goals?
2	Structure	How is the division of work done? How is authority relationships defined? Is there clear specification of responsibility? Is there a fit between the purpose and the internal structure of the organization?
3	Relationship	What type of relations exists between individuals? What type of relations exists between departments? What types of relations exists between individuals and their jobs? Is their interdependence? What is the quality of relations? What are the modes of conflict? How conflicts among people are are managed? How are conflicts with technologies resolved?
4	Rewards	Are there incentives for all the tasks? What does the organization formally reward? What do organizational members feel about rewards and punishments?
5	Leadership	Do leaders define purposes? Do they embody purposes in their programs? What is the normative style of leadership? Do they keep the boxes in balance?
6	Helping mechanism	Have we adequate coordinating technologies? Do they help accomplish goals?

In addition, one has to question the environment-organizational relationships and the impact the environmental variables make on organizational functioning.

McKinsey's 7-S Model

McKinsey Consulting[14] developed the 7-S model which comprised seven interdependent factors which are categorized into hard and soft elements given as follows:

1. *Hard elements*: Strategy, Structure and Systems
2. *Soft elements*: Shared Values, Skills, Style and Staff

The model provides an especially useful framework for reviewing the impact of change.

Table 8.7 shows the sample diagnostic questions that help examine the organization.

TABLE 8.7 Diagnostic Questions in 7-S Framework

Elements	Sample diagnostic questions
Shared values	What are the values of the organization? What is work ethic in the organization? What are the beliefs and norms that guide employee actions and decisions?
Structure	Is the structure tall or flat? Is there proper division of work, assignment of authority and responsibility? Are role definitions clear and specific? Is job design facilitative of good performance? Is structure supportive of strategy? Is the structure flexible to change with environment?
Strategy	What are the mission and vision statements of the organization? What are the long-term goals for the organization? Is organization proactive or reactive to changes? What strategies does the organization have now? What strategies has the organization followed in recent past and with what outcomes? What are the core competencies of the organization? What kind of competitive advantage the firm has now and requires in future?
Systems	What systems are in vogue in different functional areas? Are the procedures, rules and instructions clear and well articulated? What mechanisms are in place for the effective functioning of organization?
Staff	What are the HR practices relating to hiring, training, compensating and appraising staff in organization? How effective are they?
Skills	What competencies does the organization need for different positions? What are the available skills? Is there skill gap? What measures are underway to bridge the skill gap? What initiatives are taken to promote and sustain skill development?
Style	What is the approach to decision making in the organization? Is there free flow of communication among employees? Do jobs provides desired degree of autonomy to employees? Is there employee empowerment for independent decision-making?

Eight Track Model[15]

Ralph H. Kilmann argues that there are three ways of viewing the world: one as a simple machine, second as an open system, and third as a complex hologram. He argues the need for an an integrated approach, and suggests that any quick fix inevitably will lead to failure. He identified eight tracks of organizational analysis grouped under three categories as:

1. *Infrastructure tracks (Culure, skills and team):* The purpose of the first three tracks is to create an infrastructure for making people to work and to get things done. The key diagnostic question is: Is the quantum infrastructure healthy and functional? If it is unhealthy, people will be put down and experience burnout from facing conflicts and punishments. They fail to use their talents efficiently, effectively and creatively.

2. *Directive tracks (strategy and reward):* The focus is on how the organization is channeling the contributions of members by enabling them to effectively use assumptions and skills in making group decisions, and rewarding performance.

3. *Process tracks (gradual, radical and learning):* The focus of these tracks is on creativity that has become important for competitive advantage in the present business world. They are concerned with incremental and radical innovations and institutionalization of knowledge management.

Table 8.8 illustrates diagnostic guidelines.

TABLE 8.8 Diagnostic Guidelines for 8 Track Model

Track No.	Track	Purpose	Diagnostic guidelines
1	Culture track	Enhance trust, openness, and adaptiveness	Take steps to identify the outdated culture and its consequences
2	Skills track	Coping with complex problems	Examine the skill set and assumptions in decision making for their appropriateness
3	Team track	Enable cooperative decisions to take place	Identify trouble makers and failures to solve problems collectively
4	Strategy structure	Aligning with strategy the organizational structure and resources	Examine strategy in relation to mission and its fit with environment and structure
5	Reward system	Aligning incentives with performance	Evaluate appraisal and compensation systems and their relationships and effectiveness
6	Gradual process	Improving quality and efficiency in operations	Examine total quality management
7	Radical process	Developing path breaking ideas and processes	Evaluate the initiatives like Business process reengineering
8	Learning process	Improving knowledge and creative talent in organization	Appraise the learning systems, knowledge management and creativity processes

Nadler-Tushman Congruence Model[16]

Nadler and Tushman adopted a systems approach and proposed a model that considers interrelationships of input, throughput and output. They proposed that output of an organization is dependent on the congruence of the four key elements in the throughput segment.

Throughput analysis

The variables in the throughput, that requires congruence are given as follows:

1. *Task:* The activities required by the organization and its units.

2. *Individual:* The attributes of individuals as employees in the organization.

3. *Formal organization:* The authority relationships, processes, and methods, designed for accomplishment of goals.

4. *Informal organization:* The employee relationships, processes, and norms emergent at workplace.

Congruence depends on fit. The tighter the fit, the greater is the congruence and the higher the resultant performance.

Table 8.9 presents the fits necessary for effective change.

TABLE 8.9 Fits Necessary in Throughput

Fit	Issues
Individual work	Need fulfillment and skills and knowledge matching
Individual formal organization	Need fulfillment, goal congruence and clarity in understanding organization
Individual informal organization	Need fulfillment, use of individual abilities in informal organization
Work formal organization	Adequacy of organizational setup to work performance and employee motivation
Work informal organization	Is relationship facilitative or obstructive?
Formal and informal organization	Consistency in structures, goals and rewards

To ensure thoroughness in diagnosis, it is necessary to examine the inputs as well as outputs.

Input analysis

They identified four input variables that influence the fit as well as the functioning of employees. They include history of firm, resources, strategy and environment as shown in Table 8.10.

TABLE 8.10 Input Analysis

Input variables	Sample questions
History	What are the important milestones in the history of organizations? Which achievements and failures have significant impact on the mind and behavior of organization? Which of the past behaviors are relevant to current organizational functioning?
Strategy	What strategy decisions the organization has taken in the context of the organization's history and in relation to environmental constraints, and opportunities?
Resources	What are the different tangible assets possessed by organization? What intangible resources (image etc.) of organization merit consideration?
Environment	What environmental forces have significant impact on the functioning of organization?

Output analysis

The output of an organization can be evaluated at three different levels as given in Table 8.11.

TABLE 8.11 Output Analysis

Level	Measures
Individual	Satisfaction, Commitment, Morale, Absenteeism, Lateness, Turnover etc.
Group	Intergroup communication, Collaboration, Conflict, etc.
Organization	Return on investment, Adaptability to external environmental demands, Image, etc.

FEEDING BACK

Effective feedback depends on the content, media and client groups.

1. *Content:* The content of feedback includes a description of the findings and data analysis tools used as well as the implications of the findings to the organization. It can on individuals or groups or organization-wide systems.

2. *Media:* The nature of delivery depends on the method chosen for presenting it. It can be a written report, or a presentation at a meeting.

3. *Recipients:* The client group receiving feedback may be family group of supervisor and immediate subordinates (Bowers & Franklin, 1972; Likert, 1961) or peer group-intergroup (Alderfer & Holbrook, 1973)[17]. Conventionally, organizations are viewed as a system of interlocking family groups (supervisor and subordinates) from top to bottom. When the feedback pertains to family groups, then it should be designed for them. However, the delivery decision requires understanding the relationship between supervisors and subordinates.

- If that relationship is positive–deliver it to the group.
- If it is negative, there will be open disagreement and in fighting. In such cases, either work with the supervisor alone or through pair wise interventions establish conditions for a full family group meeting.

If the feedback is on system wide issues use peer group-intergroup model.

- First, meet peer groups, which have no formal hierarchical differences among members, to deal with data pertaining to the relationship between the groups (e.g., production and marketing).
- Second, meet groups that represent different hierarchical levels (e.g., branch managers and senior vice-presidents).

Making Feeding Back Effective

Figure 8.1 shows the consequences of feedback.

1. *Help overcome anxiety:* Feedback is very stressful to the consultant-client relationship. For client, it is the period of maximum anxiety for two reasons: (i) Doubts about consultant's work (whether the consultant has got right data and conducted right analysis), and (ii) tension of knowing outcomes (what kind of problems the system has and how can they be solved). For consultant, it is a period of maximum anxiety, because his work may or may not be accepted. Sometimes, rejection may occur due to client's inability to tolerate the tension of learning about the loopholes in the system.

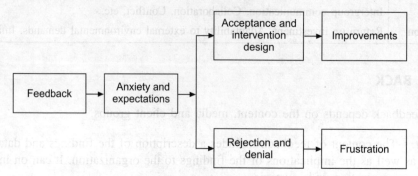

Figure 8.1   Feedback model.

2. *Structure feedback:* Whether feedback is positive or negative; it should be delivered in an appropriate way. Ensure that it is relevant to the recipients and verifiable by evidence. It should be descriptive but precise. While it should be elaborate to provide good understanding, it should be without boring, lengthy explanations. It should be timely to take follow up action at right time. In addition to oral presentation, consultants should provide some record of the analysis as evidence that the diagnosis has been completed and the contract fulfilled. This record may include simply a narrative or visuals like the charts used for presenting information during the feedback meetings.

3. *Structure the meetings:* The oral presentation of the feedback can be carried out in well structured and controlled meetings. Structure is important to ensure: (i) inclusion of right participants, and (ii) presence of people with power. Controlling through agenda and discussion leader is necessary to see that the meeting does not degenerate into chaos or aimless discussion. The presence of people with power helps to sustain energy of feedback, by maintaining direction in discussion. Otherwise, negative, ownership can be lost in conversations and energy gained from dealing directly with the problem is lost.

Motivate People to Work with Feedback

People will show energy to work the feedback data when the following conditions are fulfilled:

1. *When members think that the feedback data will provide beneficial outcomes.* If the members do not perceive benefit, they simply disown the feedback.
2. *When members (group) have appropriate power to make necessary changes.* If members have no power to make changes, the feedback meeting will become an empty exercise.

3. *When actions on feedback have support from explicit sanction and support from powerful groups.* If the top management is not in favour of changes, status quo continues.
4. *When assistance is available to decide and act on the feedback data.* If organizational members are left alone they may not be able to design right interventions due to paucity of knowledge and skills.

DEBRIEFING

Debriefing meetings which generally last for one to two hours, are held with the purpose of sharing the feedback with all the team members about the project. It offers an opportunity to provide an in-depth view of what went well and what did not go well. It helps identify the root causes of problematic issues. The follow up is important, as feedback without action planning or goal setting is unlikely to lead to change.

SUMMARY

Organizational diagnosis is the process of examining an organization to understand how it is currently functioning and suggesting the need for change interventions. In the OD process, organizational diagnosis plays a key role, and consultants should have ability to apply appropriate diagnostic tools. Like the diagnosis of physician, organizational diagnosis is a professional work. It is holistic, scientific and recursive. It can be narrow or broad as it is based on client needs and enables managers and consultants in identifying organizational ailments.

Diagnostician may take prospective or prescriptive stance. Research has shown that consultants used different approaches like individual and joint analysis. Organizational diagnosis consists of three distinct phases—entry, research and feedback. Diagnosis suggests ways to remove weakness, bring about change and innovation, and engage people in diagnostic, reflective and strategy-making processes. The inquiry methods should be structured and have validity and reliability. They must be culturally fit. A wide range of tools, such as Document analysis, Environmental scan, Behavioral observation, Individual interviews, Exit interviews, Employee opinion survey, Focus groups and Organizational audit are being used.

OD consultants and researchers have developed a wide variety of models to make approach systematic, to minimize bias of researcher to provide a mechanism for research and to provide a common language. Some of the popular models of diagnosis are—Four frames model, GRPI model, Six box model, 7-S framework, Eight track model, and Congruence model. Effective feedback depends on the content, media and client groups. Feedback helps overcome anxiety; It should be delivered in a descriptive, but precise manner to provide good understanding and to take follow up action at the right time. Debriefing sessions help share feedback and find better ways of solving problems.

EXERCISES

I. Review Questions

1. What do you mean by organizational diagnosis?
2. Explain features of organizational diagnosis process.
3. Explain the approaches to organizational diagnosis.
4. Describe the diagnostic process and its benefits.
5. List the inquiry methods used by researchers.
6. List the diagnostic models known to you.
7. How do you get and share feedback?

II. Discussion Questions

1. Explain the concept, nature and approaches to organizational diagnosis.
2. Identify the methods of inquiring the state of affairs at individual, group and organizational levels.
3. Explain any three models of organizational diagnosis.
4. Explain how feedback can be given to the client.

📖 MINI-PROJECT

Conduct organizational diagnosis for a local organization of your choice and prepare a report incorporating recommendations for change. Make a presentation in the class and elicit opinions of classmates.

WEB ASSIGNMENT

Visit, www.rtsa.ro/en/ and search for research papers in Transylvanian Review of Administrative Sciences on organizational change and diagnosis and prepare a paper on the role and methods of organizational diagnosis.

CASE STUDY

Diagnosing a Health Care Organization

It was in 1992–1993 that World Bank funded a project—"A Healthy Romania", to augment healthcare facilities in Romania. Earlier, The Social Health Insurance Bill in 1994 and Public Health Law in 1998 contributed to the financing and functioning mechanisms of hospitals. Between 1992 and 2006, major reforms were introduced in the health system, which provided for autonomy of hospitals and encouraged independent family practitioner offices.

Aim of Diagnosis

Despite the changes and reforms, it was found that the internal structure and internal management of the hospitals did not show significant improvements. This called for an assessment of both management and quality of services offered by hospitals. In light of this, Organizational Diagnosis was employed for Satu Mare County Hospital as part of a restructuring the healthcare facility and make it more flexible and responsive to the citizens needs.

Procedure

A five phase conceptual model (adapted from Rogers and Fong, 2000) was used for this:

1. Symptoms—spotting deficiencies
2. Fact finding—identification of facts
3. Causation—knowing the causal factors
4. Evaluation—appraising alternative solutions
5. Optimization—choosing right solution

The diagnostic areas chosen were the five major organizational components. They are— Organizational structure, Inputs, Processes/Management, Organizational Culture, and Output (quality of services, relation with clients, relation with other organizations, types of services provided).

Phase 1: Symptoms

The existence of serious problems (symptoms) was brought to the attention of the change management team by the employees in the casual discussions.

- Employees from the administrative department were vexed with the ways of the head of the department and planning to leave the organization
- Purchase process was slow due to tedious procedures
- Number of beds was not in accordance with the real needs
- Though there were funds, there was a lack of necessary medical products.

Phase 2: Fact finding

In this phase hospital employees were informed about the purpose and process of diagnosis. Three primary assessment techniques: survey instruments, document analysis and structured interviews were used.

- A 100 item survey structured in 5 major categories (Organizational Structure, Inputs, Processes, Organizational Culture, Outputs) to around 350 employees (from total of 1320) was conducted. The surveys helped identify the trends in the organizational procedures and practices.
- Twenty interviews were organized with the head chiefs of each department. The interviews helped gain insights into the operational areas and detect certain types of problems.

- Documents that provided information on the organization's mission, goals, objectives—strategy, organizations internal rule and procedure code, budget plans, and activity reports, were consulted. Document analysis gave an idea about organization's recent behaviors.

Phase 3   Problems and causal factors

The information gathered revealed major problems with regard to all five aspects analyzed.

1. There exist two codes of rules and procedures causing an overlap of tasks and avoidance of responsibility.
2. The allocation of space was inappropriate leading to overcrowding at some sections of the hospital and vacant spaces in other sections with very few beds occupied.
3. There were not any records about all hospital proprieties and this had lead to mismanagement.
4. Resources were inadequate and inappropriate. The medical staff complained about lack of technological resources, necessary for quality services. The IT network, was ineffective being fragmented and less operative.
5. The management adopted a fire fighting approach. The hospital had no statement of mission, vision and medium and long-term objectives. Things were dealt with on a daily basis.
6. Most of the problems were sorted out through the informal network. The relation between management and lower levels of the organization were poor.
7. Finally, the organizational culture was very weak. It was characterized by domination, rigidity, appeal to rules and procedures, and avoidance of responsibility.
8. Though there was funding for owing to lack of professionalism and low motivation in staff, the public acquisition procedure was not set right and required pharmaceutical products and equipment were not made available.
9. The outcomes were inefficiency and poor quality services. Some services were not available due to poor processes, outdated technology and non-availability of certain pharmaceutical products.

Questions for Discussion

1. Do you think the diagnosis process is effective in obtaining required information?
2. Based on the findings, draft a report presenting the current situation, available options and recommendations for improving the hospital.

Source: Adapted with permission from Cătălin Baba, Răzvan Chereches, Tudor Ticlau, and Cristina Mora, (2009) Organizational diagnosis–a management tool for change–Case study in Satumare County Hospital, Transylvanian Review of Administrative Sciences, 25E. pp. 32–39, available at about TRAS-TRAS, www.rtsa. ro/en/

REFERENCES

1. Adapted from Organizational Audit, Organisational Diagnosis, Diagnose problems... www.psyasia.com/organizational_diagnosis.php; Organization Diagnosis–Capelle Consulting, www.capelleconsulting.com/sg/business/solutions/od_diagnosis. php; Roxanne Ray and Eric Sanders 2008, AHP Cultural Transformation, Driving Positive Organizational Change, OD Practitioner, Vol. **40**(1), pp. 10–16; Dutta Roy, organizational diagnosis—Indian Statistical Institute, www.isical.ac.in/~ddroy/ odiag.html, 20 March 2001 (Human Synergistics is a consulting firm) and Human Dimension–Organizational Development Consulting. www.humandimension.org/ ODconsulting.html

2. Weisbord, Marvin R. (1978), *Organizational Diagnosis: A Workbook of Theory and Practice*, Reading, MA: Addison-Wesley.

3. Noolan, Lecture on Effective Organisational Diagnosis ... it www.COD.gov.sg, 8 Nov. 2010.

4. Alderfer, Clayton P.T. (1980), The Methodology of Organizational Diagnosis, Professional Psychology, Vol. **11**(3), June, pp. 459–468.

5. Diagnosis, 21 April 2006 ... ...www.mistyriver.net/org_diag.htm.

6. Organizational Diagnosis–Wikipractice: the Best Practices web site, 2 Jan. 2011 ... en.wikipractice.org/.../Organizational_Diagnosis–United States

7. Beckhard, R. (1969), *Organization Development: Strategies and Models*, Reading, MA: Addison-Wesley.

8. Bhattacharya, S.K., Chattopadhyay, S. and Sengupta, Subroto (1980), "Management Consulting: Its Present Status and Future Direction in India", Ahmedabad, IIM (unpublished).

9. Russell Professional Group | Organisational Development. www.rpgroup.com.au/organisational-development.php

10. Management and Organizational Sustainability Tool (MOST). www.msh.org/.../management-and-organizational-sustainability-tool...

11. Bolman and Deal (1989), *Modern Approaches to Understanding and Managing Organizations,* San Fransciso: Jossey-Bass.

12. Richard Beckhard, (1972), Optimizing Team Building Effort, *Journal of Contemporary Business,* Vol. **1**(3), 1972.

13. Weisbord, Marvin R. (1976), Organizational Diagnosis: six places to look at with or without Theory, Group and organization studies, I. pp. 430–437.

14. For Strategic Fit. www.differentiateyourbusiness.co.uk/mckinsey-7-s-framework-for-st... 2 Sep. 2011.

15. Kilmann, Ralph H. (1989), *Beyond the Quick Fix: A completely Integrated program for creating and maintaining organizational success*, San Francisco: Jossey–Bass; and

Kilmann, Ralph H. (1975), A Holistic Program and Critical Success Factors of Corporate Transformation, *European Management Journal*, Vol. **13**(2), pp. 175–186.

16. Nadler, D.A. and Tushman, M.L. (1980), A model for diagnosing organizational behavior, *Organizational Dynamics*, Autumn, pp. 35–51.

17. Bowers, D.G. and Franklin, J.L. (1972), Survey-guided development: Using human resources measurement in organizational change. *Journal of Contemporary Business,* Vol. **7**, pp. 43–55; Alderfer, C.P. and Holbrook, J. (1973), A new design for survey feedback, *Education and Urban Society,* 1973, Vol. **5**, pp. 437–464, and Likert, R. (1961), *New Patterns of Management,* New York: McGraw-Hill.

Chapter **9**

Interventions

Vignette: Variety of Interventions

The nursing director of a large hospital called Human Dimension for help to find out the cause of heavy turnover in the clerical ranks of the nursing departments and also resolving serious conflicts between nursing staff of two departments. During the study, it is found that employee morale was very low in the administrative services area. Surprisingly, it was root cause for distraction of nurses form patient care and nurse-group conflicts. The consultant offered solutions to the Director for improving morale and establishing trust and intergroup relations for better cooperation and patient care.

A sixteen year old electronics company had achieved significant growth in terms of size and operations. The owner of the company felt it necessary to devise strategic plans for consolidating the growth and move to the next stage of development. He wanted an objective view of the company—its processes, systems, employee relations and development systems—and recommendations on how to develop next stage strategic plans.

A new director of the US division of a large multinational company called Human Dimension, and assigned the task of combining two previously competing and geographically dispersed departments into one team. Both the departments harboured hostility and played a blame game for the last four years. The consultant designed team building and third party peacemaking interventions, and reduced the chasm and paved way for integration.

Due to a rapidly changing market, the IT leadership team of a large bank had problems in decision making. Through interviews and surveys, Clarity consulting discovered problems like poor information flow poor leadership and soiled decision-making. The consultant team conducted a discovery process that identified critical break points in communication and decision-making among leadership. They helped the IT leadership team design and use an operating model, that clarified information flows and decision-making, and improved cross-functional collaboration. They facilitated strategy/leadership off sites over an 18-month period on strengthening the team work and leadership ability. They offered coaching to senior team and individual leaders in one-on-one and group meetings. The follow-up interviews six and twelve months later, showed positive results like effective leadership and improved dialogue and accelerated decision-making[1].

The interventions presented above are only illustrative of the range of interventions that consultants adopt to increase organizational effectiveness. In this chapter, we will identify a wide range of interventions and describe the implementation aspects.

INTRODUCTION

Organizational change is a complex, lengthy activity and requires a well thought-out strategy. The strategy has to be evolved by integrating different organizational interventions aimed at creating improvements in various spheres of organization over a period of time. OD consultants have a wide variety of interventions that vary from standardized programs to relatively unique programs tailored for a specific group or individuals in an organization. An understanding of the interventions and their suitability to different organizational problems and change requirements is important for making right choices.

DEFINITION

Interventions are change effecting activities, which provide learning and cause change in the action stage of organization development. Johnson defined interventions as:

Structured activities used individually or in combination by the members of a client system to improve their social or task performance[2].

Georges presented the following definition:

Intervention involves purposeful action by an agent to create and facilitate change in a particular organization setting or system[3].

NATURE

Organization Development interventions differ from other types of interventions like HR interventions that aim at developing people in the organizations. Following are the points explaining the nature of OD:

1. *Change-oriented:* All OD interventions are change-oriented. They seek to bring about change, that is necessary in the light of a discrepancy or an opportunity identified.

2. *Structured:* All OD interventions, whether targeted at individual or organization, whether aimed at impacting goal setting skills or organizational culture change, are structured and delivered to ensure participation and involvement of the concerned members.

3. *Purposeful:* Every intervention has a purpose of bringing about an improvement. It can be in individual competencies, or group cooperation or organizational effectiveness. The specific goal will be decided jointly by the consultant and client.

4. *Process-oriented:* The essential feature of interventions is involvement, ownership and participation of members of client system. The client is not eager to exhibit his knowledge or design intervention which cannot be understood and appreciated by the client system. As such interventions will lay emphasis on organizational processes in contrast to substantive content.

5. *Contextual:* Interventions do not take place in a vacuum. It has to be designed in normal course to suit the environment of organization, especially the systems, culture and climate. As such, consultants consider the facilitating and inhibiting factors of the client system before finalizing the design of intervention.

6. *Agent-driven:* Interventions are supported by a behavioral scientist who acts as a change agent, sometimes referred to as a catalyst or facilitator.

7. *Theory based:* Interventions are derived from theory, practice and experimentation. Many of the interventions have conceptual theoretical material, research findings on practice and experimentation in real life situations. They are conceptualized, hypothesized, tested and proved.

8. *Strategy-linked:* Interventions are an integral part of a strategy evolved jointly by the consultant and client with reference to a corporate strategy, and change objectives and needs. They are thus an integral part of an improvement strategy of the client organization.

NEED

Interventions aimed at producing desired changes may become necessary due to the following reasons:

1. *Discrepancy/Repair:* Interventions are needed when an organization has some performance gap or has some broken pieces that have to be fixed. Interventions help set things right and create desired skills, system, processes and outcomes.

2. *Realignment:* Some parts of the organization are out of alignment, and are working at cross purposes. This may be manifest in poor coordination, conflicts and delayed responses to stakeholders. Interventions are needed to ensure smooth functioning of organization.

3. *Reformation:* Organization needs a new vision, and the necessary structures, processes, and culture to support. The changes in environment call for new outlook and new face lift. While

business continues to be the same organization may need a new logo, new work environments and new approaches to conversations with people and. employees.

4. Development: Organization needs building additional strengths to seize an unrealized opportunity. Such a need arises when organizations seek to grow through expansion and diversification or mergers and acquisitions. Such decisions give rise to a host of employee problems like work force diversity and cultural shock. Interventions that facilitate adaptation and adjustment as well as augment the system capabilities are needed.

TYPOLOGY OF INTERVENTIONS

Interventions include a wide range of procedures from simple, common place tools like experiential exercises, questionnaires, attitude surveys, interviews, and meetings to complex, sophisticated ones like behavior modeling, process consultation, appreciative inquiry, quality circles, and visioning. Box 9.1 illustrates the OD interventions offered by two Indian OD consultants.

Interventions can be classified based on two factors: (i) purpose and (ii) target members. A brief description of the two categories is provided here.

BOX 9.1   Range of Interventions Offered

Potentia, Hyderabad offers wholesome bouquet of OD services, like Organizational transformation, Culture building, Strengthening leadership quotient, Executive coaching, Enhancing team effectiveness, and People productivity optimization. Organization design and HR interventions like Performance management, HR strategy, Compensation and benefits, Employee engagement and a host of other services.

Smuday Psycon, New Delhi, offers tailor made interventions for specific requirements, which are planned, discourse free, highly participative and steered jointly by the client and the consultant. Some of their major interventions are:

- Organization design, Vision building, Collective leadership at the top, Family-business interface, Executive coaching, and Leading and managing change.
- Developing internal leaders and leadership processes, Leadership coaching, and Upgrading HR capabilities.
- Team formation, Team strengthening, Intra team resolution, and Inter-group conflicts.
- Roles, membership and self, mid career, late career review and self-renewal.

Source: Based on www.potentia.in/ and, www.samuday.com/about_us/ The list is illustrative and not exhaustive.

Based on Purpose

Interventions may also be classified according to the type of change they can effect. Illustrative list of such interventions is given under.

Organization growth and renewal

They include strategic interventions targeted at the whole organization. Their aim may be one of the following:

(i) To align with its new environment to keep pace with changing conditions,

(ii) Taking a new direction for expansion or diversification, and

(iii) Restructuring operations for creating lean, elegant organizations to improve overall performance.

The interventions are highly structured. They originate at top management level. A shared commitment and a contagious effect are created to involve people through participation, education and communication. The interventions suggested are—mission, vision and purpose, strategic planning, goal setting, visioning, scenario planning, benchmarking, SWOT, communication/strategy audit, values commitment, climate survey and culture change. According to Cummings and Worley, the intervention process includes: preparation of the large group meeting, conducting the meeting and following on meting outcomes[4].

Raising performance levels

The interventions are techno structural type and apply to work units—jobs, processes and methods. They aim at improving organization structure and performance, by introducing new technology. The interventions, in most cases, rely on deficit based approach, to rectify problems and deficiencies. The interventions include—organization restructuring, business process redesign, workplace design, knowledge management and organizational learning.

Management and leadership development

They focus on managers in the organization and aim at improving the quality of leadership in the organization. According to Corporate Leadership Council organizations take the following measures to improve leadership quality:

(i) Leadership profiling keeping in mind current business demands,

(ii) Top management commitment to leadership development,

(iii) Creation of continuous development culture, and

(iv) Customized development opportunities to have right development[5].

Interventions of this kind include: executive and professional development program, mentoring, coaching, action learning, action science, MBO, succession planning, 360 degree feedback, and participative management.

Team development

They are focused at teams and groups in organization. They aim at building team and cohesive-functional groups to create better coordination within and between groups and ultimately high level of performance. Interventions include: goal setting, role analysis, decision-making, stress management, and conflict management and communities of practice.

Personal development

They are applied to individuals. They aim at developing specific skills of individuals to be good communicators, decision makers, goal setters and performers. The common interventions are: Life-and career-planning activities, goal setting, decision-making, role play, mentoring, coaching, counseling, and interpersonal communications.

Based on a Functional Aspect

Interventions are classified based on the functional aspects like strategy, process improvements, human resource processes and development.[6]

1. *Strategic interventions:* Strategic interventions are similar to organizational growth and development interventions and include mission/vision development, strategic planning and goal setting, visioning/scenario planning, benchmarking, SWOT, communication audit/strategy, climate survey and culture change.

2. *Techno-structural interventions:* Techno-structural interventions focus on application of technology developments to structural components to improve process effectiveness, and thereby organizational effectiveness. Socio-technical system, job analysis and job design, business process redesign, and physical settings, etc. come under this category.

3. *Human resource management Interventions:* These types of OD interventions aim to improve HRM processes. Hale classified HR based interventions into three categories—information, design and consequences[7]. Table 9.1 shows them.

TABLE 9.1 HR Based Interventions

Category	Purpose	Tools
Information	Inform	Feedback, debriefing sessions, and newsletters.
	Define	Meetings and conferences
	Document	Libraries, manuals, expert systems, job aids and decision guides
Design	Organize	Reorganization, reengineering, and merging
	Standardize	TQM, Six Sigma, quality circles, and ISO series adoption
	Redesign	Safety measures, service redesign, maintenance system changes and rationalization
	Reframe	Brain storming, challenging assumptions and other lateral thinking techniques
	Counsel	Employee assistance programs, and counseling
	Develop	Training, mentoring, coaching, on-the job experiences physical fitness centers, yoga and meditation
Consequences	Measure	Balanced score card, appraisal, and benchmarks
	Reward	Pay for performance, annual recognition meetings, and publicity through notices and newsletters
	Reinforce	Preventing fire able offenses like sexual harassment, workplace violence, unethical practices through policing, whistle blowing, hotlines, monitoring and punishments

Based on Causes

Blake and Mouton identified a typology of interventions based on the causal factors given under[8].

1. *Theory interventions:* Interventions based on behavioral sciences to correct or improve the situation which is described wrong, according to an accepted theoretical knowledge.

2. *Experimentation interventions:* Interventions that test two different plans for their effectiveness to choose the better one.

3. *Dilemma interventions:* Interventions that seek to resolve an emergent dilemma by examining the underlying assumptions and choices available.

4. *Discrepancy interventions:* Interventions that seek to correct something which is not acceptable and prompts the exploration for finding ways to resolve it.

5. *Procedural interventions:* Interventions that examine whether the methods in vogue are appropriate and the best.

6. *Relationship interventions:* Interventions which examine interpersonal relationships to see whether there are strong negative feelings and find ways of removing them.

7. *Perspective interventions:* Interventions that relegate the present to the background, and focus attention on analysis of the past and the future, to ascertain whether current activities are in the right direction for achieving desired goals.

8. *Organization structure intervention:* Interventions that help identify structural weaknesses in organizations.

9. *Cultural interventions:* Interventions that examine traditions, values and belief for their relevance in the operating context of organization.

Based on Target Members

Interventions are classified based on target groups—individuals, dyads, teams and groups, inter-groups, and the total organization. Table 9.2 shows them.

TABLE 9.2 Interventions Based on Target Members

Group	Interventions
Individual	Life and career planning, Force field analysis coaching, counseling, education and training, work redesign, Gestalt OD and Grid OD phase-1.
Dyad	Role analysis and role playing, role negotiation, behavior modeling, Responsibility charting, and Gestalt OD.
Groups	Process consultation, Sensitivity training, Self-managed teams, Team building (process and task directed), Gestalt OD, Grid OD phase-2 Interdependency exercise, Visioning, Socio-technical systems, Appreciative inquiry, Appreciations and concerns exercise, Quality of Work Life, Quality circles, Organizational mirroring, Partnering, Survey feedback. Grid OD phase-3, Third party peace-making and Power Dynamics.
Organization	Mission & Vision Development, Future search, MBO, Socio technical systems, Cultural audit, Climate analysis, TQM, Quality of work life, Grid OD phase 4, 5 and 6, Workforce Diversity Management, Organizational Learning, Change Management, and Stress Management.

Interventions Based Functional Components

Yet another way of classifying interventions is in relation to the organizational functional components human resource based, technology based and structure based.

Consulcube

Blake and Mouton's developed a three-dimensional cube to make a complex display of the variety of interventions[9]. The three dimensions are given as follows:

1. Who the client is (called units of change)
2. What consultation style is used (kinds of interventions)
3. The problem(s) diagnosed (focal issues)

Units of change	Kind of interventions	Focal issues
Individual	acceptant	power/authority
Group	catalytic	morale/cohesion
Intergroup	confrontation	norms/standards
Organization	prescriptive	goals/objectives

CHOICE OF INTERVENTIONS

How do you select the appropriate intervention from the wide array of interventions available? OD interventions are integral part of an OD strategy, developed to serve a definite purpose. A sound strategy specifies objectives, interventions, schedules and evaluation methods. In practice, formulation of game plan and sequence of interventions are based on several factors as detailed here:

1. Goals: Depending upon the goal interventions vary. The goals of change can be repair, reform, realignment and development.

2. Problems: Problems are wide ranging from communication, to conflicts, individual to organizational ineffectiveness. Some problems may relate to task issues (what people do) and some others on process issues (how people go about doing it). Depending on the problem, one has to choose the intervention. If poor performance is the problem, interventions like training, coaching, counseling will be chosen. For poor leadership, appropriate interventions may be participative management and MBO.

3. Resources: Another important consideration is client and consultant resources. The client time and energy, the availability of internal facilitators, and the skills and talent pool the consultant, has, exert influence on the choice of interventions.

4. Target group: Intervention choices depend on the target group. There are interventions addressed to different units of organization—individual, dyad, group, systems and organization.

5. *Support system:* The support system in the organization is an important consideration in choosing an intervention. When support system is weak, group and organization-wide interventions cannot be successful. One has to start from base level, and gradually build support when attempting such interventions.

6. *People readiness:* If an organization is for the first time using OD, then interventions that create readiness must precede other planned interventions. Assessment of organization readiness, willingness and capacity help determine where to start and which interventions to use.

7. *Chance for success:* The chosen intervention should be one for which chances of success are high. To effect changes gradually, series of wins are essential. The consultant requires at least a moderate success to gain respect from the client.

Beckhard provides six assumptions (A-1 to A-6) on the nature and functioning of organizations that guide structuring of interventions[10].

- **A-1:** Team or group is the basic building block of an organization. Change should start from groups, not individuals. *Choose team-based intervention.*
- **A-2:** The relevant goal of a change program is increasing collaboration and reducing inappropriate competition between various units of the organization. *Choose intervention for collaboration.*
- **A-3:** Decision-making is associated to information sources and not to a particular role or level of hierarchy. *Choose interventions for restructuring organizational decision processes.*
- **A-4:** It is goals, but not controls that decide performance. Controls are at best interim measurements, not the basis of managerial strategy. People work against goals. *Choose interventions that strengthen strategy formulation and goal setting.*
- **A-5:** Healthy organizations create open communication, mutual trust, and confidence between and across levels. *Choose interventions that improve interpersonal communication and trust.*
- **A-6:** People support what they help create. *Choose interventions that allow active participation of relevant people.* Relevant people are those affected by the problem or opportunity. For instance, if the goal is to improve team effectiveness, involve the whole team.

DESIGN OF INTERVENTIONS

Designing intervention involves choosing and sequencing of intervention activities in a way they can be implemented appropriately to get desired results.

Packing-Integration

In general, Organization Development programs employ simultaneously more than one intervention. The benefits of OD can be enhanced by using a combination of several techniques instead of one. Organizations attempting smaller changes will choose one or two interventions and implement them in a phased manner. However, it serves the purpose of finding temporary solutions. To be effective, organizations should aim at a high degree of organizational change, periodically. They should employ a full range of interventions, and implement them simultaneously.

Intervention Structuring

Structural interventional activities facilitate the following:

1. Secures involvement of relevant people.
2. Provides for learning by theory (discussion with consultant), practice (experimentation) and reflection (thinking and developing improved understanding).
3. Facilitates 'learning together' in a relaxed and planned manner, without anxiety and pressure.
4. Engages the whole person, not a part of him or her. One should be able to combine skill, knowledge and attitudes or emotional and rational intelligences while participating in intervention.
5. Direct activities to problems and goals. Participants should be able to see the relevance of an activity from problems as well as goals point of view.

Sequencing: Prioritization

Michael Beer has provided six principles for sequencing interventions in a proper manner[11]. Table 9.3 shows them as well as consequences of ignoring them.

TABLE 9.3 Consequences of Violation of Principles

S.No.	Principle	Focus	Consequence of violation
1	Maximize diagnostic data	Research	Results in administering wrong interventions
2	Maximize effectiveness	Impact	Leads to cumulative ineffectiveness
3	Maximize efficiency	Resources	Causes wastage of resources and implementation of unwanted interventions
4	Maximize speed	Schedules	Results in slow development
5	Maximize relevance	Problems	Leads to loss of motivation among participants
6	Minimize psychological and organizational strain	Emotional stability	People's sense of confidence and competence will be lowered

1. *Maximize diagnostic data* (research): Organization Development combines action with research to bring about improvements in actions and enrich theory. As such, intervention should be structured in a way they provide data for diagnosis. Such data can be used to evaluate the effectiveness of the intervention and decide which intervention can be used in the next stage.

2. *Maximize effectiveness* (impact): Interventional activities are to be seen as a chain of events, each event contributing to the successive event to have progressive improvement. For example, a personal development intervention has to precede team development intervention, in order to maximize effectiveness of team development intervention.

3. *Maximize efficiency* (resources): Efficiency refers to proper use of resources and avoidance of wastages. The proper utilization of the time of the participants and money should be considered in sequencing the intervention activities.

4. *Maximize speed* (schedules): Confusion, waiting times between two activities, overlapping activities etc. will not only degenerate interest of client but also waste time. The time taken will be longer than necessary and progress will be slow.

5. *Maximize relevance* (problems): It is not unusual that participants will feel a sense of urgency to solve immediate problems. As such, interventions addressed to immediate problems will be seen relevant ones and will be readily embraced. As such, in sequencing interventions priority should be given to immediate problems.

6. *Minimize psychological and organizational strain* (emotional stability): Interventions should be sequenced and structured to take organization forward and improve its functional capabilities. As such care is to be taken, in the choice of interventions. Such interventions, which may cause anxiety, stress and dysfunctional tendencies, should be avoided.

BENEFITS OF INTERVENTIONS

The benefits of effective OD programs are myriad. This can be understood from the testimonials managers and business owners have given to OD consultants. Box 9.2 shows the comments of OD beneficiaries.

Additional Benefits

Since interventions are specific goal directed, the primary benefit of intervention is goal accomplishment. In addition, there will be other benefits as interventions are interactive, reflective and theory-based. They create some sort of positive energy and enthusiasm among participants.

1. *Discover self:* Intervention will provide new data about oneself and discover hither to unknown self.

2. *Novelty excitement:* The Hawthorne effect will be visible when intervention leads to the awareness that, "this is a new ball game", or that "we are now playing with a new set of rules".

3. *Positive sentiments:* Homans described group as a complex of three things: activities, interaction and sentiments. He suggested that increased interaction leads to increased positive sentiments[12].

4. *Broader outlook:* According to Murphy, individuals and groups in isolation tend to develop 'tunnel vision' or 'autism'. Increasing communication and exposure to new situations will counter this tendency[13].

5. *Optimism:* Increased optimism is the result of sharing views with others and discussing about future opportunities and possibilities.

BOX 9.2   Benefits of OD Interventions

Christopher Tobit, Director Sales and Operations, Airtel, appreciates workshops of OD alternatives as cathartic providing an opportunity to take a glimpse deep within oneself to discover and marvel at the hidden potential locked inside and provide a stark realization of utter inter-dependence on one another. According to him, they provide all the ingredients for true alchemy at the workplace.
 	
  K. Ravi, Formerly Head—Operations, Beam Cable System, appreciates 'Executive coaching' intervention of Potentia. He observed that the intervention helped him in understanding himself better as an individual, as a manager and as a leader. He writes, "I could feel that I have become more effective and could enhance my personal productivity. I was able to create in my team positive energy that really enhanced our collective productivity, and most importantly achieve work life balance that eludes most senior teams".
 	
  Barbara Higgins, VP Customer Experience, United Airlines appreciates Betsy (Accelera consulting group) for positively influencing and enabling her in using existing skills more effectively and be a better leader. She rates Betsy as an unparalleled thought partner in sorting through organizational and strategic issues.
 	
Source: http://www.odalternatives.com/testimonials.asp, http://www.potentia.in/ testimonials.html and http://www.acceleraconsultinggroup.com/menu/client-results/rave-reviews/. Reported with permission.

PROGRAM MANAGEMENT

OD interventions are programs comprised of specific activities, designed in relation to a problem or opportunity, to effect a specific change, over a specified period of time, in an organization. Given this, the program management involves, planning, organizing, leading and controlling of interventions. Table 9.4 presents a brief summary of important aspects in program management.

TABLE 9.4   Program Management Tasks

Function	Tasks
Planning	Defining problem or opportunity, examining current and future situations, setting goals, exploring alternative interventions, evaluating and selecting right intervention and evolving an implementation plan (goals, standards, resources, schedules, etc.)
Organizing	Identifying activities involved in intervention (activity analysis), assignment of activities along with appropriate authority and responsibility (change agents, task forces, steering committee etc.), liaising with consultants, etc.
Leading	Inspiration and support from top management, active involvement of concerned managers and supervisors, self management teams, etc.
Controlling	Setting standards and evaluation procedures, design feedback, implementation feedback, intervention feedback, maintenance feedback and corrective measures.

Prerequisites of Implementation

Success does not come automatically and very easily. The same is true with OD initiatives. OD interventions that are pursued in a sloppy, half-hearted, and faulty manner will not succeed in bringing about meaningful change. Writing in the *Academy of Management OD Newsletter,* consultant William G. Dyer identified the following prerequisites of implementation program[14]:

1. *Demonstration of relevance of intervention:* The management of client organization should communicate effectively about the intervention to the concerned members. The communication should establish two things: (i) intervention is based on accurate diagnosis of organizational conditions, and (ii) it relates to the organization's goals and overriding mission. This step will arouse curiosity and generate interest toward the proposed intervention.

2. *Awareness and knowledge:* People involved in OD can play their roles and lend support to the program only when they are informed in advance of the nature of the intervention and the nature of their involvement in it.

3. *Commitment of client system:* The concerned members in the client organization should genuinely feel ownership of the effort. Along with this, they should display their commitment to the successful implementation of the intervention. This happens when people are empowered and involved.

4. *Integration of organizational units:* The connected parts of the organization are to be integrated to make the intervention effective. The forward and backward linkages are to be visualized, and accordingly a system for implementing intervention is to be created. Part by part approach will result in isolated developments which may not be beneficial to the organization.

5. *Leadership for direction:* The entire intervention effort has to be directed by appropriate managers and guided by change agents. OD interventions require visionary leadership. Kanter, Stein and Jick express this view emphatically in the following lines.

An organization should not undertake something as challenging as large-scale change without a leader to guide, drive and inspire it. These change advocates, play a critical role in creating a company vision, motivating company employees to embrace that vision, and crafting an organizational structure that consistently rewards those who strive toward the realization of the vision[15].

Implementation

Implementation of intervention requires tactics that help smoothen the implementation process[16].

1. *Simultaneous:* Practitioner and consultant implement interventions simultaneously in all divisions of the enterprise.

2. *Familiar:* Begin implementation in units which have already experienced with some OD interventions.

3. Power association: Start with a group that is most influential in terms of power and relationships. A suitable project may be team building activity conducted with the manager and his staff.

4. Pilot project: Consultant conducts a pilot project and achieves success, to create confidence among organizational members. The initial success will be a trigger to future successes.

5. Control through action research: Consultant implements intervention in one unit, which is called control group. The results are measured and disseminated to other groups. Based on the experience and appreciation, the intervention is administered in other units. When compared to pilot project, this approach involves tight controls and limited scope.

6. Ongoing activity: Some times, involvement in an ongoing project or change that the organization has been implementing, may be a safe route to successful implementation of proposed intervention.

EVALUATION

Managers investing resources in OD are increasingly bothered by the questions, like whether the result justifies the expenditures in terms of hard, bottom-line outcomes? Whether to continue the change program, or modify it, or terminate it and try something else? To find right answers to guide them, companies are looking for appropriate evaluation methods.

Success requires not only commitment and effort but also standards that, describe it. Before implementation, the consultant and client firm should decide a program of evaluation. Evaluation is a process of finding the worth or effectiveness of the aspect under consideration. The effectiveness measurement provides feedback to practitioners and organization members to take decisions on intervention and resource allocation. The important considerations in evaluation are:

- When to evaluate—before, during and after implementation of intervention.
- What to evaluate—measures or indices for assessment of intervention design, implementation or impact.
- How to evaluate—method of measuring the variables.

When to Evaluate?

In a continuous process, the results of actions are to be measured and evaluated continuously to facilitate formulation of new action plans, if necessary to effect desired changes. Decisions about the measurement of relevant variables and the design of the evaluation process should be made early in the OD cycle so that evaluation choices can be integrated with intervention decisions. If holistic view is taken, we should expand our view of evaluation to include before, during and after implementation stages as shown in Table 9.5. Evaluation carried out to provide guidance to implementation is called implementation feedback. The measurement of impact—both short- and long-term—to evaluate outcomes may be called intervention evaluation feedback.

TABLE 9.5 Effectiveness Measures

When	What	Basis	Measures
Before	Intervention design effectiveness	Theory–assumptions, process and principles	Relevance
During	Implementation effectiveness	Progress in program and internalization	Milestones, targets, Member participation, commitment and satisfaction levels, Cost measures
After	Intervention effectiveness	Change in behavior (thinking and doing) and improved performance-immediate and long-term results	Goal accomplishment, Results vs standards Cost-benefits measures.

Before: Design effectiveness feedback

In fact, organizational diagnosis is the starting point and it helps identify particular organizational problems or areas for improvement, as well as likely causes underlying them. Based on the assessment of situation, consultants and clients look for interventions. From the wide array of interventions, consultant helps client choose appropriate interventions. The choice is based on the practice theory built by the researchers. Next, the designs the intervention by structuring its activities, and preparing an implementation plan and schedule.

During intervention: Implementation effectiveness feedback

The implementation begins with general guidelines and the process is flexible to accommodate changes necessary to make it effective. The managers and employees follow the guidelines and translate them into specific behaviors and procedures. The information on the progress of intervention, provides implementation feedback to consultant and client for taking suitable decisions like making modifications or allowing continuation.

It is advisable to collect such implementation data at short intervals to have a series of snapshots about how the intervention is progressing and when to plan for the next implementation.

After implementation: Intervention effectiveness feedback

The intervention evaluation feedback begins, immediately after implementation. Evaluation feedback is concerned with results expected, as stated in the purpose of the intervention. It is concerned not only with the short-term but also long-term impacts. The feedback may be negative or positive.

1. Positive results indicate effectiveness of intervention and encourage the client firm to initiate measures to institutionalize the changes.
2. Negative results indicate either that the initial diagnosis was wrong or intervention choice was in appropriate. Corrective measures like conducting additional diagnosis and search for better intervention might be taken.

What to Evaluate?

The feedback should be qualitative consisting of how people felt about the effort as well as quantitative to measure tangible results—the improvement in skills, performance, satisfaction, etc.

Outcome measures

The outcome measures vary for each intervention and may include qualitative and quantitative measures. Select the right variables to measure. Table 9.6 provides an illustrative list of measures for some interventions.

TABLE 9.6 Program Outcomes

S.No.	Interventions	Quantitative measures	Qualitative measures
1	QWL programs	Reduced turnover, profitability and goal attainment	Increased job satisfaction and Organizational effectiveness
2	TQM	Productivity and profitability	Job satisfaction, commitment, and group cohesiveness
3	Executive coaching	Improved performance measures like savings in cost and time	Self confidence, self efficacy, and stress levels
4	Role analysis technique	Rise in output	Role clarity, Improved inter personal relations
5	Work/life programs	Recruitment costs and benefits (Time to Fill, New Hire Turnover, Cost per Hire, Cost of Individual Recruiting Components and Applicant Conversion Rate) Productivity	Raise in morale, Best workplace reputation

Changes as a measure

Change in the select variables impacted by interventions can be measured by two types of analysis.

1. *Comparative analysis:* The measure obtained by evaluation is compared with a preselected organization or unit, or predetermined targets or standards or chosen benchmarks.

2. *Longitudinal analysis:* Change is measured over time. Measurements are taken at two different times and the change is found. Ideally, the data collection should start before the change program and continue over a predetermined period considered reasonable for producing expected results.

Research has shown occurrence of three types of measurements of change: (i) change in the level of a variable, (ii) change in the perception about variable, and (iii) change in the very definition of variable. Any one of these changes, explained as follows, may occur as a result of an intervention[17].

1. *Alpha change:* It refers to movement along a measure that reflects stable dimensions of reality. For example, if perceived employee trust (a stable variable) shows an increase after a team building program, it represents alpha change caused by the program.
2. *Beta change:* If involves the recalibration of the intervals along some constant measure of reality. If there is a change in the perception of employee about factors influencing trust, the measurement approach will change. This kind of change is called beta change.
3. *Gamma change:* If employee redefines the measure, in view of the change in framework, it is called gamma change. If after the OD intervention, trust may be seen as less relevant, it represents gamma change.

How to Evaluate?

The measurement of chosen variables for evaluation requires a scientific method. The use of research process and techniques is quite common. OD practitioners have a wide variety of research approaches to conduct evaluation research. The research methods should be appropriate and rigorous. For drawing statistically valid conclusions, three important conditions are:

- Good metrics—Measures and measuring instruments are valid and reliable
- Sampling procedures are adequate
- Statistical tests applied for interpreting outcomes are appropriate

Variety of metrics

Cost is defined as a measure of resource sacrifice (e.g., time, money) incurred to obtain a benefit or service. Time measure is used to measure the response (quick or slow) and speed at which a task is completed (faster or slower). Volume is a measure of output (tangible or intangible) traditionally measured in units produced, number of incidents, or in frequency of events. Income is a measure of revenue or profit in monetary terms. Quality indicates compliance to predetermined standards often manifested in units of error, returns and reworks. Stakeholder reaction measures are internal (e.g., satisfaction, engagement) and external (e.g., market share price).

Basic computation methods include rate, ratio, average and index. Measures can be longitudinal or cross-sectional.

1. Longitudinal measures help observe changes over a period of time, by computing measures for two different time periods.
2. Cross-sectional analysis options are: (1) organization structure/division, (e.g., department, location, product-line); (2) socio-demographics (e.g., age, gender, ethnicity/race, education level, language preference); (3) employment status (e.g., union/non-union, full-time, part-time); (4) job-type (e.g., exempt or non-exempt, management or line staff); and (5) longevity or tenure (e.g., seniority level, time in position, time with organization)[18].

Designing measures

Metric goodness requires the development of measures that are psychometrically sound. It means they should be credible (e.g., perceived authoritative or believable), meaningful (e.g., possessing managerial value), legitimate (e.g., perceived fairness and openness), accurate (e.g., perceived as correct), and considered strategically valuable by the users (e.g., decision-makers, evaluators of performance). The measures should be operational, reliable and valid.

1. *Operational definition:* For the purpose of measurement, it is important to convert concepts into measurable variables. For example, consider job satisfaction. For measuring it, first one can visualize it as a feeling with different levels of intensity (high and low). Second, it can be taken as a single variable, or a complex construct determined by multiple variables, like relationship with boss, work environment, job, relationship with peers, etc.

2. *Reliability:* Measures should be consistent, stable, and repeatable. If an instrument yields different results on repeated trials (when everything remained same), it is unreliable. Reliability or the ability to show consistency in the results is an important quality of instrument, especially when data is gathered at different times.

3. *Validity:* It refers to the ability of an instrument to measure what it is supposed to measure. When a phenomenon is taken for measurement, the chosen metrics should reflect all its properties (content validity), represent the construct it purports to measure (construct validity), agree with results of other metrics being captured at the same time (concurrent validity), and be able to predict future results (predictive validity).

For example, when the instrument of job satisfaction is constructed, various items (statements or words) that represent the dimensions of job satisfaction like: satisfaction with job, satisfaction with superiors, peers, subordinates, satisfaction with career growth opportunities etc., are included in the instrument.

The items chosen should be checked for accuracy and representativeness. The number of items chosen should be adequate to measure the chosen variable. It should be able to produce same results when administered on same type of individuals and help predict the outcomes when interventions based on the dimensions (say job design or role analysis) are introduced.

INSTITUTIONALIZATION

Institutionalization refers to making changes a permanent part of the organization's normal functioning. When an intervention is institutionalized, it takes on a life of its own. It will be valued for itself and acquires immortality. If there is a change, questioning its relevance, it redefines itself.

Firms direct attention at institutionalizing those changes, which were found effective in creating desired results. However, some organizations view institutionalization as an unnecessary exercise, as the environment in which organizations operate has become more turbulent. Today, change has become the focus of institutionalization and 'Ability to change' has become a prized quality of organizations. When an organization seeks to institutionalize a change, it has to ensure that the change has right attributes and follow a process that is appropriate.

Determinants

The following features of the change considered for institutionalization are important for embedding change in organizational practices. Figure 9.1 shows the model of institutionalization[19].

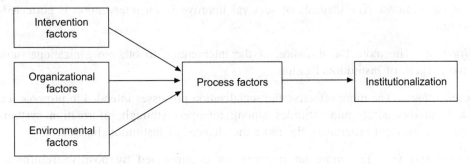

Figure 9.1 Model of institutionalization.

Intervention factors

An intervention that complements or augments an organization process or systems, with a specific goal and defined activity has better chance of becoming a permanent part of an organization.

1. *Congruence:* The more the intervention is in harmony with the organization's philosophy, strategy, structure and current environment, the more the chances of institutionalizing the change.

2. *Goal specificity:* The more specific the goals of intervention, the more effective the socialization process (for example, training and orienting new members) that leads to institutionalization of change.

3. *Programmability:* The more the changes can be programmed (the extent to which the different intervention activities can be specified clearly in advance) the more the chances of institutionalizing the change.

4. *Level of change target:* The more the extent to which the change target is the total organization, (rather than a department or small work group), the more the chances of institutionalizing the change.

Organizational factors

Interventions supported by the top management as well as people related to the intervention survive.

1. *Sponsorship:* The more an intervention is supported by a powerful sponsor, especially from the top management, the more the chances of institutionalizing the change.

Instances of interventions collapsing abruptly when the sponsor, usually a top administrator, left the organization are many.

2. *Internal support:* The more the strength of internal support system to guide the change process, the more the chances of institutionalizing the change.

Process factors

Intervention succeeds when there is widespread awareness, learning and rewards leading to a sense of commitment. The chances of survival improve when intervention is corrected from time to time.

1. *Diffusion:* The more the diffusion of the intervention to other organizational units the more the chances of institutionalization.

2. *Socialization:* The more effective the socialization processes intended to promote learning of new behaviors, skills and attitudes among members (though information systems and employee involvement programs), the more the chances of institutionalization.

3. *Reward system:* The more an intervention is supported by positive reinforcements (a variety of rewards linked to it) the more the chances of institutionalizing the change.

4. *Commitment:* The more the strength and distribution of commitment in the organization, the more the chances of institutionalization.

5. *Sensing and calibration:* The more the organization, lays emphasis on sensing and correcting the process of intervention, the more the chances of institutionalization.

Environmental factors

The external factors like unions and technology can exert influence on the success of intervention.

1. *Union support:* The more the strength of cordial relationship between union and management, the more the chances of institutionalizing the change. If the relationship is hostile, change cannot be implemented as expected.

2. *Stability of environment and technology:* The more the stability of the organization's environment and technology, the more the chances of institutionalizing the change. If environment changes, organization has to change and in the new change context, the intervention may become irrelevant.

Measures of Institutionalization

Institutionalization refers to the degree of persistence and penetration of an intervention. The following five indicators can be used to assess the level of institutionalization of an OD intervention[20].

1. *Knowledge:* It refers to the extent to which organization members has enough working knowledge of the intervention, to perform the behaviors and to recognize the consequences of the performance.

2. *Preferences:* It refers to the level of preference of employees for the intervention. High preference level indicates better chances for internalization.

3. *Normative consensus:* It refers to the extent to which organizational member agree about the appropriateness of the intervention and feel that they should support it. An intervention will be absorbed by an organization when it has gained normative consensus of members of the organization.

4. *Value consensus:* It refers to the extent the intervention has fitted into the value system of the organization. Value is both judgmental and normative. They help people to decide what is important and what acceptable. An intervention that fits into the value system of an organization will be easily internalized by the organizations. It continues to stay as long as the value system does not change.

5. *Performance:* It refers to the working of the intervention and favorable results it is producing in the organization.

An OD intervention is fully institutionalized when all factors—knowledge, preferences, norms, values and performance are in favor of the intervention adoption in organization.

SUMAMRY

OD interventions are change effecting activities which provide learning and cause change in the action stage of organization development. OD interventions are change-oriented, structured, theory based, contextual, strategy-linked, purposeful, process oriented, driven by a catalyst or facilitator. Interventions are necessary for fixing repair, realignment, reformation, and development.

Interventions can be classified based on several factors. OD interventions are integral part of an OD strategy. They are chosen by considering goals, problems, resources, target group, support system, people readiness, and chances for success. Beckhard (1969) suggested six guidelines: (i) Choose team based intervention, (ii) Choose intervention for collaboration, (iii) Choose interventions for restructuring organizational decision processes, (iv) Choose interventions that strengthen strategy formulation and goal setting, (v) Choose interventions that improve interpersonal communication and trust and (vi) Choose interventions that allow active participation of relevant people.

Designing intervention involves choosing and sequencing of intervention activities in a way they can be implemented appropriately to get desired results. Michael Beer (1980) has provided six principles for sequencing interventions in a proper manner. They are—maximize diagnostic data, maximize effectiveness, maximize efficiency, maximize speed, maximize relevance and minimize psychological and organizational strain.

Right interventions create some sort of positive energy and enthusiasm among participants, when properly implemented. William G. Dyer identified the following prerequisites of implementation program: demonstration of relevance of intervention, awareness and knowledge, commitment of client system, integration of organizational units, and leadership for direction. Program management involves, planning, organizing, leading and controlling of interventions.

Evaluation carried out to provide guidance to implementation is called implementation feedback. The measurement of impact–both short- and long-term to evaluate outcomes may be called intervention evaluation feedback. The feedback should be qualitative consisting of how people felt about the effort as well as quantitative to measure tangible results—the improvement in skills, performance, satisfaction, etc.

Institutionalization refers to making changes a permanent part of the organization's normal functioning. When an intervention is institutionalized, it takes on a life of its own. It will be valued for itself and acquires immortality.

EXERCISES

I. Review Questions

1. Define and classify OD interventions.

2. Explain the nature of OD interventions.

3. Examine the factors that influence the selection of interventions.

4. How do you design interventions?

5. Identify the issues concerned with program management.

6. How do you evaluate the implementation of interventions?

7. Discuss the measures necessary for institutionalizing interventions.

II. Discussion Questions

1. Explain the meaning and nature of OD interventions. How do you classify OD interventions?

2. For what reasons OD interventions are chosen for implementation in organizations. Explain with case examples.

3. How do you design and implement OD interventions?

4. Explain the methods of evaluation of OD interventions? How do you institutionalize interventions?

📖 MINI-PROJECT

Management institutes use team work as a way of learning. Elicit views on team as tool of learning, from about 30 students using the following questionnaire. Prepare a report with suggestions to improve the tool based on the responses.

Instructions: You had experience of working in groups. Based on the experience, please answer the following questions. Do not spend long time on any one question. Provide brief and concise answers that reflect your initial reaction.

1. List your expectations by ticking

S.No.	Expectations	Response
1	I expect others to understand me	Yes/No
2	I will be able to learn how to understand others	Yes/No
3	I can work with others on a give and take basis	Yes/No
4	I can learn how to negotiate with others	Yes/No
5	I can improve my ability to cooperate with others	Yes/No

2. To what extent you could learn skills through your team participation?

S.No.	Skills	Learnt
1	I learnt to be understanding and not critical to what others say	Yes/No
2	I learnt to be confident in my interactions with team members	Yes/No
3	I learnt to work with people having cultural and gender differences	Yes/No
4	I learnt to give to and take assignments from others	Yes/No
5	I learnt to deal with conflict among team members	Yes/No
6	I learnt to negotiate solutions that are agreeable to the members	Yes/No
7	I learnt to lead a group during times of cooperation and conflict	Yes/No
8	I learnt active listening of views of other members	Yes/No
9	I learnt the art of clear and logical expression of ideas	Yes/No

WEB ASSIGNMENT

From the following source, and other similar sources, develop a paper on the approach of Centre for Leadership Development (CLD) in design and implementation of interventions

Four Stage OD Intervention Leads To Measurable...

cldonline.in/cld_case_18_four_satge_od_intervention_%20leads_to_...

CASE STUDY

Institutionalizing Interventions

Since its inception in 1995, Bharti has pioneered in the telecom sector with many firsts and innovations to its credit. It is the first private basic telephone service in India and comprehensive telecom service provider outside India. Its strategic goals are:

- Delight its customers;
- Build the best global team;
- Leverage its scale and scope;
- Expand its market boundaries;
- Be a responsible business; and
- Provide superior returns to shareholders.

The company has three individual strategic business units—mobile services, Broadband and telephone services and Enterprise Services. The third one, Airtel Enterprise solutions (AES) includes Voice services, Mobile services, Satellite services, Managed data and internet services, Managed e-business services and Managed customized integrated solutions.

Problem

The high pace of growth in terms of number of people and revenue has drawn the attention of senior management to the issues, like employee engagement, satisfaction and ownership. To find out the organizational health from the point of view of employees, employee engagement surveys and other feedback mechanisms were put in place. OD Alternatives (ODA) was hired to create a climate of care and trust and inter personal bonds.

Diagnosis

The consultants conducted deep structured interviews with key stake holders and designed interventions based on the feedback. The feedback suggested the need for a providing a fresh outlook that stresses the importance of team work. As such, the focus was placed on team building activities that connect the members emotionally and functionally.

Structure of the Intervention

The intervention was supposed to break down formal boundaries and barriers of social interaction. As such, groups were formed by drawing members from different functions and hierarchy levels. The interventions adopted an outbound experiential format. The outbound program was for 2 days and 1 night.

A 2 day intervention was planned for around 1000 participants. The participants were divided into 4 regions and taken to offbeat locations that provided a safe, secluded and ideal place for learning and bonding. They are: (i) South—Forest in the High ranges of Palghat in Kerala and Elagiri, a small hill station near Chennai, (ii) North—Jim Corbett, Sataal, Simla and Naukutiataal (iii) East—Gangtok and (iv) West-Lonawala.

The CEO in his personal letter to the participants explained the purpose of the intervention. This indicated how much CEO is concerned about this. In each region, an ODA consultant in coordination with a representative from Airtel managed the lodging and boarding of the participants as well as indoor and outdoor training. Each workshop was facilitated by two ODA facilitators and one adventure leadership expert. In all three consultants spent around 75 days on site for this workshop.

Tools Used

Belbin, Theatre and various outdoor activities were used. Belbin gave participants an opportunity: (i) to know at their behavior; (ii) look at behaviors of others; and (iii) understand their key strengths. It helped participants gain insight that while an individual can never be perfect, a team can be. The outdoor activities were organized to facilitate an understanding of team dynamics and improve inter personal skills. Theater helped participants to understand 'Role clarity' and connect with others at a deeper human level breaking boundaries and hierarchies.

A social networking site was created with the objective of creating a sharing ground to enhance the learning's of the intervention and cement the relationships created. However, it did not create much traffic.

Feedback

Three evaluation questions were asked to gain feedback on the interventions.

Rating: 5–Excellent 4–Very good 3–Good 2–Average 1–Poor

S.No.	Aspect	Scale				
1	How useful was the program in creating interpersonal connect and bonding?	5	4	3	2	1
2	How effective do you feel the facilitators were?	5	4	3	2	1
3	Food	5	4	3	2	1
4	Place	5	4.	3	2	1
5	Services and comfort	5	4	3	2	1

Questions for Discussion

1. Critically evaluate the interventions employed by OD Alternatives.
2. Is the feedback form, adequate in assessing effectiveness of the programs?
3. What steps in your view are necessary to institutionalize the benefits of the interventions?

Source: Adapted with permission from: http://www.odalternatives.com/Team-Effectiveness-for-Airtel-Enterprise-Group.asp.

REFERENCES

1. Adapted with permission from Human Dimension—Our Company, www.humandimension.org/ourcompany.html and Clarity Consulting: What We Do: Examples Of Our Work, www.clarityconsulting.com/ what-we-do/examples-of-our-work.php

2. Johnson, Richard A. (1976), *Management Systems and Society: An Introduction*, Pacific Palisades, California: Goodyear Publishing, pp. 224–226.

3. Romme, A. Georges, L. (2011), Organizational Development Interventions—An Artifaction Perspective, *The Journal of Applied Behavioral Science*, Vol. **47**(1), pp. 8–32.

4. Cummings, T.G., Worley, C.G. (2001), *Organization Development and Change*, Cincinnati: Southwestern College Publishing.

5. Corporate Leadership Council (2001), *Women and Minorities in Leadership Development*. Corporate Executive Board, Washington, DC.

6. Kormanik, Martin B. (2005), OD Systems in Organizational Development (OD) Interventions, armandojusto.blogspot.com/.../organizational-development-od.html.

7. Hale, Judith (2006), The Performance Consultant's Fieldbook: Tools and Techniques for Improving Organizations and People, John Wiley & Sons, available at www.explorehr.org/articles/.../Types_of_OD_Intervention.html

8. Blake R. Robert and Mouton, Jane, S. (1964), *The Managerial Grid*, Houston: Gulf, pp. 281–283.

9. Blake, R.R. and Mouton, J.S. (1983), *Consultation: A Handbook For Individual and Organizational Development,* Reading Mass: Addison-Wesley.

10. Beckhard, Richard (1969), *Organization Development: Strategies and Models*. Reading, Mass: Addison-Wesley, p. 114.

11. Beer, M. (1980), *Organizational Change and Development*: *A Systems View*, Santa Monica, C.A.: Goodyear Publishing.

12. Homans, George (1950), *The Human Group*, New York: Harcourt, Brace & Co.

13. Murphy, Gardner (1945), The Freeing of Intelligence, *Psychological Bulletin*, 42, pp. 1–19.

14. Dyer, William G. (1989), "Team Building: A Microcosm of the Past, Present, and Future of OD" *Academy of Management OD Newsletter,* Winter.

15. Kanter, R.M., Stein, B.A., and Jick, T.D. (1992), *The Challenge of Organization Development,* New York: The Free Press.

16. Evaluating and Institutionalizing Organization Development ... www.zainbooks.com/.../organization-development_25_evaluating-an...

17. Quality & Equality: OD in Focus, www.quality-equality.com/publications/qe-articles/od-in-focus/.

18. Measuring Conflict: Both The Hidden Costs and the Benefits of ... www.lawmemo.com/articles/measuring.htm

19. Buller P.F. and Evo, McGlenn, M. (1989), Determinants of the Institutionalization of Planned Organizational Change, *Group and Organizaiton Studies*, Vol. **14**(1).

20. OD Intervention Success Indicators—Best website on HR ... www.explorehr.org/.../OD_Intervention_Success_Indicators.html

Chapter 10

Techno-structural Interventions

Learning Objectives

After studying this chapter, you will be able to:

- Explain the purpose of techno-structural interventions
- Know the process involved in the interventions
- Understand the merits and limitations of the interventions
- Know issues concerned with program management
- Identify the precautions to be taken in implementing the interventions

Vignette: Job Redesign Improves Service

Few of hospitals in Australia experimented with new initiatives to achieve the objectives of quality improvement and cost control. As people are the key for good service, focus was laid on staff skills and functions. It is found that the patient care units in the hospitals are staffed with different categories of healthcare workers, like cleaning staff, ward attendant, catering staff, porter, etc. There is rigid demarcation of work, creating different categories of staff akin to the patterns of manufacturing industry. However, the results indicated that this kind of job design does not work in health care units. Problems like overstaffing, inflexibility in deployment of staff, and narrow approach to duty are found. Attitudinally, there is a lack of sense of responsibility in patient care.

In view of the above, the need to redefine the jobs, by replacing the various categories of workers with only one generic classification of multi-skilled workers is considered. For achieving this, a detailed job analysis is carried out. A new generic classification of hospital workers, called as Patient Care Assistants is made. Appropriate selection and training initiatives are taken to find persons with a holistic view of servicing patients. The selected candidates are given training in multi-skilling on a unit basis.

In india, we find a similar scenario. A study by Srilatha in Public Hospital in India revealed that sanitation and hygiene are poor in many hospitals. The poorly maintained toilets and infrequent mopping of floors in the hospital are the major causes for this problem. As a result, there is patient dissatisfaction. Another patient satisfaction survey by Institute of Health Systems on 30 hospitals managed by Andhra Pradesh Vaidya Vid Parishad (APVVP), collected opinions of 1382 inpatients has found mixed results. While the composite scores of patient satisfaction level is at 71%, about 36% of the respondents have made caustic comments on the general cleanliness, shortage of drug supply and toilet maintenance[1].

Emulating the Australian hospitals, Indian hospitals may consider reviewing existing job designs to create a new model, which can improve coordination among staff, enhance quality of hospital services and reduce costs. The case points out the need for innovative thinking to improve performance levels through techno-structural solutions. In this chapter, we will discuss techno-structural interventions in detail.

INTRODUCTION

Technology has been changing the lives of people in the society and the work life in organizations. The adoption of new technology brings to light two interrelated questions—what is it adding? What is it replacing? With the advent of computers there is paperless office and with robots there is people less firm. In India, we need technology that makes jobs challenging as well as rewarding. Jobs associated with technology are not only satisfying to people but also pleasing to organizations as they are producing desirable results like quality, productivity and profitability. However creating and sustaining profitable socio-technical systems requires continual design of jobs, roles and systems. It is a mammoth task that requires the expertise of OD consultants.

EMPLOYEE INVOLVEMENT (EI)

Employee involvement refers to structural and process interventions that create an environment in which people have an impact on decisions and actions that affect their jobs. The interventions lead to an increase in information, knowledge, power and rewards, and enable employees perform better.

EI—A Powerful Tool

Each of the three strategies—process reengineering, Total Quality Management (TQM) and employee involvement produces an effect, but it is Employee Involvement which is the stronger driver of financial performance. While TQM focuses on work methods and process control, process reengineering advocates downsizing or layoffs. In contrast, employee involvement focuses on upgrading workers' knowledge and skills.

According to a study of Fortune 1000 firms by Edward Lawler, a professor of management at the University of Southern California, among HR initiatives, the winner is Employee

Involvement[2]. In India, for the year 2011, MakeMyTrip Pvt. Ltd. is adjudged as one of the best companies in Employee Involvement and collaboration[3].

Approaches to Employee Involvement

In practice, we find a wide range of mechanisms, programs, and strategies that provide participation opportunities for employees. They include—self-managed work teams, employee committees or task forces, continuous improvement teams, participative decision making and employee suggestion forums, such as a suggestion box and monthly meetings. Box 10.1 provides a brief description of employee involvement practices. Table 10.1 provides a classification of the programs.

BOX 10.1 Employee Involvement

At Raymonds, employee involvement is valued and encouraged. It is expected to facilitate continuous improvement, sound decision-making and development of an open and transparent organization. Open forums provide a foundation of people centric policies by providing opportunities to information sharing among employees. An online HR Manual accessible to all employees ensures transparency in HR processes. Kaizen, Quality Circles and Suggestion Schemes are instituted to foster creativity among organizational members. Raymond Interchange, the top management groups think-tank, is a driver of employee involvement. It encourages employees to express their views business strategy.

Steelscape, a Kalama, WA-based manufacturing company, which produces cold-rolled, metallic-coated and painted steel coils for the construction market, believes in self-directed work teams. It being a company operating round the clock, in the night shift, employees in the plant must make key, on-the-spot decisions. As such, the company allows a team select its own members. A candidate who is qualified in skill tests will then be interviewed by a team of six to eight peers. He is rated in: commitment to safety, environment and quality; interpersonal skills; teamwork and cooperation; initiative and motivation; and use of rational processes. A human resources professional attends the interview, to serve as a consultant and not as an interviewer. As a result, the team assumes ownership for performance and functions effectively under all circumstances.

Source: Based on Raymond HR Practices, www.raymondindia.com/crs_hr_pplproc.aspv and PHWP: Employee Involvement, www.phwa.org/resources/.../ employeeinvolvement/

Information sharing

Regular staff meetings and newsletters provide periodically information to employees. Websites and social media can be used to display latest updates. Social media can be used to connect and converse with employees. Ideas campaigns by placing dry-erase boards in each department and rewarding good ideas with small gifts, like a coffee cup or other company logo product will promote partnership in continuous improvement decisions. Employee feedback through organizational climate survey and employee suggestion programs help understand employees and take measures to improve their roles.

TABLE 10.1   Employee Involvement Practices

Category	Practices
Information sharing	Information sharing forums Survey feedback
Leadership practices	Democratic management Open-book management Worker representation on corporate boards of directors
Team approach	Team-based work structures Safety and health committees Union management cooperative projects Self-managing work teams
Quality management initiatives	Total quality management Quality circles Quality of work life programs
Reward linked programs	Gain-sharing and profit-sharing plans Employee ownership programs
Work improvement designs	Job design Business process reengineering Knowledge management programs

Leadership practices

Practices, such as sharing of critical information through open book, sharing of power through democratic leadership, and putting workers on the top level management boards, encourage employees to take a level of responsibility for organizing and doing their jobs with less or no dependence on management.

Team approach

Teams can take over leadership roles as they become more experienced in decision-making. A more formal mechanism, such as a joint consultative committee can ensure that employees' views are taken into account. Occupational Health and Safety (OHS), Environment Improvement and Corporate Social Responsibility (CSR) task forces are just some of the joint committees. Many organizations also set up cross-functional teams to tackle specific problems and strengthen integration. Unions are a channel to greater employee participation in decision making, to canvass ideas and to obtain feedback. Self-managed teams generate greater motivation than individuals or loosely connected groups and produce high level of performance.

Quality management initiatives

Success of all quality management initiatives depend on people's motivation, commitment and ability to work together in well-organized teams. Total Quality Management (TQM) is a way of life in organizations that guides people to manage in such a way that customer satisfaction is ensured at every stage. When combined with effective leadership, it results in an organization, that does the right things right, first time. Quality circles are teams or small groups that meet periodically to analyze, and review working practices to using a wide variety of tools, like flow charts, pareto charts, 5-whys, fish bone diagrams, and others. Based on the analysis, they think creatively and come up with suggestions for improvements. Quality-of-work-life programs go beyond work/life programs and consider employee needs at workplace and outside of work. The initiatives include open communications, mentoring programs, alternate work arrangements (flexi work, and work at home), job redesign, and self-managed teams that enhance satisfaction and reduce stress.

Reward linked programmes

Since rewards have motivational potential, some companies make use of reward linked programs. Gainsharing is a system of management in which an organization seeks higher levels of performance by rewarding people based on performance. It is a team approach; and payout is based on operational measures (productivity, quality, spending and service). Payout is preferably in case and is made often monthly or quarterly. Employees think more like owners and share responsibility of owners when they are provided with stock options. A perceptible shift in how decisions are made is found in organizations, which used this method. According to one CEO, instead of complaining about shortage of staff and resources, and making suggestions to spend more money or hire more people, employees have started thinking of other solutions[4].

Work improvement designs

Changes in job content and context provide a chance to increase both the quality of the employees' work life, and their on-the-job productivity. Scientific management argued that well-structured, repetitive tasks produce efficiency and effectiveness. However, its application led to dull, repetitive, seemingly meaningless jobs that offered little challenge or autonomy, and caused discontent among workers. As a result, experiments with designing jobs based on the characteristics that have motivation potential gained momentum. Task variety, task identity, significance, autonomy, and feedback are identified as the core characteristics of a job. All these initiatives have resulted in six ways of job design as given under[5]:

1. *Job engineering*: Maximizing efficiency through application of work study techniques
2. *Job enlargement*: Adding more tasks to the job to provide variety
3. *Job enrichment*: Making job interesting by increasing autonomy and variety
4. *Job rotation*: Giving different jobs to provide variety
5. *Goal setting*: Using objectives to decide and structure job components
6. *Socio-technical*: Making individual or group responsible for the job and balancing technical and human dimensions.

Business process improvement or functional process improvement has caught attention of managers to achieve excellence and stay competitive in the market place. Two approaches to improvements are developed:

1. Continuous improvement which examines the as is process and brings improvements in it as shown in Figure 10.1.

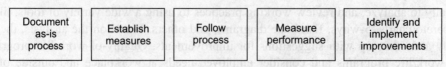

Figure 10.1 Continuous process improvement.

2. Break through reengineering model which considers the current process irrelevant and starts with a clean slate perspective. It creates a vision for the future and design new business processes and develops an action plan that helps bridge the gap between as-is process and to-be process as shown in Figure 10.2.

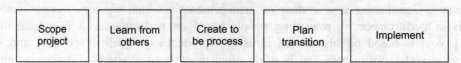

Figure 10.2 Breakthrough reengineering model.

A Knowledge Management (KM) program, focused on supporting innovation and learning, and drawing on flows of new knowledge, including knowledge from outside can be a motivator to employees in sharing and testing their knowledge. When conducted with clear goals, vibrant communities of practice, effective use of IT and social media and valid metrics it can make difference in the organizations.

Involvement Process Guidelines

Employee Involvement is not easy to implement. The implementation problems include the following:

1. *Resistance to change:* This is found in superiors who have to share power with employees.

2. *Mistrust in motives of management:* Employees may view the whole program as another gimmick to squeeze more output from them for fewer wages. This mistrust is owing to the earlier traditional management practices which emphasized compliance and discouraged creativity.

3. *Lack of clarity in expectations:* Both the managers and employees should behave clear expectations of their contribution and benefits they would get.

4. *Lack of participative skills:* As involvement requires new skills of team work, creativity and decision-making.

5. *Lack of executive commitment:* Many employee involvement programs have failed due to lack of top management commitment.

As such the employee involvement program should be documented before the start to provide sound basis for implementation. It should contain the following:

1. *Objectives:* What goals are planned for accomplishment through the program? Is it intended to increase productivity, improve quality; enhance employee commitment, strengthen teamwork, etc.

2. *Roles and responsibilities:* Who will be steering it? What kind of support services (education, training, information, etc.) are made available? What is role of line managers?

3. *Program process:* What is the procedure? How is it implemented?

4. *Rewards and recognition:* What kind of motivation rewards are announced? How are they administered?

5. *Monitor and improve:* What kind of arrangements is made for getting feedback and taking measures based on that? Who is responsible for that and to whom he or she has to report?

SOCIO-TECHNICAL SYSTEM (STS) DESIGN

The Tavistock Institute for Human Relations in London pioneered the concept and practice of STS design, beginning in the 1940's. The term socio-technical systems was originally coined by Emery and Trist to describe systems that involve a complex interaction between humans, machines and the environment[6]. Its focus was on the design of work systems in factories and offices, to foster and improve relations between the dehumanized employees and employers.

During the 1960's through 1980's, a number of Scandinavian projects focused on STS for use of computers in manufacturing organizations and office work. The focus of STS is expanded from mere adaptation to systems to user participative, interactive and creative designs. Improved workplace democratization characterized the politics of labour conditions and influenced labour-management conflicts. Key terms used to denote this proposition include user involvement, participatory design, user satisfaction, human relations, and for the political dimension, workplace democracy[7]. The guiding principle of STS is: *If a technical system is created at the expense of a social system, the results obtained will be sub-optimal.*

For STS design a wide range of methods are available. Gordon Baxter and Ian Sommerville[8] identified four methods useful in different stages of software development life cycle as shown in Table 10.2.

TABLE 10.2 STS Methods for Software Developers

Method	General	Analysis	Design	Evaluation
Cognitive work analysis		Yes	Yes	
The socio-technical method		Yes	Yes	
Ethnographic workplace analysis		Yes	Yes	
Contextual design	Yes	Yes	Yes	

1. **Cognitive work analysis** helps in analyzing the kind of work that a complex socio-technical system can perform. It is predictive and carries out work analysis to identify the work flows and human involvement contexts.

2. **The socio-technical method** helps design work systems. It analyzes the working of systems to identify tasks that have to be allocated to machines and the tasks that humans as individuals or teams have to perform. This method has general use to make function allocations of socio-technical work systems.

3. **Ethnographic workplace analysis** helps reveal the importance of awareness of the physical workplace and its influence on performance. It focuses on the operational issues that affect the functionality and use of a system and studies the relation of workarounds and dynamic process modifications.

4. **Contextual design** has focus on users. It is based on the notion that every system has a particular way of working and that it should be convenient to users. The key question therefore is—How the users work with the system? Its focus is on understanding the functional styles of people and designing machines or products based on such understanding.

JOB REDESIGN

For over three decades, job design and redesign initiatives have been considered by organizations in different contexts. Recently, in the context of lean organizations, it has come into limelight. The survivors of organizational restructuring, downsizing and lay-off failed in general, to absorb and cope with increased work load. However, preoccupied with the problem of how to survive the transitional period, management paid less attention to this problem, and it led to a decline in intrinsic job dissatisfaction. Brockner, Grover, Reed and Dewitt argued that job redesign that enhances the intrinsic job quality is necessary to help survivors cope with increased job scope and depth[9].

Job Redesign Approach

Job redesign task is to be approached with a systems view for better results. Every job is a link in a process chain and the interdependencies are as important as the job content itself. As such, diagnosis requires focus on the following questions:

1. What are job characteristics and what improvements are necessary?
2. To which jobs, the job in question is related? On which job or jobs it is dependent? What modifications it requires from the interdependent point of view?
3. To which output the job is contributing? What modifications are needed in the job to secure the desired output?
4. Who performs the job? What design elements need attention from the human point of view?

Job Characteristics Model

The efforts of job redesign require an understanding of job characteristics. Hackman and Oldham argued that the intrinsic value and motivating potential of a job are based on certain task dimensions: task variety, autonomy, identity, significance feedback and skills variety[10]. They were proved right by researchers who studied the effects of work redesign on employee perception, attitudes (job satisfaction and commitment), and behaviors[11]. The dimension of the job proposed by Hackman and Oldham are:

1. *Skill variety:* The perceived variety and complexity of skills and talents required to perform the job.

2. *Task Identity:* The extent the job is seen as involving a whole, identifiable task.

3. *Task significance:* The extent that the job affects the well-being of others.

4. *Autonomy:* The extent the job is seen as allowing for personal initiative in performing the work.

5. *Feedback from the job:* The extent that the job, itself, provides information about job performance.

These characteristics when found right in a job, will lead to a positive psychological state that represents motivation and job satisfaction.

Design Analysis Approaches

Job redesign analysis can be undertaken by using the following approaches: (i) designer analysis, and (ii) employee analysis.

Designer analysis

The job design consultant will perform the following tasks:

- Prepares a list of characteristics of the job
- Develops a check list of questions or statements that help describe and rate each characteristic
- Using the check list he or she collects data by observation
- Based on the filled in check list solutions (actions to be taken) are suggested

Employee analysis

In this approach, the employees doing the job are involved in discussion on the nature and challenges of job. Employees will be able not only to provide complex information with deep insights into the job but also offer appropriate suggestions. The outcome will be more realistic and motivating to employees (Box 10.2).

BOX 10.2 Empowering employees
Colgate-Palmolive (Labrador, Australia facility, each year shuts down their factory for one or two days and arranges a meeting of all the employees working in the building together. They were asked to say what were holding us back and which were pushing us toward better performance. At one such Renewal retreats, the managers asked for more authority to make decisions and the change of the authority to decide levels saved the company close to $300,000.
Source: An Organization Redesign Process: Redesigning Your Workplace... www.leadership-and-motivation-training.com/organization-redesign.

Job Redesign Process

The various steps involved in job redesign are presented in Table 10.3.

TABLE 10.3 Job Redesign Process

S.No.	Step	Tasks
1	Assess current work	Examine need for job redesign Discuss with employees and supervisors
2	Analyse tasks	Know who is doing a job and his or her skills Identify the outcomes of the job Divide the job in to measurable tasks and find time taken for each task Find the equipment or technology needed to complete tasks Identify problem areas
3	Analyse inter-dependencies	Find out input and output linkages and how the work is affected by such linkages
4	Design the job	Identify the methods for doing the work, rest periods, and work schedules
5	Implement gradually	Start on small scale with a pilot Train employees in new procedures, equipment and goals. Allow time for adjustment
6	Revaluate job design	Make necessary adjustments. Set up a committee of workers, union members and supervisors to monitor progress Communicate the job redesign to employees and be open to receive feedback

Approaches to Job Design

Campion and Thayer identified that there exist four individual approaches: mechanistic, motivational, biological, and perceptual/motor[12]. Each one focuses on different characteristics of a job. As such, each one is associated with different outcomes, costs, and benefits when applied to a job redesign. Box 10.3 describes a job redesign endeavor.

1. *Mechanical:* Used for low level factory jobs. The job redesign is done to facilitate specialization, simplification and defining skill requirements.

2. *Motivational:* Applied for managerial and professional jobs. Job redesign can be done either by job enlargement or enrichment.

3. *Biological:* Typically used for heavy industry or lighter repetitive jobs. Job redesign is done through knowledge of ergonomics. Various disciplines, like bio-mechanics, occupational medicine, etc. are used to design movements for safety at work place.

4. *Perceptual motor:* Used for all jobs, typically for not one position. The redesign seeks to maximize effort, but not beyond one's mental capabilities. This approach is adopted along with other ones.

BOX 10.3 The Redesign Endeavor

The redesign project team is concerned with the work of nursing assistants. They asked the nursing staff, in two units (orthopedic and cardiac surgery units) three specific questions: (i) What is the outcome of your job and what kind of outcome is viable in the present environment? (ii) What is your view of your way of doing it? Is it efficient and can it be done more simply or more efficiently? (iii) Are you qualified and trained to do this job?

The inquiry and discussion involved the staff in the process of brain storming, on all the individual jobs/tasks that they performed on a regular basis on the patient care units. The ideas and problems are pasted on $12'' \times 12''$ wall. It provided the framework for future course of design.

The team then reviewed the qualifications and experience. Copies of state regulations served as a guideline in the review process. The tasks that could be performed by were then sorted into clinical and non-clinical categories and two roles for the patient care—technician role (a clinical role) and the patient care service associate role (a guest services role), were created.

The patient care technician role serve as another set of eyes for the nurses. The tasks include setting up of equipment, assisting patients with their activities of daily living, taking vital signs and noting changes in patient status.

The patient care service associate is a multi-skilled worker who assists with, among other activities, transporting, cleaning of patient rooms, and restocking of supplies.

The task delineation and assignments step of the redesign gave the staff nurses, ownership in this redesign effort. Since it is the nurses that ultimately determined what tasks were appropriately delegated to each level of service personnel, this involvement benefited the exercise.

The nursing unit assistants became excited as they saw growth potential for their own job and they subsequently went through the Patient Care Technician Program. The patient care service associate became an integral part of the unit team, rather than outsider and it started a team building process that is continuing even today.

Source: Aged & Community Services, SA & NT Inc©, Job Redesign Project—Mature Workers Matters Strategies & Activities.
www.agedcommunity.asn.au/mature-workers.../job-redesign-project...

WORKPLACE REDESIGN

Nowadays an office space is more than physical product, it is viewed from different perspectives—as a place that stimulates people to work better, a place which saves energy, a place where interactions are smooth and creative, and a place which enhances image of the company. The workplace design sensibilities are maturing. The interventions of architects, facility managers interior designers and OD consultants are called for, to integrate workplace design with organizational processes, values and strategy.

Strategic Work Place Design

Workplace design is need based and goal oriented (see Box 10.4). When considered for long-term benefits it will become a strategic decision requiring a comprehensive and integrated approach.

BOX 10.4 Case of Workplace Redesign

The leader of a major social services organization realized the need to consider workplace redesign, given the mission—rich but resource—spare agenda. There is reduction in resources due to economic recession while there is huge rise in demand for their services. The generations old, out-of-date, compartmentalized, and walnut-panelled space dragged on their energy and purpose.

First he carried out a sort of research in workplace design and interacted with architects, designers and furniture manufacturers. He then, formed a vision of the workspace and described it as the open, collaborative, agile and responsive. With this clarity, he embarked on a major program to find and design the right type of space. He then moved his organization in. The new space stimulated cultural change and he acted as a facilitator for it to take shape.

Source: The latest *workplace design trends* << archizoo
archizoo.com/2010/05/14/the-latest-workplace-design-trends/

So far attention was paid to workplace design from ambience (physical and aesthetic aspects) and employee comfort and convenience. Less attention is paid to group and organizational processes and outputs. However, the Environmental Design Research Association's (ERDA, 2005) workplace network group and others have pointed out the need for new approach[13]. One comprehensives analytical approach is Workplace 20–20 a methodology for linking workplace to organizational goals and strategy. It involves the following steps:

1. *Organization context analysis:* The client engagement process begins with the analysis of the context of organization by a multi-disciplinary team. Discussions, interviews and exercises will be used to understand and describe the context.

2. *Visioning:* The employees are now asked to visualize the future of organization to foresee future needs besides current needs.

3. *Balanced score card (BSC) analysis:* A BSC (Kaplan and Norton, 1999) linking workplace design to organizational effectiveness is developed[14].

4. *Charette process:* Based on the findings of organization context analysis, the design concepts will be evolved and prioritized using a charrette-like process.

It involves several small groups simultaneously discussing parts of the "big picture. The groups will pass their ideas on to the next group for improvements.

5. *Strategy map:* It provides direction and key concepts in design. In fact, the use of BSC serves two purposes—(i) to initiate discussion on goals, Mission, external constraints, etc. and

(ii) development of a strategy map and a measurement matrix. Table 10.4 shows an example of the matrix.

TABLE 10.4 Matrix of Measurement for Workplace Design

Desired change	Workplace strategy	Measures	ES	BP	HC	F
Better coordination	Reduce visual and spatial barriers within and between groups	Observation and survey of interactions		X		
Improvement in sharing of knowledge	Provide more space for meetings, workshops and conferences	Information requirements survey	X	X	X	X

ES—Employee satisfaction,   BP—Business processes,   HC—Human capital,   F—Financial.

REENGINEERING

According to Hammer, reengineering is the fundamental rethinking and radical redesign of business processes to achieve dramatic improvements in critical, contemporary measures of performance such as cost, quality, service and speed[15].

Characteristics

Some of the important characteristic features of reengineering are as given under:

1. *It considers fundamentals:* It suggests looking at the basics and starting from roots.
2. *It is process oriented:* A process is defined as a series of steps designed to produce a product or a service to a customer. Reengineering focuses on processes that enable an organization function properly.
3. *It is radical in approach:* Reengineering in a political form is similar to a coup than to a parliamentary democracy. It calls for throwing out everything that exists and reconstituting a new organization based on fresh ideas.
4. *It produces dramatic improvements:* It does not believe in small improvements; it aims at total reinvention. It is an all-or-nothing proposition that produces dramatically impressive results. Reengineering... can't be carried out in small and cautious steps. In political form, it is much closer to a coup d'état than to the methods of a parliamentary democracy.

Steps in Reengineering

We find differences in the steps suggested by different writers, though the purpose is same. For instance, Harrison and Pratt suggested a five step model[16]: (i) Determine customer requirements and goals for the process; (ii) Map and Measure the existing process; (iii) Analyze and modify existing process; (iv) Design a reengineered process and (v) Implement the reengineered process.

Relatively with simple labels, Manganelli, and Klein proposed the following steps[17]:

(i) Preparation
(ii) Identification
(iii) Vision
(iv) Technical and social design
(v) Transformation

Table 10.5 presents a typical reengineering process[18].

TABLE 10.5 Steps in BPR

S.No.	Phase	Tasks
1	Prepare for BPR	Consensus and approval Cross functional team formation Vision development
2	Map and analyse	Process mapping Activity based costing
3	Design new processes	Benchmark processes Design new processes
4	Implement reengineered processes	Managing resistance Making alignment Establish process linkages Demonstration of new process operations Training people for new operations
5	Monitor and improve	Monitoring Collecting feedback Making improvements

Prepare for BPR

The question that rings bell for the reengineering process is: Is BPR necessary?

1. Consensus and approval: A survey of executive opinions and meetings for discussing the need for change and ideas for transformation will help provide answers to the question. Once a consensus is built on the need for change, and the breakthrough business goals, approval for reengineering is obtained from top management.

2. Cross-functional teams: A cross-functional team with key players is established. It has to operate without any dislocation to normal functioning of the organization and work on the game plan for change.

3. Vision development: Keeping in view the strategic direction supplied by top management and changes in environment and customer requirements the mission or vision statement is formulated. It helps establish guidelines for change. Also it can act as the flag around which to rally the troops when the morale begins to sag and it provides the yard stick for measuring the company's progress.

Map and Analyse Process

In the second phase process analysis is carried out.

1. *Process mapping:* Just as companies have organization charts, to understand authority flows, reengineering needs process maps to give a picture of how work flows through the company. It can be used to better understand and significantly improve business processes and bottom-line performance.

While some organizations prefer the Hammer and Champy way of designing a new process, without examining the existing process, some other build a new process based on a thorough understanding of the existing one[19]. The former approach seeks to evolve a more imaginative, theoretically sound model, and the second one combines practical outlook with imagination in its creative exploration.

2. *Activity-Based Costing (ABC):* After the identification of various processes with their interconnections, the consultant will make an estimate of the amount of time necessary for the activity.

Design New Processes

In this phase the aim is to produce alternatives to current processes.

1. *Benchmarking:* As the main idea of reengineering is to create a radical design, it is important to know how good the processes are in other organizations. Hence, this phase starts with benchmarking. Benchmarking is the comparing of both the performance of the organization's processes and the way those processes are conducted with those relevant peer organizations to obtain ideas for improvement.

2. *Design new processes:* The design process involves selection of right processes for integration. The choice is based on three criteria:

- *Dysfunction*: Which processes, from functional point of view, are the worst?
- *Importance*: Which are the most critical and influential in terms of customer satisfaction?
- *Feasibility*: Which processes are most likely to be reengineered?

On the completion of the design with the potential improvements to the existing processes, the model is to be subjected to ABC to analyze factors, like the time and cost involved.

Implement the New Process

The full scale launch of the process redesign involves the following steps[20]:

1. *Managing resistance:* As there will be resistance to change, it would be prudent to run a culture change program simultaneously with the reengineering process. The change program should aim at 'winning the hearts and minds of everyone involved in the BPR effort'.

2. *Alignment:* Once this has been done, the next step is to moving from existing one to the new process. During the transition steps are taken to align the organizational structure, systems, and styles with the redesigned processes.

3. *Process linkages:*   Use of Work Breakdown Structure (WBS) or the BPR software technologies will be helpful in defining the causal and time sequential relationships between the activities planned.

4. *Validation:*   Using prototyping and simulation techniques, the transition plan is validated.

5. *Demonstration:*   Pilot versions are designed and demonstrated to establish credibility among employees.

6. *Training:*   Suitable need based training programs for the workers are initiated.·

Monitor and Improve

Implementation does not end with installation; it is an ongoing process of internalization and improvization.

1. *Monitoring:*   The first step is monitoring two things—the progress of action and the results. The progress of action is measured by the extent of acceptance and accommodation of the new process in the organization. This can be found from employee attitudes, customer perceptions, supplier responsiveness, etc. Information can be obtained through attitude surveys and discrete fireside chats with members of reengineering team.

2. *Feedback:*   A performance tracking system through ongoing measurement of performance, team reviewing and feedback loop provides valuable data for correction and improvements.

3. *Improvements:*   Continuous improvement of performance is ensured by periodical exercises of remapping and redesigning. The incremental changes will strengthen stability as well as quality of the system. In fact, it is desirable to integrate TQM with BPR, which when complement each other, and produce wonderful results.

Box 10.5 provides guidelines to ERP implementation.

BOX 10.5   Guidelines to ERP implementation

Jet Airways, implemented ERP first in 2000 in response to IT developments; again in 2005, when it moved to international operations. In both the cases there is realignment of its processes in the area of human resources and other concerned departments. The process necessitated people involvement and changes in their working styles. According to the CIO, the entire exercise was viewed positively within the organization. Based on the experience the CIO provides following guidelines:

- *Process documentation:*   First of all, a CIO and his team should make efforts to understand the existing processes, and document the details like—activities, persons doing them, time and cost.
- *Change management plan:*   The team must evolve a change management plan. The team should be clear about the implementation process and be aware of process automation's impact.

- *Estimation of benefits:* The objectives of the project in terms of cost reductions, revenue earnings, manpower reductions required, etc. should be identified and estimated. The benefits will be the project's return on investment and an understanding of the expected benefits serves as a monitoring mechanism after the project goes live.
- *Environment sensitivity:* A CIO should keep in mind that business is never constant. He should keep his project environment sensitive to identify requirements that keep on changing. No company should project plans for more than three years.
- *Stakeholder involvement:* Business stakeholders have an important role as there will be two sides—those who have face challenge of playing new roles and those who benefited by simplification of roles. As such, the exercise needs partnership between business and IT.
- *CIO as a business guy:* He has to communicate in the language of business and win support. IT projects involve manpower downsizing and learning. As such there is resistance from the lowest level to the middle management level.

Source: Yuga Chaudhari, Business process reengineering: A sensitive issue for Indian organizations available at http://..searchcio.techtarget.in/news/1370433.

ORGANIZATIONAL RESTRUCTURING

The need to change structures, roles, and functions and realigning them with the new objectives arises whenever organizations adopts to changing environment and develops new strategies. The case of restructuring of Defence Research Development Organization (DRDO) given in Box 10.6, succinctly explains why restructuring is important for organizations. It also outlines the action plan of restructuring.

BOX 10.6 DRDO Restructuring in the Pipeline

Prime Minister Manmohan Singh, asked the state-owned Defence Research and Development Organization (DRDO) to speed-up research and development of new military technology as "our competitors have often moved at a faster pace." He said, organizationally, DRDO should aim at becoming leaner and making the best use of its human, financial and technological resources". It is criticized that, the DRDO was set-up in 1958 as the primary technology generator and systems developer for the Indian defence forces, has failed in its mission of making India self-reliant in the development and production of defence hardware. The failure is attributed to the inefficiency and underperformance caused by the highly centralized and top heavy institutional set up of DRDO. Critics point out that from the outset, DRDO has been buffeted by a variety of problems including a lack of vision and motivation and wrong and distorted policies due to interference from bureaucracy, military establishment and powerful export lobby.

(Contd.)

BOX 10.6   DRDO Restructuring in the Pipeline (*Contd.*)

Defence Minister, A.K. Antony, ordered restructuring of the 50-year-old organization. DRDO will be made a lean organization and its 47 laboratories will be trimmed by a merging process. The merger may be among the laboratories or with other public-funded institutions with similar discipline[21]. A technology commission, chaired by the defence minister will be at the helm of affairs to guide DRDO on futuristic strategic technologies. The management of DRDO will be decentralized by forming seven clusters on specific areas, each headed by a Director General. Aviation cluster will be at Bangalore and the missile cluster will be in Hyderabad. The Director Generals of these clusters will report to Chairman, DRDO on timely execution of various projects. A new commercial arm of DRDO will be created as a private limited company to deal only with spin-off products and technologies meant for civilian use. A human resource consultant will be hired to examine its man power policies and suggest innovative ideas for induction of talented persons.

Source: DRDO restructuring in the pipeline, www.deccanherald.com > National, 13 May 2010, and DRDO Restructuring: Boosting Self-Reliance? by Radhakrishna Rao
www.ipcs.org/.../drdo-restructuring-boosting-self-reliance-3172.html.

Strategies for Restructuring

There are different strategic initiatives like mergers and acquisitions, new product development, joint ventures, strategic alliances, diversification and outsourcing, that call for organizational restructuring. Box 10.7 presents the case of Bharti Airtel. It is suggested that voluntary or pre-emptive restructuring can provide more benefits than the restructuring done under the imminent threat of bankruptcy or a hostile takeover. The case of Jet Airways substantiates this point of view.

The rise in fuel prices and the crisis of the financial markets globally had led to the downturn in traffic. It entered into a code-sharing alliance with No. 2 carrier Kingfisher Airlines to cut costs, and has put its international expansion plans on hold and trimmed capacity. It retrenched 800 flight attendants and 1100 employees across all categories and departments. However, the protests from retrenched and political parties had made it to take back the decision[22].

BOX 10.7   Organizational Restructuring by Bharti Airtel

Bharti Airtel, which has operations in 19 countries across Asia and Africa, announced a new organization structure that came into effect from August 1, 2011. Mr. Sunil Bharti Mittal, Chairman & Managing Director, described the new organization structure as a major step towards building an organization of the future.

The vision of Airtel is to be the most loved brand enriching the lives of millions and the restructuring exercise aimed at creating a de-layered and more agile organization, with business and functional synergies to realize the vision. The new structure is proactively created as an integrated customer-centric organization and it provides a common interface to customers. It will have two distinct Customer Business Units (CBU) with clear focus on B2C (Business to Customer) and B2B (Business to Business) segments. The B2C business unit is designed to provide a solid platform to offer comprehensive services to the retail consumers, homes and small offices, by combining the erstwhile business units—Mobile, Digital TV, Telemedia and other emerging businesses, like M-commerce, M-advertising, M-health, etc. It focuses on customer experience, product and service and builds an ecosystem around the B2C services.

The company is expected to announce changes to over 3,000 job positions to create more meaningful, empowered roles to employees.

Source: Bharti Airtel Announces Organisational ... www.worldofgprs.com/.../ bharti-airtel-announces-organisational.

Restructuring Process

Restructuring is similar to reengineering and comprises the following steps:

Developing a case for change

This step involves assessing existing structure, identify deficiencies in view of current and future needs, and preparing an appropriate redesign plan. Michael Goold and Andrew Campbell proposed nine tests to assess existing organizational structures[23]. Table 10.6 and Table 10.7 present them as fitness tests for growth and performance respectively. If answers for any one of them fall short of the benchmark, these are probably the right places to initiate change process..

TABLE 10.6 Four Growth Fitness Tests

Fitness drivers	Tests of fitness	Description
Service strategy	Service advantage test	Does the present design facilitate proper attention to the priorities in each service area?
Corporate strategy	Parenting test	Does the design support the strategic initiatives and add value to the organization?
Innovation and adaptation	Flexibility test	Does the design facilitate new ideas and experimentation? Is it flexible enough to adapt to future changes?
Constraints	Feasibility test	Does the design overcome performance constraints?

TABLE 10.7 Five performance fitness tests

Fitness drivers	Tests of fitness	Description
People	People test	Does the design provide congenial climate for motivation and display of strengths available in people?
Knowledge and competence	Redundant hierarchy test	Do positions at all levels in the organization add value?
Specialization	Specialist culture test	Does the structure foster specialization culture and protects it from the dominant culture?
Coordination	Difficult links test	Does the organization have coordination difficulties on a networking basis?
Control and commitment	Accountability test	Does the design provide control processes that are motivating and economical?

Formulate a new business strategy

Develop new strategy keeping in mind the changes in market, technology and economy. For this constitute a high level cross-functional internal team. Depending on the need it may be supported by an external consultant team. The team will evolve a strategy by conducting organization-environment analysis.

1. *Identify gaps which warrant change:* The next step is conducting a study of as-is business processes, and examine the possible impact of change on the organization. Identify gaps or add-on features to make the processes suitable to the new organization.

2. *Develop and execute a change management plan:* This the critical stage in the change process. Based on the analysis develop a structural change plan. Identify vision and flexible road map for restructuring. Choose a team to manage the project, which can take lead in communicating, motivating and coordinating the change. Integrate organization-wide changes, and align the structural changes with systems, culture, HR, strategy and so on. Identify the affected stakeholders and consult them. Involve employees to help them cope with and work through the change cycle.

3. *Define performance metrics:* For the proposed changes, develop suitable metrics for evaluation of process, value additions, and outcomes.

4. *Review and improve:* Conduct periodical reviews to find whether the changes are in accordance with road map and yielding expected outcomes. Capturing learning for improving future redesigns.

An illustrative case of restructuring is given in Box 10.8.

BOX 10.8 Restructuring by P&G

On 28 January, 2005, P&G announced its decision to acquire 100% of the Gillette company. The companies have over 138,000 employees and 30,000 people employed in different countries. A day before the formal announcement, the news of merger was leaked to the employees and created a sense of shock and fear in the minds of the employees.

- *Collaboration:* The decision was taken collectively by the CEOs of the two leading and profitable ones with the objective of creating the greatest consumer products company. The CEO of Gillette, Jim Kilts, and the CEO of P&G, Alan Lafley, had a friendly process of negotiations that signified collaboration. There were no lawyers or bankers present at their first meetings.
- *Culture problems:* There were many similarities as well important differences between the two companies. P&G was like a family and Gillette was like a team. With clear role definitions and goal setting, Gillette instilled performance and commitment culture. This gave the organization agility. On the other hand, P&G emphasized on consensus, and lacked decision-making speed. Michelle Stacey, who headed Gillette's sales to dental professionals observed that at P&G, people tended to put everything on paper, in meetings, whereas in Gillette PowerPoint presentations are common. P&G has she focus, whereas Gillette has he focus, from

marketing point-of-view. P&G employees always make a reference to company's Purpose, Values, and Principles (PVP) in discussions and decisions and this is peculiar to Gillette people.

- *Partnership:* The integration was smoothly managed by the personal involvement of senior members of the management and support given by consultant, grow talent. At each stage of the project, they worked with commitment, to secure the best results. Two teams—a core integration team and a cross-functional team were formed, and due diligence of all the departments was carried out and all possible impediments were removed.

- *Communication:* As the leak of the merger news sent shock waves among employees, the very next day, CEOs personally explained the rationale of the decision and most of the employees were convinced. Some of the talented employees of P&G left while some others expressed unwillingness to join the merged company. They were given severance package along with the employees found surplus.

- *Transition support:* One post-merger challenge was design of sales and distribution model. P&G, in India followed a Golden Eye distributor model according to which 30 key distributors with their own sales officers were chosen to operate across India. In contrast, Gillette chose 700 distributors and operated through company-employed sales officers and field personnel. Gillette provided transition support to minimize impact on business and successful distributor disengagement. The pay package of employees of Gillette was protected. Efforts were made to see that those leaving organization had at least one job offer in hand.

- *Training and career planning:* Wit the support of Grow Talent the company took several steps to support employees.
  - One day training program for existing employees from Gillette and also to those who were to leave the company.
  - A three day career fair was held in 4 locations. About 37 best employers were contacted in India, across various sectors and the interested organizations were invited to the fair. To those organizations who could not participate in the career résumés of suitable candidates were submitted.

- *Mentoring and counselling:* Support had come from many sources to the employees in dealing with anxiety, handling the transition news with friends and family and in making career choices. The sources included:
  - Leaders both at the corporate and divisional level
  - Grow Talent consultants
  - Internal mentors at Gillette
  - Peers

The supportive organization culture built by Gillette over the years reflected in the support services. The employees and the ex-employees were like a family with members looking out for each other. The ex-Gillette employees gladly stepped in to counsel, guide and even look for job opportunities for employees, who chose to quit the organization.

(Contd.)

BOX 10.8 Restructuring by P&G (*Contd.*)
• **Workshops:** To enable managers to handle separation meetings and handling employee reactions, and support the reemployment campaign, workshops were organized. For impacted employees also workshops were conducted aimed at providing emotional, intellectual and landing support. Emotional support programs helped employees share the job loss news with friends, relatives and family, and deal with consultants approaching with job offers or opportunities. Intellectual support was provided by organizing 10 workshops across 4 locations in India. In addition one-on-one coaching support was made available and a '30 second commercial'—a brief to introduce oneself' was presented. Landing support was provided by skill development programs by undertaking skill enhancement workshops, providing e-learning initiatives—access to 'Right from Home' web link, and helping candidates in preparing effective resumes and personal marketing campaigns.
• **Outcomes:** The results of career transition support were impressive. Gillette won the DMA Erehwon Innovation Award for 2006 for its career fair idea. Other important benefits were good will and a league of strong brand ambassadors for Gillette and no loss to business momentum.

Source: Yasmeen Rizvi, 'Picking the flowers'; Acquisition strategy as a tool for survival and growth. A case analysis of the acquisition of Gillette India Limited by Procter & Gamble. Available at www. iitk.ac.in/.../Marketing and Case Study pef.czu.cz/~kaderabkovat/.../PS_procter_and_gamble_gillette.pdf

SUMMARY

Technology has been changing the lives of people in the society and the work life in organizations. It is capable of producing quality, productivity and profitability to organizations. Employee involvement refers to structural and process interventions that increase information, knowledge, power, and rewards and enable employees perform better. Employee involvement practices include—information sharing, leadership practices, team approach, quality management initiatives, Reward linked programs and work improvement designs.

The focus of socio-technical systems is on the design of work systems in factories and offices, to foster and improve relations between the dehumanized employees and employers. The guiding principle of Socio-technical systems is: *If a technical system is created at the expense of a social system, the results obtained will be sub-optimal.*

Job redesign has gained significance recently in the context of lean organizations. Hackman and Oldham (1976) argued that the intrinsic value and motivating potential of a job are based on certain task dimensions: task variety, autonomy, identity, significance feedback and skills variety. The critical psychological states include the following:

(i) Experienced meaningfulness of work
(ii) Felt responsibility
(iii) Knowledge of results
(iv) Internal work motivation

(v) Job satisfaction

(vi) Growth satisfaction

There are different approaches to job redesign—mechanical, motivational, biological, and perceptual and motor. Job redesign analysis involves: (i) designer analysis, and (ii) employee analysis. Workplace design is need-based and goal-oriented. One comprehensive analytical approach is 'Workplace 20–20' a methodology for linking workplace to organizational goals and strategy. According to Hammer (1993) reengineering is the fundamental rethinking and radical redesign of business processes. Harrrison and Pratt (1993) suggested a five step model[16]:

(i) Determine customer requirements and goals for the process

(ii) Map and measure the existing process

(iii) Analyze and modify existing process

(iv) Design a reengineered process

(v) Implement the reengineered process

Organizational restructuring may occur when organizations adapt to changing environment and develop new strategies. Restructuring is similar to reengineering and comprises the following steps:

(i) Developing a case for change

(ii) Formulate a new business strategy

(iii) Identify gaps which warrant change

(iv) Develop and execute a change management plan

(v) Define performance metrics and

(vi) Review and improve

EXERCISES

I. Review Questions

1. Explain the purpose of interventions.

2. How is job redesign done?

3. How is work place design implemented?

4. Explain the purpose and process of organizational restructuring.

5. What is reengineering and how is it carried out?

6. Explain the dimensions of socio-technical design.

II. Discussion Questions

1. Discuss when and how the following interventions are implemented: (i) Job redesign, (ii) Work place redesign and (iii) Socio-technical design.

2. Explain with case examples: (i) Reengineering and (ii) Organizational restructuring.

3. Explain the purpose of techno-structural interventions. What are their merits and limitations of the interventions? List the precautions to be taken in implementing the interventions.

📖 **MINI-PROJECT**

In your management institute, find the involvement of students in various activities and decision-making. Interview 20 active students and find out from them their expectations regarding their involvement in design of programs that enhance academic excellence and institute image.

 WEB ASSIGNMENT

Read the following research article and prepare a brief not exceeding 600 words for classroom discussion.

Effect of Employees Involvement in Techno-structural interventions ...
www.cluteinstitute.com/proceedings/2010.../Article%20327.pdf

CASE STUDY

IT Reengineering at IOC

Indian Oil Corporation Limited (IOCL) is today the largest commercial enterprise in India (in terms of sales turnover) and the first Indian company to find a place among Fortune's Global 500 list of the world's largest companies (ranked 232 in 1999). Its success can be attributed to clear vision, effective management, and adoption of changing technology. M.S. Ramachandran, Chairman of Indian Oil, "IT has always played a strategic role in the development of our company. IT helped in giving us a competitive edge, but has also helped in increasing the sales of our products, and improved efficiency of our refinery and pipeline divisions."

Background

Beginning with punch cards in 1960s, for applications in sales and finance, the company migrated in 1972–73, to second generation computer systems. During 1976–77, third generation computer systems were imported from East European countries, and COBOL-based applications were used. Around 1983–84, the company employed RDBMS applications, in collaboration with HCL, TCIL and Wipro. In 1987–88, IOCL shifted to an online transaction processing system. The software was developed in-house. Around 1992–93, the company introduced SCADA (Supervisory Control Administration System), which helped the company monitor, control and administer its activities. However, the company faced a problem of incompatibility of the systems working in different branches as they had separate systems administrators. The need to consolidate infrastructure and bring in operational efficiency was felt due to the following pressing demands.

Lot of processing time was wasted. The company deals with almost 0.75 million transactions happening per month, and the number was only increasing. Also, due to the wide geographical spread, data had to be transported from all locations to a centralized point. To keep track of all these transactions and for providing quality service to its customers, the company needed a robust communication system based on very high-end software, which could handle these transactions. Thus, IOC felt the need for IT reengineering to integrate the islands of information across the company.

Embraces SAP

IOCL launched Project *Manthan* in 1996, to transform IOCL into a transnational integrated energy company. The company appointed M/s Price Waterhouse Associates (PWA) and with their support designed *Manthan* project. The project comprised four stages: (i) Conceptualization and design, (ii) Development and debugging, (iii) Trial implementation, and (iv) Stabilization and standardization.

SAP/R3 along with the associated oil and gas specific software IS-OIL and CIN was selected as Enterprise Resource Planning (ERP) solution for customization and implementation across the company, integrating important functions, such as finance and controlling, human resources, production planning, sale and distribution, material management, plant maintenance, project system and quality management. Several add-ons, that addressed vital functions such as demand forecasting, distribution planning, crude selection and refinery planning were planned. The Company had implemented in March 2004, SAP/R3 at 292 out of 530 sites at a cost of ₹ 182 crore (against the initial estimate of ₹ 95.95 crore including hardware software and consultancy).

Audit Report

The IT audit report highlighted the following failures of the company in implementation of the project.

1. It failed to evolve a long range plan and strategy, duly documented with performance indicators and targets.
2. The company was not able to identify the tangible benefits of the project.
3. The company had not appointed an exclusive committee to monitor the IT reengineering project.
4. There was a lack of coordination and it resulted in a delay of over two years.
5. The company did not develop adequate in-house expertize and hired five outside consultants at an expenditure of ₹ 9.56 crore. This was an avoidable expenditure.
6. The company relied heavily on PWC and asked them to select the ERP software. It was not in the work scope of the consultants.
7. The company had not prepared a proper IT road map and failed to communicate about IT project and future to people at all levels of the organization.
8. There was total negligence in providing training to all users for operating in the new technological environment.
9. The company did not configure all as-is and to-be business processes into SAP. This failure had resulted in gaps in the functionalities provided by SAP and the business processes.
10. There was no check on the performance of consultants. A system of regular reviews to evaluate delivery of consultants, as laid out in contract, was not instituted.

11. There was a total failure in achieving Critical Success Factors (CSFs) though implementation of SAP at 292 sites was completed.
12. Whatever, improvements were obtained; they were not ingrained into all the relevant processes of the organization as a whole.

Discussion Questions

1. Identify the goals of the Manthan project?
2. Based on the theoretical model of BPR implementation, identify in what stages the company has failed?
3. Based on your observations in the case, what guidelines do you suggest to companies embarking on BPR.

Source: Indian Oil Corporation Limited Reengineering Project (Manthan)
www.intosaiitaudit.org/hosted_external.../India_1IOCL.pdf and
IOCL fuels IT infrastructure growth with SAN—Storage Special...
www.expresscomputeronline.com/20020826/storage4.shtml, 26 Aug. 2002.

REFERENCES

1. Adapted with permission from Sanjay Kumar Arya, D.K. Sharma, Shyama S. Natarajan and Vipin Kaushal (2003), Job Redesigning-Key to cost containment and TQM in Hospitals, *Journal of the Academy of Hospital Administration,* Vol. **15**(1), available at www.indmedica.com/journals.php?journalid=6&issueid=23...

2. Quoted in Apostolos Apostolou (2000), Employee involvement, Report produced for the EC funded project, available at ww.urenio.org/tools/en/employee_involvement.pdf

3. Best Companies To Work for 2011: Special Category Awards ... articles.economictimes. indiatimes.com > ... > Agilent Technologies, 24 Jun. 2011.

4. *Quote*: *Employee Ownership*, Motivating Employees Article-Inc ... www.inc.com > Leadership and Managing > Employee Benefits

5. Hellriegel, D., and Slocum, J. (1979), *Organizational Behavior*, St. Paul, MN: West Publishing.

6. Emery, F.E. and Trist, E.L. (1960), Socio-technical systems. In C.W. Churchman, & Verhulst, M. (Ed.), *Management Science Models and Techniques,* Pergamon, Oxford: Vol. **2**, pp. 83–97.

7. Kling, R. and Scacchi, W. (1980), Computing as Social Action: The Social Dynamics of Computing in Complex Organizations, in M.C. Yovits (Ed.), *Advances in Computers*, **19**, pp. 249–327.

8. Socio-technical systems: From design methods to systems... lscits.cs.bris.ac.uk/docs/BaxterSommervilleSTSE%20IwCAccepted.pdf

9. Brockner, J., Grover, S.L., Reed, T.F., & Dewitt. R.L. (1992), Layoffs, job insecurity and survivors' work effort: Evidence of inverted-U relationship. *Academy of Management Journal*, **35**: pp. 413–425.

10. Hackman, J.R. & Oldham, G. (1976), Motivating through the design of work: Test of a theory. *Organizational behavior and performance*, Vol. **16**: pp. 250–279.

11. Salanick, G. & Pfeffer, J. (1978), A social information processing approach to job and task design. *Administrative Science Quarterly*, Vol. **23**: pp. 224–253; Weiner, Y. and Verdi, Y. (1980). Relationships between job, organization, and career commitments and work outcomes—An integrative approach, *Organizational Behavior and Human Performance,* Vol. **26**, pp. 81–96, and Griffin, R.W. (1991), Effects of work redesign on employee perceptions, attitudes and behaviors: A long-term investigation, *Academy of Management Journal*, **34**(2), pp. 425–435.

12. Campion, M. & Thayer, P. (1987), Job design: Approaches, Outcomes, and Trade-offs, *Organizational Dynamics*, Vol. **15**, pp. 66–79.

13. Designing for Organizational Effectiveness | Whole Building Design... www.wbdg.org/resources/design_orgeff.php?r=cafm

14. Kaplan, R.S. and Norton, D.P. (1996), The *Balanced Scorecard: Translating Strategy into Action*. Harvard Business School Press, Boston, MA.

15. Hammer, M. and Champy, J. (1993), *Reengineering the Corporation: A Manifesto for Business Revolution.,* London: Harper Collins.

16. Harrison, Brian, D., Pratt, Maurice D. (1993), A methodology for Reengineering Business, *Planning Review*, Vol. **21**(2), pp. 6–11.

17. Manganelli, Raymond, L., Klein, Mark, M., (1994), The Reengineering Handbook: A Step-by-Step Guide to Business Transformation, New York: American Management Association.

18. Subramanian Muthu, Larry Whitman, and S. Hossein Cheraghi (1999), Business process reengineering: A consolidated methodology, National Conference on Industrial Engineering Theory, Applications and Practice, November 17–20, San Antonio, Texas, USA available at Business Process Reengineering: A Consolidated ... webs.twsu.edu/whitman/papers/ijii99muthu.pdf

19. Hammer, M., Champy J. (1993), *Reengineering the Corporation: A Manifesto for Business Revolution.*, London: Harper Collins.

20. Reengineering—Strassmann, Inc., www.strassmann.com/pubs/reengineering.html

21. Political bureau, Organizational restructuring in DRDO in the offing, The Financial express, available at www.financialexpress.com/.../organisational-restructuring.../296157/13 April 2008. Sujana Metal retains TSMG on organisational restructuring, Sunday, July 20, 2008, news.oneindia.in/.../sujana-metal-retains-tsmg-on-organisational-restr...

22. Jet Airways to lay off 1100 more employees www.financialexpress.com/.../jet-airways...lay-off...employees/37408...16 Oct 2008.

23. Goold, Michael and Campbell, Andrew (2002), Designing effective organisations, New York: John Wiley & Sons, and Do You Have a Well-Designed Organization?—mbaNERDs,your ... mbanerds.com/index.php?title=Do_You_Have_a_Well...

Strategy Interventions

Vignette: Strategic Support

The Indian arm of Finnish company, global leader in the field, evolved an ambitious plan of becoming a billion Euro company from 150 million Euro company in short span of 2 years. Potentia was engaged to make the BHAG (the Big Hairy Audacious Goal) into an implementable plan comprising of SBU/Function/Department goals and individual Key Result Areas (KRAs). Potentia developed vision, mission, values and strategy in close association with the top management. In a short span of eight weeks, Potentia facilitated the process through strategy alignment, SMART goals to individual managers, and action plans for implementation. It set-up a robust mechanism for individual review and monitoring of goal achievement.

One of the largest regional private Internet Service Providers (ISP) was facing the challenge of growth. It has targeted five-fold growth to be achieved in five quarters. This required a new thrust on leadership and high performance culture. The organization consulted Potentia to devise appropriate interventions. Potentia identified the need to catalyze the leadership development and design of a focused strategy for realizing the fast-paced growth. They employed AI-based intervention to create awareness and appreciation and a positive mindset for fast-paced change. The 'working session' that followed it resulted in enhanced clarity, high commitment and impact on the organizational culture.

A zoological institution that had three distinct departments that were not aligned or cooperating with each other. While they shared a passion for the mission of the zoo and for conservation, there was an inordinate amount of time spent on employees in conflict. This affected internal efficiency, employee satisfaction and ultimately, the quality of the customer experience. Accelera was roped in to bring about a change. The consultant conducted an assessment and found that while the organization's mission was shared, the three departments had very distinct goals and professional standards. She initiated a strategic partnering project for teams to identify the key cross-functional processes and develop synergies for partnering at essential decision points. She conducted work sessions among the departments for teams to develop solutions for improved cooperation and decide on standards to guide their interactions with one another. As a result, conflicts between departments dramatically decreased, employees discovered new ways to cooperate and, together, they developed new programs to greatly enhance the customer experience[1].

The above cases provide a view on strategy interventions designed by OD consultants. In this chapter, we will discuss a variety of interventions in the area of strategy making.

INTRODUCTION

When environments were stable, companies were function-centric and they focused on internal efficiencies and productivity, to be successful. The dynamic environment of today, has changed the rules of the game and companies have become customer-centric. They are focusing on innovative value additions to enhance competitiveness. As changes from current sate to a future state have become rapid and uncertain, the ability to predict the future and prepare for future markets through strategic planning has gained significance. In view of this, we find a rise in the number of OD consultants. They have been offering a wide variety of services to enable and support organizations in designing and implementing strategic interventions.

RANGE OF INTERVENTIONS

What kind of interventions do we find in this category? To have an idea, let us consider what a consultant does. Box 11.1 presents an over view of the interventions from a practitioner's perspective.

BOX 11.1 Strategic Interventions—A Practitioner's Perspective

Strategic Interventions can be done across the life cycle of a business group, a single organization, a Business Unit (BU/SBU) or for a product/service. To initiate such an interventions, a Business Baselining exercise for the business is often carried out which could include a Gap analysis (as-is analysis), historical financial analysis (at least 3–5 years), market and competitive analysis, scenario analysis, business risk analysis, staff skill/competency analysis, supply/demand chain analysis, econometric analysis or a visioning and discovery exercise.

Using a combination of the above exercises, it is possible to identify the following critical parameters (illustrative) for the business where the interventions need to be applied, namely,

(Contd.)

BOX 11.1	Strategic Interventions—A Practitioner's Perspective (*Contd.*)

- Business momentum (sustainable rate of growth)
- Cash flow cycles (cash to cash conversion cycle)
- Investment cycles (capital commitment cycles)
- Revenue mix (quality of revenue streams)
- Product mix (economic life of products on the maturity curve)
- Resource productivity and capacity (equipment, people, supply chain)
- Econometrics (market competitiveness)
- Governance, Risk and Compliance (degree of market freedom)
- Learning & Development (skill and competency)
- Goal congruence (stakeholders alignment to business goals)

Using the above context, the firm's stated need and intervention context is assessed which could include the following business situations (illustrative):

- Incubation
- Growth
- Change
- Modernization
- Diversification
- Divestment
- Merger and acquisition
- Business process alignment
- Business maturity
- Innovation

Based on the above 2 sets of inputs, a set of impact or outcome statements are generated that capture the tangible expectation of the client and grouped into a set of SMART Goals, that can be measured on a periodic basis. A group of interventions is then picked as part of the call-to-action exercise which could include programs, activities and tools that impact different organizational aspects, as given in the Table below:

Interventions	Examples	Tools (Genre)
Corporate	• Visioning and Discovery workshop/workouts • Product/Service portfolio analysis • Business transformation workouts • Research and Innovation workouts • Business excellence framework (EFQM) • Organization Development exercises • Coaching and Mentoring of business leaders/managers • Growth/change management programs	• Gap analysis • Scenario analysis • Vision-driven goal setting • Strategy maps • Revenue cycle analysis • Ratio analysis • Enterprise valuation • Econometric analysis • Market analysis • EQFM assessment • Balanced scorecard (company)

Interventions	Examples	Tools (Genre)
Functional/ Cross functional	• Functional transformation/alignment exercises (Finance, HR, Procurement, Materials, supply chain, marketing, sales, sourcing, IT, IS, Governance, etc.) • Value engineering • Process reengineering • Technology and process automation • Business analytics • Build and detail • Measurement and review • E-commerce	• Business Blueprinting • Process modeling • Product life cycle analysis • Value Stream mapping • SPC/SQC • BPR/BPM • Lean/Six Sigma • Toyota production system • Business intelligence tools • Agile tools • ITIL standards • CRM standards • Quality systems • Business/Operational audits • Cross functional audits • Capability maturity assessment
People	• Organization structure analysis • Organization effectiveness analysis • Work unit sizing and modeling (scale/expansion) • Organization and work unit performance • Assessment and development centers • Interpersonal and group behavioral dynamics • Compensation modeling • Employee incentives and rewards • Creative and transformational leadership	• Competency assessment (MBTI, BEI, E-DISC) • Balanced Scorecard (unit) • KRA/KPI measurement • Organization performance summary (bell curve) • Experiential learning tools • Employee Satisfaction surveys • Compensation frameworks • Reward frameworks • ESOP frameworks
Special	• Incubation of new businesses • Social impact programs • Corporate Social responsibility • Sustainable development programs	• Due diligence frameworks • ROI analysis • Triple bottom line reporting • Social impact analysis

Source: Prof. Ranganath Iyengar, Managing Partner & Founder
© SIIPL Entrepreneur Research and Resource Center 2012
Strategic Interventions India Pvt. Ltd. (www.siiplconsulting.com)

INTEGRATED STRATEGIC CHANGE MANAGEMENT

The simultaneity of strategy and organizational design in the context of external and/or internal disruption is the essence of integrated strategic change (ISC) management.

Features

ISC is characterized by the following features[2].

1. ISC considers three-time states: The present, the transition, and the desirable future
2. ISC seeks to align systems with strategy and strategy with environment
3. It is a highly participative process. The traditional strategic change planning was confined to top management. The ISC integrate strategic change from the top down, and across silos to achieve their target goals
4. It has four iterative and overlapping phases: strategic analysis, strategic choice, designing the change plan, and implementing the plan

Strategic Change Process

The strategic change process is a four step model.

Strategic analysis

It involves examination of organization strategy and environment fit. The study involves:

(i) Analysis of an organization's external environment
(ii) Current strategic orientation of the company
(iii) The degree of the effectiveness of the strategy in fulfilling the mission and objectives of the organization.

Strategic change may be prompted by positive changes, like transition to a global economy, and changing industry structure or negative forces, like intensifying competition and technological obsolescence in the environment. It may be driven by progressive steps, like diversification or expansion or threats like suboptimal or declining organizational performance, and stakeholder dissatisfaction. Sometimes, with changes in environment, the present strategies may be outdated and require new orientation.

Strategy making

It requires an integrated approach and in-depth analysis of organizational capabilities. It involves the following steps:

1. *Vision development:* The change initiative starts with the creation of a dynamic strategic vision. This requires support from the top to the bottom. It should be an outcome of a holistic perspective and integrated participation at all levels.

2. *Strategic goal development:* The CEO and Senior Leadership Team (SLT) together prepare measurable, strategic goals and get approval from the board.

- The goals should be able to direct future effort towards creation of significant, sustainable, and scalable increases in shareholder value.
- To integrate past with present, the goals should take into account the past three to five years of actual performance and future three to five years.

- To ensure measurability, they should be stated in quantitative terms. Examples: employee and customer satisfaction (in per cent), employee turnover (in per cent), margins (in per cent), market share (in per cent) and return on assets (in per cent).
- To gain support from lower level employees, they are cascaded down into the business units and departments.
- To maintain focus and align priorities within the organization in conjunction with other challenges and initiatives. The quantitative strategic goals should be tracked and communicated to all stakeholders on a quarterly basis.

3. *Establishing strategic initiatives:* The next step is developing initiatives to achieve the goals. Two approaches are found in practice.

- *Outside-in approach* looks at organization to know how things are being done with reference to values and capabilities. By considering them, it seeks to shape vision, goals and strategy.
- *Inside-out approach* seeks to know how things are being done with reference to external changes. It looks at an external opportunity and develops strategy for realigning internal processes and capabilities towards it.

It is better to create a chart, showing various initiatives. It helps understand interdependencies of each initiative throughout the organization and identify gaps or overlaps, if any, to mitigate implementation resource challenges. Examples of strategic initiatives include: brand repositioning, talent development, new product development, and reorganise sales force. For example, a client organization decided to strengthen the company's goal of increasing market share in Asia and Europe by appointing new president, CFO, and two new directors. A global search was planned and executed to achieve the goal.

Strategic plan design

At this stage, identification of enabling strategic assets, is very important. Organizations must make inventory assets available, as some of them may be helpful to support strategic initiatives. For instance, an agile organization can more effectively share and integrate assets across organizational units than a less agile one. Examples of strategic assets are: agility, governance, talent, creativity, image, technology, brands, culture, intellectual property, distribution, financial resources, location, services, etc.

The mapping of enabling assets helps organizations to recognize gaps between the assets required and assets available for effective implementation of the strategic initiatives. As a prerequisite to launching strategic initiatives, organizations, should take steps to build the required assets. For instance, a client organization chose to develop value-added product enhancements. It found the need to upgrade its technology infrastructure to enable the initiative. When the assets were mapped it was found that they did not have skilled technology program managers competent to effectively manage internal and external resources. Immediately, steps were taken to appoint senior program managers.

Anticipation of resistance and developing counter strategies should be an integral part of the design process. For instance, an organization aims to upgrade its technology; its employees should have change readiness. When an employee attitude survey indicates a significant degree of resistance to innovation, the company may adopt gradual implementation strategy. It can begin the change process with a pilot group comprised of a few enthusiastic employees.

Employees are to be explicitly communicated about strategic orientation of change and the road map of change process. Specific roles are to be assigned to right candidates to play roles of change agents.

Implementation of the plan

The transition from old to new will be smooth and effective, when proper control measures are developed and communicated to people concerned. The measures include: budgets and timetables, specification of responsibility, allocation of resources, employee commitment and satisfaction, etc. By proper monitoring mechanisms, implementation is made effective.

ORGANIZATION DNA ANALYSIS

Successful organizations like 3M, HP, Johnson & Johnson, Motorola, and Walt Disney could not only perpetuate but also outperform competitors owing to their unique traits which are codified by the familiar metaphor of DNA. Booz & Company developed organizational DNA framework to understand the organization's personality and identify its idiosyncratic behaviors. DNA is the genetic blueprint that determines the features of a cell, a body and, an organization[4].

In many organizations, people talk about the roadblocks to progress in various ways as illustrated here.

"It's a great idea; of course, in our organization it'll never happen." I do not think I should go an extra mile; what is in it for me".

Organizational DNA analysis helps to overcome such problems. Like the four nucleotides that comprise human DNA, the DNA of the living organization has four bases.

1. **Structure:** Type of organizational hierarchy, number of layers and reporting relationships, etc.
2. **Decision rights:** How and by whom decisions are truly made, beyond the lines and boxes of the organization chart.
3. **Motivators:** What objectives, incentives, and career alternatives do people have?
4. **Information:** Metrics of performance, coordination of activities, knowledge transfers, expectations and progress, etc.

The Seven Organization Types

Based on the way the four bases are made functional, we find seven organizational types as given in Table 11.1. Three of them just-in-time, military precision and resilient work can execute and produce better results. The other four—fits-and-starts, over managed, outgrown and passive-aggressive cannot effectively implement their strategies, and therefore, tend to perform poorly[3].

TABLE 11.1 Seven Types of Organizations

S.No.	Type	Problem	Action
1	Passive-aggressive	People agree but not act. Resistance to change due to apathy	Create an enthusiasm to change and willingness to be in the lead position
2	Fits and starts	People come up with ideas and work but in the absence of strong direction from the top and a solid foundation of common values below, there are clashes of interests	Retain people by permitting freedom, but set up systems for coordination. Establish values and direction from top
3	Outgrown	A well-coordinated efficient organization faces the burden of growth. Though opportunities are there, ability to respond is low. The failure is partly due to top-down approach.	Undertake organizational restructuring, decentralization and leadership development
4	Over managed	Organisation has too many layers Over analysis by managers leads, bureaucratic functioning, and political decision-making.	Undertake organizational restructuring.
5	Just-in –time	Despite absence of consistent, disciplined structures and processes, the organization has talent to respond to opportunities just-in-time.	People supportive structures are needed. Design flexible organic structures.
6	Military precision	It is a hierarchical organization and operates under a highly controlled management model. Fails to meet the unexpected changes.	Design flexible organic structures
7	Resilient	The organizations are flexible, forward looking. They attract team players. They keep changing.	Reinforce the positive attitudes and improve skills

Workshops

A DNA (Deoxyribonucleic acid) Workshop focuses on vision and strategy development of an organization. It can help develop a brand definition for the organization, define core values and principles by which the organization stands, identify problems and prioritize action goals. The process involves three phases: discovery, navigation and action[4].

1. In discovery phase, the heart of the leader is probed, key factors for success are researched and the competitive landscape is understood.
2. In the navigation phase, the courses of action are planned for journey into the future.
3. In the action phase, the implementation plan with metrics is developed.

Box 11.2 describes one-day off site workshop for senior management conducted by Booz & Company.

BOX 11.2 Org DNA Workshop

The off-site workshop delivers the greatest impact when it involves the senior and upper-middle management ranks of large organizations. The process begins with Booz & company setting up a customized, password-protected *Org DNA Profiler®* Website for the client. A cross-section of the organization (typically between fifty and five hundred or more individuals) designated by the client take the survey. There are questions on demographics, to help compare groups. The data is analyzed and provided as an input to the one day workshop. Discussion in the morning is based on results of the *Org DNA Profiler®*. In the afternoon, organizational roadblocks are identified and solutions are suggested with the assistance of Booz & Company facilitators. Breakout discussions help bring senior managers from different parts of the organization together to take part in problem solving processes.

Source: OrgDNA: Improve your organization, www.orgdna.com/apta/improve.cfm, An Org DNA Profiler®—is available on the webpage www.OrgDNA.com, of Booz & Allen.

ORGANIZATIONAL TRANSFORMATION

Transformation, by definition, is an emergent phenomena, it is neither predictable nor controllable. Living systems transform themselves in an evolutionary manner. The transformation of very complex systems are beyond simple knowledge, design and control. It requires a recursive, iterative, feedback process to accomplish the change[5].

Benefits

Organizational transformation helps organizations achieve excellence which can be measured by various measures, like time-to-market, operational costs and productivity. Generally, firms hire consultants when overall business performance is deteriorating, employee dissatisfaction is increasing, or there is a general decline in economy.

Process

Organizational transformations initiative looks across a whole organization to discover the right way to initiate a change process. A simple 3-step approach to implementing lasting change is unfreezing, changing, and then refreezing of business practices. The process can be explained as follows:

Stage 1: *Break with the past*

The step involves additions and deletions. The Board of the company may introduce outsiders with expertise onto the top management team. Several structural changes, like rotation of managers, promotion of trustworthy young managers, utilization of project teams, designing a suitable bonus/incentive system may be introduced. Some mechanisms that worked in the past may be removed. Some companies may modify traditional command-and-control management style to achieve more rapid implementation of change; others may switch over to democratic leadership style to strengthen latest demands, like customer relationships, innovation and R&D. Some organizations create a sense of crisis as a lever for organizational change.

Stage 2: Manage the present

The top-down approach may be continues to break with the past in some parts of the organization. Three important measures to maintain or quicken the pace of change are:

1. *Empowerment of employees:* Employees may trained to acquire the ability to learn and exercise authority to act.

2. *Benchmarking:* Positive move can be achieved by identifying and adopting the best practices with and other organizations. This will require a well organized knowledge management system.

3. *Resource management:* Reconfigure, divest and integrate resources. This involves everything from streamlining business systems to removing non-aligned employees to consolidating new acquisitions operationally and culturally.

Stage 3: Invest in the future

The consolidation of new approaches and rationalization of old practices and systems will continue till satisfactory change is achieved. The process continues to give final touch by looking into future.

1. *Continue exploration of new ideas and business practices:* This can be achieved by encouraging innovation. Routinize trial and experimentation by developing a culture which encourages informed risk-taking and learning from mistakes. Simultaneously, developing new capabilities is also required.

2. *Create new paths:* This is possible when new capabilities are employed for creating radical innovations that will help secure sustainable competitive advantage to the firm.

Thus, by involving outside consultants, key managers, and active employees, organizations can react successfully to changes in the environment by establishing new developmental pathways. Box 11.3 describes how Maya Townsend (Founder, Partnering Resources) transformed a losing concern into a profit making one.

BOX 11.3 Organizational Transformation

Maya Townsend has helped the new CEO turn around a software company by energizing employees with the information on the strengths of new strategy initiatives. The new CEO felt that turnaround needs more than restructring, He told the consultant: "I wanted to look introspectively to determine fundamentally who we are, what is important to us, and where do we want to go."

First the consultant developed a plan to get the executive team to think creatively about the company and its future. The executive team made elaborate discussion and identified the core purpose and values and evolved a strategy for the company.

(Contd.)

BOX 11.3 Organizational Transformation (*Contd.*)

As next step, the team was asked how they would implement it without any hitch. They felt the need to communicate it to the managers and involve them in the action plan. Accordingly, to gain acceptance as well as benefit from their experience, managers were engaged in defining actions needed to achieve the strategy. The executive team presented the strategy to all employees in an energized, creative meeting. It facilitated employees see their role and understand how their goals contributed to the core purpose of the company. The CEO expressing satisfaction on the outcome observed: "… the management of the company is more energized. We have built the foundation to be a truly great company."

Source: Adapted with permission from OD Network. www.odnetwork.org/

Box 11.4 presents a case of organizational transformation which is focused on team building.

BOX 11.4 Transformation by Clarity Consulting

A leading global enterprise software firm initiated a major change by way of restructuring. The massive change was necessitated by the increasing demands of their customer base and making organization more nimble, creative and responsive. While different functional areas have achieved significant changes, the Marketing organization, under its maverick leader, lagged behind. The initial diagnostic revealed that success would require harnessing the entrepreneurial spirit of the people towards a shared goal and fostering cross-functional teams for service delivery.

Clarity consulting worked side-by-side with multiple client project teams for three-weeks to diagnose the organization. They facilitated a two-day leadership meeting to identify strategic initiatives and partnered with senior leaders to set up cross-functional project teams (requiring substantial stakeholder engagement) for each initiative. They structured and led a comprehensive stakeholder engagement approach including, targeted communications. They developed and managed a robust governance and communications approach for the transformation. At the end of the first phase of work, the results of the project teams were such that they attracted the attention of the senior leaders of the organization.

Source: Adapted with permission from Clarity Consulting: What We Do: Examples Of Our Work, www.clarityconsulting.com/what-we-do/examples-of-our-work.php.

DOWNSIZING

Downsizing has become common today. In response to external/internal pressures and motivated by the need to control costs and make organizations more agile, sleek and effective , strategies for downsizing (reducing the number of employees) or delayering (removing excess layers of management) are employed. Like any other strategy, it can be either proactive or reactive. Here are some cases of job cuts and closure of branches.

Owing to the economic slowdown HSBC, a multinational bank announced that it would slash 1,200 jobs, in 2012. The number equals to one-fifth of its Indian head count. Other foreign banks, such as Citibank and BNP Paribas are pressurizing employees to perform better. Other firms that laid-off executives in India, in 2011, include Daiwa Securities, Bank of America Merrill Lynch, Nomura and UBS. Currently, the life insurers are not only downsizing employees but also closing branches due to the slump in the business. According to IRDA, private life insuring companies shut down 593 branches during 2010–11. The largest private insurer, ICICI Prudential Life, itself closed down 100 branches in the past year[6].

Major Concerns in Downsizing Process

The decision to downsize should take into consideration the human as well as organizational concerns. There will be major change in the employment relationship and the way people perceive, think and behave at work. A sense of insecurity and a need for taking care of their employability and career development will spread through the organization.

Human side issues

Downsizing impacts the psychological and functional aspects of three main groups. The reactions of each group will be different and call for attention of management.

1. *Losers:* The employees who are given pink slip will experience fear, anger and frustration. They need counseling, rehabilitation and retraining as well as referrals to secure jobs in other organizations.

2. *Survivors:* The employees who remain with the organization may experience survivor syndrome. Psychologically they will be disturbed and functionally challenged. They will not have same confidence and zeal to work for the organization. They may be assigned new tasks or additional workloads. They may require learning new skills and working for longer hours. Also, they may face the threat of withdrawal of some benefits and privileges. The end result may be suspicion, distrust, and poor morale which lead to fall in productivity and quality of work.

3. *Managers:* The managers of the victims of downsizing will lose respect and confidence of employees. As such, there is a need to inform employees about downsizing and make the process fair and transparent. For this, managers are to be equipped with good interpersonal skills and patience to handle the sensitive cases. The managers of survivors have to take measures to restore their confidence and enhance morale. They should be capable of handling the work load and training problems in a tactical way.

Organization side issues

Downsizing will create some problems and challenges to organization. The unintended consequences may include detrimental effects on innovation, productivity and morale.

1. *Organization restructuring:* There may redesign of organization due to closure of branches or departments and delayering.

2. *Attrition:* If downsizing is done through Voluntary Retirement Scheme (VRS), there may be more applications than expected. This happens when industry is growing and job opportunities are attractive.

3. *Loss of key personnel:* An important problem is the loss of important skills. The challenge of finding suitable replacement or rehiring in place of the experts and experienced who quit organization, is a difficult one.

4. *Equality and diversity affected:* Downsizing may create an imbalance on equality and diversity in organization which was hitherto appreciated. Future recruitment and promotion decisions are to be directed to restore both of them.

Support services

The role of consultants and HR department is critical when downsizing is made on a large scale. The steps like identification of jobs and employees for downsizing and handling separation require expertise and they cannot be left to Line Managers. Some of them may be not capable; some of them may be sensitive, and hold feelings of guilt. Some of them may be unprepared to handle the situations. As such, it is important to train line and HR managers.

Steps in Downsizing

Institution builders and other consulting firms have suggested the following steps for effective downsizing[7].

Envision your organization

Identify the changes that may take place in the environment that impact the organization and figure out what the organization will be in the next 2 year period. Prepare a half-yearly vision statement in terms of size, customers, capabilities and culture. Each of the six months assessments, help organization progressively downsize employees. The survivors at the end of the 24 months are the core team.

The manpower planning exercise involves the following aspects:

1. *Demand estimation of employment needs:* There should be careful assessment of assessing the skills or jobs needed for meeting current and future demands. A skill matrix maybe developed.

2. *Manpower inventorying:* It involves taking stock of employee number, skills and contributions.

3. *Identification of new jobs/skills:* A comparison of future needs and available manpower will help know the need for new skills or jobs.

4. *Identification of excess manpower:* An important fall out of this exercise is the identification of surplus manpower and identification of the need for downsizing. The jobs/skills that are no longer necessary in the organization are to be identified and critically examined for their relevance and possible modifications for continuing.

Get your core team onboard

Some companies make the mistake of not involving or at least informing the employees who are supposed to be part of the core team. As a consequence, the capable ones required by the organization, start looking out for a job, and even secure a job outside. It is a common fact that capable ones get jobs even in a downturn. When they leave, the organization loses talent required for its effective functioning. In view of this, companies are advised to make key people the part of its planning and implementation team for revival and growth.

Define criteria for go decisions

This is the most critical part of downsizing. Different departments and different jobs vary in respect of their criticality for the organizational performance. A common observation is the classic case of separating the wheat from the chaff and letting go the wheat. If this should not happen, criteria are to be laid out and decisions should be made by groups. The factors for evaluation may include—nature of employment, experience, value add to business, and performance. The feedback may be from both internal and external customers. After spelling out criteria and approach to feedback, panels consisting of two eminent external members, two assessment experts and two internal senior managers may be constituted to decide on the downsizing numbers.

Developing Realistic Downsizing Preview (RDP)

An overview of organization consisting of information about the downsizing, explanation of reasons for and consequences of downsizing and details of current and future vision and strategies of the organization to employees is to be prepared and communicated to both survivors and terminated. The aim of the RDP is to induce positive thinking and elicit positive response from employees.

Clearly communicate RDP

Downsizing will be unethical when it does not reflect honesty and concern for employees. Informing employees that organization is facing difficult times, and reducing people is the only option that can help handling the entire process with respect and dignity. Leadership has a key role, as leaders need to be sensitive and develop a clear transition support plan.

Communication of RDP can be done through different media: e-mails, public notices, meetings and training programs. Survivors may be informed of the opportunities to cope with the post-downsizing situation to sustain their motivation to perform better. Terminated may be prepared in advance to cope with the stress caused by pain of separation and anxiety associated with job search.

Provide career transition support

Concern for people leaving organization will help make separation less painful. It will take 3 months or more for a person to find a job. Instead of leaving one to his or her fate, help them by providing transition support. The support may be provided in terms of training, coaching and counseling to increase career self management skills and employability. Assistance in job search can be rendered by providing on-line job vacancy lists and references.

1. *Coaching:* Workshop-based coaching or one to one coaching to help a person in the following aspects: (i) overcome grief, shame, anxiety and anger and regain emotional stability, (ii) identify strengths and weaknesses, especially the attitudes that so far hindered progress. Sometimes, the sessions may help rediscover a hidden skill that may change career direction, and (iii) Chart a career path.

2. *Counseling:* Counseling will help employees to ventilate their ill feelings and regain composure is an essential part of support program. Onsite counselors/telephonic support may be arranged.

3. *Training program:* Training programs necessary for enriching the skills of employees are to be planned.

4. *Placement company:* Sometimes signing up with a placement company may be of some help in placing people. The downside of this initiative is placement companies, in their self interest, may persuade employees to accept a wrong job or a wrong company, from employee point-of-view.

Prepare for the D day

No employee will be delighted by the separation decision. The reaction will be grief and depression. When the Line Manager and HR managers cannot handle the separation brief, the Head of the Department may be involved.

It would be better when scripts on the business case for the decision are made and given to Line Managers and HR mangers to enable them speak in brief, with concern and objectivity.

The duration of the meeting should not be more than 10 minutes. Prolonged meeting will prove more painful to all the participants. At the end of the meeting, direct the employee to see a coach or a counselor to get transition support. With the news of job search support, the employees find some relief and leave with hope.

Communicate with survivors

Reconnecting with survivors is important. The parting of some employees will be painful to the survivors. Let them mourn and maintain contact with the terminated. However, take measures to periodically inform the employees on how the career transition support is helping the downsized employees. Some of them might have started their own units and become your customers or suppliers. Some of them might have got better jobs in Indian or foreign companies. The good news will help rebuild confidence and commitment toward the organization.

Rebuild the organization

Take a freshlook at the organization, its people, processes and technology. It is time to redefine and rebuild the organization to make it more relevant and agile. Consistent with the vision and mission of the business define a long-term plan of development. Seek answers to the questions and let employees know about them.

- What is our business?
- Who are our customers?
- What are our differentiators?

Engage and align employees

Assign leadership roles to the core team and direct them to engage the entire employee force. Involve employees in shaping culture and team building. Gradually, align employees to the new vision and create a new climate and culture.

Create company alumni

As the organization grows, new job opportunities arise. If the company has maintained good relations with terminated employees, some of them may come back and bring with them rich experiences and competencies. It will be a sort of home coming after a sabbatical leave and something worthy of celebration.

OUTSOURCING

Outsourcing refers to assigning a function or service to another, on a contractual basis. The functions outsourced can be simple operational services, like janitorial and landscaping operations to specialized strategic ones, like payroll, software development and customer services. Box 11.5 shows the range of services offered by some consultants operating in India.

BOX 11.5   Outsourcing Consultants

Accenture is world leader with capabilities in application outsourcing, infrastructure out-sourcing, business process outsourcing and bundled outsourcing. With more than 2,44,000 people serving clients in more than 120 countries, its global outsourcing services touch almost all industries and business processes. They assure services that transform their clients' operations, and make them smarter, faster and cheaper. They are experienced in working with visionary organizations and creating innovations in strategic outsourcing.

Outsourcing Consultants specialized in varied services–Logistic Solutions & Supply Chain Management, Distribution Network and Inventory Management, Franchising, IT Services, Flexible Packaging and Labelling, and Imports and Exports.

Madaan & Co., provides services that include IT, BPO, KPO, manufacturing and other fields. Their consultants and lawyers include those admitted to bar in the United States of America and India and have handled legal matters in the USA, India and Europe. They are well-versed with the multi-cultural and the multi-jurisdictional aspects of international business.

Source: Global Management Consulting, Technology and Outsourcing... www.accenture.com/Outsourcing Consultants, www.foroutsourcing.com/; outsourcing Consultants, Offshore Outsourcing...madaan.com/outsourcingconsultants.html.

Strategic Decision

For far too long, there was debate on outsourcing versus insourcing. The reality is some companies do well by outsourcing, as it is done with a strategic intent. Bob Carlson, former group head of IT and telecommunications at HSBC observes[8]:

"Sourcing is not a strategy in itself—it has to be the business strategy that drives the sourcing decision."

The common thread running through different organizations, like Hero Honda Motors, Bharti Tele-Ventures Limited, the National Stock Exchange (NSE), HDFC Bank, Sony Entertainment Television, Hyatt Services India Pvt. Ltd., and HPCL is all of them have chosen outsourcing as a strategic business decision.

Merits and Limitations

It is, important to appreciate the risks as well as the opportunities of outsourcing. In a fast changing environment, outsourcing offers a key advantage. It supports a strategy of rapid expansion without consuming much time scaling up of internal IT and the upfront costs that it requires. Also, it can give a company the opportunity to play on a global scale. However, outsourcing should not be used indiscriminately. Some things, like core competencies and critical problems should not be outsourced.

Process

Outsourcing process involves the following stages:

Strategic analysis

It involves understanding the services or jobs that can be outsourced and the purpose of outsourcing. What does the company seek to improve—quality, reliability, timeliness, cost savings or strategic advantage? The introspective question is: can someone else do it better, faster and cheaper; safely than us? The resultant understanding helps develop a blue print for successful outsourcing, with clear goals and expected end results.

Service provider selection

This step involves developing outsourcing projects and identification of potential locations for the work to be done. Then it is followed by search for services providers and evaluating them for assigning contract. Not every provider is right one to choose. As such, gather information on the provider's business and know their safety record, reputation, strengths and weaknesses, work ethic, performance metrics and current customers. Conduct suitable analysis and evaluate the operations with reference to chosen criteria.

1. *Choose right provider:* The right partner is one who understands the company's business, values, needs and expectations, and is willing to complete the work safely, better, faster and cheaper than the company can.

2. *Contract development:* A long-term agreement is worked out keeping in mind the legal factors pertinent to it, and negotiated pricing and Service Level Agreement (SLA) terms.

3. *Governance:* This is concerned with evaluation of the performance of the service provider. Design a reliable system for tracking in terms of cost, quality, etc. The client company continues the relationship, as long as they have a need, and a service provider can ably satisfy it.

Factors Influencing Choices

Today there are many outsourcing solution providers and they offer variety of services related to different business areas, like IT, finance, HR, and so on. The decision to outsource is a major one, carrying significant risks as well as benefits. It should never be undertaken without due cognizance. The decision requires consideration of the following:

1. *Competencies:* The assessment of the competencies of outsourcing agency is the first step in making the choice. The technical and economic aspects are to be examined from the point-of-view of the services required and expected period of relationship. If the outsourcing agency is not sound financially, there is a risk of failure and the company will be in trouble.

2. *Attitudes and values:* Another important consideration is how outsourcers see the world. Do they see it the same way as customers of the company? Especially, in case of offshore outsourcing cultural fit is critical. There is a difference in nationality and culture and the attendant problems.

3. *Distance:* The more distant the offshorer, the more the challenge of coordination. Distance brings problems of connectivity and reach.

4. *Relationship:* Managing the relationship is important from partnership and cost point-of-view. Relationship must be well-defined. Flexibility and goodwill are far more important than service level agreements and price. Situations are dynamic and everything about the contract keep changing over time, often rapidly, making renegotiation necessary. In fact, the first clause of the contract is the exit clause.

5. *Costs:* The consideration of costs in service as well as exit should be noted. In case of exit, the company should have a way to recover their intellectual property, data and systems.

6. *Contract:* The contract and the relationship must be designed between the firms and it should be independent of the signatories. People may move on causing new problems. Outsourcing is not a transaction, it's a commitment. It is a commitment that must be reciprocated. It is a joint venture and both the parties have skin in the game.

CULTURE ASSESSMENT AND DEVELOPMENT

New firms face the challenge of building right culture consistent with the spirit of entrepreneur whereas going firms show concern for maintaining or changing the culture that governs decisions and actions of people.

Developing Culture

The entrepreneur seeks to build a culture that matches his style and comfort zone. Box 11.6 describes show entrepreneur shapes firm culture.

BOX 11.6   Entrepreneur Shapes Culture

The Founder and CEO of a start-up high-tech firm was interested in establishing a result oriented performance culture. He was operating for the last six months with an initial team of five members. He was playing many roles and was now interested in hiring people and assigning roles to them. He was interested in making people accountable and aligned to goals, with focus on results. He hired Culture Strategy Fit—an organizational culture alignment consultant to define and provide a cultural frame.

   The consultant worked with the group and explored the culture that had evolved to date and the areas that needed attention. The culture discussion helped the team develop shared understanding of the culture fit requirements for new staff. The consultant employed the tool "Leading Culture Snapshot" which allowed the team to confidentially input what was being experienced on a day-to-day basis. It encouraged a non-confrontational discussion on delicate topics that needed to be addressed such as empowerment, accountability and job definitions.

Source: Adapted with permission from: Employee Cultural and Performance Survey | Corporate...
www.culturestrategysurvey.com/

Culture Change

Bringing about a change in entrenched culture is not an easy task. W. Chan Kim and Renee Mauborgne (Blue Ocean Strategy) identified four hurdles that a manager may face when trying to institute broad change in an organization[9].

1. *Cognitive:*   Lack of proper understanding of the proposed change.

2. *Resources:*   Shifting resources away from some areas and towards others, causes temporary loss of authority.

3. *Motivation:*   The drive to facilitate or adapt to the change may be weak.

4. *Institutional politics:*   The political wrangles may lead to apathy. People complain often in such organizations: "In our organization, you get shot down before you stand up."

   To overcome the hurdles, they suggested four measures:

1. *A "tipping point" approach to management*:   Focus on changing people who are influential. Shine a spotlight on their accomplishments; as the message spreds, others start changing.
2. *Get people face realities to learn*:   Unless exposed to the problematic issues or persons learning will remain theoretical and incomplete. Put managers in the front line to solve problems.
3. *Redistribute resources toward "hot spots"*:   Keep resources away from "cold spots" or areas with large resource demands, but relatively low impact.
4. *Appoint a "consigliere"*:   Give importance to an active vocal advocate of right policies and procedures in devising strategies for change.

Suite of Survey Tools

Consultants have evolved different types of assessment tools to analyze cultures, people readiness to change and draw culture road maps[10].

Culture snapshot

It is a broad scan of culture patterns and its report provides a culture scorecard, of an organization's culture strengths and development areas, including priority areas for attention making use of eight dimensions. Table 11.2 presents the dimensions.

TABLE 11.2 Dimensions of Culture

S.No.	Dimensions	Variables
1	Agility	Adaptability, external focus, flexibility, intuition, proactive change
2	Direction	Future orientation, goal alignment (vertical)
3	Engagement	Autonomy, identity, involvement, mastery, purpose
4	Discipline	Execution, process discipline, rational decision-making
5	Performance orientation	Accountability, results focus, work expectations
6	Risk management	Compliance, risk avoidance
7	Collaboration	Cooperation, goal alignment, interpersonal relations
8	Trust	Candour, information sharing, disclosure

Leading culture snapshot

Culture strategy fit is a kind of 360 degree feedback tool that looks at leadership from a culture and organizational systems lens. It helps understand how their actions and speeches shape culture and influence people around them. It provides feedback in four areas:

1. *Explorer Index:* It indicates how the leader demonstrates and supports agility and learning.

2. *Conductor Index:* It measures the ways the leader influences direction, discipline, performance and risk.

3. *Steward index:* It explores how the leader demonstrates collaboration, engagement, openness and trust.

4. *Exemplar index:* It examines the ways that the leader role models the organization's value proposition (e.g. customer experience, innovation, reliability or operational excellence) or primary value driver (e.g. collaboration, performance, or learning).

Workshops

Consultants organize workshops to create awareness of their organization's culture and its subcultures and provide direction for shaping the culture. For instance, culture safari (workshop) of culture strategy fit consists of two modules:

- Module 1 explores the current culture of the organization or group) and based on this understanding.
- Module 2 develops the organization or group needs for the future.

They also offer a one day 'Future-state Culture Executive Workshop' that focuses on articulating the future-state culture needed for the delivery of goals and strategies. Similar assessment tools are designed and used by OD consultants.

Balanced Scorecard

Kaplan and Norton (1992) developed Balanced Scorecard (BSC). It is a multi-dimensional performance scorecard[11]. With mission and vision of the company at the core, it translates the company's strategic objectives into a coherent set of performance measures through four different perspectives as given in Table 11.3.

TABLE 11.3 Components of BSC

Balanced scorecard category	Main objective(s)	Key measure(s)	Target(s)	Overall initiative(s)
Financial	Increase net revenue	Manufacturing costs	Cut manufacturing costs by 10% in this year	Introduce six sigma to increase efficiencies
Customer	Improve customer retention	Repeat purchases	Rise purchases of existing customer from 40 to 50%	Implement customer care program
Internal business processes	Faster order fulfilment	Average time form warehouse to customer door	Reduce average time from 4 days to 2 days	Introduce new quicker shipper order fulfilling system closely related to courier system
Learning and innovation system	More and better improved input from employees	Number of employee suggestions	Increase employee suggestions from present 20–30 to 100	Workshops on creativity and incentive program

Benefits

The most important benefit of the tools is balanced view. Earlier managers adopted a single-minded focus on bottom-line earnings, to the exclusion of other important issues. By forcing to watch all of the key performance factors, the Balanced ScoreCard strikes the right balance in evaluation. It was implemented by several companies in various countries including India. Tata Motors' Commercial Vehicles Business Unit (CVBU) entered the Balanced Scorecard Hall of Fame. Box 11.7 presents two success stories.

BOX 11.7 The Triumph of Balanced Scorecard

Karen Ponce, CEO of Shat-R-Shield, has a mantra: "As President, my job is to work On the business, not In the business." Shat-R-Shield is a manufacturing concern. It produces plastic coated shatter-resistant lamps for the food and consumer products processing and packaging industries. In order to orient the organization toward common goals, Karen introduced the discipline of strategic planning into the business. In course of time, her team learnt to make use of strategy tools like Vision, Mission, SWOT analysis, BHAGs, and Customer Value Propositions. In 2005, Karen came to know about KPI balanced scorecard and decided to try the approach. It took her three years to lay a good foundation for its successful use because for the first time the company is measuring things that were really important, but cared less. Now the company had over 20 objectives.

Tata Motors' Commercial Vehicles Business Unit (CVBU) in 2000, was in financial doldrums. The management deployed Balanced Scorecard taking assistance of mPOWER, known for execution of strategies focused on bringing in solutions based on the Balanced Scorecard and Performance Management Framework. It is the largest implementation and automation of the Balanced ScoreCard methodology with more than 400 scorecards, 8 levels of cascade in the organizational structure and 20,000 measures and 3000 objective owners. It incorporated SQDCM (Safety, Quality, Delivery, Cost and Morale) and VMCDR (Volume, Market share, Customer satisfaction, Dealer satisfaction and Receivables). Through the defining, cascading and communicating strategies across the organization, transparency and proper alignment were created. The company showed tangible improvement in performance just within 2 years of implementation. There was a 40% growth in revenue.

Source: Success stories, Associates of the Balanced Scorecard Institute
www.balancedscorecard.org/AbouttheInstitute/.../tabid/.../Default.asp.
Clients—MPOWER, www.mpowerasia.com/clients.html www.tata.com > ... > Tata companies > Tata Motors > Media releases, 31 Oct. 2003.

Guidelines for Implementation

Companies implementing BSC for the first time may make a few critical mistakes. Here are few guidelines for developing a proper BSC.

1. Be clear with mission and vision statements. They guide the development of goals and performance measures.
2. Start with the data you have on hand, and refine it as you go along.
3. Be objective. The approach is most effective when it is clear. To get right perspectives, take the standard perspective and adjust it to meet the needs of your department or organization.
4. For each perspective, identify leading and lagging indicators. Generally, organizations may not find problem with the financial, process and customer service measures. Difficulty is, found in respect of the innovation and learning perspective.

BSC for HRM

The Balanced Scorecard can be applied to HRM[12]. It leverages the traditional measures for human resources with metrics of performance from four additional perspectives—Financial, customers, internal business processes and learning and growth. Balanced Scorecard will be effective only when important measures relating to objective are identified and aligned with the company's strategic plan.

We will now illustrate how it works with recruitment. Say, the vision of the company is to be an efficient, competitive organization, the objective of recruitment is to reduce employee turnover and improve effectiveness of new hires. HR managers have to develop effective recruiting methods and new-hire orientation methods to optimize the retention of new hires.

To streamline, HR managers have to identify key attributes of loyal and capable employees, utilize technology for recruiting and screening applications, set up right selection methods, integrate branding efforts into recruiting and revise orientation program to ensure new-hire retention. Figure 11.1 shows the BSC for HRM.

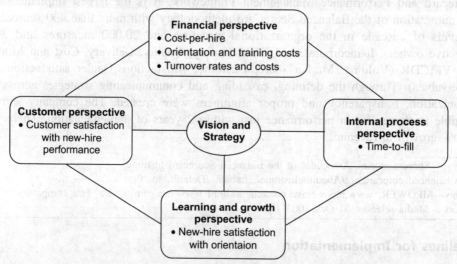

Figure 11.1 Balanced Scorecard for HRM with reference to hiring.

SUMMARY

The dynamic environment of today has changed the rules of the game and strategic planning has gained significance. The interventions are varied from visioning to integrated strategic change management. The simultaneity of strategy and organizational design in the context of external and/or internal disruption is the essence of Integrated Strategic Change (ISC) management. The strategic change process is a four step model: (i) Strategic analysis, (ii) Strategy making, (iii) Vision development, and (iv) Strategic goal development.

Booz & Company developed organizational DNA framework to understand the organization's personality and identify its idiosyncratic behaviors. Like the four nucleotides that comprise human DNA, the DNA of the living organization has four bases—structure, decision rights, motivators and information. Seven organizational types are identified out of which just-in-time, military precision and resilient work can execute and produce better results. The other four- fits-and-starts, over managed, outgrown and passive-aggressive cannot effectively implement their strategies and therefore tend to perform poorly. Organizational transformation involves assessment, strategic planning, communication planning, and transformation. Transformation involves three steps: freezing, moving and unfreezing or break with the past, manage the present and invest for the future.

Downsizing can be either proactive or reactive. Downsizing impacts the psychological and functional aspects of three main groups—losers, survivors and managers. Outsourcing refers to assigning a function or service to another, on a contractual basis. The functions outsourced can be simple operational services, like janitorial and landscaping operations to specialized strategic ones, like payroll, software development and customer services. Today, sourcing is not a strategy in itself—it has to be the business strategy that drives the sourcing decision.

New firms face the challenge of building right culture consistent with the spirit of entrepreneur whereas going firms show concern for maintaining or changing the culture that governs decisions and actions of people. Kaplan and Norton (1992) developed Balanced Scorecard. It translates the company's strategic objectives into a coherent set of performance measures through four different perspectives—Financial Perspective, customer perspective, internal business perspective and innovation and learning perspective.

EXERCISES

I. Review Questions

1. Give a brief description of strategy related interventions.
2. Explain the purpose of integrated strategic change. What type of tools are employed for it?
3. What is organizational DNA analysis?
4. Explain what do you understand by organizational transformation.
5. Discuss the need for outsourcing.
6. Why do firms resort to culture change?
7. What is Balanced Scorecard?

II. Discussion Questions

1. Explain any two of the following: (i) Outsourcing, (ii) Balanced Scorecard, and (iii) organizational DNA analysis.
2. How is integrated strategic change implemented in organizations? What is the role of consultant?
3. If you were a consultant how do you help organizations in (i) Organizational transformation, and (ii) Culture change.

MINI-PROJECT

Identify the performance measures of any two local organizations and prepare balanced score-cards, for them. Make a presentation in the classroom for discussion.

 WEB ASSIGNMENT

Read the following papers and prepare a paper on "Shaping DNA of culture and innovation":

(i) Dr. Reena Agrawal, Innovation: A DNA of Organizational Success
dspace.iimk.ac.in/bitstream/2259/475/1/185-194+.pdf.

(ii) D.K. Srivastava, 'Culture' is the key to an organisation's DNA,
www.deccanherald.com>supplements >DH Avenues.

CASE STUDY

Changing Culture

Culture strategy fit was hired by an organization to study the prevailing culture and make recommendations to bring about changes consistent with the strategy.

Strategy

The company has chosen to become a world class performer and customer-centric firm. It seeks to focus on operational excellence in key business processes, implement its new strategic account management process for development of deeper customer relationships and innovative solutions to meet customers' global needs.

Culture Change Needs

The shift to new strategy required changes in the ways of working and innovating in the organization. Employees must improve efficiency and effectiveness, develop a positive attitude to sharing and exchanging knowledge and building networks and optimize the productive use of existing resources. Managers have to be ready to lead the employees in creating a culture for future success.

Objective of Culture Survey

A culture snapshot is taken with the objective of identifying primary culture strengths and opportunity areas and identify priorities for culture change. The culture highlights are as given under.

Discipline

It is found that people are efficient and disciplined, process-oriented. Decision-making is highly analytic and fact-based. Policies, procedures and processes are followed. Table CS-1 shows the survey results.

TABLE CS-1 Discipline in Organization

Aspect	Statement	(%) agree
Execution	We always finish what we start	77
	We follow through to make sure that our plans are fully implemented	75
	We carefully monitor our progress when implementing an initiative	80
Process discipline	Processes are implemented consistently for similar types of work throughout the organization	80
	Processes are designed to achieve consistency across the organization	75
	Processes are consistently followed	64
Rational decision-making	It is important to have all the facts before making a decision	80
	We conduct a thorough and detailed analysis before making a decision	75
	We rely heavily on hard facts and data when making difficult decisions	84

Agility

While discipline is a culture strength, it has contributed to a strong, internal focus and emphasis on doing what we do well. There is lack of external focus and reluctance to question the relevance of current way of working. They are reactive to external change. Table CS-2 presents the survey findings.

TABLE CS-2 Agility of Organization

Aspect	Statement	(%) agree
Adaptability	We are constantly challenging our assumptions about the way that things are done around here	45
	We are constantly looking for better ways of doing things	45
	We are constantly trying out new ways of doing things	49
External focus	We keep abreast of developments in our sector or industry	52
	We assess the potential impact that external changes may have on our organization	51
	We constantly look outside of our organization for better ways of doing things	52
Proactive change	We anticipate changes in the external environment that may affect us	35
	We make changes in anticipation of external developments that may affect us	33
	We make changes before the need to change is obvious	41

Differences among Organizational Members

Significant differences are found both level wise and department-wise. Tables CS-3 and CS-4 show the data:

- While senior team members are consistently and significantly more positive in their responses to adaptability, other team members are not.
- Sales and marketing staff are adaptive where as administration, operations, quality and supply chain are less adaptive.

TABLE CS-3   Adaptability of Members—Across Level

Statement	Total	Senior leaders	Area leaders	Regional directors	Managers	Other team members
We are constantly challenging our assumptions about the way that things are done around here	45	100	79	67	57	38
We are constantly looking for better ways of doing things	45	100	82	63	62	36
We are constantly trying out new ways of doing things	49	100	87	79	65	39

TABLE CS-4   Adaptability of Members—Across Department

Statement	Total	Adminis-tration	Operations	Quality	Sales & marketing	Supply chain
We are constantly challenging our assumptions about the way that things are done around here	48	62	37	6	78	34
We are constantly looking for better ways of doing things	45	58	34	6	76	26
We are constantly trying out new ways of doing things	49	66	31	6	78	28

Recommendations

For setting priorities, it is important to focus on those with greatest leverage to positively influence the change and also focus on only limited priorities, say 1 or 2. Accordingly the consultant identified the following priorities.

1. Strengthening adaptability across the organization.
2. Strengthening understanding between managers and staff.

Discussion Questions

1. Examine the methodology adopted to obtain information on culture in the client organization.

2. What social, managing, operating or organizational learning practices might be introduced to strengthen adaptability?

Source: This case is adapted with permission from: Employee Cultural & Performance Survey | Corporate ... www.culturestrategysurvey.com/

REFERENCES

1. Adapted with permission from: About us–Potentia, http://www.potentia.in/casestudies2.html, and Accelera Consulting Group, www.acceleraconsultinggroup.com/.. ./organization-development-101...

2. Worley, C., Hitchin, D. & Ross, W. (1996), Integrated Strategic Change. Reading, MA: Addison-Wesley Publishing Company.

3. David Dye, David Kletter & Walter McFarland, The Case of the Passive Aggressive Culture: Transform the Organizational DNA... infinityconcepts.net/services/branding/dna-workshop/

4. OVERVIEW A DNA Workshop is a dynamic two-session and Organizational DNA workshops, Organisational DNA consultants... www.odalternatives.com/Organizational-DNA-workshops.asp.

5. Organization Transformation Solutions, www.avanco.com/sol_org_transform.html. and Organizational Transformation and Change, www.rsvpbusiness.com/.../Organizational Transformation and Change....

6. Life insurance companies downsizing to save costs, www.insuringindia.com/Global/NewsBlog.aspx?id=365, 31 Jan 2011.

7. A Guide to Downsizing for Organization Leaders—Institution Builders institutionbuilders.com/.../ AGuidetoDownsizingforOrganizationLead.

8. Outsourcing—A Strategic Decision?—Cover Story—Network... www.networkmagazineindia.com/200410/coverstory01.shtml

9. How to Change Your Organization's Culture—Management—WSJ.com guides.wsj.com/.../how-to-change-your-organizations-culture/

10. Find out about the Leading Culture Survey—Changing Corporate... www.culturestrategyfit.com/cart-view-all

11. Kaplan, Robert, S. and Norton, David, P. (1992). "The Balanced Scorecard: Measures that Drive Performance," *Harvard Business Review*, Vol. **70**(1), January-February, pp. 71–79 and Tata Motors awarded the Balanced Scorecard ... Tata Group www.tata.com > ... > Tata companies > Tata Motors > Media releases, 31 Oct. 2003.

12. How cans the balanced scorecard be applied to HR? | SHRM India. www.shrmindia.org/how-can-balanced-scorecard-applied-hr.

Chapter 12

Planning and Training Interventions

Learning Objectives

After studying this chapter, you will be able to:

- Identify interventions for individual development through planning and training
- Describe the design and application aspects of such interventions

Vignette: Potentia Delivers Solutions

The CEO of a fast growing mid-sized company contacted Potentia, OD consultants. He was concerned with the impact of a key executive and wanted to give a try before opting for "hit below the belt" solution. Potentia offered Executive Coaching for the key executive, with the aim of catalyzing his thought process, enhance the result-orientation and boost self-confidence. After ten coaching sessions spread over six months the outcome was astounding. The coaching objectives were met. Employee productivity went up by 50%, giving a big boost to the internal HR processes implementation. Eventually, he was adjudged the best CXO and given the role of a strategic business manager.

A Potentia consultant was called, when the Head of Operations, wanted to improve his team performance. The organization required dynamic leader to upgrade the product value chain. Interviews with the executive and informal talks with others revealed that he was caught in the vicious cycle of low self-esteem → insecurity → poor performance. Coaching sessions helped him regain the confidence. The facilitated discussions with the dyadic team of CEO + CXO resulted in this CXO discovering the virtuous cycle of performance → recognition → high self esteem. Impressed with the results, the CEO decided to spend time periodically with the consultant.

The Managing Director of a hi-tech consulting company faced several issues of strategy deployment, employee development, cultivating performance orientation, etc. Potentia Team conducted a deeper analysis and found the need to deal with the interpersonal and collaboration issues amongst the Directors. A customized individual coaching and team interventions were offered. Coaching helped each of the directors, to expand his horizons of thinking and decision making. The group work involving them led to expanding awareness of oneself as well as others, established mutual trust and respect and finally the much desired atmosphere for high collaboration.

The mid-level managers working in the Indian center of an American Software Development company were wasting a number of billable hours. Potentia analyzed the problem. They found lack of proper planning and scheduling as well as poor communication skills led spending more time on conference calls and meetings. They offered a customized communication skills program and it included classroom training, real time critiquing, and one on one coaching. As a result, there was about 30% saving in the time spent[1].

The above cases signify the need for interventions. In this chapter, we will discuss some interventions required, for growing organizations.

INTRODUCTION

"Learning is a way of life in organizations," says Eduardo Salas, a psychological scientist from the University of Central Florida. Modern organizations are employing training and development interventions for the purpose of skill development and changes in attitudes of people. Researchers found that business leaders who view training as a whole system and not a one-time event are more successful in achieving their development goals. This means that what happens before and after the actual training is just as important as the training itself[2]. Whether it is development of an individual or an organization, it should start with planning, and continue to take place with proper monitoring. In this chapter, we will examine different interventions that support development of individuals and groups in organizations.

PLANNING INTERVENTIONS

Richard Beckhard wrote emphasising the need for planning and development of people as follows:

"... in our rapidly changing environment, new organization forms must be developed; more effective goal-setting and planning processes must be learned, and practiced teams of independent people must spend real-time improving their methods of working, decision-making and communicating[3]."

The interventions that help assess and develop future plans and strategies, like the life and career planning, organizational mirroring, future search, visioning, and force field analysis are briefly described here.

LIFE AND CAREER PLANNING

In the present environment, opportunities and risks are on the rise. Single and stable careers are concepts of the past. Today, people are changing jobs and even careers. To have control on their careers, they are empowering themselves with new qualifications and skills. Organizations are responding to the career ambitions of employees, by preparing career paths and succession plans. They are developing employee engagement programs, to retain them for longer periods. In this connection, they are engaging HR consultants who can offer required services.

Career Planning and Management Inc., is a typical HR solutions firm. It works with client organizations to formulate innovative approaches for developing human resources, and enhancing competitive strength of the organization. They provide the following services: organizational career development programs, career counseling, talent management and workforce planning, career development workshops and seminars, skills/competency profiling, professional development, coaching, career audit and intervention, etc.

Career Planning Exercise

Career planning involves looking into the future, and considering personal interests and emerging job opportunities[4].

Chart your career path up to the present

Look into the past to connect it with the present and future. Compiling information on the jobs held by you in the past can be done based on the following headings:

- Jobs held
- Duration
- Emoluments
- What I liked?
- What I disliked?
- Reasons for choosing the job
- Comments on your decision on job

Reflect on current interests and motives

As today's decisions focus on moulding career that fulfils both rational and emotional needs, self-introspection is necessary. For example, some people in midlife do not want to continue with the same career. They want to make a difference, and some people look for progress in the same career. It is hence, important to figure out career interests and motives before making career choices. The following information is necessary for you to move on in career planning:

1. Identification of career anchor and its strength
2. Figure out your interest in career-continuing in the same career or change for a new career.
3. Provide justifications for your decisions

Identify the transferable skills

Take a look at your skills and identify the skills that are transferable to other jobs. In retrospect, trace the development of skills and list the strong ones. From this list, identify the skill cluster (such as plan, teach, calculate, and so on) which in your view will be useful to jobs you prefer to hold in future. It helps recognize career paths in which you can comfortably take.

- Jobs held ...
- Skills used ...

Identify the job trends

Explore the job market and identify the jobs that are fast emerging as prized ones, which are good from growth, status and remuneration point-of-view. Make a list of the jobs and details of career progress.

Set career goals

This is the critical phase of career planning. Evaluate the career options. What exactly are you looking for in work-life? What are your expectations of career? Decide the criteria and evaluate the job options (see Table 12.1).

TABLE 12.1 Evaluating Job Options

Option	Money	Interest	Status	Growth
Continue in the same job in the same organization				
Make a job switch–within the same company				
Make a job switch–within the country				
Make a job switch–go to a foreign country				
Make a career change–Career–A (work as a consultant or set-up own unit)				
Make a career change–Career–B (take a different job)				

Develop an action plan

Recognize the nature and extent of preparation needed for the future jobs. The questions that demand answers from you are:

- *Skill development needs:* How I can grow in my current job, or find a better-fitting job in my current company? What kind of skills is needed for career change?
- *Job search:* What sort of job search strategy should I adopt for finding a new position?

Life mapping with career anchors

Planning for success is about mapping the different aspects of our life. Here is a six-step process to prepare a life map.

- Origin
- Destination
- Vehicle
- Travel bag
- Landmarks and route
- Anticipate turns, detours, and potholes

1. *Origin:* Who am I? This indicates the origin of your career journey. To be clear about who you are, you can try the following exercises:

    (i) Introduce yourself to a friend of yours.

    (ii) Ask your close friend to introduce you to a stranger.

2. *Destination:* "Who I want to be?" Every journey has a destination. "What is my destination? What are my inclinations to pursue physical, emotional, intellectual, and spiritual needs of life and I want to achieve?" To help you in this phase, a good variety of exercises are available. Box 12.1 presents four typical exercises.

BOX 12.1   Destination Identification Exercises

Magic Fairy Exercise—Imagine you've just met the magic fairy. She is thin, translucent and surprisingly able to fulfill any wish you could possibly have. She whispers in your ears in crystal clear voice "*I can fulfill you 3 wishes*". Since she fulfills whatever you ask, you have to be careful in asking. They should be the ones you really need.

Obituary—It may be embarrassing, but your own obituary is one simple way of taking stock of your life goals and where you are in actualizing them.

- *Write your own obituary:* Writing your obituary, many years before your death, gives you a unique opportunity to think about how you'd like to be remembered by people known to you. It helps get perspective on what you've done and where you'd like to go.
- *Friends writing your obituary:* Imagine what your friend would write to another friend about you when you died.

Goal collage—The visual presentation of goals is one sure fire way to find and achieve goals. Creation of a goal collage is very simple.

- *Fix your goals for life:* What do you want, to make yourself happy and satisfied? They can be anything from your office, dream home, cars to pictures of your holiday destinations and the like.
- *Gather materials:* Start to search out pictures that best represent the collection of goals. You can find them from news papers, magazines, and internet. Cut and paste them. You may need a chart/news paper, scissor, glue/paste, poster board, paint brush, pictures, pencils, sketch pens, etc. to display the goals.
- *Watch them:* It is a fun way to keep you focussed on your goals. Even the act of constantly looking for pictures to add to your collage will be helpful to keep you on the success track.

Brainstorming—Another simple way of setting goals for life is by listing the important areas of life and thinking about achievements relating to them. Some illustrative areas are: career, financials, education, family, cultural and literary pursuits, religion and social services. Have a brainstorming session to generate goals in the areas of importance for you. Then select one or more goals in each category that you genuinely want to achieve. Then consider trimming again so that you have a small number of goals that you can focus on. One way to finalize the list of goals that you truly want to achieve is given here.

Write your wish list and keep it aside. Pick it up the next morning and read the first goal/desire on your wish list and ask yourself, "*Is it what I truly desire? Will it make me my life any happier?*" Listen to your heart and not to your mind. If the first spontaneous response is "yes!" put a "+"next to that goal; otherwise put a "–" next to it. Likewise place + or – next to all the goals in the list. Every morning re-read the list and put the appropriate signs next to the goals. After 30 days, you will notice that some of the goals have a lot of "+", Identify those with more + signs. They are your core goals. Concentrate on them.

Source: Roua, Dragos Goal Setting: The Magic Fairy Exercise, www.dragosroua.com > Personal Development, 6 April 2010; Goal-Setting: Developing a Vision & Goals for Your Career Plan ...hrweb. berkeley.edu > ... > Career Development > Goal-Setting, Goal Collage, www.self-help-healing-arts-journal.com/goal-collage-article.html, and Brainstorming Process—Businessballs, www.businessballs. com › teambuilding/games.

3. *Vehicle:* The driving force for any person is passion and mission. Find what you are passionate about. Develop a mission statement and check whether your passion supports the mission. Examine whether it matches your true interests. Vision statements and mission statements tend to collect dust if there isn't a passion driving them. People who are inspired by a passion move mountains.

4. *Travel bag:* Identify and figure out your knowledge, skills, and attitude. Assess their adequacy for attaining your vision. This assessment will helps you develop a travel map with specific landmarks or milestones.

5. *Landmarks and route:* To make long range goals (destination) clear and attainable set short-term actionable goals. They become landmarks to keep you on the right track. The short-term goals must be SMART (Specific, Measurable, Attainable, Realistic and Time bound).

6. *Anticipate turns, detours, and potholes:* The purpose of your life map is to minimize chances of failure due to hasty decisions and diversions in life. However, it may sometimes necessary to modify your plans due to some inconveniences, delays, and other situations beyond your control.

Career anchor analysis

People will have their own prioritized career anchors. Edgar Schein[5] identified eight such career anchor themes as given in Table 12.2. Score each anchor by assigning a number 0 to 5 (where 0 is nil and 5 is a great deal).

After completing this tool, you can know whether you are in the right sort of job or that you need a change. This assessment will give you insight into your future goals and objectives.

ORGANIZATION MIRRORING

A mirror is an object that reflects our image. The *organization mirror* is used when a particular organizational group seeks to identify and improve its image. It involves the following steps[6].

TABLE 12.2 Value of Career Anchors

Anchors	How important this aspect of career to you?	How does this match with your current post?
Technical/functional competence		
Managerial competence		
Autonomy/Independence		
Security/Stability		
Entrepreneurial creativity		
Service/dedication to a cause		
Pure challenge		
Life style		

1. It starts when an organizational group, experiencing some difficulties with other organizational units likes to have feedback from them to improve its functioning and relationships. It invites a consultant to facilitate the process.
2. The consultant holds interviews with key people of other units to get a sense of the problems and their magnitude. It helps prepare the participants, to discuss issues openly.
3. The organizational group hosts a meeting with key people from the related departments. Fishbowl conversation is employed. In fishbowl, there is an inner circle consisting of four or five chairs and outer circle with many chairs. The members giving feedback will sit in the inside chairs and host unit members sit in outside chairs.
4. The manager of the host group sets the climate by stating that the host group is genuinely interested in making changes in its style of functioning based on the views of the participant members.
5. The consultant feeds back to the total group information from the interviews.
6. The participants speak about the host unit in a natural, uninterrupted way while the host group members listen and learn.
7. The host group members seek clarifications to understand the information they have heard. A summary of the discussion is prepared with subheads like—positives, negatives and expectations.
8. Subgroups composed of both host group members and invited participants are formed to identify changes required to improve the host unit's effectiveness.
9. Meeting is again convened. The subgroups make their presentations to the total group. Action plans are drawn, target dates are set and responsibilities are fixed.
10. After some time, on an agreed upon date, a follow-up meeting is held to review the progress and initiate suitable measures.

The Consultant plays a key role in creating a conducive, non-threatening climate, for people to actively participate.

VISIONING

Visioning is used by many organizations to guide them forward. It is designed to create preferred future states and images of potential.

Why Vision?

The vision statement is main spring of inspiration for people and the framework for strategic planning of the organization. It is important when building a new organization, or managing an organization in a turbulent, ever changing environment. A clear compelling vision sets the direction for an organization. It keeps organization focused and motivated and also secure support from other organizations.

Qualities of Vision

A challenging yet achievable vision embodies the tension between what an organization wants and what it can have. Effective organizational vision is said to have the following qualities[7]:

1. *Easy visualization:* It shows a future achievement aims in an easy to visualize forms. It is worded in the present tense for giving a feel that it is happening right at the moment.

2. *Knowledge based:* It is evolved based on the contributions from a variety of sources and active involvement of individuals with required skills.

3. *Values based:* It reflects the personal values of the prospective supporters.

4. *Motivation:* It is easy to communicate and serves as a strong motivator.

Process

The following procedure will help develop compelling vision[8].

Preparing for visioning

1. *Decide the unit:* Decide the focus of the vision development. Is it a division or whole organization?

2. *Decide time frame:* Vision statements can be prepared for two to 10 years. However, five years is common planning as Indian government has adopted five year planning system.

3. *Look at positive in the past:* Focus on positive things about organization and the participating members. This will provide a base on which you can build a platform for future success. Make it brief.

Visioning

1. Develop a worksheet with a list of key questions on unique features of the organization and its values, trends and, challenges and desired future state and goals.

2. Divide people to work in small groups. They will answer all the questions.
3. All the groups assemble and share their answers with other small groups.
4. Small groups individually will then draft a vision statement that embodies these answers.
5. They meet again to work as a big group and prepare a vision statement, agreeable to all.

There are different approaches to writing a vision statement. We outline some of them as follows:

1. *Narrative:* Let each person write their own version of a vision statement. Then he passes their paper on to the next person. The person underlines the keywords and phrases, and passes the paper onto the next person. He does the same thing. Repeat the process until everyone has seen and underlined key phrases or words in vision statements of all other members. Use this as a basis for crafting the final statement of vision. Form a nominal group to do it.

2. *Story:* Let each person in the group write the future story of organization that made headlines of a news paper.

3. *Collage:* Describe the future state with words, pictures and photos.

Testing

The one test of effective vision is, it should be inspiring to one and all in the organization. In writing vision statement, one should therefore have an understanding of how the stakeholders measure the success of an organization. He should use the language of success and write as if the vision has already happened.

Tips to writing vision statement

The following guidelines will be helpful in developing an effective vision statement:

1. *Identify expectations.* Identify your stakeholders. Figure out their expectations and needs.
2. *Have larger picture.* Recognize the trends in environment that impact the organization in the future.
3. *Think big.* Set somewhat ambitious goals. Be creative and think out-of-box.
4. *View long-term.* Make projections for a long period, depending on your ability and interest.
5. *Dream your vision.* Imagine yourself, your people and your organization, sharing the joy of success. Know what benefits the success brings to each group.
6. *Have passion.* Write the vision with a passion. It should be exciting and inspiring to you.
7. *Be objective.* Keep in mind the resource constraints and other possible hurdles. Vision should be realistic too. It should be attainable.
8. *Be open.* Be open to other's ideas and inputs. Share your vision with others. Make corrections if need be and begin to build a plan for implementation.

CONFRONTATION MEETING

Confrontation meeting is a large change methodology, developed by Richard Beckhard[9] in 1965. This is a one-day meeting, but can be conducted for different durations (half day, a full day, or an evening and a morning). It can bring together the management team, or the entire unit or system. It allows entire management group, composed of individual from all levels of the organization to identify problems and to set action plan for solving them.

Process

Table 12.3 outlines the phases in the confrontation meeting. Box 12.2 describes how a consultant conducted confrontation meeting to transform a hospital.

TABLE 12.3   Phases in Confrontation Meeting

S.No.	Phase	Time (minutes)	Activity
1	Climate setting	15	Top manager explain the goals and the opportunity to influence the organization through free expression and group deliberations
2	Information collecting	15	Small, cross-functional groups without any reporting relationships, identify problems and demotivators
3	Information sharing	60	The groups report their conclusions. The meeting leader classifies information for analysis
4(a)	Priority setting	15	Group assembles and reviews the data. The members discuss and develop categories. In each category, relevant items are placed
4(b)	Group action planning	60	The group form functional, natural work units and set priorities for action
5	Organization action planning	60–120	Top management responds to the issues raised by different units
6	Immediate follow up by top team	60–180	The top management team meets, informs commitment to the groups in a few days
7	Progress review	120	Four to six weeks later, top management reviews the progress of confrontation meeting

Source: Based on the description in consulting today, www.consultingtoday.com/.../Consulting Today.

SURVEY FEEDBACK

Survey feedback is a participative data collection approach[10]. It involves the members engaged in managing the work environment in giving feedback on the performance and suggestions to improve it. The stakeholders may be peers, superiors, subordinates and customers. The data collection tool may be a survey, one-to-one interview, focus group interviews and 360 degree feedback. The steps in the three stages of survey feedback can be outlined as given Table 12.4.

BOX 12.2	Confrontation Meeting for Turn Around

NHS Trust Hospital, a market leader for a number of years, had numerous problems like drop in quality, and product recalls. They were about to lose their ISO 9000 accreditation. Summing up the situation, the Managing Director told Thinking Consultancy, "the company's survival is at risk and we need to change some attitudes".

The consultants employed Confrontation Meeting to quickly bring tangible results. As there were 700+ staff to 'process' the exercise was limited to 24 meetings. The meetings were held three weeks apart, and involved supervisors of shop floor operatives comprising a mix of trades, grades and manufacturing locations. Each person was to attend two of these meetings, and the Director was present in all the 12 second meetings. At the first meeting the group discussed issues and incidents that affected quality. At the second meeting, the participants discussed incidents they observed during the intervening three weeks and reported to the Director. They also presented him their recommendations. For each issue raised, the Director came up with a measurable action plans. The consultants recorded the 'action plans' and the target dates.

The action plans comprised a list of specialist equipment required, grassroot feedback on the causes of bottlenecks, a comprehensive list of training needs, list of redundant, ineffective procedures and causes of waste, duplication etc. The intervention worked. Tangible results, demonstrating that attitudes were changing and quality was improving, became visible.

Source: Paul, The *Confrontation Meeting* | LinkedIn
www.linkedin.com/.../Confrontation-Meeting-3778835.S.78070465.

TABLE 12.4 Survey Feedback Process

Design stage	Implementation	Action planning
Define the need and objectives of process	Conduct interviews and focus groups	Team leaders hold meetings for action planning
Brief team leaders and employees about the process	Train leaders on facilitating team discussions	Leaders present reports on progress and results to Senior Management
Design survey and approaches to organize it	Analyze the data and construct a report	Follow-up by senior leadership to ensure progress and accountability
	Provide feedback to leaders	

1. *Design stage:*   In this stage, the change management team will gain an understanding of the focus areas of inquiry and secure participation of employees and team leaders. With the support provided by them, they design appropriate data collection instruments.

2. *Implementation stage:*   In this stage, data are collected through instruments designed for the purpose. Box 12.3 lists questions that may be asked during the interview. The team prepares report based on the data obtained and provide feedback to leaders.

3. *Action planning stage:*   In this final stage, the role of leader is critical. It is the responsibility of leader to familiarize the team with the findings and outlining appropriate solutions for critical examination. Feedback should go into a comprehensive strategy that includes goals, responsibilities, time frames, revisions and reviews.

A series of meetings become necessary. After the initial meeting, leaders have to document the action plans and circulate them for future discussion. To be successful leaders should possess facilitation skills. The following tips will be helpful to them.

- Be optimistic; take steps with good expectations. Express positive points
- Be excited about the information and process
- Be supportive. Work with team members through different stages
- Show clear commitment to utilize the survey feedback

BOX 12.3 Survey Questions

Here are the sample questions that can be asked during the interview:

- What is your organization's vision? Is it realistic? If not how do you redefine it?
- What are the strategic goals of your organization? Are they pragmatic? Do they need reformulation?
- What is your opinion on the style of your superior as a leader? Is the style appropriate? Do you suggest him or her to make some changes?
- What type of culture do you have in your organization? Is it performance-oriented? Does it need modifications? If yes, in what direction?
- Are relationships between persons and groups positive among business units? Are they stressful? What can be done to improve them?
- Are policies and procedures updated? Do they facilitate achievement of desired outcomes? What can be done to make them effective?
- Are there mechanisms to sense and understand impact of environment on the organization? Is organization adaptive? What suggestions do you have to make it more effective?

FORCE FIELD ANALYSIS

Force field analysis is a diagnostic technique developed by Kurt Lewin, It helps identify the variables involved in planning and implementing a program.[11] Lewin posited that in any situation there will be both driving and restraining forces that influence. Driving forces are positive; they push in the desirable direction. Restraining forces are negative; they push in the undesirable direction. Equilibrium is reached when the sum of the driving forces equals the sum of the restraining forces.

How to Develop Force Field?

The steps involved in developing a force field analysis are as follows:

- Choose a scale for assigning a score to indicate the strength of the forces.
- Identify the plan (a course of action) proposed for implementation.

- List the driving forces acting in support of it and assign to each force a score on a scale.
- List the restraining forces and assign a score to each force, from 1 (weak) to 5 (strong).
- Take steps to balance them.

Uses

Force field analysis is useful to make decisions: (i) by identifying the need for change and (ii) by evaluating alternative courses of action.

Need for change

Consider the following situation and forces in the situation:

The supervisor is autocratic; he puts continuous pressure by using stick approach to exceed standards. The organization has good incentive system and fosters competition. Though workers are earning good incentives, they have lost commitment and developed antagonism. It is manifest in absenteeism. They blame work environment and equipment as well as supervision for their loss of interest in work.

Driving forces (D): Autocratic supervision, incentive earnings, and competition
Restraining forces (R): Poor work environment, poor maintenance of equipment and apathy

You are the new manager. You are interested in raising productivity. Increase the strength of driving forces and reduce the strength of restraining forces. If autocratic supervision has a score of 3 (on a five point scale of 5-high and 1-low) and the loss of commitment due to it has a score of 4, then, it should be discarded. A new leadership style is warranted.

Evaluating an alternative plan

Let us develop a work sheet for a project:

Introduction of new technology to expand capacity of production. List the forces as given in Table 12.5 and assign a score on a 5-point scale (5-High, 1-Low)

TABLE 12.5 Forces

Driving forces	Score		Restraining forces	Score
Growth in markets	3		Staff fear for new technology	4
Economies of scale	3	Expansion by new technology	Loss of over time for staff	4
Improve customer retention	2		Environmental impact	2
Competitive advantage	1		Cost	1
Total	9		Total	11

The restraining forces are stronger (11) than driving forces (9). Hence, the project is rejected.

If the management decides to implement it, it requires additional effort to make it successful. The analysis shows that the staff resistance is the major problem. It can be overcome by taking steps like: education (explaining how expansion is important for survival), training (improving skills to overcome fear), and showing advantage (the loss overtime is compensated by a new interesting jobs and higher earnings due to new incentive plan). Measures that reduce environmental impact can reduce the strength of another restraining force.

CULTURAL AUDIT

Culture is how employees describe their workplace and perceive their membership and role in the organization. Building a strong workplace culture is essential for attracting talent and success of the organization. To remain competitive, organizations have to evaluate its values and practices to ensure that they are aligned with their corporate strategy.

A culture audit gives a comprehensive diagnostic of current culture. It helps know whether employee actions and decisions are consistent with the espoused values and norms of the organization. It provides a detailed understanding of the culture desired for the organization. In doing so, it helps develop a road map for cultural transformation.

Process

A cultural audit consists of three stages: assessment, analysis and recommendation.

Assessment

In this stage data regarding culture is obtained from the following measures:

- Review of internal documents
- Review of print and other media (radio, TV, newspaper, magazine, web content, etc.)
- Site visits
- Focus groups
- Surveys and interviews with stakeholders to define desired outcomes.

The Kets de Vries Institute (KDVI) has developed a simple, easy-to-use, psychometrically valid tool for conducting Organizational Culture Audit (OCA). It consists of a questionnaire covering 12 dimensions of organizational culture[12]. Table 12.6 shows the dimensions.

TABLE 12.6 Dimensions of Organizational Culture

Competitiveness	Team work	Learning environment
Social responsibility	Fun	Results orientation
Client/stakeholder orientation	Responsibility and accountability	Respect for the individual
Change orientation	Trust	Entrepreneurship

Analysis

The collected data is analyzed to identify the values and practices in the chosen areas and find gaps between desired and current cultural practices.

Recommendation

Based on the culture gap, future courses of action are outlined.

TRAINING INTERVENTIONS

The interventions aim at enhancing knowledge, skills and attitudes of employees and help them do their jobs effectively during normal and difficult times. We find a myriad of interventions developed and used by consultants. We will limit our discussion to the following interventions: education and training, appreciations and concerns, coaching, counseling, leadership development, mentoring, communication and transactional analysis.

EDUCATION AND TRAINING

Education and training programs can be effective in improving attitudes, knowledge and skills of employees faced with the threat of obsolescence in a dynamic environment. Box 12.4 illustrates how companies encourage continuous enhancement of knowledge.

BOX 12.4   Continuous Enhancement at Tata Steel

Tata Steel lays emphasis on continuous enhancement of knowledge, skills and capabilities of its employees. Tata Steel's training and education programs are designed to realize vision, facilitate career progression and enhance employee performance. Safety training, based on Dupont guidelines is given top priority. Development in managerial competencies and leadership are being addressed through a variety of methods. Reputed organizations, like TMTC, XLRI and IIMs conduct in-house training programs for its managers. On-the-job training is provided through new job assignments, rotations, working in task forces and committees. The company encourages self-study by providing leave facility for higher education and sponsorship for Masters/Doctoral level programs at world-class institutes.

Source: Careers at Tata Steel & Its Training Facilities, careers.tatasteelindia.com/working.../learning-and-development.asp

---

Box 12.5 explains how an organization encourages self-study method of education.

BOX 12.5   Education at WNS

Keshav R. Murugesh, Group CEO, WNS Global Services observed, "At WNS, our focus is not only on career building, but also honing the academic skills of our employees. We believe in the concept of learn while you earn." Consistent with this commitment, they have set-up the WNS Learning Academy, which imparts professional development training to the employees in soft skills and languages.

WNS (Holdings) Limited, is a leading BPO services provider. During 23rd November and 9th December 2010, WNS learning Academy organized an education fair, for the benefit of its over 18,000 employees working in different locations in India and showcased over 100 courses including management, domain certification, and foreign languages of 21 leading educational institutions across the globe. The courses were specially designed for the employees, to suit their time availability and schedules and were offered for a low course fee ₹ 6,000 to ₹ 2,00,000.

Source: WNS creates higher education opportunities for employees,
www.financialexpress.com/news/...education...employees/719333/, 2 Dec. 2010.

Training specialists conduct a wide array of programs, like orientation and on-the-job training for new employees; interpersonal effectiveness and leadership development for supervisors, cross-cultural adaptation programs for expatriates, and language and voice training for BPO employees, They may also design and offer individualized training plans to strengthen existing skills or teach new ones to employees. Trainers also offer situation specific programs to assist employees to cope with changes due to mergers and acquisitions, or new technologies. Box 12.6 describes the initiatives of Punjab National Bank.

BOX 12.6   Customer Service Sensitization

Punjab National Bank (PNB) has contracted Centum Learning, a leading training and development multinational organization, to provide training to 30,000 employees across the country. Centum Learning has already been working with many other companies of repute like American Express, Deutsche Bank, HSBC, Axis Bank, Bajaj Finance, UCO Bank, Allahabad Bank.

The initiative included a customer service sensitization program for a period of 10 months to improve the customer service levels in nearly 65 circles comprising a total of 5,247 branches spread across the country. More than 1,000 certified trainers will train both external and internal customer-facing employees at various levels, including branch managers as well.

The program would focus on necessary soft-skills required to better serve the bank's end customers, through initiating a set of actions around external customer service, and putting an effective coordination mechanism in place for internal customers while ensuring consistent quality and uniform messaging. The content designed in consultation with PNB will be delivered through instructor-led-training mode. Appropriate methodologies to monitor impact of the training solution will be put in place. It is expected that besides helping staff communicate better with customers, the training will also enhance team bonding between officers, clerical staff and sub-staff.

Source: Adapted with permission from Centum Learning to Train Punjab National Bank Employees, August 06, 2012 available at Press releases, www.centumlearning.com/

APPRECIATIONS AND CONCERNS

People at work interact with their co-employees. During these interactions, there will be occasions that require one to express appreciation for good work of others or show interest in discussing work related concerns or sorting out irritations. If they lack this kind of competencies, they cannot make effective team members.

Kouzes and Posner[13] in their book *The Leadership Challenge* wrote: "Feeling affirmed and appreciated increases a person's sense of self-worth, which in turn precipitates success in all areas of one's life. If we have someone in our life who believes in us, and who constantly reinforces that belief when interacting with us, we're strongly influenced by that support".

There will always be challenges and problems at workplace and what is required is the right attitude. Instead of lamenting at the problems, one should see them as opportunities to work with others. In view of these skill requirements of employees, this intervention is designed. It seeks to assess the ability of members in expressing appreciation, and confronting concerns and irritations. This can be done as follows:

1. Assemble a group of people who work together.
2. Distribute the paper with names of members and space to write appreciations and concerns (see Table 12.7). Alternatively, you may separate sheets for each member.

TABLE 12.7 Sample Sheet

S.No.	Name of group member	Appreciation	Concerns
1		1. 2. 3.	1. 2. 3.

3. Ask each member of the group to write down three (any number) positive things in appreciation for each member of the group.
4. Ask each member to write down three (any number) irritations or concerns in interaction with each person of the group.
5. The appreciations and concerns of each member are presented to group to validate. Sometimes, a new perspective may emerge from the discussion.

On the positive side, sometimes raising concerns in a team setting can provide an opportunity for others to validate what is being perceived or to provide another perspective.

COACHING

The recurring themes for the failure of executives across different nations are: inability to cope with transition challenges, interpersonal conflicts, and failure in visioning and meeting strategic challenges. The importance of people holding executive positions need not be overemphasized. We find some people to be some effective; some ineffective. Not surprisingly, people who report to ineffective ones, make comments as:

- "He needs to give up the one-man show. Times have changed; but he didn't."
- "He should quit rubbing people the wrong way."
- "He should be told: stop talking; start listening".
- "She needs to be tough; kindness does not work here."

Obviously, executives need coaching to improve their ways. According to the Executive Coaching Forum, executive coaching is an experiential and individualized leader development process that builds a leader's capability to achieve short- and long-term organizational goals. Box 12.7 describes how coaching is valued by large companies. With more number of companies recognizing and employing coaching method, there is a rise in the number of professional coaches. Box 12.8 describes the emergence of coaching as a new career option.

Assumptions

Coaching is based on the assumption that the person being coached is an individual who likes to excel whether in business, relationships, or personal growth.

1. *Communication skills:* Coaching helps individuals become aware their weak points and learn new ways to communicate.
2. *Emotional intelligence:* Coaching helps people become aware of their emotional strength and stability and learn to interact with others in healthier ways.
3. *Relationship:* Coaching helps two or more people improve their interaction for the good of a larger group.
4. *Performance:* Coaching helps people better understand their job requirements, the competencies needed to fulfill them, gaps in performance, and improvement strategies.
5. *Development:* Coaching helps executives analyze the 360-degree feedback and chalk out a development plan.

Coaching for Different Levels

Coaching can be performed at three different levels—performance, change and transformation. It can be offered to employees at different levels.

1. *Transition/on boarding coaching:* It helps new leaders and executives to learn ways of coping with the challenges on the new job. More important it helps the executive to avoid making costly mistakes that are too difficult to undo.

2. *Succession coaching:* It helps prepare potential candidates for senior management positions in organizations expecting retirements or turnover.

3. *Cohort/team coaching:* It helps in shaping individuals as effective members especially in cross-cultural teams. Each team member will have a coach and internal mentor, who help him a Professional Development Plan (PDP).

BOX 12.7   Coaching in Indian Organizations

Coaches act as objective sounding boards. Top executives like Former SBI Chief OP Bhatt, felt the need for someone with whom they could vet his ideas. Natarajan of Bausch & Lomb observed that Indian executives are mindful of hierarchy and this restricted their sharing of expectations and conflicting points of view with colleagues and juniors. His coach, McRobb, US-based coach felicity, worked on this and helped him to overcome this problem. He was also helped to cultivate professional aggression in making presentations to the Board members. Natarajan is now sending his other senior team members for similar intervention.

In the case of a US-based apparel retailer, coaching helped grooming the new chief. When the India head quit, the company identified a candidate and gave him a coach. Now the firm is considering its new country head for a bigger role at the Asia-Pacific level. Senior leaders of Honeywell India participated in a workshop on 'Leader as a Coach'. Aditya Birla Group organized group coaching for their executives. Airtel rolled out one-on-one coaching intervention for its COOs in the North-East and Assam circles. At Tata Teleservices, Rajiv Arora, Head (HR, business excellence & BPR), a certified coach, trains six to seven top performing executives within the company.

Source: Pande, Bhanu, ET Bureau (2011) Companies from Tata Group, M&M, HUL to HCL hire corporate mentors, *The Economic Times,* August 23.available at Companies from Tata Group, M&M, HUL to HCL hire corporate ...articles.economictimes.indiatimes.com > Collections > Companies, 23 Aug. 2011.

Process

Coaching involves the following steps[14]:

1. First the coach determines the world view of the client by asking him to fill out a self-assessment instrument. Coach discusses the situation of the client—the goals, challenges, strengths, and any other concerns. They build rapport and ensure that the fit is right between them.

2. The coach helps the employee to gather critical data to have full and accurate picture of his or her current reality. Data may be collected from the key stakeholders (peers, customers, supervisors, reports, HR/OD). This data is collected in various ways: (1) Confidential interviews of people who work with the employee (peers, superiors, current and past direct reports, clients, etc.); (2) 360 assessment, such as the Denison® Leadership Survey; and (3) Myers-Briggs® Type Indicator, for a personality assessment. To this the observations of coach may be added, if possible.

3. Next the coach and client review the data, and decide goals for development. They are codified in a Professional Development Plan (PDP). The employee's manager, and the Human Resources or Talent Management representative will be asked to review it. After incorporating their suggestions, the PDP will be put into action.

4. Coaching is done in person, or over the phone. During the coaching period, e-mail or phone contact will be maintained.

5. A minimum of 10 sessions, each session 45 minutes long on an average, are conducted. In some cases, they can be much longer, spread over for a period of six months to one year. Larger part of coaching engagement is spent gaining a clear and accurate picture of the client reality. As such, in terms of the coach's time investment, coaching engagements are front-end loaded.

BOX 12.8 Coaching—A New Career Option

Harvard Business Review estimates, executive coaching is over $1-billion industry in the world. In India, the market is valued between ₹ 650 crore and ₹ 2,000 crore. As the understanding of executive coaching is growing the industry is moving to a high-growth trajectory.

According to Manchester Consulting Group study of Fortune 100 executives, coaching resulted in a Return on Investment (RoI) of almost six times the program cost as well as a 77% improvement in relationships, 67% improvement in teamwork, 61% improvement in job satisfaction and 48% improvement in quality, Similarly, a study of Fortune 500 telecommunications company, Matrix Global, found executive coaching resulted in a 529% RoI.

The demand for certified and competent coaches is on the rise. Some companies have internal coaches. Engineers India Limited adopted the concept of 'manager as coach' and about 20–25 managers doubled up as coaches. Max group, NIIT, Idea Telecom, Aircel have their own internal coaches. In view of this, senior executives are increasingly considering coaching as an alternative career. The president, Fortis Healthcare and former MD, ICI took to coaching and has already coached around 20 executives at Fortis. Youngsters, like Rahul Rai, 39, a mid-career high-performing professional in an IT MNC, quit his company to take up coaching as his career.

Currently, there are two schools in India offering International Coach Federation (ICF) certifications—Coach for Life, in partnership with OD Alternative and Result Coaching Systems in partnership with Franklin Covey India. Australian coaching firm, Coach U, is likely to set-up its office here. These schools offer accredited coach training apart from coaching.

Source: Pande, Bhanu, ET Bureau (2011) Companies from Tata Group, M&M, HUL to HCL hire corporate mentors, *The Economic Times*, August 23.available at Companies from Tata Group, M&M, HUL to HCL hire corporate ...articles.economictimes.indiatimes.com > Collections > Companies, 23 Aug. 2011.

COUNSELING

Counseling is an enabling process. It helps people by encouraging them to use their own rational, emotional and spiritual intelligence, to find ways for solving problems and grabbing opportunities related to work and life. The goal of counseling is changing the attitudes and behavior of the client and enhancing satisfaction.

Types

Counseling has varied contexts—from remedial to preventive. It could be anything from helping people cope with stress, preparing people for a change, becoming appropriately assertive, communicating more harmoniously with team members, to choosing a career option. A broad categorization of counseling types can be as follows:

Performance counseling

Some workplace problems, like interpersonal conflicts, stress due to targets and deadlines, failure to make right decisions, etc. may manifest in poor performance levels. In such case, counseling is employed to deal with performance related aspects, to help employee find solutions and improve performance.

Personal and family well-being

Since organizations hire not merely the hands or mind but the whole person, family related matters also come into focus in employee counseling. Many a times, employees carry the baggage of personal problems to their workplaces and due to it, fail to deliver good performance. Observing this, firms have started offering family counseling. The issues range from work-life balance to health problems.

Functions

Counseling process influences positively the emotional and mental states of the client. It can perform four functions as outlined here.

1. Reassurance: Counselor provides a sense of confidence in the client, by declaring his support and helping his discover his hidden strengths. He provides assurance by providing positive strokes like appreciation.

2. Communication: Counseling involves speaking and listening. It requires observation of non-verbal signs to get real meaning of client's words.

3. Emotional release: It helps client open up, pour out his emotions and release his tensions.

4. Clarified thinking: The client speaks out his problems and possible solutions. He expresses his dilemmas and his preferred actions. Thus, he thinks in the presence of counselor and understands about himself, and his view of the situation.

Process

There are three types of counseling processes as shown in Table 12.8.

Guidelines

Counseling is a planned, structured dialogue between a supervisor and employee to improve or correct behaviors and/or performance[15].

TABLE 12.8 Types of Counseling Processes

Type	Role of counselor	Role of client	Purpose
Directive	Leads the session completely giving advice and reassurance	Speaks out problems. Listens to advice and seeks clarifications	Releasing emotional tension and regaining emotional balance
Non-directive	Only listens, understands the problem but does not offer any solutions	Discusses the situation and finds solution	Decision-making
Cooperative	Participates in discussion offering his view and also suggests ideas for solution	Discusses the situation and finds solution taking ideas and views of counselor	Decision-making

Before

As a counselor define your objectives. Have all documentation relating to the person to be counseled and review all the facts. Create an outline for discussion. Then arrange for privacy. It is time to verbally inform the employee in person and in private, what the meeting is all about, and where and when it is to take place.

During

How you behave and what you say during the session determines the outcome. Be aware of this throughout the session. Set a positive tone. Describe the problem to the client. Ask for opinions and viewpoints. Listen attentively and sympathetically. Make inquiries and necessary corrections to obtain the right picture. Conclude the session in a friendly manner. Have series of meetings. The time between meetings will help client to introspect and reflect on the issues discussed and helps him become more clear about himself and the issue.

After

The client discovers solutions and presents them during discussion. Give guidance to client to arrive at right course of action. Follow up to ensure client follows the guidelines.

LEADERSHIP DEVELOPMENT

The importance of leadership skills for managers needs no emphasis. The rapidly changing nature of work today makes it more important than ever. Team leaders and senior managers need to learn how to act as role models to employees, and how to inspire and influence performance and development of individuals and teams. The implication is organizations have to initiate measures to continuously develop people occupying positions that need leadership skills and attitudes. Box 12.9 describes the leadership development at Infosys and the commitment of Wipro to promote leadership.

BOX 12.9 Leadership Journey at Two IT Majors

The Infosys Leadership Institute (ILI), the biggest corporate training facility in the world, adopts a scientific approach to nurture talent. Powered by intellect, driven by values'— Infosys has been at the forefront of a new India Inc. since 1981. *Leadership @ Infosys* is the first book to codify Infosys' unique history, values and leadership practices and describes the dimensions of leadership model: strategic leadership, change leadership, operational leadership, talent leadership, relationship and networking leadership, content leadership and entrepreneurial leadership.

Based on the most advanced psychometrics, employees can plan their own leadership development using ILI's Leadership Journey Series. Developing roadmaps that leaders can follow, ILI uses a number of 'vehicles', such as mentoring, technology-enabled simulations, blended learning and books, e-learning, in-person workshops, 'Leaders Teach' sessions and other means for nurturing leaders.

Wipro in 2007, became the first Indian company to win the Dale Carnegie global leadership award. Wipro has built global leaders not only for its own organization, but also for the IT industry as well. Wipro is said to be exceptional on three accounts. One, exposure and challenge—by placing top talent in critical positions; two, formal and informal mentoring and three, a good process and board involvement in developing the leadership pipeline. At Wipro, leadership development training is not an event, but a process. It is a cyclical process of learning, participating and measuring.

Source: Infosys—Leadership Development Models | Talent Leadership... www.infosys.com/leadership-institute/programs.../pages/index.aspx and Wipro among top global companies for leaders—CIOL News Reports.
www.ciol.com/News/News-Reports/Wipro-among-top...leaders/.../0/

MENTORING

Mentoring is a long-term support process by which a superior helps an individual employee in acquiring the skills required for current job as well as for career progression. The mentee is less informed and less experienced, whereas the mentor is more knowledgeable and resourceful.

How Does it Work?

The mentee sets an agenda of own development needs. The mentor provides guidance to mentee in achieving the desired goals. Mentoring can be classified into different types as given in Table 12.9.

Mentoring Program

Organizations should take care in establishing, monitoring and evaluating mentoring programs to reap the full benefits from it[16].

TABLE 12.9 Types of Mentoring

S.No.	Type	Description
1	One-to-one mentoring	A mentor provides guidance to only one mentee
2	Group mentoring (or mentoring circles)	Several mentees and mentors, with the ratio of one mentor for every two to three mentees
3	Peer learning alliances	Participants having similar levels of experience preferably in different areas become partners and guide each other
4	Remote mentoring/ e-mentoring	Mentor and mentee work in different locations. Mentoring is done over the phone or via email or social networking

Establishment

This phase involves awareness building and creating a setting for mentoring.

- First the purpose and method of mentoring are communicated to all the employees in the organization.
- Second, guidelines on mentoring are publicized.
- Third, training programs are organized for mentors, to equip them with the skills of mentoring.
- Fourth, the mentors and mentees are matched.

Monitoring

The effectiveness of mentoring depends on the monitoring mechanisms set up by the organization. Monitoring can be done by asking mentors to record the meetings. The record provides a summary of discussion and action points and helps make assessment of the progress in relationship.

1. *Expectations:* Mentee's needs for current performance and future career growth as understood by mentee and mentor.

2. *Progress in relationship:* After six months, assess how well the relationship is working.

3. *Outcomes:* After 12 months, measure the developments in mentee in terms of expectations fulfilled.

Evaluation

It is important to evaluate the mentors as well as the program. To evaluate the program, mentees and mentors may be asked to give feedback on the effectiveness of the mentoring relationship. Feedback may be collected through the following ways:

1. *Report:* The participants may write a narrative providing their assessment of the mentoring in terms of purpose, process and outcomes.

2. *Questionnaire:* A questionnaire may be given to the participants to answer specific questions about the program. It acts as a guide to the participants to provide a structured response covering assessment points.

3. *Interview:* A more flexible alternative to questionnaire, it helps capture the finer points in the assessment, which a questionnaire cannot help record.

Guidelines to Mentoring

A poorly planned and unstructured mentoring relationship can be a waste of time for both the mentor and mentee. Here is a four step model for effective mentoring[17]:

Step 1: *Building the relationship*

Spending time getting to know the mentor is one of the most important things that a mentee should know. When both mentor and mentee take time to build a trusting relationship, sharing the goals and discussing the challenges, becomes a very comfortable process. The relationship should being with acquaintance and progress to the point of appreciation. It requires time to open up, to share views and experiences, and developing mutual trust. Don't rush this vital first step. Relax and work as if becoming acquainted is the goal of this process.

Step 2: *Negotiating agreements*

After mutual rapport is built, strive to create a set of operating agreements for mentoring relationship. Mentor and mentee define their roles, determine when and where to meet decide the duration of meetings, and clarify preferences and limitations. Negotiating to arrive at mutual agreeable working patterns is essential for the smooth functioning of mentoring. It removes the possibilities of misunderstanding and conflict.

Step 3: *Developing the mentee*

Developing the mentee is the essence of the process and will comprise most of the efforts of mentee and mentor. During this step, the mentoring partners will set one or more goals and select development activities to achieve the chosen objectives. Mentor faces the following challenges in this phase.

1. In goal setting, mentee may come up with goals which are vague and too many. Mentor has to help mentee in pruning and clarifying them to make the goal realistic and attainable.
2. In choosing the development paths and plans, mentor has to help mentee. Based on his experience and wisdom, he or she should be able to counsel the mentee.
3. In developing the mentee, the mentor has to play the role of coach and ensure that the mentee gains the knowledge and skills as expected.

Step 4: *Ending the relationship*

Mentor and mentee have to end their formal relationship, to celebrate accomplishments and plan for the future. It signals the beginning of a new informal relationship between mentor and mentee. It provides a sense of completion and achievement. It helps mentor and mentee to plan for future activities. Mentee and mentor may, however, keep in touch to share interesting experiences, problems and successes.

COMMUNICATION

The problem of poor communication in organizations is almost universal. It is a well-known fact that poor communication sabotages every positive thing that an organization is doing. As such managers have to place heavy emphasis on development of communication by taking appropriate measures.

They may hire consultants to improve communication efficiencies. Box 12.10 describes the work of Mincu & Associates.

BOX 12.10 Communication Training

Mincu & Associates first determine where the communication breakdown is occurring and suggest appropriate interventions. Here is a brief description of their approach[19].

Workshops: The workshops are tailor-made to identified target groups—new supervisors (skills for giving feedback and direction), middle managers (skills for empowering employees), teams (skills for communicating with members in different styles), and managers (skills for holding meetings).

Training programs: Communication is integrated with programs like team development, leadership development, new supervisory skills and diversity training. A bank division wanted its managers to learn behaviors that facilitate empowerment of their staff. Training encompassed seven 2-hour modules. The content has three components—empowerment, leadership style and communication skills.

Coaching: One-to-one coaching is offered to help individuals in overcoming specific communication problems. For effective oral communication, role-play, conversation, and public speaking are employed. For developing campaigns and formulating messages training in written communication is emphasized.

To improve relationships between superior and subordinates, training programs focused on giving feedback are offered.

Source: Adapted with permission from about Mincu & Associates, www.bonniemincu.com/about.

TRANSACTIONAL ANALYSIS

Eric Berne (*Games People Play*) and Thomas Harris (*I'm OK, You're OK*) popularized this technique of analyzing interpersonal communication. It is explained through ego states, transactions, stroking and life positions[18].

Ego States

Berne defines an ego state as "A consistent pattern of feeling and experience directly related to a corresponding consistent pattern of behavior". Every person will have three ego states: Child, Adult, and Parent.

1. *Child ego (C):* The child state shows immaturity in behavior. The individual behaviors are emotional and range from innocence to arrogance, submissiveness to aggressiveness, benevolent to manipulative. The Child ego state may represent a (i) natural child (hedonistic or rebellious), (ii) little professor (new ideas or tricks) and (iii) adapted child (submissive and grateful).

2. *Adult ego (A):* The adult ego state is represented by 'cool-headed,' rational behavior, calculative, objectivity, fairness, gathering and analyzing information, logical choice, etc.

3. *Parent ego (P):* In the Parent ego state, individual acts like controlling parent (why did you do this?) or nurturing parent (I will help you. Don't worry).

Transactions

Transactions between two or more individuals can be classified into three types:

1. *Complementary trasactions:* Transactions are complementary, if the message sent and received are as intended. Figure 12.1 shows them.

- *Adult-Adult:* Production Supervisor (Adult ego) asks the Foreman (Adult ego) suggesting measures to reduce the cost of production. The Foreman (Adult ego) identifies the low cost sources and suggests measures to foreman (Adult ego).
- *Parent-child and child-parent:* For example, a production supervisor (Parent ego) tells the foreman (Child ego) to change the schedule. The foreman (Child ego) simply obeys the order of foreman (Parent ego).

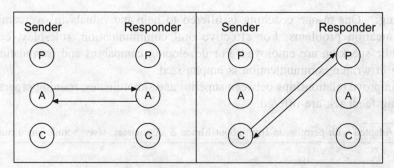

Figure 12.1 Complementary transactions.

2. *Crossed transactions:* Crossed transaction occurs when the message or the behavior of one person's ego state is not in accordance with the expected ego state. Crossed transactions are the sources of interpersonal conflict. Consider this example.

- *Adult ego:* "Will you tell me what time it is?" (Sounding that it is time to go to bed) is addressed to an adult in others.
- *Child ego responds:* "Why are you always rushing me?"

This is a crossed transaction. If the response has come from the Adult ego state ("Can I finish this and go to bed?"), it is complementary. Figure 12.2 shows such cross transaction.

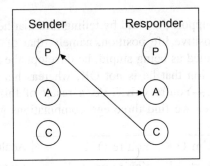

Figure 12.2   Crossed transactions.

3. *Ulterior transactions:*   The ulterior transactions involve at least two ego states one manifest and another hidden. The individual may say one thing, but may mean quite another. These transactions are very complicated and result in interpersonal conflict.

Stroking

Eric Berne defined a stroke as a "unit of human recognition". A stroke can be a look, a nod, a smile, a spoken word, a touch. It may be positive, negative, sarcastic or mixed. Small recognition such as "hello" is a positive stroke and can nourish a person. Negative strokes (like asking are you crazy?) collect bad feelings in the individual. The feelings collected in the form of positive or negative strokes are called trading stamps. A person who has collected angry feelings may blow up at a co-worker or his wife or any other individual. He is thus redeeming his negative trading stamp.

Games people play

Games are ongoing series of complementary transactions, with an underlying message of the game and a predictable pay off. Recall the frequent 'homework game' which students like to play. Students who forget to do homework, play games to get favorable reaction from the teacher. If the teacher does not accept explanations, such as "I have not had time", or "I forgot and will bring the work the next day", they will use gimmicks and get their payoff. They concoct a cock and bull story highlighting hurdles to doing homework.

Scripts

In TA language, people live by their scripts. Scripts are generally selected in childhood. For example, where the parent tell the child consistently that he will be successful and famous one day, the child when he grows up develops this as his life script, trying to become famous all the time. This concept of script writing can be used to develop a new positive script that encourages employees to excel on their jobs. Leadership training focuses on this script writing for their followers.

Life Positions

Where the parents always support the child by telling him that he will become famous one day, the child may develop a positive life position, namely, that of "I'm O.K." As against this, if the child is constantly ridiculed as being stupid, he develops the position and script of "I'm not O.K." and makes a conclusion that he is not OK, whereas his parents are O.K. He develops the position "I'm not O.K.—You're O.K.". As a result of this transaction process, between different parents and children we find three ego combinations given under.

1. I'm O.K., You're O.K.	Adult–adult
2. I'm O.K., You're not O.K	Parent–child
3. I'm not O.K., You're O.K.	Child–parent

In organizations, when superior takes the role of parents who tell not O.K., subordinates lose confidence and assume not O.K. position. They fail in their jobs due to this poor psychological state. Consultants counsel employees to change from "I am not O.K" to "I am O.K".

SUMMARY

Planning and development of people and organizations is critical in our rapidly changing environment. Career management is to be done in a partnership with employees and by using different techniques, like career anchors, magic fairy exercise, brainstorming and life mapping.

The organization mirror is used when a particular organizational group seeks to identify and improve its image. Future search is a planning meeting, and is a proven method of improving organizational systems and abilities. Visioning is used by many organizations to guide them forward. It is designed to create preferred future states and images of potential. Confrontation Meeting is a one-day meeting that brings together the management team, or the entire unit or system to identify problems and to set action plan for solving them. Survey feedback is a participative data collection approach. The data collection tool may be a survey, one-to-one interview, focus group interviews and 360 degree feedback. Force field analysis helps identify both driving and restraining forces that influences business functioning. A culture audit gives a comprehensive diagnostic of current culture. It provides a detailed understanding of the culture desired and helps develop a road map for cultural transformation.

Training interventions aim at enhancing knowledge, skills and attitudes of employees and help them do their jobs effectively during normal and difficult times. Companies are encouraging self-study method of education by offering assistance. Training specialists conduct a wide array of programs, like orientation and on-the-job training for new employees;

interpersonal effectiveness and leadership development for supervisors, cross cultural adaptation programs for expatriates, and language and voice training for BPO employees. Appreciations and concerns exercise seeks to assess the ability of members in expressing appreciation, and confronting concerns and irritations. Coaching helps senior managers to sharpen their skills and refine their attitudes. Counseling is an enabling process. It helps people by encouraging them to use their own rational, emotional and spiritual intelligence, to find ways for solving problems and grabbing opportunities related to work and life. Leadership development programs are now found in almost all organizations. Mentoring is a long-term support process by which a superior helps an individual employee in acquiring the skills required for current job as well as for career progression. The problem of poor communication in organizations is almost universal. Companies are hiring consultants to improve communication efficiencies. Transactional Analysis is a tool for improving interpersonal effectiveness.

EXERCISES

I. Review Questions

1. Explain in brief life and career planning.
2. Discuss the significance of organizational mirroring.
3. Explain visioning process.
4. Elaborate the process of confrontation meeting.
5. Discuss the benefits of survey feedback.
6. Illustrate the application of force field analysis.
7. With examples, state the significance of education and training.
8. How do you organize 'appreciations and concerns' exercise?
9. Explain the need and process of coaching.
10. How do you counsel an employee?
11. With examples, substantiate the need for leadership development.
12. How do you perform the mentoring function?
13. Explain communication interventions.
14. What is transactional analysis? How do you make use of it as an intervention?

II. Discussion Questions

1. Explain the applications: (a) Life and career planning, (b) Organizational mirroring
2. How do you implement: (a) Visioning process, (b) Survey feedback, (c) Force field analysis, and (d) Confrontation meeting
3. Describe: (a) Appreciations and Concerns, and (b) Leadership development
4. Explain the importance and process of: (a) Counseling, (b) Coaching, and (c) Mentoring
5. Explain communication interventions.

MINI-PROJECT

Form into a group of 4 people. Inquire local organizations whether they have put in place leadership development porgrams. Design a half-day workshop training program on leadership for management students. Conduct it in your school and obtain feedback from participants. Prepare a report and submit it to your instructor.

 WEB ASSIGNMENT

Nine Conversations in Leadership™ is an innovative leadership intervention developed by Worlds view consulting firm and is available at
www.worldsviewconsulting.com/Nine_Conversations_in_Leadership.
Develop a brief note on the intervention and explain how it can be administered.

CASE STUDY

People Transformation

Vedanta Resources is a large metals and mining group with annual sales of $1.9 billion. It has a major market share in India and substantial operations in Zambia and Australia. With a proven transactional, operating and turnaround skills, Vendanta is seeking growth and opportunities in India and elsewhere to gain competitive advantage. It has defined its goal as follows: "To generate strong financial returns and create a world-class metals and mining group". The strategy evolved to realize the goal includes initiative to debottleneck plants, improve efficiency, expand output, and reduce costs.

Problems

The acquisition of major share in Konkola Copper Mines, Zambia, employing more than 10,000 workers, posed the problem of differences in culture and required interventions for integration. The transition process, post acquisition, found resistance to change. It was largely due to lack of professional practices and suspicion. To add fuel to the fire, the internal politics played a negative role. In this context, to facilitate change, and align operations to the strategy OD Alternatives Consultancy was brought in.

Diagnosis

This interventions focused on 1500 employees, who were administered by three consultants. The design took 20 days and implementation was spread over 90 days. The diagnosis was done with the help of climate surveys and deep structured interviews. They helped the identification of the existing culture of the organization and the attitudes of employees toward change.

Interventions

To create change readiness and ownership for change different groups were chosen and interventions were administered.

1. *Project team drive:* A project team was set up to drive the transformation. A two day interventions focusing on issues like creating escape velocity, resolving people issues and building team spirit were carried out.
2. *Change leaders workshop:* A group of professionals to prepare employees to change by communicating the message of change and clarifying doubts was set-up. Two day workshops were conducted for about 200 middle managers from three business units.
3. *Train the trainer workshops:* About 40 people including employees and some of the union representatives were chosen to be internal training resources. They were made capable of organizing a one day inspirational session for the workers using appreciative Inquiry model.
4. *Workshops for workers:* Large number of workers was involved in an appreciative Inquiry processes in one day workshops.

Alignment and Leadership

The restructuring resulted in the formation of several SOU (Strategic Operating Units). To align the new teams to the new business model two day workshops for around 200 middle management professional were held. The two day leadership workshop with upper middle management engaged participants in visioning exercise and five leadership competencies listed as follows:

1. Lead by example
2. Inspire a shared vision
3. Break out of comfort zone
4. Empowering others
5. Encourage the heart

Participants were assessed with a 360 assessment tool, before and after workshops.

Cultural Differences

It was found that there were differences of opinion and conflicts between Indian and African executives. A one day intervention on culture sensitivity and conflict resolution was designed. The facilitation helped the teams identify differences and develop common working norms for cooperation.

Functional Conflicts

The organization decided to streamline commercial/purchase process, by creating separate department. Earlier the purchase decisions were taken by the operations department. The decision led to huge conflict between the operations and commercial department. A series of facilitated sessions, were conducted for the two departments.

Questions for Discussion

1. What challenges and issues were faced by OD consultants?

2. Identify the interventions implemented to resolve the different issues.

3. If you were the consultant, would you adopt a different approach and different interventions? Justify your answer.

Source: Adapted with permission from: OD Alternatives, *www.odalternatives.com.*

REFERENCES

1. Adapted with permission from http://www.potentia.in/casestudies.html

2. Hyde, Lucy, *Training and Development in Organizations: What Matters, What ...* www.psychologicalscience.org/.../the-science-of-training-and-develo... 13 Jun 2012

3. Beckhard Richard (1969), *Organizational Development: Strategies and Models*, New York: Addison-Wesley.

4. A Little Goal Setting Exercise that Can Change Your Life. www.arinanikitina.com/a-little-goal-setting-exercise-that-can-change-... Goal Collage, www.self-help-healing-arts-journal.com/goal-collage-article.html and Goal Setting: The Magic Fairy Exercise, www.dragosroua.com/the-magic-fairy-exercise/

5. Schein, E. (1996), Career Anchors, Discovering your Real Values. Pfeiffer. Oxford: www.goalsettingstrategies.com/life_mapping_a_vision_of_success.html life mapping | examples of smart goals and objectives | life map,

6. Kondalkar, (2009), *Organization Effectiveness and Change Management*, New Delhi: PHI Learning.

7. Johnson, Martin (1999), A feasibility test for corporate vision, *Strategic Change*, 8, September-October, pp. 335–348.

8. Overview of Vision and the Visioning Process, uwcc.wisc.edu/coopcare/docs/vision.pdf 8 Steps to Creating a Great Vision | Inc.com, www.inc.com/ss/8-steps-to-creating-a-great-vision.

9. Beckhard, R. (1967), "The Confrontation Meeting", *Harvard Business Review*, Vol. **45**(2), pp. 149–155.

10. Managers Guide to Survey Feedback, www.ipacweb.org/files/mgrsurveyguide.pdf— United States and Customer Feedback Survey, www.infosurv.com/customer-feedback-survey/

11. Force field analysis. www.accel-team.com/techniques/force_field_analysis.html Force Field Analysis (Force field Analysis)—Decision-Making Skills ... www.mindtools.com > Decision Making

12. Organizational Culture Audit (OCA)—Kets De Vries Institute www.kdvi.com/Page/Organizational_Cultural_Audit

13. Quoted in the Power of Appreciation—How to Praise your ... —Careerbright careerbright.com/.../the-power-of-appreciation-how-to-praise-your-...

14. Human Dimension—Coaching and Personality Assessments, www.humandimension. org/coaching.html and The Framework for the Strategic Executive Coaching Process, www.excn.com/pages/articles/framework_SEC.html

15. Counseling and Discipline—Employee and Labor Relations—Stony ... www.stonybrook. edu/lrweb/counseling/, GOER—Supervisors' Guide to Counseling: How to Conduct a ... www.buffalostate.edu/offices/hr/goer/how.asp and Coaching and Counseling Skills for Managers, cscfrs-si.org/class/Counseling%20Skills%20for%20Managers.doc

16. A Proven Process for Successful Mentoring www.mediapro.com/.../mentoring/...Using mentoring to boost employee performance | Business Link www.businesslink.gov.uk > ... > Staff motivation and performance

17. Key Steps in the Mentoring Process. wiki.tafensw.edu.au/.../a/.../Key_steps_in_the_ Mentoring_Process.pd...

18. Berne, E. (1961), *Transactional Analysis in Psychotherapy*, Grove Press Inc. New York Berne, E. (1964), Games People Play. Penguin: Harmondsworth and Harris, Thomas (2004) *I'm O.K., You're O.K.* New York: Harper.

Chapter 13

Role and Team Interventions

Vignette: Interventions at BHEL

Way back in 1976, in its Bhopal division, Bharat Heavy Electricals Ltd. (BHEL) set up 'Human Resources Committee' to develop and improve the effectiveness of the human resources in the organization. It was designated as a central body for implementation of all OD efforts with the help of external and internal resource persons. A wide range of OD interventions were contemplated, designed and implemented.

In Hardwar unit, job redesign was undertaken and the experiment lasted for around 4 years. It gave encouraging results, such as more satisfying jobs due to increased variety and relief from boredom and monotony, personal development by learning of additional skills and leadership qualities, increased self-esteem and pride, team spirit, improved communication and reduction in health/safety hazards. Diagnostic surveys and workshops were conducted to identify training needs. The heads of the departments took active part in the survey, and provided information on training needs in their departments. The workshops on various themes generated valuable ideas on thrust areas of training and development. Based on the diagnostic information, specific training and development programs were designed.

For effective role definitions, role analysis was considered. The Corporate Personnel worked with the Personnel/Training (HRD)/Divisional heads, on evolving database for helping the executives to visualize their roles more clearly and become more effective in their present and future jobs. The performance appraisal and potential appraisal were revamped by introducing performance feedback and counseling. The superior who was hither to acting as the single judge for evaluation, was given the new role of counselor. The passive appraisee was encouraged to become more involved in self evaluation and engage in constructive dialogue with his or her superior. A good number of workshops on performance feedback and counseling were conducted to enable employees to practice it.

The interventions had included career planning and development of employees. Learning by study was encouraged by creating sponsorship program. Employees seeking higher educational programs in IIMs/IITs were supported. Further, employees were encouraged and trained to plan their own career paths. Merit was given due importance by introducing time-cum-merit based promotion system[1].

The case suggests how a multi-pronged approach becomes necessary in going organizations to keep their human resources effective and enhance performance. In this chapter, we will discuss interventions that help improve role performance, team development, conflict management and performance and quality improvements in organizations.

INTRODUCTION

A successful organization is one which has integrated systems and teams that work cohesively to achieve the goals. Good team work not only enhances the performance of organizations but also contributes the development and satisfaction of team participants. It generates a sense of belonging, provides mutual support, facilitates learning, and empowers people to play their roles more effectively. As such, organizations have to address the challenge of developing teams and also roles of members. There are several interventions that help define roles and develop teams.

ROLE INTERVENTIONS

Besides formal job description a role description includes the identification of informal relationships and expectations that determine the way an employee acts in the organization. Due to the dynamic nature of organizations, behaviors required of people occupying jobs, also keep changing requiring redefinition and clarification. The three concepts that provide basis for understanding role play are:

1. *Role conception*: The attitude or thinking of people towards their work roles
2. *Role expectation*: The expectation of a person with regards to another person's job role
3. *Role behavior*: The activities of people in their job function

When there is a lack of clarity in any of these three factors, role ambiguity arises and results in confusion and conflict. Role confusion not only lowers productivity but also results in dysfunctional conflict. Four important interventions helpful in clarifying roles are:

- Role analysis
- Role negotiation
- Interdependency exercise
- Responsibility charting

ROLE ANALYSIS AND COMPETENCY PROFILING

Competency profiling and role analysis are the modern approaches to job analysis[2]. The traditional approach to job analysis adopted content analysis approach in describing the job or position in an organization and provided a description of activities associated with it. The competency profiling approach adopted a diagnostic functional approach to define role of the job in the organization context, to make it capable of contributing maximum performance. The former is task-focussed, whereas the latter is outcome or results-focussed.

Even today, job descriptions are important in the hiring process. However, in place of the question "What duties, tasks, and responsibilities are involved in this job?", we ask "What competencies are required to succeed on the job?"

Focus and Outcomes

Role analysis focusses on identification and description of two dimensions of a role:

- *Activities:* Tasks, duties and responsibilities relating to the job.
- *Competencies:* The knowledge, and skills, as well as personal characteristics required for competent performance of the job.

Knowledge refers to awareness and understanding one domain area essential to perform a job. For example, a Spanish translator may need to have knowledge of technical vocabulary. Skills can be technical or managerial. Examples of technical skills are welding, drafting, technical writing, and accounting. Examples of management skills are planning and organizing, interpersonal decision making, and leadership. Attributes are characteristics that motivate an employee to perform well. For instance, a salesperson is happy interacting with different types of people, and conducting presentations.

The focus and outcome of Competency profiling are shown in Figure 13.1.

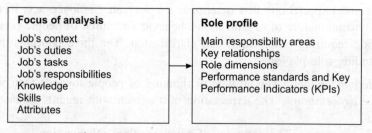

Focus of analysis	Role profile
Job's context	Main responsibility areas
Job's duties	Key relationships
Job's tasks	Role dimensions
Job's responsibilities	Performance standards and Key
Knowledge	Performance Indicators (KPIs)
Skills	
Attributes	

Figure 13.1 Competency profiling.

Application Contexts

Role analysis can be done as follows:

1. Single role: When a minor change has resulted in role ambiguity of a job, then that role becomes focal role.

2. *Multiple role:* Company-wide analysis of all roles becomes necessary when there is major change, and redesign has become necessary for ensuring that all business functions are properly aligned.

Role analysis is beneficial in many ways. The HR functions, such as recruitment and selection, training, performance appraisal, pay and benefits, career pathing and promotion decisions are based on role analysis.

Process

Role analysis is a collaborative process that involves all the related persons and uses multiple data collection tools.

1. In the first phase, interviews are conducted with focal role incumbent to understand how the role is actually performed. Then his expectations about other related roles are gathered.
2. In the second phase, the expectations of others about the desired role behavior of focal role are collected through interviews or questionnaires.
3. In the third phase, a meeting is conducted to facilitate discussion on focal role. Through exchange of views, members reach an agreement on what the role is.
4. In the last phase, role/competency profile is prepared. It is reviewed by the members concerned and then finalized for documentation.

Commitment and enthusiasm from the senior managers is important. Therefore, they should be involved from the start. They are frequently involved in communicating the process and its results to all members of staff.

Data Collection Tools

Information is collected from records, job incumbent, managers, and others familiar with the role. The data collection tools include: observations, interviews, critical incidents, questionnaires, visioning, etc.

1. *Job observation:* Observe role incumbents and make a note of what they are doing.

2. *Interviews:* Develop the interview questions ahead of time. They should focus on learning about their key responsibilities, the types of problems they need to solve, the interactions they may have with others, the most difficult part of their job, and the skills and abilities they feel are necessary for success.

3. *Critical incidents:* Facilitate meetings with the supervisors of the focal role incumbent and ask them to provide specific examples of times when he or she demonstrated highly effective and highly ineffective behaviors.

4. *Visioning:* Facilitate meetings with people who are visionaries—people who really know the jobs, the organization, and most important, the future of the jobs and the organization.

ROLE NEGOTIATION

Roger Harrison developed this method[3]. The issues of authority, power and responsibility are often left unresolved in organizational design and change processes. Consider the following situations:

- A CFO is worried that Heads of field divisions are delaying quarterly figures. As a result, there are deadlines and closer supervision. There is passive resistance among concerned employers.
- The Chief Marketing Officer and the VP of Sales. Various product managers are making competing demands for the time of sales people. From sales people, there are some limitations. Marketing people think that sales people are less cooperative.

To resolve such issues, and clearly defined roles, role negotiation is utilized. Role negotiation is a structured process of identifying sources of role conflict among group members, and resolving them for redefining the role of an individual in a group. In this process, it helps group members to negotiate specific changes in each others' behavior which are mutually satisfying. It is satisfying because, it facilitates open discussion of issues hindering productivity and then negotiating a settlement among the parties involved.

Assumptions

Role negotiation is based on the following assumptions:

1. Most people prefer a fair, negotiated settlement to a state of unresolved conflict.
2. People are willing to invest some time and make some modest concessions in order to achieve a solution.
3. People are willing to take a small, but significant risk of being open for exchanging views and modifying roles.

Method

It is a small group intervention that can be used for negotiation between individuals as well as units. The maximum number of members is ten. It may take one and a half to four hours depending on the number of members and their ability to communicate with each other and negotiate the roles. The process can be made effective in terms of time and clarity, by using message forms. The focus is on three things: (i) doing things better, (ii) stop doing or doing less, and (iii) continue doing. Table 13.1 presents the form. Table 13.2 shows the summary form, which presents the views of self and other members (A to H in this case).

TABLE 13.1   Issue Diagnosis Form

Expected to	Activities
Continue doing as now	
Stop doing or doing less	
Doing more or better	

TABLE 13.2 Summary Form

Category	Self	A	B	C	D	E	F	G	H
Continue									
Stop or less									
Do more or better									

Process

According to Roger Harrison, role negotiation process involves four steps[4] as shown in Table 13.3.

TABLE 13.3 Role Negotiation Process

Step	Activity
Contract setting	Discuss issues related to power, influence, performance and productivity manifested in relation to your group and individual members. The focus is on identifying the power and influence: (i) you believe you have, (ii) others believe you have, and (iii) you believe you should have.
	Think about required changes for better working relationships and productivity. Who and what things should: (i) continue to be the same, or (ii) change
Issue diagnosis	Use issue diagnosis form (Table 13.1) to get messages from members. Use one for self to figure out your views.
	Exchange the lists within your group. Everyone will have his or her views along with those of others. Summarize them for each individual.
	Members write the summary on a flip chart and post it for the group to see. (Table 13.2)
Negotiation period	Discuss openly rising questions like—"What", "Why" and "How"? Be positive and constructive in identifying the changes you prefer and others require.
	Develop agenda for change—(i) items willing to change for others, (ii) items which you prefer others to change and negotiate by offering "If you do X, I will do Y." Negotiation ends when all parties are satisfied.
Follow up meet	Write the agreement and circulate it among the members of the group. The members discuss to assess the effectiveness of agreement or contract.

Guidelines

The following guidelines are important to make the process effective:

1. *Be rational:* Do not probe anyone's feelings or emotions.

2. *Be open:* The success of the method depends on one's ability to frankly express his or her views to others.

3. *Be ready for trading:* Give and take is the core of a negotiation process.

4. *Be positive:* More than threats and pressures, positive incentives yield greater results.

5. *Be clear in giving feedback:* Abstract feedback makes negotiation difficult. Use written media to communicate expectations and demands. It helps one to remember and reflect for a long time.

Delayed feedback, is "gunnysacking". A series of reactions are stored and then dumped at once. It causes difficulty in negotiations.

6. *Be fair:* Play the negotiation straight. If you use tactics or manipulation, then people will suspect you and the process fails to deliver the expected results.

7. *Be polite:* If the request is easy and beneficial, you can say "Of course! I will accede to your request", if the request is ethically or functionally impossible you say "Sorry! I can't do that because......".., if an exchange is desirable, you can say "I would be prepared to meet your request if you would help me with this one of mine".

INTERDEPENDENCY EXERCISE

This intervention is helpful to groups facing inter-group cooperation problems. It helps in surfacing problems that are latent and not previously examined. The exercise will be effective if the number of participants is between 10–35 members. It is ideal for 10 people, especially when top level managers are involved. The intervention may require 3 to 4 hours[5]. When a large number of participants are involved the exercise can be structured as outlined in Table 13.4. Before assembling the participants, consultant/facilitator will collect data from members of the different groups in the organization diagnostic data and identifies the nature of problems. This activity will stimulate thought processes among the participants.

TABLE 13.4   Interdependency Exercise

Step	Time (minutes)	Activity
1	10	The leader explains participant groups the objectives of the exercise. The facilitator hands over the schedule to them. Leader answers the questions of participant groups.
2	15	Facilitator presents the diagnostic data results to the participants. The consultant and participants discuss the results and draw inferences.
3	60	Form sub groups. The sub groups elect a leader and discuss the problems faced by the groups. The problems are recorded on a paper.
4	60	A fish bowl exercise is arranged. The sub-groups make a presentation to the whole group the problems identified by them. The whole group prepares the final list of problems.
5	45	Based on similarity, the problems are classified to form clusters. Each cluster is given a title.
6	30	The clusters are assigned to sub-groups based on skills and knowledge of the subgroups. Those problems which cannot be assigned to sub-groups may be assigned to specially formed committees.

When there are about ten participants, the exercise can be structured as follows[6]:

***Step* 1:** (*10 minutes–1 interview*): The participants are asked to sit in a straight lines of 5 persons each facing each other as shown under. Participant 1 interviews the 6th member sitting opposite him/her. An interview sheet given in Box 13.1 may be used. They identify problems and develop mutual action plans.

1	2	3	4	5
6	7	8	9	10

***Step* 2:** (*40 minutes–4 interviews*): The members are asked to move to the chair next to them. That is participant 1 moves to 2 and 5 moves to 1. Members 6 to 10 remain in their seats as before. The process of interviewing and finding solutions is repeated until each member has participated in 5 interviews. For instance, participant 1 interviews 6, 7, 8, 9 and 10.

***Step* 3:** (*20 minutes*): The participants take a break and then assemble again.

***Step* 4:** (*40 minutes–4 interviews*): Each participant will interview 4 other participants. For example, participant 1 interviews 2, 3, 4 and 5 members.

***Step* 5:** A summary of the problems will be prepared based on the interviews.

BOX 13.1 Interdependency Exercise

Person being interviewed:

Unit:

What interdependencies do you recognize in our jobs?
What interdependencies do you find between our units?
Which of them, are going well?
Which of them are causing hurdles and hurting your performance?
Which of them do you think, in your view, may become obstacles?
What is your action plan to remove those hurdles?
If the interdependencies are less significant, learn a few things about the other person's job.

RESPONSIBILITY CHARTING

Responsibility is the obligation on the part of a person to report on authority exercised for decision making and achievement of results expected. It is also referred to as accountability.

At one organization, which has a tall hierarchical structure, many decisions had to be approved by managers at different levels. Managers at each level assumed that errors would be noticed and corrected at the previous level and forwarded the memos to the next level. Even the CEO did the same. He signed the forms without reading them. It resulted in sending inappropriate messages to stakeholders[7].

Responsibility chart provides a visual map showing who is responsible for consultation, for approval, for decisions, etc. It is a good intervention to use to: (i) improve the team spirit, relationship and performance of a team with their existing work, and (ii) to clarify roles and responsibilities before, during or after a change process especially when number of committees is used.

Designing a Chart

The vertical and horizontal axis on the "responsibility chart" can be first developed by the leaders. Then it can be placed for discussion by team members. It is the team that has to develop the chart[8].

1. *Establish purpose:* Introductory meetings are to be conducted to secure support of the top management.

2. *Identify the tasks:* This can be done by from the information available in process documents, flowcharts, and block diagrams. In case a new process is planned, one has to create from scratch. Brainstorming will be helpful in designing the process.

3. *Identify the responsibility areas:* Explore the linkages between stakeholders (teams, sub teams, and departments) who have linkages in connection with a process and establish them. Here comprehensiveness is important. Forgetting some individual or group can be detrimental to the success of the activity.

4. *Adopt a coding scheme:* There are different types of coding schemes used by organizations to classify the nature of the relationship between resources and tasks. One popular coding scheme RACI is given in Table 13.5.

TABLE 13.5 RACI Coding Scheme

Code	Role	Description
Responsible (R)	The doer	One who has to complete the task. The degree of responsibility is determined by person with the "A" Responsibility can be shared
Accountable (A)	The buck stops here	One who is ultimately answerable for the activity or decision. Possesses authority to say "yes" or "no" and veto power
Consult (C)	In the loop	One who is to be consulted prior to a final decision or action
Inform (I)	Keep in the picture	One who needs to be informed after a decision or action
Dash (–)	Non-behavior	Non involvement of a person with the decision

Other coding schemes are given under:

RASIN: Responsible, Approval, Consulted, I–Informed N–Needs to be consulted

RIDS: Responsible, Informed, D–does the work, S–Supports

5. *Define the relationships:* This is the difficult part of the process. It takes considerable time and requires elaborate thinking by all the team members. It is advisable to hold a workshop involving the members. They may, go through the process the first time relatively quickly, getting the initial impressions of other members. This creates a rough sketch of responsibility structure and it can be used as a basis for further discussion and improvements.

In assigning codes for each process, one may consider the current roles and responsibilities, data from flow charts and other process mapping tools. Every box need not be filled. In fact, it should not be. Again when there is difference of opinion, thorough discussion is needed before finalizing it.

6. *Review assignments:* The first draft should be subjected to critical examination to justify assignments. In fact, there will be, in general, lots of crossed-out assignments, rewritten codes, and changes in processes.

7. *Communicate:* Once the agreement is reached on the responsibility structure, it should be documented and distributed to team members and others. Meetings may be conducted with all individual and departments for reinforcement of role definitions.

Guidelines for preparation of the chart[9]

Table 13.6 shows the chart.

TABLE 13.6 Responsibility Chart-Example.

Actors ────▶ Decisions	Release manager	Project manager	Developer	Program manager
Product planning	I	A	R	C
Product development	I	I	A	R
Product release	R	A	I	I

1. *Be clear about the activities:* Do not use generic activities like "attend meetings". Be more specific like," analyze data to identify source of delay". Begin each decision with an action verb. Examples of action verbs: evaluate, approve, schedule, report, write, develop, review, record, update, inspect, determine, collect, and determine.

2. *Coding:* There is only one letter per person per task. Place A (Accountability) and R (Responsibility) at the level close to the scene of action. There can be only one A per activity. Two As indicate sharing of accountability. Vetoes should be used rarely.

3. *Use Excel chart for convenience:* Excel spread sheet may be used for easy editing. Addition and deletion of tasks can be easily done.

TEAM INTERVENTIONS

Today, team dynamics and productivity have become critical for modern organizations adopting flat structures and project management approaches. A major issue in team work is differences of opinions and attitudes that arise due to differences in personalities and professional training of the members. As such, team building and development interventions focus on:

1. Helping team members learn to value and respect differences
2. Developing capacity to understand their own and others' styles
3. Leveraging on the strengths of other team members
4. Communicating for understanding and negotiating for mutual benefit
5. Resolving conflicts in a way that they become constructive and a strong binding force in organizations

Box 13.2 shows the team building interventions of Mincu & associates and OD alternatives.

Types of Teams

There are four typed of teams: (i) work teams, (ii) parallel teams, (iii) project teams, and (iv) management teams.

1. Work teams are continuing work units responsible for production or services. Their membership is full time, stable and defined. They are now being shaped into self-managed work units, with supervisors becoming coaches.
2. Parallel teams pull employees from different units to perform tasks which the regular organization is not equipped to undertake. Examples include quality circles and task forces which make recommendations to top management.
3. Project teams are time bound. They are set up to perform a specific set of activities having a predetermined goal.
4. Management teams provide coordination to business units by assembling top managers of different units.

BOX 13.2   Team Development Interventions

Mincu & Associates help organizations in team building. Their approach is as given under:

Interviews: They start the intervention with interviews. They interview members of a team individually to understand their issues.

Team Development Workshops: Interviews are followed by sessions with the whole group to surface differences in how the team perceives itself. This is done in a creative, interactive way. Members are encouraged to open up. An effective team can lead to breakthrough results.

Live Theater Options: An exciting option is integrating live actors into a team development workshop. The consultant ropes in theater professionals, to create a unique, dynamic experience with teams.

ODA firmly believes that a team to be perfect and successful, the starting point is individual. It suggests the client to first understand and map the individual and articulate the need for change, then design team intervention and arrange a follow-up as given in figure below:

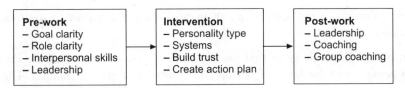

Figure Approach to team building.

Their team health check instrument measures, at an individual and at the team level four parameters: interpersonal skills and conflict management, goal orientation and alignment, role clarity and leadership. They conduct simple team bonding exercises to complex team conflict resolutions, intense problem solving sessions in the board room to outbound workshops deep in forests.

Source: Adapted with permission from Mincu & Associates: Coaching, Consulting, Training, www. bonniemincu.com/
OD consultancy, interventions, Leadership, coaching, Team building ...www.odalternatives.com/

Team Effectiveness

Team effectiveness depends on design and processes factors and is measured by outcomes as shown in Table 13.3.

TABLE 13.7 Team Effectiveness Factors

Inputs	Process	Outcomes
Task design (nature of activity) Group composition (size, member characteristics, etc.) Context of operation (reward or punishment) Environmental factors (stable or turbulent)	Internal processes, like collaboration and conflict resolution. External processes like delivery and complaint handling. Group governing processes (influence of norms, values and traditions)	Performance outcomes like production, quality, etc. Attitudinal outcomes like satisfaction, loyalty, etc. Behavioural outcomes like absenteeism, turnover, etc.

FORMAL GROUP DIAGNOSTIC MEETING

The formal group makes a critical appraisal of the performance of the members and the group and identifies problems. The diagnostic meeting can be conducted in one the following three forms[10]:

1. *Total group:* A total group discussion involving everyone to think and contribute to problem solving.

2. *Sub-group:* Dividing the entire group into sub-groups and asking them to discuss and report to the total group for further discussion.

3. *Dyad/Pair:* Forming pairs and asking them to discuss and report to the total group for further discussion.

The aim of the diagnosis is to find the direction of the movement of the groups (where is the group going?) and the level of performance (how well are we doing?). The discussion as such centers on performance and the enabling factors. The leading questions can be as given as:

1. *Abilities:* What are the strengths and weaknesses of the group? What steps should be taken to enhance competences?

2. *Relationships:* What is the quality of relationships among members of the group? What is the quality of relationships of the group with other related groups? What steps should be taken to improve relationships?

3. *Problems:* What problems does the group have that restrict its performance? What supportive factors are available to the group to enhance performance? What steps should be taken to mitigate problems and utilize support?

4. *Opportunities:* What opportunities does the group have? Are they identified and tapped? What opportunities should the group take advantage of?

5. *Outcomes:* Is the performance of the group satisfactory in terms of expected outcomes? What should be done to improve performance?

Benefits

The diagnostic meeting offers several benefits.

1. *Reenergize participants:* The meeting helps participants to gain fresh outlook on the group relationships, problems and performance.

2. *Solving problems:* Linking the diagnosis to problem-solving, discussion can be carried out on issues, in a problem-solving session. It may involve two steps:

   (i) Grouping of issues and labeling them as planning problems, operational problems, and control problems.
   (ii) Finding solutions to the problems by assigning different categories of problems to different sub-groups or special task forces.

3. *Keeps groups ahead of problems:* It requires half day or one day to hold the meeting. It can be conducted half-yearly to stay ahead of problems.

SENSITIVITY TRAINING

Sensitivity training in its original form was used for improving work practices within groups. It focused on group process, and emphasized 'here-and-now' orientation and immediate feedback. The T-group which is referred to as encounter groups, human relations training, or study groups was considered as a base for this. However, T-groups focus more on job related skills, whereas sensitivity training focuses on personal growth and relationships. Sensitivity training is now being used to addresses concerns arising from work force diversity like gender sensitivity (with more women joining corporate) and cultural sensitivity (with global cross-cultural operations of organizations). Sensitivity-training programs vary in duration depending upon the purpose from a few days, to several weeks[11].

Purposes

Sensitivity training aims at making people understand about themselves and others by developing in them social sensitivity and behavioral flexibility. Social sensitivity refers empathy—the ability of an individual to sense what others feel and think from their own point-of-view. Behavioral flexibility is ability to adopt behavior in accordance with the new awareness and knowledge.

Procedure

The training is carried out as detailed below. Figure 13.2 shows the change process[12].

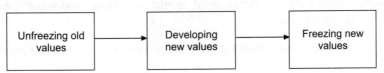

Figure 13.2 Change process in sensitivity training.

1. *Group formation:* In this, an unstructured group of 10–15 people has no agenda, no leader and no predetermined goals. The members look for guidance, but trainer refuses to intervene.

2. *Unfreezing:* The group members struggle, to form into a working group. There may be disagreement on who can be the leader, and what can be done by the group. The interaction brings to surface differences in values, beliefs and interests of group members. Trainee finds that conflict can be resolved by looking from a different perspective and new values.

3. *Developing new values:* The trainer, at this stage, offers support to trainees in examining their interpersonal behaviors. He encourages them to exchange feedback and discuss the reasoning of the feedbacks. Based on the discussion, the trainees identify desirable values and behaviors. The trainees test the new behaviors and values by employing them in their interactions.

4. *Refreezing the new ones:* The new behaviors and values are adopted in future interactions. The learned behaviors may be reinforced by a word of appreciation by the superiors.

T-GROUPS

According to Robert T. Golembiewski, T-groups is distinguished from other group-based programs by its approach. It is a learning laboratory with focus on learning how to learn[13].

1. The numbers of trainees is limited to 10 to 15 persons.
2. Face to face interaction is encouraged. The limited size facilitates regular interaction among participants throughout the training program.
3. An unstructured group is formed without a goal, a designated leader and an agenda.
4. The group members are given an assignment, like case study or role play.
5. The group members struggle to create something meaningful for themselves. They may develop group norms, communication patterns, and collective decision-making patterns.
6. The members are encouraged to express freely their feelings and viewpoints. They are also encouraged to understand the behavior and feelings others[14].

T-group training helps participants express need for change, develop ability to contribute to goal accomplishment, gain empathy in working with others and build competence to maintain interpersonal effectiveness, by resolving conflicts.

BEHAVIOUR MODELING

The behavior modeling approach is based on social learning theory. A number of trainers are finding it effective in shaping the behavior of employees. Three important considerations in making the program effective are:

1. *Attention:* Make sure those trainees are paying attention to the model behavior presented to them.

2. *Retention:* Help trainees remember what they observed and practiced.

3. *Reinforcement:* Reward good performance based on the new model behaviour.

Procedure

The steps involved in behavior modeling are described as follows[15]:

1. *Identify skills to be modeled:* The trainer identifies the skills to be imparted to the trainees and designs some kind of process or behavior. He may choose an expert to exhibit such behaviors or make a videotape of the expert's behavior.

2. *Explain to trainees:* The trainer introduces the model behavior by explaining its relevance, rationale and validity. The trainees are given instructions for observing and noting down the specific points or critical behaviors, when they watch the model behavior.

3. *Exhibit a model:* The trainees observe the demonstration by expert or watch the video.

4. *Encourage practicing:* The trainees are encouraged to practice the behavior. The trainer may use experiential methods like a role play or simulation to encourage trainees.

5. *Reinforce behavior:* Reinforcement of the model behavior is encouraged by appropriate motivational measures.

GRID TRAINING

Grid training, developed by Blake and Mouton is a comprehensive and systematic OD program based on the assumption managerial and team effectiveness can be taught to managers with outside assistance. The managerial grid offers a variety of positions on 9×9 grid. The 5 positions discussed for the sake of simplicity are: impoverished management (1, 1) country club management (1, 9), task management (9, 1), dampened pendulum/middle of the road management (5, 5) and team management (9, 9). Though team management is valued by many, different organizations employ different positions depending upon their culture and situations.

Change Process

The change process from the present to the desired style involves three simple steps:

1. Identification of current style based on the recent behaviors in communication, planning and controlling situations.
2. Knowing which styles is good. For instance, during economic hardship task orientation is desirable and during merger, people orientation is appropriate, and
3. Adopting the behaviors that define the desired style.

To develop the team management (9, 9) style of the grid, a six-phase change program is necessary as shown in Table 13.8. The process utilizes a variety of instruments for developing effectiveness of individuals, groups, and the organization[16].

TABLE 13.8 Grid OD Process

S.No.	Phase	Goal	Activity
1	Managerial grid	Assessing managerial skills	Off-site training program for 9 groups for assessing communication skills, problem-solving, team work and style based on managerial grid
2	Team work development	Perfecting team skills for 9, 9 position on grid	On-site training program. Analyzing team cul-ture, traditions, goal-setting, and problem-solving. Each person develops a conflict resolution strategy to test his or her position. 9, 1 and 1, 9 are ineffec-tive in conflict resolution
3	Intergroup development	Move from win-lose to win-win, ideal relations	Two member teams analyze ideal intergroup rela-tionships. They share with other groups. Next action plan to move from present model to idea is developed

(Contd.)

TABLE 13.8 Grid OD Process (*Contd.*)

S.No.	Phase	Goal	Activity
4	Ideal strategic corporate model-development	Learning concepts and skills of corporate logic for corporate excellence	Top management team develops a strategic model and presents to organizational members for their views. Enthusiastic persons from different functional areas contribute. Top management develops the ideal model based on the inputs. This process may take one year
5	Ideal strategic corporate model-implementation	Development of implementation plan.	An additional planning team is formed to facilitate design action plan and oversee implementation.
6	Systematic critique	Moving organization to the ideal	A critical evaluation of the results obtained like effective decisions, improved team work, cooperation, and organizational effectiveness is made to validate the process.

GESTALT OD

Gestalt theory was developed at the Gestalt Institute of Cleveland to incorporate using Gestalt in coaching and OD consulting. In 1960, Edwin Nevis and Richard Wallen popularized the application of gestalt concepts to organization development. Around 1974, Edwin Nevis, John Carter, Carolyn Lukensmeyer, Leonard Hirsch, and Elaine Kepner founded the Organization and Systems Development Center at the Gestalt Institute of Cleveland[17].

Assumptions

The design of the method is based on the following assumptions[18]:

About learning

1. Learning occurs through examination of 'here and now' experience.
2. Growth occurs at the contact boundary, between what is known and that which is unknown or rejected.
3. Awareness is the precursor to effective action; awareness leads to choice.

Client

1. There is an inherent drive for people to behave as effectively as possible.
2. Individual autonomy is crucial to healthy adjustment.
3. Change is the responsibility of the client, not the coach.

Consultant

1. Growth is facilitated by the interaction of client and coach. The presence of the coach is a critical element.
2. The coach's task is to help client learn new behaviors.

Role of Consultant

An active and contributory role is envisaged for the consultant. The consultant is an awareness expert, sharing his observations with the client, and providing support in diagnosis and change experiment. He acts as a teacher. He shows client how to identify habitualized behavioral patterns, and how to safely experiment with other ways of behaving that might prove to be more effective within the organization. The consultant needs specific knowledge and skills, for shaping and supervising a good variety of experiments. Obviously, experiments vary in design based on the client's specific needs, situation and environment.

Dialogue

The mode of consultant-client interaction will be more of a dialogue, rather than a discussion. Discussion and dialogue operate by opposing processes. According to Ellinor & Gerard[19], "dialogue is about gathering or unfolding meaning that comes from many parts, while discussion is about breaking the whole down into many parts". Table 13.9 captures the differences. Discussion emphasizes the idea of analysis, focuses on persuading others and leads to a conclusion or agreement. Conversely, dialogue suspends judgment giving value to curiosity in further knowing and provides for inquiry within and between people.

TABLE 13.9 Discussion vs Dialogue

Discussion	Dialogue
Breaking the issue/problem into parts	Seeing the whole among the parts
Seeing distinctions between the parts	Seeing the connections between the parts
Justifying/defending assumptions	Inquiring into assumptions
Persuading [through declaration and assertion]	Learning through inquiry and disclosure
Gaining agreement on one meaning	Creating shared meaning among many

Experiments

Experiments provide a new awareness in a natural way and are more powerful than other methods of learning. Gestalt experiments are referred to as "creating a safe emergency," and are carried at different levels of organization. They vary from changing individual to a division. They begin small to allow experimentation at less cost. The basis of Gestalt experiment (or pilot) is that "all living systems start small."

Role of Client

For the experiment to be a valuable learning experience, the client needs to pass through the five steps of the *experiential cycle of learning*. It begins with an awareness of what is and moves to "what should be," and tries with a new process, or technique. In the safety of the experiment, the client is able to learn a new concept or adopt a new behavior or a different way of working without risking personal or organizational resources.

Process

The process of intervention can be described as given in Table 13.10. The discovery process may help identify a problem of conflict between two polar points which clients have to resolve with the support of consultant.

TABLE 13.10 Gestalt OD Process

Phase	Key question	Activity
The beginning	Assessing "what is"	Heightening the client's awareness of what already "is" by describing, defining, and assessing the current situation
Transition	Choosing what to attend to	When required energy/support to move is building around a topic, the consultant can select what to attend to
Middle	Acting on the choice	Consultant articulates themes that include the energy for change and the energy for the status quo (sameness). The polar points provide for dialogue. An experiment could be proposed that would further heighten the awareness of the situation
Transition	Closing out the Activity-I	Consultant spends more time for discoveries or accomplishments have a chance to be acknowledged and digested by the individual or group
The end	Closing out the Activity-II	Appreciation, recognition, and assimilation are critical. Consultant organized discussion for each person to express what is new or different. It leads to shared meaning and clearer understanding of the new "what is" emerges

Box 13.3 describes the zero point process.

BOX 13.3 Zero Point Process for a CEO

A CEO experiencing polar tension may be asked the following questions to enable him to explore the opposing perceptions so as to rediscover our zero point.

Part I: Positive pole questions
- Recall the times when you most felt like a CEO? Describe the circumstances during that time.
- Were there times when you took pride of being a CEO? Explain the reasons?
- What are the significant to you as CEO? Why?

Part II: Negative pole questions
- Recall the times when you least felt like a CEO? Describe the circumstances during that time?
- Were there times when you were embarrassed to be a CEO? Why?
- What difficulties or inconvenience did you face being a CEO? Why?

Part III: Zero point questions
- Imagine you had a magic wand that granted three wishes for you. What wishes do you ask to fully become the CEO?
- What action do you plan to make the three wishes come true?
- What did you learn from the experience of being CEO? Mention three important things.

Source: Paradox: A Gestalt Theory of Change, www.clevelandconsultinggroup.com/ .../paradoxical_theory_of_chan...

SELF-MANAGED TEAMS

Today, self-directed teams are set-up in organizations to improve performance and manage change. Self-managed teams differ from other employee participation methods, like quality circles. In quality circles, employees of same work unit voluntarily think and design quality improvements. On the other hand, self-managed teams are operations oriented. They seek to increase production and productive efficiency. The important characteristics of the self-managed teams are[20]:

1. Associated with terms describing high performance and autonomy.
2. Consists of multi-skilled members drawn from different functional units.
3. Empowered with necessary authority and is held responsible for results.
4. Makes decisions on processes to achieve the team goal.
5. Maintains a high degree of collaboration and accept more difficult challenges

Companies implementing self-managed team replace supervisors with coaches. The coach seeks to develop the capabilities of team members by holding discussions, asking questions, and providing explanations to raise the team's level of thinking, commitment and performance.

Development

The effectiveness of self-management teams depend on the following factors[21]:

1. *Communication:* Regular team meetings with core group of team leaders and periodic all-hands meetings.

2. *Competence:* Training to improve skills required from time-to-time.

3. *Change readiness:* The team should be willing to take up new responsibilities. They should be ready to absorb various supervisory routines into their daily functions, especially administrative matters.

INTER-GROUP TEAM-BUILDING

The intervention includes diagnosis, data feedback, prioritizing, problem-solving, process intervention action planning and control mechanisms. This is essential when teams require mutual understanding and appreciation for working together. Consider the following situations:

1. Sales and Engineering departments are frequently at loggerheads over the limits to customizing the product line.
2. The Marketing department complains that IT department is insensitive to their system needs.

A serious breakdown between units or departments calls for dialogue. The dialogue process may vary from one day spent together in a room to several shorter meetings. The intervention focuses on strengthening cooperation and weakening dysfunctional competition between the teams.

Process

The process consists of the following steps[22]:

Step 1: The consultant meets the leaders of the two groups. In some cases the consultant may also choose to meet the members of the two teams. The inquiry focuses on the two questions:

(i) Do you think the relations between the two groups can be better.

(ii) Are you willing to search for mechanisms or procedures that may improve inter group relations.

Step 2: The two groups (say A and B) are assembled in separate rooms. The members are asked to discuss and build two lists.

List 1: List of their views, attitudes, feelings, and of the other group.

List 2: List of the views, attitudes, feelings, the other group might have about their group.

Step 3: The two groups (say A and B) come together and share with each other the information on the lists:

(i) Group A reads its list and Group B listens.

(ii) Group B reads its list and Group A listens.

No discussion of the items on the lists is allowed. However, questions that seek clarification of the meaning of the items are allowed.

Step 4: The two groups are now asked to reassemble in their rooms and perform two tasks:

(i) First, each group compares the lists—one prepared by them and another by the other group. It helps resolve the misperception and miscommunication between the two groups.

(ii) Second, each group makes a list of the priority issues that still need to be resolved between the two groups.

Step 5: The two groups are assembled in the same room. Together they work as follows:
(i) Compare the lists of unresolved issues and problems to be solved.
(ii) Set priorities on the items in terms of importance and immediacy.
(iii) They generate action steps for resolving the issues.
(iv) Assign responsibilities for the actions. "Who will do what when" is agreed upon for the most important items.

Step 6: As a follow-up a meeting of the two groups or their leaders is conducted. They examine the progress and determine steps to be taken in the future.

THIRD-PARTY PEACEMAKING

Third party intervention involves three roles—two parties and one consultant.

Consultant

The role of consultant is critical. Sometimes, a third party group is formed from the two groups involved in conflict. The third party should be a skilled practitioner, who is impartial and capable of listening carefully and respectfully to both the parties. He has to be fair and balanced. He should have confidence and empathy. He is to be the facilitator, not the judge to deliver a decision.

Setting

The setting should be neutral and informal. It is essential not to meet on the turf of either group or their allies. A comfortable and congenial atmosphere is necessary for conflicting groups to interact.

Method

The interventions may include the following[23]:

1. Interviewing the parties before a confrontation meeting, helping to set the agenda, and attending to the pace of the dialogue.
2. Arranging a series of informal and flexible small group discussions which focus directly on the nature of the conflict and the relationship between the parties.
3. Recording what was said during the meeting, and writing up a short report summarizing the discussions and agreements that were reached.

PARTNERING

Inter-organizational partnerships involve a distinct set of challenges and demands. They require a level of collaboration and consultation that goes well beyond typical patterns of working relationships. By adopting a reengineering mentality and focussing on the creation, maintenance, and assessment-related issues, the strength of partnerships can be enhanced as shown in Table 13.11.

TABLE 13.11 Partnership Issues

S.No.	Category	Issues
1	Creation related	Clarity of strategic objectives and inter-firm expectations
		Mutuality of business needs of partners
		Mutuality of inter-firm need(s) for partnership
		Relative core competencies: own and partner(s)
		Strength of top management support, commitment and direction
		Extent of mutual incentives/profit
		Partnership control/degree of parity between partners
		Appropriateness of alliance structure/architecture
		Flexibility/Adaptability to emerging opportunities and threats

(Contd.)

TABLE 13.11 Partnership Issues (*Contd.*)

S.No.	Category	Issues
2	Maintenance related	Relationship-related issues Attention to inter-firm communication, understanding, trust-building and fairness Sharing and accuracy of information and timeliness of feedback between partners Partnership champions: existence, visibility, effectiveness Unwritten expectations associated with legal agreement Sense of teamwork between partners Degree of inter-firm commitment to partnership Availability of appropriate technical assistance
3	Evaluation related	Measurement against mutually agreed on goals and targets Problem solving: decision processes, resource availability, inter-firm cooperation Protection of core competencies: own and partner(s) Clarity and effectiveness of work flow: appropriateness of inter-firm linkages, shared ways of operating, areas for improvement

Five key dimensions emerge as important parameters in reengineering such partnerships:

   (i) Reconceptualizing competitive essence;
  (ii) Redesigning inter-organizational processes;
 (iii) Restructuring the inter-organizational architecture;
 (iv) Reorienting individuals; and
  (v) Recreating a partnership-oriented culture.

We will now discuss them in the following sections:

Reconceptualizing Competitive Essence

An understanding of the role of partners on a different plane is important for partnership to work. It is necessary to build a strategy around core competencies based on a critical re-examination of the factors that drive the firms. In the context of partnership, the assessment should go beyond benchmarking a firm's visible manifestations—end products, market share, financial performance, and so forth, to include organizational responsiveness in past partnerships, which can be a good predictor of how an organization will operate in emerging alliances.

Redesigning Inter-organizational Processes

Since processes are key for partnerships success, the following initiatives are necessary[24]:

1. Learning each other's business;
2. Engaging in joint planning and vision development;
3. Assessing partner's willingness to commit resources to the venture; and
4. Engaging in ongoing interpersonal contact and interaction, especially at operational levels.

As part of this process, the following process related initiatives are to be undertaken:

1. Exploring of process alternatives that meet strategic objectives:
2. Mapping out current process flows and collecting documentation;
3. Working with operations personnel;
4. Probing and questioning why different activities take place; documenting the processes;
5. Benchmarking against industry leaders; and so forth.

It is important to focus on (inevitable) mistakes or problems as they emerge, and on correcting them. Box 13.4 presents how shortsightedness leads to problems.

BOX 13.4 Problems Unexpected

Hindustan Unilever (HUL) partnered with ACCESS Microfinance Alliance (AMA) to sell its Pure-It water filters on credit to villagers in Andhra Pradesh. The AMA branches purchased the filters, sold them at a price of ₹ 1800 through their loan officers. Customers purchased them and paid a monthly installment of ₹ 100. The program showed good results initially. In the meetings held at village centers, loan officers demonstrated the products, made sales, and collected payments.

Nevertheless, some operational problems showed up in course of time. AMA faced working capital shortages to maintain an inventory of filters and cover distribution costs. The transportation by auto-rikshaws proved difficult and costly. Further, after-sales service posed a challenge to AMA.

Although the program was a valuable learning experience, it underscored that MFIs should not underestimate the challenges of taking a direct role as traders or distributors of third-party products.

Source: Stretching the Fabric of MFI Networks, www.mim.monitor.com/.../whitepaper-MFI-networks-screen.pdf

---

Restructuring the Interorganizational Architecture

Partnership redefines the orientations and responsibilities of the participating firms. Table 13.12, shows the differences between partnership and traditional vendor-customer relations. Change can be established by restructuring the architecture. Two measures given under may be helpful in this regard:

1. Create dedicated positions for specific roles in the partnership. Define responsibilities of the new roles and clearly communicate to alliance team members as well as to the broader organizational population.
2. Identify appropriate personnel in the partner organization who could serve as role-related liaisons or area representatives.

This process can be accelerated by matching organizational chart.

TABLE 13.12   Traditional vs Partnership Perspectives

Dimension	Traditional relationship	Partnership
Time frame	Short-term, Renewable	Long-term, Sustainable
Strategic orientation	Subcontracting	Strategic outsourcing
Interfirm relationship	Superior-Subordinate	Leader-team member
Information flow	One way	Two way
Decision-making	Precise, from Firm to OEM: Unilateral	Guidelines, between work units Consensus-oriented
Planning	Few Executives, Experts	Many managers, Line and staff
Product improvement	Defined by contract	Ever-changing, Fluid
Control	Traditional hierarchy	Multidisciplinary, teamwork
Primary objective	Price	Quality, Price, Timing
Profit orientation	Buyer controlled	Mutually controlled

Reorienting Individuals

Organizations must realize that successful partnerships depend on the contribution of organizational members Training should focus on developing skills and attitudes in three areas:

1. *Performance:* Skills like initiative, problem-solving, and communication to work well on their jobs.

2. *Team work:* Team skills, like cooperation, trust, conflict resolution are important to act as partners.

3. *Change:* Reengineering for partnership often creates anxiety often based on fatalistic expectations. Training should focus on building trust and confidence in management.

Recreating a Partnership-Oriented Culture

Partnership dynamics depend on cultural orientations and range from fully collaborative partnership to limited interactions. The failures in partnership are often associated with gaps in commitment, values and authority. As such the following initiatives are required:

1. Examining partner commitment towards the common goal.
2. Knowing partner firm values statements and assessing the extent to which these core values are embedded in organizational orientations and behaviors.
3. Assessing willingness to jointly create, and adhere to a partnership-based values statement.

Reducing hierarchy gap and re-creating a partnership-oriented culture can be achieved by interpersonal/relationship-building sessions, joint meetings and site visits/tours for appropriate operational personnel.

TRANSORGANIZATIONAL DEVELOPMENT (TD) NETWORKING

OD consultants are facing the challenge of moving beyond the single organization in its turbulent environment focus, to the global playing field of TD networks as business in the globalized context is concerned with multi-organization network development. Transorganizational Development (TD) took birth in 1970s, with the contribution of Samuel A. Culbert, J. Max Elden, Will McWhinney, Warren Schmidt and Bob Tannenbaum[25].

Definitions

There are different definitions of TD.

Culbert, et al., defined TD as a planned change in the collective relationships of a variety of stakeholders to accomplish something beyond the capability of any single organization or individual[26].

Boje explained it as a story creating process. A collective story is being shaped and co-constructed among the network of (organizational) participants. Each stakeholder (organization) is negotiating the meaning of the collective story. Each story is a fragment, a perspective on the whole. Some are problem-based, issue-based, solution-based or just fantasy-based. Each is a candidate to become the dominant collective story[27].

At practical level, it includes a wide range of consulting strategies, such as information technology, reengineering, knowledge management, learning organizations, appreciative inquiry, participative democracy, Socio-economic Approach to Management (SEAM); Socio-technical systems, network organization design, supply and value chain management, military cyber–war game simulations, and various postmodern approaches, such as restorying spectacles of mass production and consumption with more ecocentric and socially responsible ethics.

ICEND Model

David Boje developed a story-based model of TD labeled as ICEND, which denote the following[28]:

  I—Interactive-Share stories around issues
  C—Communicative-Stories of the collective
  E—Experiential
  N—Network
  D—Development

Collective storytelling around issues leads to development of network for action and change. The method suggests steps, like convening people to interact, communicate their stories, and form common experience, to develop network for change actions. The intervention envisages formation of three subsystems—TD1, TD2 and TD3. As shown in Table 13.13.

1. *Monological TD* **(TD1):** The first type of transorganizational network tells the good story of progress through business, and explains negatives like layoffs through logical reasoning, like reengineering and downsizing. The market acts as a transorganizational means of discipline.

CEOs and managers are trained how to fabricate and narrate the reengineering change as a story with several acts.

2. *Middle Range* TD1/TD2:   There are middle range approaches between TD1 and TD2 or involving combinations of both. For example, many firms apply learning organization, appreciative inquiry, or partnering to bring business practices into more sustainable and socially responsible praxis. The middle range approaches deviate from the profit maximization, free market economy view of TD1. They are based on ecological approach.

3. *Dialogical TD* (TD2):   Both TD1 and TD2 processes interpenetrate the same systems. TD1 facilitates the formation of the second subsystem TD2. The TD2 networking seeks to resist or modify the behavior of TD1 networks and take advocacy position. Participative democracy search conferences focus on crystallizing issues, identifying leaders, forming a temporary organization to facilitate change. The consulting process of TD becomes one of inviting more voices into the collective story construction, deconstruction, and reconstruction work of the network of players.

TD3—The change initiated in TD2 is seen in a wider perspective and temporary organization is withdrawn. Change is institutionalized.

TABLE 13.13   TD Systems

Subsystem	Description	Tasks
One	Outside process consultation cycle	Diagnosis–Involvement–Active Intervention–Support–Evaluation
Two	Internal problem solving and networking cycle	Issue crystallization (issues that bring form community)–Locate stakeholders–Expanded stakeholder involvement–Search conferences and focus group intervention–Convene temporary organization–Withdrawal of temporary organization (before bureaucracy sets in)—Assessment and Evaluation.
Three	Extended network involvement cycle	Issue perceived more widely in the extended network–initial organizational involvement beyond temporary organization–Discovery of under-employed resources–Breakdown of status quo response patterns (subsystem II interventions in extended field)–Demand builds for greater organizational involvement–Breakdown of status quo responses.

SUMMARY

A successful organization is one which individual has definite role and teams have clear goals to achieve. There are several interventions that help define roles and develop teams. The three concepts that provide basis for understanding role play are—role conception, role expectation and role behavior. Four important interventions helpful in clarifying roles are—role analysis, role negotiation, interdependency exercise and responsibility charting. The role analysis and competency profiling approach adopts a diagnostic functional approach to define role of the job in the organization context, to make it capable of contributing maximum performance. Role negotiation is a structured process of identifying sources of role conflict among group members, and resolving them for redefining the role of an individual in a group. Interdependency exercise helps in surfacing problems that are latent and not previously examined. The exercise will be effective if the number of participants is between 10–35 members. Responsibility chart provides a visual map showing who is responsible for consultation, for approval, for decisions, etc.

Today, team dynamics and productivity have become critical for modern organizations adopting flat structures and project management approaches. The formal group diagnostic meeting aims at finding the direction of the movement of the groups (where is the group going?) and the level of performance (how well are we doing?). Sensitivity training emphasizes 'here-and-now' orientation and immediate feedback. T-groups are a learning laboratory with focus on learning how to learn. The behavior modeling approach is based on social learning theory. Grid training, developed by Blake and Mouton offers a variety of positions on 9×9 grid, though the 5 positions given under are usually discussed for the sake of simplicity. Gestalt theory assumes that learning occurs through examination of 'here and now' experience. The coach's task here is to help client learn new behaviors through a journey of experimentation and learning.

Self managed teams operate with autonomy and seek to increase production and productive efficiency. Intergroup team building includes diagnosis, data feedback, prioritizing, problem-solving, process intervention action planning and control mechanisms. In third party intervention consultant acts as a facilitator, to help groups reach an agreement adopting a reengineering mentality and focusing on the creation-, maintenance- and assessment-related issues. OD consultants are facing the challenge of moving beyond the single organization in its turbulent environment focus, to the global playing field of TD networks development.

EXERCISES

I. Review Questions

1. Explain when and how you employ role analysis and role negotiation.
2. Describe: (i) Interdependency exercise, (ii) Responsibility charting.
3. Outline the procedure for Formal Group diagnostic meeting and third party peacemaking.
4. Elaborate the process of sensitivity training, and behavior modeling.
5. What are T-groups? Explain inter-group team building and self managed team development.
6. Explain grid training. What is Gestalt OD?
7. Describe the two interventions: (i) Partnering, (ii) Trans-organizational development.

II. Discusssion Questions

1. Explain role related interventions with suitable examples.
2. Discuss team related interventions with suitable examples.
3. Is transorganizational development network, next generation OD? Explain it in brief.

📖 MINI-PROJECT

Take the role of Professor/Director in your academic organization and conduct role analysis. Make a report and share with your class mates.

WEB ASSIGNMENT

Visit the website given under and read "Leadership Inquiry method" explained through a UNI case study and prepare a paper for presentation in the class.

"Self managed teams, www.leadership-development-coaching.com/self-managed-teams. html".

CASE STUDY

Life Cycle Approach to Talent Development

Verizon Data Services India is a 100% subsidiary of Verizon Communications, head quartered at US. Established in 2001, it employs around 5000 people from across the country and performs a range of IT and non-IT functions at four facilities in Chennai and Hyderabad.

Inspired Working

At VDS India, one gets the opportunity to work on the most advanced wave of communication and broadband technologies. When it comes to rewards the compensation package is competitive. Further, there are well-defined professional development pathways, a diverse, vibrant work environment and timely performance recognition and rewards. It was at 22, on Business Week's list of *"Best Places to Start a Career"* and won third position in Training magazine's 2011 list of Top 125 Training Organizations in America. This is the 10th consecutive year that Verizon Wireless has been named on Training magazine's list.

Ethics and Culture

Verizon is known for its ethical standards. The professed core values are—integrity, respect, performance excellence and accountability. The credo of the organization relating to employees and values is represented by the following statements:

1. We know teamwork enables us to serve our customers better and faster. We embrace diversity and personal development not only because it's the right thing to do, but also because it's smart business.
2. We believe integrity is at the core of who we are. It establishes the trust that is critical to the relationships we have.
3. Everything we do is built on the strong foundation of our corporate values.

Employee Driven Initiatives

The organization has developed number of employee-driven initiatives to nurture an inclusive and diverse work culture, foster a strong sense of belonging to the value system and extend their collective ability to the community at large to make a difference.

Development for New Roles

The organization offers good career opportunities to its employees that are domain-intensive, and rewarding both intellectually and financially. It has adopted a lifecycle approach to development starting right from induction and on boarding. Every employee prepares an individual development plan in consultation with his or her supervisor. It identifies clearly the corresponding training and development needs. Learning is encouraged in different ways as given under:

1. A bridge development programs to help employees succeed in new responsibilities.
2. Access to a vast and diverse knowledge resource to go for self-paced learning.
3. Encouragement to participate in peer learning and coaching.
4. Support to continuation of formal education including certifications. VDS India framed its Education Assistance Policy to provide financial assistance to support employees' higher education plans. The option is open to employees for Distance Higher Education Programs, Certification courses and management education, during their employment with the company.
5. Provision for classroom training, online self-paced classes and on the job learning.
6. Participation in employee forums set up for enhancing presentation skills, public speaking abilities, communication skills, etc.

Every employee typically goes through a minimum of 80 hours of training in a year. The developed employees are moved into more complex roles and then the cycle starts again.

Performance Recognition

The performance recognition programs for individual or team excellence are devised to boost performance or encourage achievements, like patent filing. Performance standards are closely tied with the strategic initiatives and values of the organization.

Diversity Council

VDS India focusses on sustaining an inclusive work culture. The thrust on diversity is so much strong because leadership at the top measures its progress like any other business objective. Because of this we find women and people of different regions make up 60% of the Verizon Workforce. Speaking on the stand of Verizon on diversity, Magda Yrizarry, Chief Diversity Officer, Verizon observes: "Our goal has always been to leverage the diversity of employees, customers, suppliers and community partners to better serve our customers around the globe." It has two forums for diversity.

1. The Diversity Council organizes events and celebrations that create appreciation for the different cultures of the nation.
2. Women's Association of VDSI Employees (WAVE provides a forum for women employees to interact and discuss common interests and challenges for professional advancement and personal enrichment.

The annual Diversity State showcase is a visual treat. In a colourful tableau, various states of the country are represented. The celebrations include a diversity quiz and a food festival showcasing cuisines from all over the country. For its commitment to diversity, Verizon was featured in Working Mother magazine's 2009 list of "100 Best Companies for Working Women" for 9 years and listed at 12 on Diversity Inc. 2009 list of the "Top 50 Companies for Diversity."

Other than Work Roles

Employees are encouraged to develop talent related to their interest in arts and sports. The music and dance club conducts events to display employee talents The annual Beats and Feet shows is a great occasion for music and dance lovers. The company has won many laurels in corporate wide sports events in cricket, volleyball, swimming, athletics, tennis, badminton, karting, dart and many others. In-house game options, like snooker, foot ball, table tennis, and carrom are available for employees to refresh themselves between work.

Social Roles

Verizon Foundation, the philanthropic arm of Verizon offers funding to community development programs. SPICE (Software Professionals Inspiring Community Empowerment) is forum of Verizon that reaches out to communities through education enrichment activities, and other initiatives. Employees make voluntary contributions and take part in varied service activities in areas, like education and literacy, safety and health and relief works during calamities. Some of the works are undertaken by having strategic partnerships with non-profit organizations. For instance, the employees in Chennai have been working with Olcott Memorial High School to provide computer education to primary class children. The computer lab and allied infrastructure was funded by the Verizon Foundation.

Questions for Discussion

1. Examine the approach of Verizon to employees and values.
2. Analyze the opportunities for individual and team development at Verizon.
3. What additional initiatives may be considered by Verizon to foster team culture and development?

Source: Gopalakrishnan, Hema, *We have a lifecycle approach to talent development—The Hindu*, www. thehindu.com/todays-paper/tp- features/tp.../article3574647.ece
27 Jun 2012, and Life in Verizon Data Services India, Life in VDSI India, Verizon India ...
https://verizoninindia.verizon.com/WhatisInside.aspx

REFERENCES

1. Datta, G.D. (1978), Worker's participation at BHEL:II, *Vikalapa*, Vol. **3**(3), pp. 167–17; and De. N.R. (1979), India: *New forms of work organization*, Vol. **2**, Geneva: International Labour Organization.

2. In many organizations Competency Profiling has replaced ... www.nicheconsulting. co.nz/pdfs/job_analysis.pdf and Competency Profiling—Role Analysis 2009, www.cgr. co.uk/pdf/competency-profiling-role-analysis.pdf

3. Harrison, Roger (1976), "Role Negotiation: A Tough-Minded Approach to Team Development," *Social Technology of Organization Development*, La Jolla, California: University Associates.

4. Role Negotiation Process, Purpose to provide a structural method ... www.cfar.com/ cf/index.cfm?fuseaction=Publications...52.

5. Rothwell, William J. and Sullivan, Roland (2005), *Practicing Organization Development: A Guide for Consultants,* Peiffer, San Fransisco: CA.

6. French, Wendell, L. and Bell Jr., Cecil H. (2000), *Organization Development*, New Delhi: Prentice-Hall of India.

7. Role and responsibility charting and mapping, www.toolpack.com/charting.html

8. JISC infoNet–Responsibility Charting, www. .jiscinfonet.ac.uk > infoKits > Change Management and RASI..Responsibility charting, yousigma.com/tools/raciresponsibility charting.html

9. Responsibility Charting–NHS Institute for Innovation and Improvement. www.institute. nhs.uk/.../project_management

10. French, Wendell L. and Bell Jr., Cecil H. (2000), *Organization Development*, New Delhi: Prentice-Hall of India.

11. Sensitivity Training—strategy, organization, examples, model, type ... www.referenceforbusiness.com > Sc-Str

12. Sensitivity Training. traininganddevelopment.naukrihub.com > Methods of Training.

13. Golembiewski, Robert T., and Arthur Blumberg, eds. (1973), *Sensitivity Training and the Laboratory Approach: Readings about Concepts and Applications,* Inc. Itasca, IL: F.E. Peacock Publishers.

14. T. Group Training—Shvoong, www.shvoong.com > Business & Finance, 26 May 2008.

15. Behavior Modeling, Overview of Behavior Modeling Training, traininganddevelopment. naukrihub.com > ... > Games and Simulations, and Behavior Modeling in Training— Best website on HR Management ... www.explorehr.org/.../Training.../Behavior_ Modeling_in_Training.h

16. Blake Mouton Managerial Grid—Leadership Training from ... www.mindtools.com > Leadership Skills and The Managerial Grid, www.change.freeuk.com/learning/ business/managegrid.html

17. Consulting, www.clevelandconsultinggroup.com/pdfs/gestalt_consulting.pdf, Gestalt.

18. Nevis, Edwin (1987), *Organizational Consulting: A Gestalt Approach.* New York: Gardner Press.

19. Ellinor, Linda, and Glenna Gerard (1998), *Dialogue*, New York: John Wiley & Sons.

20. Merritt, Edward A. and Reynolds, Dennis E. (2003), *The Effect of Self-Managing Teams on Manager Commitment and Organizational Tenure in Private Clubs*, available at Self-managed teams, www.csupomona.edu/~jis/2003/Merritt_Reynolds.pdf.

21. Team–Wikipedia, the free encyclopedia, en.wikipedia.org/wiki/Team

22. French Wendell L., Bell, Jr. Cecil H. and Vohra, Veena (2006), *Organization Development*, New Delhi: Pearson Education.

23. Third Party Intervention, www.colorado. edu/conflict/peace/treatment/3ptyint.htm

24. Reengineering partnerships: process intervention in strategic alliances. www. thefreelibrary.com > ... > March 22, 1997.

25. TD-Transorganizational Development: And Introduction and ... web.nmsu.edu/~dboje/ TDtransorgtext.html–United States and Transorganizational development boje, D.M. & Hillon ...D3779995.u30.infinology.com/.../...

26. Culbert, Samuel A., James Max Elden, Will McWhinney, Warren Schmidt and Bob Tannenbaum (1972), "Trans-organizational praxis: A search beyond organizational development," *International Associations*, XXIV (10, October).

27. Boje, D.M. (1979), "The Change Agent as Revolutionary: Activist Interventions into Inter Organizational Networks," Transorganizational Development Session of the Academy of Management Meetings, Atlanta, Georgia.

28. Boje, D.M. (1982), "A Networking Approach to the Problem of Securing Hi Tech Jobs for Unemployed Minority Autoworkers" available at IADB 2000 Critical Postmodern OT Track Schedule, web.nmsu.edu/~dboje/TDdeathofod.html-United States.

Chapter 14

Learning and Large Scale Interventions

Learning Objectives

After studying this chapter, you will be able to:

- Describe how learning and innovation can be promoted in organizations
- Discuss interventions related to performance management
- Explain how large scale interventions take place

Vignette: Learning Solutions[1]

Centum Learning developed a learning solution for sales people of PepsiCo India. It conducted needs assessment study in collaboration with PepsiCo's Sales Academy, and prepared a detailed roadmap of training. The learning solution comprised instructor-led training and workplace projects. A follow-up process to monitor skill enhancement post this intervention was also included. Before the launch of Zen and Estilo, Maruti Udyog engaged Centum Learning for conducting a learning program to equip its over 8,000 dealers and sales people with the product presentation and customer handling skills The training included instructor-led interactive sessions and a virtual tour of the product. The sessions were interactive with components, such as quizzes, puzzles, role plays and outdoor games.

Human dimension has helped a large multinational company, in training and coaching new hires. As the MNC has recruited several young men and women it has become necessary to conduct cost-effective training programs for all of them. A global consulting company contacted Human dimension to develop their own executive coaches in North America and Asia. In the Chinese division of a European company, the turnover rate was as high 200% a year. As such, recruitment and training became a constant feature. Human dimension made an assessment of reasons for turnover and designed appropriate training program.

A large Fortune 100 company with multiple divisions and lines of businesses was concerned about the exorbitant spending on training. Labor costs and costs associated with the immediate lost productivity costs of leaders and employees attending training prevented the company from experiencing a strong return on investment. Their goal was to decrease costs to conduct training while increasing the relevance and effectiveness of training initiatives. To address the situation, Accelera consulting organization conducted a series of interviews and focus groups with key stakeholders, clients and training employees to identify gaps, local requirements and global opportunities.

They facilitated a group discussion with identified change champions to develop a new training structure. They established and worked with an internal project team which piloted and implemented the new structure. Also, they provided leadership and organizational coaching to the new leader of this organization to ensure sustainability. Over time, the centralized structure resulted in desired improvements.

The above cases illustrate the need for learning interventions as well as the concerns in introducing, such interventions in organizations. In this chapter, we will learn how to create learning organization for continuous innovation.

INTRODUCTION

A main challenge organizations face today is from innovation and technological advancement. To encounter this, organizations have to foster learning and encourage knowledge sharing and creation. There is a need to shift from an episodic learning to a learning culture. Training systems are designed in general to offer learning interventions rather than establishing learning as a way of life.

When learning is continuous, there will be continuous as well as radical innovations that give enterprises competitive edge. When environment and operations change over the years, changes become massive calling for large scale interventions. As such, OD consultants are required for growth companies to assist in moulding learning and innovative organizations and introducing large scale changes.

LEARNING INTERVENTIONS

Managers are usually preoccupied with operational issues and deadlines and they view learning as an interruption and non-value added function. They do not recognize the value of learning as a strategic business thrust. As such, learning interventions have become necessary to change the style of management from management of learning to leadership of learning. We will now briefly discuss the following interventions:

1. Learning organization
2. Parallel learning structures
3. Knowledge management
4. Performance management

LEARNING ORGANIZATION

Learning organizations according to Peter Senge are systems where people continually expand their capacity to create the results they truly desire, where new and expansive patterns of thinking are nurtured, where collective aspiration is set free, and where people are continually learning to see the whole together[2].

Building Blocks

Senge identified five dimensions, given under, that an organization has to take into cognisance for building a learning organization.

1. *Systems thinking:* It refers to the holistic view of seeing each part in relation to the whole and understanding how each part and the whole, function together to achieve the desired goals.

2. *Personal mastery:* Mastery requires continuous learning and application of knowledge. Acquisition of knowledge helps people discover their shortcomings and improve their ability to excel in their work.

3. *Mental models:* This refers to the uncovering assumptions and process generalizations regarding a phenomenon. Flexibility and openness for validating the ideas and improving are the focus of this component.

4. *Building shared vision:* The emphasis is on a shared vision for collaborative and creative work. As people talk, the vision grows clearer and as it gets clearer, enthusiasm for its benefits grows and commitment develops.

5. *Team learning:* Teams are essential and people have to learn to work and learn together. It is important to have team culture and discipline to enhance the quality of the team's discussions and insights.

Features of a Learning Organization

The learning organization can be created by changes in the structure and processes of an organization.

1. Structure is decentralized and carefully aligned with strategy, avoiding the development of "silos" and minimizing unnecessary levels of hierarchy.
2. Leadership is committed to learning and clearly communicates that learning is critical to organizational success.
3. A supportive learning culture, in which failures and unintended outcomes are the focus of constructive discussions leading to new approaches.
4. Communication systems facilitate the lateral transfer of information and knowledge.
5. Adequate resources are allocated for learning in terms of time, space, support staff, and budgets.

Box 14.1 describes how Apple Japan created a learning organization.

BOX 14.1 Creating a Learning Organization

Apple, Japan, the Japanese arm of the multinational Apple Computing Corporation, launched a drive to increase Apple's presence in the market and accelerated change. It approached the management consultant firm, Arthur D. Little. They planned brand repositioning, expansion of distribution, improvements in customer relations management, and creation of learning organization. Apple was advised to tackle the five disciplines, which are essential to a learning organization.

1. Team learning was facilitated by stretching the normal group meetings to allow more time for group discussions and team education.
2. Shared vision was created through communication process and each member was encouraged to work towards the same goal irrespective of their position.
3. Mental models: By fostering team spirit and action, the consultant made an attempt to ceate common mental model.
4. Personal mastery was facilitated by strengthening e-learning processes. Training programs were conducted to help managers to set challenging goals.
5. Systems thinking: They were trained to take holistic approach and find solutions from system perspective.

When most of the companies were talking about competency models, Apple has taken a page from learning organization books. They begin capturing the essence of Apple's executive performance and philosophy in digital form for leaders on into the future. Apple, founded Apple University in 2008 "to teach Apple employees how to think like Steve Jobs and make decisions he would make."

Source: Learning Organisations, www.ee.ed.ac.uk/~gerard/MENG/MEAB/lo_index.html. and The Real Succession Plan For Steve Jobs: Apple Thinks Different ...www.bersin.com > Analyst Blogs > Josh Bersin's Blog, 26 Aug. 2011.

Building a Learning Organization

The key components[3] of the process of building a learning organization include:

1. *Organizational assessment:* Make an assessment of organization with particular focus on culture, leadership, and the organization's tolerance for change.

2. *Creating a strategic plan:* Develop a strategic plan and align this plan with the organization's mission, vision, and values.

3. *Documenting knowledge:* Collect knowledge contained in various written media through job audits and other collection methods.

4. *Laying down procedures:* Establish standard operating procedures and work instructions to make knowledge portable.

5. *Training and education:* Introduce performance and training initiatives to make each worker improve skills and knowledge and contribute more fully to the organization.

6. *Technology support:* Introduce technology for easy access of information and knowledge, and future changes.

7. *Communication:* Develop communication strategies before, during and after implementation.

8. *Continuous evaluation:* Put in place, mechanisms to monitor the on-going progress and suggest corrective measures.

KNOWLEDGE MANAGEMENT

Knowledge is the result of learning and it provides the sustainable competitive advantage to the firms, especially those in information technology sector. Box 14.2 shows how Wipro excelled in this. Knowledge Management (KM) is a process which has to be infused in each and every individual, and group (department) of an organization.

BOX 14.2 Wipro—The Leader in KM

Wipro Technologies has been running, since 2000, a structured knowledge management program. Since its inception, Wipro InfoTech, has adopted open culture, and showed interest in cultivating knowledge. It implemented an enterprize wide KM system to meet three objectives: growth of organization to a competency-based and knowledge-driven organization, adoption of new technology for diversification and growth and expansion of competency framework to create new business opportunities.

The KM framework has three components: (i) *Learning* (specialized training and personalized instruction through e-learning, workshops, online mentoring and contact sessions), (ii) KEEP (Knowledge Enhancement, Extraction, and Practice) and CARE (Competency Augmentation with Research Excellence). The system enables its 75,000 plus employees spread all over the world, to access the expertise lying in the organization. Wipro has implemented a web-enabled portal built on Microsoft Share point to manage documented knowledge and operate virtual communities of practice. For delivering value-based customer knowledge, the Global MAKE (Most Admired Knowledge Enterprises) award was given to Wipro Technologies third time in a row.

Source: State of Knowledge Management in Indian IT Companies
www.isrj.net/PublishArticles/456.aspx and Wipro tops in global MAKE award 2007 | Dalal Street, www.dalalstreet.biz/.../2007/11/wipro-tops-in-global-make-award-20...

The goal of KM is the systematic advancement of organizational learning to strengthen core competencies and spread knowledge and skills organization-wide. The knowledge that flows continuously across the organization is to be categorized, processed, shared, stored and retrieved. For this, every company needs a knowledge management strategy. The following actions are part of such strategies[4].

- Coding the existing raw data and developing a knowledge base for organizations, for future processing and sharing.

- Capturing information from experts through asking methods like interview, dialogue and panel discussions and written methods like websites, memoirs, autobiographies, biographies, research papers, etc.
- Storing data by converting it into audio and video formats to suit the knowledge requirements.
- Sharing through meetings, seminars, workshops, group discussions and other kind of gatherings.

PARALLEL LEARNING STRUCTURES

Parallel learning structures (also known as Communities of Practice) are knowledge management practice. They promote innovation and change in large bureaucratic organizations. Groups representing various levels and functions are formed to work parallel to the normal, hierarchical structure. They exchange information that helps enhance knowledge, improve practices and promote innovation[5]. Box 14.3 presents how these groups came into existence in Xerox and other organizations.

BOX 14.3   Parallel Learning Structures

Xerox found that its technical representatives were gathering in common areas (the local parts warehouse or coffee pot) and exchanging information about how to repair machines better. Rich knowledge transfer took place through these conversations. As such, Xerox decided to expand them in the name of learning and innovation. The corporation set-up Eureka—an electronic "knowledge refinery". It organizes and categorizes tips provided by the field staff. All technical representatives, regardless of rank, can submit a tip. There is no incentive other than recognition as a good knowledgeable colleague.

At National Semiconductor, an informal community of engineers began advising on new chip designs. The service attracted different product groups and they approached them. The group gradually won wide reputation for excellence and led to the formation of Communities of Practices (CoPs).

Source: John Seely Brown and Estee Solomon Gray (2007), The People Are the Company, December 18, The Fast company, I-pad edition. Available at http://www.fastcompany.com/magazine/01/people.html.

INNOVATION INTERVENTIONS

The success of business largely depends on its ability to create value for the customers. Value is created by developing innovations in tune with an ever-changing environment. However, most organizations view the process of idea creation, as an expense and as an activity outside the operations. Unfortunately, they are not aware, that it is the building of an organization skill and competence, that turns the so-called intangible asset into a tangible one. To those enterprises looking to go beyond operations and creating next frontier businesses, consultants are available to help. Box 14.4 provides a brief on the role played an innovation developing consultant.

BOX 14.4 Inspiring Innovation
Confianzys, a consulting firm offers assistance to companies in demolishing boundaries and bringing together expertise in ideation with a strong product and market intervention capability. I-Qube is the Confianzys Incubation Center that provides support in the form of innovation, incubation and investment. It supports start-up teams tossing with an idea by providing strategic thinking to build a viable innovation. It helps going concerns build a culture of innovation and deliver market-relevant innovative products. It inspires established companies to stretch their capabilities and look beyond current lines of business. Confianzys founding team, act as mentors to help clients question existing assumptions and beliefs, and look at varied sources for innovation, such as customer experiences, technological developments for creating the "next" frontier business. Opposite thinking, question the questions, sport the absurdities, customer experiences, outsider experience, and extreme push are the innovative thinking tools of Confianzys.
Source: Based on Innovation Interventions—Confianzys Consulting is a Product ... www.confianzys.com/innovation_interventions.html.

In this section, we will discuss four innovation related interventions, given under:

1. Total Quality Management
2. Continuous Improvement
3. Quality of Life
4. Benchmarking

TOTAL QUALITY MANAGEMENT

Quality has become a dominant concern in all organizations. Total Quality Management (TQM) has evolved as a consequence of this. It is defined as a leadership philosophy and strategy that is based on continuous improvement of every process, empowerment of people, continuous learning, and institutionalizing a culture of efficiency and innovation. TQM initiatives were first taken in India in the early 1980s and thee credit for introducing quality circles goes to Bharat Heavy Electricals Ltd (BHEL), Trichy and Bharat Electronics Ltd. (BEL), Bangalore[6].

Prerequisites

Since introduction of TQM, goes beyond lip service and tinkering with the organization, caution is necessary in introducing it. There will be a radical change in the culture—the way organization works and values results.

1. *Leadership:* The leadership style should be participatory to empower employees with necessary authority to make decisions, and experiment with new ideas. A personal program of leadership is essential to assess the fitness of existing leadership to the TQM culture.

2. *Employee attitude and skills:* The new culture requires employees to change the traditional beliefs and values to accept a new role. They should be willing to undergo training for acquiring the competences needed to think creatively, participate in meetings and discussions, and experiment with new ideas and produce quality products and services.

3. *Systems:* Various systems like human resource system (job design, selection, orientation, training, appraisal, reward and others), and communication systems should be align to support the TQM culture.

4. *Structure:* To facilitate participative leadership, layers of organization is to be reduced, and roles are to be redesigned.

5. *Results:* The evaluation of the results in terms of continuous improvements, increase in efficiency and savings of resources, etc.

CONTINUOUS IMPROVEMENT

Continuous improvement refers to adaptation to the evolutionary changes to make sure that the product, process or system continues to be effective. It requires as such the following initiatives:

1. Feedback from various sources of environment, on firm's outcomes and processes.
2. Free discussion on the information and issues by teams at different levels and areas.
3. A system to evaluate and choose new ideas and carry them out.
4. Systematic ways to measure your progress and the outcomes of the changes.
5. A real desire to do it, even if it means changing power relationships and doing some things that leaders do not completely agree with.

Box 14.5 shows how Tata Motors and Tata Steel improved quality.

BOX 14.5 Tata's Win Quality Award

Tata Motors is the largest commercial vehicle manufacturer in the country and among the top ten commercial vehicle manufacturers in the world. The Passenger Car Business Unit (PCBU) of Tata Motors has received the coveted 'certificate of approval' of its Quality Management System (QMS) from Bureau Veritas Certification (BVC), for compliance with ISO/TS 16949:2002. It has received this prestigious recognition because it has developed a QMS with a variety of quality tools for continual improvement, defect prevention, and reduction of variation and waste in the supply chain. The system is firmly rooted in the plan-do-check-act (PDCA) philosophy of Total Quality Management (TQM). It adopted a process approach that focusses on process outputs and customer satisfaction, and works back into the process. Each process is evaluated to find how it might be done faster and better, to enhance customer satisfaction.

Tata steel won the Deming prize in 2008 for the application of total quality management (TQM). TQM initiatives began in the late 1980s and several quality activities—quality circles, ISO certification, quality improvements using Juran methods, etc were taken. In 2005, a TQM diagnosis was conducted to understand the status of the TQM implementation.

Strategies and policy management issues were examined for relevance, balanced score card analyzes were made and areas that required changes were identified. The day-to-day operations were standardized and incremental improvements were encouraged. People involvement was encouraged through quality circles, suggestion management, knowledge *manthan*, etc. Six examination units were set up and 26 examiners, having a lot of experience were appointed. They examine each department for 2 days and cover all the 52 departments within 12 days.

Two major challenges were: (i) to bring quality to the forefront. For this, customer focused objectives and strategies were formulated in various divisions and departments; (ii) to create a mindset that values and seeks improvements in activities. The challenge is formidable given the organization employs more than 35,000 employees. This was done through workshops and by explicitly stating and documenting improvement targets.

Source: Tata Group | Tata Motors | Media releases | Tata Motors gets Bureau ... www.tata.com > ... > Tata companies › Tata Motors › Media releases and Winning the Deming prize–Tata Group www.tata.com > ... > Tata companies > Tata Steel > Interviews.

Many continuous improvement efforts focus on processes. A common framework for continuous improvement, is called "plan-do-check-act.[7]" Once a shortfall is sighted, people plan their changes; implement them (do), evaluate their impact (check), and then move on to further changes (act). Continuous improvement is the central part of the balanced scorecard for some companies. Box 14.6 shows how TQMI provided quality consulting.

BOX 14.6 Quality Consulting

Total Quality Management International (TQMI) Private Ltd. was approached by a leading refined products distribution company in UAE, having foreseen a stiff challenge from its competitors. A project team was set up to improve the filling station operations. First, current process map of filling station operations was prepared. It highlighted the macro level process, the particulars of cost data and the detailed tasks of the current process. After deep review, all Non-Value-Adding (NVA) activities were eliminated. Through site surveys, customer perceptions were obtained and root cause analysis was done for key issues. Proposed process maps were developed indicating revised cost and time data. The revised process was implemented by installing daily routine activity management across the organisation. As a result, waiting time of customers during peak hours was reduced by 30%. It improved the Customer Satisfaction Index by 20%, reduced the cost of filling station operations by 29%.

A large multinational company in the financial sector faced a problem in the financial processes. The lack of consistency in the processes (accounts receivable, accounts payable, financial reporting, and payroll) has resulted in delays in executive decisions and rise in costs in their transactions with their internal (domestic and international project offices), and external customers. TQMI worked with internal managers and found that corporate finance function was viewed as cost center with no ability to add value to business or customers. They launched four cross-functional process improvement teams. They were

(Contd.)

BOX 14.6 Quality Consulting (*Contd.*)

given minimal training in process analysis. For the four critical financial processes, they conducted current state analysis and developed future state design. This step took eight weeks and 80 hours of meeting time. They facilitated interviews with stakeholders to establish clear customer requirements for financial reporting process. The result was standardized financial processes that enhanced savings in time and costs.

Source: Adapted with permission from Case studies, TQM International Pvt. Ltd. (TQMI) >> History ::: Quality Management ...www.tqmi.com/history.asp.

QUALITY OF LIFE

Quality of work life is a major determinant of performance and productivity in organizations. Quality of life makes an organization a great place to work. Robert Levering, Co-Founder, Great Place to Work® says, "A great place to work is one in which you trust the people you work for, have pride in what you do, and enjoy the people you work with."

Quality of work life can be ensured through good HR philosophy and practices. It comprises overall well-being of an employee. It consists of the three dimensions given under:

1. *Physical well-being:* The hygiene factors (the focus on scientific management and Factories Act in India).

2. *Mental well-being:* The satisfaction factors (the people-centric human resource management practices, wage and welfare legislation in India, work force diversity as well as the voluntary CSR (corporate social responsibility) approaches.

3. *Spiritual well-being:* The programs that address workplace stress, like yoga, meditation, prayers, etc., and work-life balance programs.

Great Place to Work® Institute, a global management research and advisory firm, assists organizations in assessment and establishment of right policies and programs for creating right work environment. Their approach is as:

1. *Awareness:* Providing an understanding of what makes a great workplace.

2. *Diagnostic:* Identifying strengths and improvement areas.

3. *Insights:* Unpeeling the layers to discover the root causes.

4. *Change:* Identification and prioritization of action areas and creation of a road map for change.

5. *Implementation:* Power implementation with understanding of best practices and processes.

Box 14.7 presents an approach to create a great place to work.

BOX 14.7 Creating Great Place to Work

Great Place to Work, believes that great organizations create cultures in which everyone is inspired and has the opportunity to contribute their best. They take a holistic picture of organization, and make assessment of culture and policies in relation to employees' experiences and the benefits and identify gaps between the organization's intended outcomes and the real effect of the policies and culture. According to them, programs in such organizations will have five qualities: variety, originality, all-inclusiveness, degree of human touch, and integration with the culture.

They conduct annually surveys to identify great places to work using two lens models that maps employee perceptions and management practices: The Trust Index Employee survey (2/3 weightage) and the Culture audit Management questionnaire (1/3 weightage).

The trust assessment is made by asking employees about behaviors that measure the following five dimensions: (i) Credibility (communication, competence and integrity), (ii) Respect (support, collaborating and caring), (iii) Fairness (equity, impartiality and justice), (iv) Pride (personal job, team, company), and (v) Camaraderie (intimacy, hospitality and community).

The Culture Audit consists of two parts: (i) employee demographics (e.g. number of employees, voluntary turnover, ethnic breakdowns, tenure, etc.), information about the organization (e.g. year founded, revenues); and employee benefits and perks like allowances, insurance, and holidays) and (ii) a series of open-ended questions, on company philosophy and people related practices (hiring, communication, employee development, company celebrations and so on).

They suggest 9 program areas for creating a great work place: inspiring, speaking, listening, thanking, developing, caring, celebrating, sharing and hiring.

Source: Great Place to Work® India, www.greatplacetowork.in/and http://www.greatplacetowork.in/storage/documents/Indias_Best_Companies_to_Work_For_-_2012_Study_-_Information_Brochure.pdf.

BENCHMARKING

Benchmarking is a process of comparing the product, process, system or outcomes of an organization with that of a successful unit or organization, either internal or external, to understand the best practices behind its excellent performance, and applying them appropriately, to improve performance of the organization. There are five key stages in benchmarking[8]:

1. ***Proto-planning:*** In this stage, the following decisions are taken:
   - Unit under question—What is to be benchmarked?
   - Benchmark—Against whom it is to be benchmarked?
   - Measures—What kind of metrics will be taken up for benchmarking? What kind of data is to be collected and how?

2. ***Data collection:*** In this stage, the following actions are performed.
   - Secondary/background research is made to collect contextual information.
   - Primary research is done to gather data from the benchmark unit.

3. *Analysis:* This stage involves the following:
   - Identification of gaps between organization measures and benchmark measures
   - Identification of enablers and bottlenecks

4. *Implementation:* In this stage, two aspects are critical:
   - Implementation planning
   - Roll-out of new modus operandi (changes)

5. *Monitoring:* In this final stage, progress in emulation of the best practices will be evaluated and corrective measures are taken. Thus it involves following decisions.
   - Authority to evaluate
   - Metrics used for evaluation
   - Iterative change

There are consultants who specialized in benchmarking services. Box 14.8 provides a view of two such organizations.

BOX 14.8 Benchmarking Consultants

Synergy Consultants provide benchmarking services in different areas. For instance, they conduct compensation surveys for evolving competitive compensation structure. The surveys collect data on the organization levels of hierarchy, salary grades, and incentives, etc. Benchmarking Consultants.com is a division JJA Consultants Inc., an international consulting, training and research company. It provides products, services, tools, techniques, methodologies and systems supporting six types of benchmarking–competitive, generic, professional, functional, internal and self-unit. The Benchmarking Network (TBN) consultants offer a wide range of specialized services to their clients, including onsite benchmarking training for the employees. They also lead their sponsors to site visits at the "Best Practices" companies. Their Fasttrakk™ study is a rapid methodology that uses questionnaire on up to 15 process and measures.

Source: Based on Synergy Consultants: Recent salary & compensation studies in India.... www.synergyindia.com/recent_compensation.htm, Benchmarking Consultants.com–About Benchmarking Consultants ... www.benchmarkingconsultants.com/about.htm and Newspaper Benchmarking | Benchmarking Business Process Best ..... newspaperbenchmarking.com/.

PERFORMANCE MANAGEMENT

Performance management is a systematic process of planning and controlling of individuals and groups, and thereby organizational effectiveness in the accomplishment of its short and long term goals. Employee performance requires decisions and actions in five areas as shown in Table 14.1.

Box 14.9 describes performance management intervention by Clarity consultants.

TABLE 14.1 Performance Management System

Subsystem	Action	Intervention
Planning	Identifying goals and performance expectations	Goal setting, MBO, TQM
Organizing	Teams and work assignments	Team building, self-management teams
Leading	Communicating and motivating to enable people to achieve	Coaching, counselling, mentoring, communication skills
Controlling	Monitoring performance to get results and rewarding good performance	Benchmarking, feedback processing and reporting

---

BOX 14.9 Performance Management by Clarity

As sales of mobile application frameworks targeted at corporate IT departments faced a steep decline the company analyzed the reasons and identified that they had the technical prowess to succeed, but lacked skills in executing critical deals. They hired clarity consultants. Their diagnosis revealed the following weak points:

- *In adequate resources:* The company was following an aggressive marketing, but on too many fronts at once. As a result, the resources spread were too thin.
- *Lack of direction:* The unresolved differences in the opinions of executives about which strategic path was best, had led to pursuing three strategies simultaneously. As such, there was lack of coordination and concerted effort.

Clarity initiated the following improvement measures:

- *Goal setting:* Planning sessions were designed to help them clarify priorities and develop a plan of attack.
- *Strategies:* Through strategic dialogue all conflicting issues were resolved and a strategy was evolved.
- *Implementation support:* Direct support to the product and business development teams for executing the new plans was provided.
- *Leader development:* Coaching was given to senior team and individual leaders in one-on-one and group meetings.

Source: Adapted with permission from Driving New Market Growth at a Software Company, http://www.clarityconsulting.com/what-we-do/software.php

---

Two of the components of performance management system will be discussed here:

1. Management by Objectives (MBO)
2. 360 degree feedback

MANAGEMENT BY OBJECTIVES

It is a simple 5-step process of working in accordance with the objectives set for performance.

- Set corporate objectives
- Set and align employee objectives
- Monitor performance
- Evaluate performance
- Reward good performance

Objectives form the core of the MBO process. However, setting good objectives is a difficult task. Employees need assistance and training in identifying and defining their objectives. The second aspect that requires attention is the performance monitoring. With an MBO solution, managers have to develop certain milestone and check the progress of employees against them. Performance appraisal requires quantitative and qualitative measures to be effective. The third step relates to rewards. Designing rewards for successful accomplishment of objectives and implementing them is critical for the success of MBO.

MBO is often misused by managers who did not realize its spirit and purpose. It seeks to empower employees with a set of self controls. However, superior managers use this to put constant pressure on the subordinate to set higher goals and produce results. Sometimes, it is made ineffective by managers who do not have the interpersonal skills to have a dialogue with their subordinate managers.

Making MBO Effective

MBO can be effective when attention is paid to the following elements of the system[9].

1. *Mission development:*   The development of an overall organizational mission.

2. *Role design:*   The development of role descriptions–functions and relationship.

3. *Performance guides:*   Effectiveness areas, or key results areas that determine contribution of an employee and indicators and standards of effective performance.

4. *Objectives:*   Specific statements about what is to be accomplished in relation to particular performance standards.

5. *Action plans:*   Plans that outline how the objectives are going to be accomplished.

6. *Standards for appraisal and procedures:*   The way a manager has to review performance and hold discussion.

360-DEGREE FEEDBACK

360-degree feedback is a positive addition to the current performance management system. Human Resource and Organizational Development professionals are turning to 360-degree feedback to improve performance and increase people's job satisfaction. It is an elaborate method that provides each employee the opportunity to have performance feedback from multiple sources.

- Supervisor
- Peers (four to eight peers)
- Reporting staff members
- Coworkers
- Customers
- Self

360-degree feedback is a powerful tool, and as such, impose a degree of risk. If not administered well, its results may do harm. The effectiveness of the feedback depends basically on two things:

- Design and administration of assessment tool
- Support services

The assessment tools are to be designed with dimensions that yield operational relevance. They should have face validity and reliability. Many consultants are available to offer support. To understand the range of support they can offer consider the following offer of The York Consulting Team, Inc.[10] a full service provider of 360° feedback interventions. They provide the following assurances:

1. We can manage your entire 360° feedback program.
2. We partner with internal resources to support current processes.
3. We train internal resources to be self-sufficient.
4. We supplement your efforts with surveys and reports.
5. We assist you in planning for cascading involvement of multiple layers of management.
6. We utilize our own web-based interaction tool to efficiently distribute and receive 360° feedback surveys.

INSTITUTION BUILDING

Since the early 70's, the United Nations Development Program (UNDP) offered guidance for its staff and governments on "institution building". In 1991, it is termed as "capacity building[11]."

Institution building, is a process of strengthening existing institutions by capacity building and creation of good governance practices. Good governance embodies processes that are participatory, consensus oriented, accountable, transparent, responsive, effective and efficient, equitable and inclusive, and which follow the rule of law.

Growing Concern

Reforms are initiated when government fails to deliver services to the citizens due to problems like political crisis, corruption, inefficiency, shortage of trained and educated manpower and others. Therefore, a major task is building state institutions. The focus will be on improvement of efficiency and effectiveness of existing institutions, the restoration of destroyed institutions and the enhancement of professionalism of authorities. In India, the economic reforms in 1990s, introduced liberalization, privatization and globalization policies and envisaged an active participation of private organizations, in different sectors of our economy. As such, capacity building has become a major activity in both public and private organizations[12].

Approach to Institution Building

National Dairy Development Board (NDDB) observes the following aims of institution building:

1. *Good governance:* Focuses on enabling a cooperative to become a viable, salient and truly member-owned and controlled enterprise.

2. *Good performance:* Helps the cooperative achieve immediate improvements in its "physical and financial" performance, and self-sustaining all around improvement over the long term.

   Box 14.10 describes the institution building by NDDB.

BOX 14.10   NDDB's Approach to Institution Building

The capacity building program at NDDB covers primary members, management committee members and staff of village Dairy Cooperative Societies (DCS) as also the professionals and elected boards of Milk Producers' Cooperative Unions.

Shared vision: The first step focuses on achieving a shared vision. The board or the management committee evolved a set of organizational values and the mission. This is followed by development of a strategic plan, with long-term objectives and the derivative action plan detailing the activities to be undertaken to achieve its objectives.

Capacity building: Education and training programs on DCS activities, member responsibilities and rights, managing committee member duties and tasks focussing on empowerment of women are undertaken. They helped develop women's leadership skills, create thrift and credit groups and promoted health, education and economic activities. The activities helped raise women's awareness both of their rights and responsibilities as cooperative members, and increased their participation in the membership and governance.

Source: Adapted from *Institution Building*—NDDB
www.nddb.org/core_competencies/coop-ib.html.

Institution Building Consultancy

Besides Talent Management, Executive Coaching, Leadership Development, and Organizational Change, Anahat (a consultant firm) offers services for institution building. Human Dynamics (a consultant firm) partners with clients in all regions of the world, at international, national, regional and local levels, to implement institutional and capacity development projects within a country's public administration[13].

LARGE SCALE SYSTEMS CHANGE

Large Scale Intervention (LSI) is a trajectory for change or learning in which stakeholders of the whole system participate and contribute to the change. It works with the "whole system in the room". The most widely known ones are: (i) Future Search, (ii) World Café, (iii) Open Space, (iv) Real Time Strategic change (Whole Scale Change®) and (v) Hybrids of the methods above.

FUTURE SEARCH

Future search is a Planning meeting and is a proven method of improving organizational systems and abilities. Box 14.11 present how IKEA benefited from Future search. The steps in conducting are as follows:[14]

1. *Task definition:*   Decide the planning task and announce it to the members.

2. *Assemble people:*   Bring together large number of people with resources, expertise, formal authority and need. Assemble them in one or in parallel rooms.

3. *Historical review:*   Members begin the discussion first by exploring their shared past by examining patterns, telling stories and describing events. If clashing perspectives come up, they are simply understood and acknowledged. No attempt is made to resolve them. They are guided to return their attention to the theme—the shared milestones in their history.

4. *Analysis of present:*   They look at the current trends to create a detailed "mind map" of the trends on a giant sheet of paper. They discuss the major issues, prioritize trends as they impact the organization, and share freely their views shifting their positions as and when required.

BOX 14.11   Success of Future Search
IKEA, the furniture company, has manufacturing facilities around the world. It offers 11 major product lines through 140 stores, and has on rolls thousands of staff involved in tracking and managing the system. It adapted the FUTURE SEARCH method to a single product, the "Ektorp" sofa, to revamp IKEA's global distribution system and realise ambitious goals set for it: double sales, improve quality and cut the price 30% without cutting profit, make sofa shopping easier for customers, and cut delivery times.   A three day FUTURE SEARCH workshop was conducted in which 52 stakeholders including suppliers, executives starting with the company president and top staff and line people, and several Ektorp customers took part. They described the existing system, documented required changes, proposed a variety of new systems, agreed on an implementation plan and got buy-in from all relevant levels and function in the organization.   Seven task forces were constituted and within a month, they helped redoing every aspect of the system. A regular conference call buttressed by emails facilitated coordination. Besides accomplishment of the goal there are other outcomes. Perhaps the most significant outcomes were: (1) involving customers in product development from the start, and (2) decentralizing systems control and coordination to meet local conditions. A kind of self-organizing ability was developed, which was not previously seen. The Ektorp sofa was used as a way of visualizing a very complex global system. No one predicted that after the Future Search it would become the world's best selling sofa!
Source: Adapted with permission from Marvin Weisbord, Co-Director, Future Search Network: A Model for Re-Designing Product Lines at Ikea. available at www.futuresearch.net/method/applications/uploads/business/ikea.pdf.

5. *Small group brainstorming:* The diverse stakeholders are now formed into sub-groups to develop futures. They do this by imagining themselves 5, 10 and 20 years in the future.

6. *Development of plans:* The sub-groups make presentations of their futures to others. Then they develop lists of common futures (what they agree they want), and potential projects (how to get there).

WORLD CAFÉ

The World Café is a flexible, easy-to-use process rooted in the philosophy of conversational leadership. Based on living systems thinking, the approach creates dynamic networks of conversation that can catalyze an organization's own collective intelligence around its change needs. The seven principles involved in the World Café are[15]:

- Create context
- Create hospitable space
- Explore questions that matter
- Encourage everyone's contribution
- Cross pollinate and connect diverse perspectives
- Listen together for patterns, insights and deeper questions
- Harvest and share collective discoveries

OPEN SPACE

Open Space enables people, in organization, to create inspired meetings and events.

With membership ranging from 5 to 2000+ people, groups participate in one-day workshops, three-day conferences, or the regular weekly staff meeting to make processes effective. It works best when complex issues, involving diverse people.

Process

What happens when a group gets into the open space cannot be exactly predicted, as it is known for surprises with its apparent lack of structure. However, there is a guarantee that the following things happen[16]:

1. Most important issues to the participants will be raised.
2. The issues will be addressed by the participants capable of working on them.
3. Within a short time of one or two days all the issues will be addressed and report will be prepared.
4. In a matter of a few hours, the important ones can be focused and prioritized even in a large group of 100s.
5. After an event, the results can be made available to an entire organization.
6. The results can be planned and implemented faster.

REAL TIME STRATEGIC CHANGE

This intervention was created in 1994 by Robert "Jake" Jacobs and Frank McKeown. It can be used in groups ranging from 40 to 4000. Real Time Strategic Change (RTSC) differs from other large scale interventions, like Future Search and Open Space in one aspect. In this, the leaders first propose a "straw-horse" model for review and feedback. Then a forum for analysis and dialogue is created. Box 14.12 presents an illustrative case of RTSC.

BOX 14.12 Real Time Strategic Change

The Board of Directors of a 7000 member professional association developed a long-term plan for improving the performance of the organization. A Real Time Strategic Change event was planned to obtain views of the leaders of different chapters located at different places. However, the attendance was made voluntary. Over 100 individuals attended the meet.

On the first day, the large group event was organized with the goal of "reaching consensus on the business plan strategies". The event helped members contribute idea for making modifications and enhancements. The members by their participation had improved their association. They also developed a sense of ownership in the strategy as it reflected the feedback of the participants. The Board and the paid administrative staff were able to implement the plan successfully.

Source: Silverman, Lori L. (2000), Using Real Time Strategic Change For Strategy Implementation, *The Quality Management Forum*, Fall, Vol. **26**(4). available at Using Real Time Strategic Change for strategy ... www.partnersforprogress.com/articles/largegroupinterventions.pdf

---

Process

It is a highly structured and organized process and involves the following steps[17]:

1. First the participants interact with their leaders and outside experts.
2. Then they exchange ideas among them. They analyze issues and formulate strategies.
3. They present their analysis and strategies to their leaders.
4. Based on mutual feedback, leaders revise the organization's approach to action and communicate it to the participants.
5. Participants are ready to act as they have contributed their ideas to the strategy development.

Guidelines

To create this kind of result, consultants make sure of the following[18]:

1. *Leader's initiative:*   A commitment from leadership to be open, honest and responsive.

2. *Formation of a cross-functional design team:*   Participants are those who can represent a maximum mix of organizational viewpoints.

3. *Instructions:* Participants are given guidelines and instruction for completing tasks and for managing their small groups.

4. *Participation:* They are encouraged to contribute their viewpoint and feedback. Feedback is shared publicly at frequent intervals. Voting is used to achieve consensus Also there is frequent moving from different types of work to ensure participants talk to other people at the event; from small groups, whole room work, and flipchart marking.

5. *Forum for discussion:* It is important to organize a workshop(s), that is well-designed and well-planned, both procedurally and logistically.

6. *Logistics management:* A logistics team behind-the-scenes and during the event is important to look into location, table arrangements, audio-visuals, handouts, and materials, meal and accommodation.

7. *Facilitators:* At least one outside facilitator and one or more internal consultants are essential to guide the design team in creating specific goal and an agenda. During the intervention, they ensure that the event takes place as planned. They restructure the agenda real-time, if needed, based on the outcome of the activities that occur during the dialogue process.

SUMMARY

Organizations are designing interventions for learning, knowledge management, innovation, quality of life, large scale interventions and institution building. The learning organization is decentralized in authority, flat in structure, with leadership committed to learning, and having a supportive learning culture, good communication systems and adequate resources for transfer of information and knowledge. The goal of KM is the systematic advancement of organizational learning. For this, coding the existing raw data and developing a knowledge base, capturing information from experts and other sources, storing data by converting it into audio and video formats and sharing through meetings, seminars, workshops, etc. are necessary. Innovations provide organizations, a competitive edge.

The innovation interventions include: Total Quality Management, Continuous improvement, Quality of life and Benchmarking. TQM introduction needs participative leadership, for creating TQM culture, new skills for employees, well-designed systems that support quality concerns, new roles for employees and evaluation of results in terms of quality. Continuous improvement refers to adaptation to the evolutionary changes to make sure that the product, process or system continues to be effective. It requires feedback from various sources of environment, on firm's outcomes and processes and changes according to it. Quality of work life is a major determinant of performance and productivity in organizations. Quality of life makes an organization a great place to work. It consists of the three dimensions: physical, mental and spiritual well-being. Benchmarking is a process of comparing the product, process, system or outcomes of an organization with that of a successful unit or organization, either internal or external, to understand the best practices behind its excellent performance, and applying them appropriately, to improve performance of the organization. Performance management is a systematic process of planning and controlling of individuals and groups, and thereby, the organizational effectiveness in the accomplishment of its short-and-long term goals.

Institution building is a process of strengthening existing institutions by capacity building and creation of good governance practices. Large Scale Intervention (LSI) is a trajectory for change or learning in which stakeholders of the whole system participate and contribute to the change. It works with the "whole system in the room". The most widely known ones are: (i) Future Search, (ii) World Café, (iii) Open Space, (iv) Real Time Strategic Change (Whole Scale Change®), and (v) Hybrids of the methods above.

EXERCISES

I. Review Quesitons

1. Explain the features of learning organization.
2. Explain when parallel learning structures are used?
3. How is knowledge management system developed in organizatons?
4. What are the components of TQM?
5. How is continuous improvement achieved in organizations?
6. What are the ways of promoting quality of life?
7. Explain benchmarking process.
8. How is performance encouraged in organizations?
9. Explain one large scale intervention.
10. How much important leadership is to institution building?

II. Discussion Questions

1. Discuss how learning organization and knowledge management can be set up for a large manufacturing unit.
2. How do you promote innovation and quality in a large scale service organization?
3. Explain: (a) quality of life, (b) benchmarking, (c) performance management.
4. Describe the procedure involved in any three large scale interventions.
5. Describe a case of institution building and highlighting the interventions employed.

📖 MINI-PROJECT

Visit a local educational institution. Identify the learning processes of teachers and administrators. Figure out how knowledge is secured, stored and shared by them. Make a report and share the information with classmates.

🖱 WEB ASSIGNMENT

Visit the following website and develop a paper on orgnaizational transformation
21-Organizational Transformation Strategy
https://www.fareham.gov.uk/council/general/cpa/orgtransstrategy.pdf

Leaders and Institution Building

Dr. Vikram Sarabhai was a rare combination of an innovative scientist, forward looking industrial organizer and imaginative builder of institutions. He was associated with a large number of institutions in diverse fields. He was a visionary; he could sense opportunities where none existed. He taught many others how to dream and realize them through application of mind and relentless effort. The success of India's space program is a great testimony to his approach.

He never ran away from taking up new responsibilities or challenges. When asked to take up responsibilities of the office of the Chairman, Atomic Energy Commission in 1966, he had substantive responsibilities in three areas: Physical Research Laboratory as Director and Professor of Cosmic Ray Physics, Chairman of the Indian National Committee for Space Research Program and family business interests, centered around chemicals and pharmaceuticals. He accepted the offer and was at the helm of both atomic energy and space research programs in India till his death. Ahmedabad Textile Industry's Research Association (ATIRA) and the Physical Research Laboratory (PRL) are among the many institutions he developed.

Early Initiative

Sarabhai was born into a wealthy, elite family that has close ties with national leaders and interest in social reforms. He had opportunity to work closely with C.V. Raman and Homi Bhabha. His mission as a creator and cultivator of institutions came to light, when at the age of twenty eight, he persuaded charitable trusts controlled by his family and friends to endow a research institution, the Physical Research Laboratory, in Ahmedabad.

Leadership Choice

Sarabhai had to held the position of Honorary director of ATIRA for nine years, as the right person could not be found. In 1956, Helmut Wakeham, an American was selected as the first full-time director of ATIRA. About the selection, Vikram Sarabhai opined like this. "I have no doubt, however, that you are fully aware of the human relations side of a man that is necessary in order that he might fit into our environment ..." However, for PRL, Mr. K.R. Ramanathan was selected as the first full-time director even before the institute was set up. He was director of Indian Meteorological Department, Poona, and Sarabhai was impressed with his leadership style.

Choice of Location

Sarabhai felt identifying the right location was important. For ATIRA, Ahmedabad, the Manchester of India, was an obvious location. Further, there was full support from the Ahmedabad Millowners' Association. As Sarabhai had already established a small research laboratory at the "Retreat" (his home) where he was doing cosmic rays research, PRL was located at Ahmedabad.

Recruitment and Development

Sarabhai insisted on recruiting fresh candidates with knowledge of scientific methodology for ATIRA. The reason is: fresh and trained young mind would be able to produce better results in the textile industry than the applications of previous experience gained in industry. The research workers were apprenticed to periods varying from 6 months to a year to a textile mill with the object of learning about the technology and the problems of the textile industry. At the PRL, young students with training in scientific methodology were admitted in the post-graduate and doctoral programs in the two areas of atmospheric physics and cosmic rays. They undertook research under the guidance of Ramanathan and Sarabhai. This led not only to student development but also to institutional development.

Enculturation

According to Sarabhai, the appropriate operating culture is created not by the formal organizational structure, but by the assumptions and behavioral norms of people working in it. Sarabhai, Bhatnagar, and Krishnan played important roles not only in the formulation of scientific research programs but also in creation of appropriate operating cultures in ATIRA and PRL. The operating culture of these institutions was characterized by the supportive role and actions of administration to the research.

Interacting and Overlapping Clusters

An important strategy employed by Sarabhai was the creation of clusters of individuals with whom he interacted, and through whom he interacted with others. This is similar to the modern networks concept. Three interacting clusters played a significant role in the growth of ATIRA. The first interacting cluster was at the policy level, second was at the research level, and the third consisted of young managing agents related to the millowner-members. Sarabhai represented all three clusters, and thus could link them.

All the members of the first cluster were involved in the institution building activity. Their mutual trust and commitment to helping each other's institution building activities added strength. At PRL, Sarabhai used the same strategy of institution building.

Leadership Style

Sarabhai had an uncanny ability of judging a person from the sparkle in his/her eyes and gauging the capability of a person just by talking to him for a few minutes. He believed in development and focused on developing himself and people who worked with him.

According to him, there is no leader and there is no led. A leader has to be a cultivator rather than a manufacturer. He has to provide the soil and the overall climate and the environment in which the seed can grow. He is not like those, who think issuing instructions to others is leading. He exercised leadership by setting an example through his own creativity, love of nature and dedication to what one may call the 'scientific method.' He encouraged young researchers to try out new ideas. He himself generated ideas constantly and inspired them.

- *Decision-making and structuring:* Sarabhai took part actively both in policy making at the council level and in implementing it in ATIRA and PRL. He promoted committee system and a committee was set up for every research and for every administrative unit. The chairman of each committee as well as the members of the committee reported to him directly.
- *Learning by doing:* At ATIRA, the routine administrative work was left to the research workers. Since everyone was new to the textile industry, Sarabhai, worked with them and jointly identified relevant areas of enquiry and helped them in planning their own budgets and implementation procedures. Thus, in place of hierarchical controls, horizontal controls were more in operation. At PRL also similar approach was employed.
- *Trust:* Trust was an important element of both personal and organizational relationship for Sarabhai. He moved across various groups and inspired trust.
- *Concern and care:* When he was Director of PRL and Chairman of ISRO, Sarabhai had called a senior accountant from Bangalore for a discussion on an issue. The moment the accountant entered Dr. Sarabhai's room, he enquired about his family and asked him why he was worried. When the accountant revealed that his father was not well, Dr. Sarabhai arranged for his leave and postponed the discussion. Many such incidents were recalled by the people who worked under him.
- *Development of people:* Sarabhai believed in developing people in a systematic and phased manner. He preferred to take young people and provide them with opportunities for development. Sarabhai was always accessible to all in both the institutions because he was convinced of the importance of the role played by feedback in managing organizations.

Identity Building

Sarabhai's image as a scientist helped in creation of an identity to both the PRL and ATIRA. Sarabhai, as a young managing agent, interacted with other managing agents, and developed the identity of ATIRA as a cooperative, technological venture serving the needs of the textile industry. For PRL, the task was easy as the scientists had an established reputation in the scientific community both in India and abroad.

Questions for Discussion

1. What are the essential components in institution building?
2. What kind of interventions do you employ to develop institutional leaders and promote institutional building?
3. Is Sarabhai's approach valid for organizations, which are in maturity stage?

Source: Adapted from Vikram Sarabhai, www.vigyanprasar .gov.in/scientists/Vikram%20Sarabhai.htm, Ganesh, S.R. and Padmanabh Joshi (1985), Institution building: Lessons from Vikrarn Sarabhai's leadership, *Vikalpa*, Vol. **10**(4), October-December, pp. 399–413 and Raman Srinivasan No Free Launch: Designing the Indian National Satellite available at chapter 16, history.nasa.gov/SP-4217/ch16.htm

REFERENCES

1. Adapted with permission from Human Dimension—Our Company, www. humandimension.org/ourcompany.html Learning Management Companies India Employability ... www.centumlearning.com/contactus.asp and Organization Development 101 | Accelera Consulting Group www.acceleraconsultinggroup.com/.../ organization-development-101.

2. Senge, P.M. (1990), *The Fifth Discipline*, London : Century Business.

3. Building a Learning Organization—FlashPoint,www.flashpointhr.com/images/building-a-learning-organization.pdf

4. Abdullah, Rusli et al. (2005), A Framework for Knowledge Management System Implementation in Collaborative Environment For Higher Learning Institution, *Journal of Knowledge Management Practice*, March.

5. Organizational Learning Strategies: Parallel Learning Structures. www.humtech.com/opm/grtl/ols/ols6.cfm

6. TQM Implementation and Organizational Development among Indian odsummitindia. org/content/html/.../Mostafa%20Moballeghi.pdf

7. The Deming Cycle—Management Methods | Management Models ... www. valuebasedmanagement.net/methods_demingcycle.html

8. Benchmarking Consultant—Steps in benchmarking—Five key stages. www.training-management.info/benchmarking/steps.htm and Benchmarking Quality Digest, www. qualitydigest.com/feb/benchmark.html

9. Management by Objectives (MBO)—focus on achievable ... www.1000ventures.com/business_guide/mgmt_mbo_main.html

10. Consultant Bios—The York Consulting Team, Inc., www.yorkteam.com/consultantbios. html

11. Capacity building—Wikipedia, the free encyclopedia. en.wikipedia.org/wiki/Capacity_building

12. Institution Building. www.sais-jhu.edu/cmtoolkit/.../statebuilding/institution-building. htm

13. Career Management & Self Development: Janaki and Mahesh have ... www.anahat. in/businesssolutions.php; Institution building & good governance | Human Dynamics, humandynamics.org/institution-building-good-governance.

14. Future Search, www.co-intelligence.org/P-futuresearch.html, and Future Search—The Method—What is Future Search? www.futuresearch.net/method/whatis/index.cfm

15. OD Interventions—World Cafe—Eclectic Change. www.eclecticchange.com/2009/01/od-interventions-world-cafe/

16. Open space technology, available at http://www.openspaceworld.org/cgi/wiki.cgi a link to www.odnetwork.org/?page=Links

17. Real-Time Strategic Change, www.cmperme.com/pdf/cmp9605.pdf

18. Silverman, Lori L., (2000), Using Real Time Strategic Change For Strategy Implementation, *The Quality Management Forum*, Fall, Vol. **26**(4), Available at Using real time strategic change for strategy ... www.partnersforprogress.com/articles/largegroupinterventions.pdf.

Part Five: Future Trends

Chapter 15

Future of Organization Development

Learning Objectives

After studying this chapter, you will be able to:

- Explain the changes and their implications to the future of Organization Development (OD)
- Identify the strengths of OD
- Emphasize the need for ethical standards in OD
- Gain some understanding of research on OD

Vignette: HR and OD Interventions

Punjab National Bank (PNB) has contracted Centum Learning, a leading training and development multinational organization, to provide training to 30,000 employees across the country. Centum Learning has already been working with many other companies of repute like American Express, Deutsche Bank, HSBC, Axis Bank, Bajaj Finance, UCO Bank and Allahabad Bank.

The initiative included a customer service sensitization program for a period of 10 months to improve the customer service levels in nearly 65 circles comprising a total of 5,247 branches spread across the country. The program is focussed on necessary soft-skills required to better serve the Bank's end customers. A set of actions around external customer service and putting an effective coordination mechanism in place for internal customers while ensuring consistent quality and uniform messaging are contemplated.

The content designed in consultation with PNB will be delivered through instructor-led-training mode. More than 1,000 certified trainers will train both external and internal customer-facing employees at various levels, including branch managers as well. Appropriate methodologies to monitor impact of the training solution will be put in place. It is expected that besides helping staff communicate better with customers, the training will also enhance team bonding between officers, clerical staff and sub-staff.

Centum Learning conducted a program—which incorporated the Experiential Learning methodology, a revolutionary concept in learning effectiveness, for over 50 Sales Managers from the Oncology and Nephrology divisions of a leading pharmaceutical company. The learning was made interactive and simple by including activities such as Flag Hoisting, Egg Drop exercise, Australian Walk and Municipal Blues. It helped build team identity and competitive spirit, enhanced capabilities in creative decision making and delivering under resource crunch, and ensured effective communication, coordination and self-discipline.

Centum Learning trained top performing sales teams of an International Banking chain towards forming a cohesive group of people who are really rooted in organization's vision, willing to go that extra mile and delight internal and external customers. An experiential learning program was conducted for over 70 best performers and their business leaders of the client's sales teams in the North, South and West Zones. Participants experienced a highly interactive and energetic program, which included multiple activities[1].

The cases point out the need to think development as a holistic one. It is the combination of OD and HR, that is happening today. In this chapter, we discuss the future of OD and the possibility of its emergence as a strategic tool in the coming years.

INTRODUCTION

Is OD on the path of progress or is it still struggling to gain an identity as a specialized profession? The question has less relevance today, as there are many OD consultants in India and they are able to succeed in getting clients and also in earning a good image for their expertise and diversified consulting. The practitioners have formed professional associations, evolved a code of conduct for the members and leveraged alliances with global practitioners. Meanwhile, OD as an extension to Human Resource Management, and development has become a field of study and research. On the demand side, client organizations are growing in number and some companies have plans to set up in-house OD departments. With all these developments one can say, OD is poised for growth in India.

CHANGES IN MANAGEMENT

What environmental forces are impacting the growth of OD? What kind of developments are taking place in OD practice? We try to answer these questions in the following lines:

New management viewpoints started emerging in the 21st century with the onset of information revolution and other concomitant developments. The major influencing factors are:

1. Globalization, with growing trends to include global customers with wide open choices, leading to increasingly specialized products and services, and need to use specialized knowledge.
2. Information and communication technology developments, causing rapidly changing needs and creation of communities of excellence.
3. Liberalization and privatization reforms that led to emergence of new public management and new forms of governance in government and non-governmental organizations.

We witnessed waves of transformation caused first by IT, then by two movements in social sphere of organizations, that have brought values and spirituality to the center stage of management.

IT-based Management

The emergence of information technology has led to a new era of management. E-commerce, Knowledge Management, Lean production, Business Process Reengineering (BPR), TQM (Total Quality Management), and Innovation management like processes required knowledge workers and team spirit. Information technology facilitated global markets and 24/7 work systems, which in one way intensified competition and in another way provided means to face competition. They have also created stress and work-life balance challenges to which employers and employees had tried to respond positively.

E-commerce is to the Information Revolution what the railroad was to the Industrial Revolution—a totally new, totally unprecedented, totally unexpected development. And like the railroad 170 years ago, e-commerce is creating a new and distinct boom, rapidly changing the economy, society and politics. Information Revolution has routinized traditional processes in an untold number of areas. They have been routinized, step-by-step, with a tremendous saving in time and, often cost.

Knowledge management is a direct outcome of information revolution. What has made it possible to routinize processes is not machinery; the computer is only the trigger. The key is not electronics; it is cognitive science. This means that the key to maintaining leadership in the emerging economy and the technology is the social position of knowledge professionals and social acceptance of their values.

According to the IBM Global CEO Study 2006, which polled more than 750 top CEOs worldwide, CEOs are increasingly focused on innovation through business models and operations as the key mechanism to drive change. In fact, 76% of CEOs rank business partner and customer collaboration as key sources for new ideas[2]. Creativity as a mental ability belongs to the domains of psychology and cognitive science. Innovative thinking, brainstorming, and lateral thinking exercises are encouraged and used by forward thinking businesses and corporations to successfully plan, create, and sell products and services.

Dominance of project structures and emergence of virtual organizations are visible in this era. Virtual organization design facilitates concentration on new services and products, especially those with intensive information and knowledge characteristics. It goes beyond outsourcing and strategic alliances and is more flexible because:

- It has continuously changing partners
- The arrangements are loose and goal oriented
- It emphasizes the use of knowledge to create new products and services
- Its processes can change quickly by agreement of the partners

Value-based Management

One comprehensive approach to management that saw light in the recent times is, "Value-based Management" or "VBM" developed by the Center for Economic and Social Justice (CESJ) in Arlington, Virginia[3]. Simply put, VBM is a business philosophy and management system for competing effectively in the global marketplace, based upon the inherent value, dignity and empowerment of each person-particularly each employee, customer and supplier. Value-based Management marries the quality, educational and participation aspects of Total Quality Management and Open Book Management, with the equity and ownership concepts underlying employee stock ownership plans (ESOPs). VBM builds checks-and-balances in the company's governance and accountability system. Within a VBM system, these aspects of value can be implemented in a business by:

1. Creating structures of corporate governance and management based on shared moral values, as expressed in a written set of:
   - Company core values (ethical principles which define the culture and clarify the social purposes and mission of the organization); and
   - A code of ethics (describing a set of virtues or habits to be encouraged, which guide individual behavior toward strengthening the company's culture and interpersonal harmony).
2. Maximizing value for the customer. Within a VBM culture, everyone in the company has a self-interest in providing "service to the customer," because ultimately it is the customer who "signs" every employee's paycheck.
3. Structuring the company's compensation and reward system to enable every person in the company to be rewarded for the value of their contributions to the company.

The development of values to guide business behavior and the commitment of the top management to values in WIPRO is described in Box 15.1.

BOX 15.1   Wipro Designs Values

In the mid-1970s, Premji decided to make a formal statement of the values to make explicit what the company stands for. The exercise began with executives examining the ethics and values statements of high-profile companies worldwide. Next they talked to business ethicists in academia. As a next step, group discussions involving managers and rank-and-file employees were held. They were asked: 'What do you think is true to us? What is the quest we should build the company around?" The participants came up with a list of six values: (a) Respect the individual, (b) Be a business leader, (c) Accomplish all tasks in a superior manner, (d) Maintain the highest ethical standards, (e) Serve customers well, and (f) Measure performance based on long-term profitability.

Premji made it a point to reexamine the company's beliefs with an idea of engaging managers and employees in an exercise that would put them in touch with one another and think about the organization. By the late 1990s, Wirpo required complete transformation as it was found suffering an identity crisis due to its multiple businesses. What was Wipro? What should it mean to employees, customers and partners? Shining Strategic Design (SSD), was hired to for a complete brand makeover.

First a survey firm interviewed Indian customers about their opinions of Wipro. It was found that the company was seen as a low-profile one, cold business unit. This finding changed the project from a brand touch-up into a major revamp of the company's identity.

The project took two years. SSD performed a series of in-depth focus groups of business partners, consumers and middlemen in each of India's regions. A series of discussions with the company's executives were organized to develop a new value statement tied in with the new brand identity.

The company's old logo, a large black W is changed to a "rainbow flower" providing a symbolic meaning to stakeholders. Yellow meant prosperity; blue, openness; and red, integrity. As the focus groups felt that the petals of the flower were too sharp, they were modified to look soft. After several iterations, "Applying Thought" was chosen as the tag line. To be seen as a global company, Wipro vetted its logo with Western customers including Microsoft, Cisco Systems, and Allied Signal.

To gain acceptance of employees, the proposed changes were debated throughout the company. Some employees, including senior managers objected to the new logo and slogan. A flower was considered inappropriate for a tech company. Some opined that the slogan might give impression that employees sit around all day thinking rather than getting things done. Even the top management, including Premji balked at some of the changes. Premji would not agree to the idea of dropping integrity as one of the company's values. The new code, renamed Wipro Values, had four pieces, as they were stated on Wipro's website: Human values, Inegrity, Innovative solutions and value for money. The values were later called Wipro Promises, and printed on the back of business card briefly as follows:

"With utmost respect to Human Values, we promise to serve our customer with Integrity, through Innovative, Value for Money solutions, by Applying Thought, day after day."

Source: How Wipro's values came to be—Express Computer, www.expresscomputeronline.com/20061204/technologylife03.shtml, 4 Dec. 2006. For elaborate story see Steve Hamm (2007), *Bangalore Tiger*, New Delhi: Tata McGraw-Hill.

Spirituality-based Management

Another development concomitant with value based management is movement towards spirituality. To the list of enterprise economic (competition, profit, economic value-added), political (power and democracy), technological (innovations, new processes, new equipment, and new products), and social (individual dignity, relationships, harmony, and team work) values, the spiritual values (holistic view, self-realization, enlightened leadership, blissful satisfaction) are added.

Various developments that advanced civilization contributed to improvement in the material standards of life on one side and on the other presented a dismal picture of society and business on human side. There is a prevalent feeling of restlessness and dismay found among people. With this, businesses looking outward started looking upward for guidance and confidence. Thus, spirituality took roots in business organizations.

Having observed this trend, researchers and practitioners started developing and applying spirituality concepts and principles, to the management of business and industrial organizations.

Environmentalists and scientists also started advocating spiritual thoughts and green business concepts.

Theoretical Foundations

A review of developments in theoretical perspectives that guided the practice of management from scientific management is shown in Table 15.1.

TABLE 15.1 Management Schools and Contributions

Schools	Contributions
Scientific management	Specialization, efficiency, training and productivity
Behavioral management	Team work, creativity, sharing the gains of productivity and equality
Quantitative School	Effectiveness in decisions in respect of resource allocation and utilization
Systems and contingency management	Situational thinking, Stake-holder concept, Business-society integration, and Change management
Socio-technical systems management	Adaptation to new technology, Project management, 24/7 routines, and Outsourcing
Value-based management	Shared values, Value-based management, Ethical behavior, Social responsibility, and Corporate governance.
Spirituality management	Self-realization and growth, Integration by devotion, and Blissful satisfaction.

Contemporary Outlook

The contemporary management is relatively more professionalized and broader in outlook. The managers are tech-savvy, and are entrepreneurial. In a recent survey of Indian CEO's, it was suggested that Indian management leaders were less dependent on their personal charisma, but they emphasized logical and step by step implementation processes. Indian leaders focused on empowerment and accountability in cases of critical turnaround challenges, innovative technology, product planning and marketing or when other similar challenges were encountered[4]. Indeed, Chatterjee and Pearson argued, with supporting empirical evidence from 421 senior level Indian managers, that many of the traditional Indian values (respect for seniority, status and group affiliation) have been complemented by newer areas of attention that are more usually linked to globalization, such as work quality, customer service and innovation[5]. The most important work related attribute of the study was the opportunity to learn new things at work.

Emphasis on scientific selection of employees, team work, creativity, empowerment, gender mainstreaming, performance management, training for updating knowledge and skills, etc., is evident in current practices. Corporate Social Responsibility has become the hallmark of modern management. Table 15.2 draws comparisons between modern and traditional management.

TABLE 15.2   Traditional and Contemporary Indian Management

Management practices	Traditional Indian management	Contemporary Indian management
Employee requirements	Family relation and caste memberships of employees	Relevant educational background and experience that match task requirements
Leadership style	Leaders provided nurturance, contingent upon the subordinate's task accomplishment	Increasingly participative management style where subordinates' opinions and input are solicited
Motivational aspects and rewards	Work was viewed as a means to an end, i.e. for the sake of satisfying family needs. Little demand for changing work tasks, only the compensation is relevant	Elements such as job rotation, enrichment, autonomy, team work and competitive rewards are increasingly considered to motivate employees
Human resource management practices	Nepotism and caste considerations affected selection and compensation. Training was less emphasized	Objective selection criteria, Training programs and performance related compensation are valued

Source: Li Choy Chong, *Rediscovering Indian Management*, www.lim.ethz.ch/lehre/fruehjahrssemester/... management/R3 and Modern and Traditional Business Management: An Overview of Two ... www. changeisgood.nl/MasterScriptie-Viola.pdf.

FUTURE OF OD

In the coming decades, the demand for OD will relatively increase and OD practitioners will have to innovate interventions to tackle unforeseen and unusual problems which arise in the future environment.

1. *Fluid environment:*   Future environments will become more fluid and organizations will become more complex, with constant state of flux. The implication is change management continues to be a challenge to organizations.

2. *Organizations will be organic and innovative:*   Organizing will aim at creating virtual, flexible networks and partnerships. This trend point to the importance of CEO as a strategist and HR's role as a strategic partner in capacity building and implementation of organization-wide change. The need for developing and maintaining organization culture that is entrepreneurial and innovative will be stronger.

3. *Employee competencies decisive:*   In the innovation driven economies, the ability to successfully innovate, will be critical to the organizations. OD practices which can be of direct value regarding performance management like goal setting, employee skills and learning, appraisals, reward systems, career planning and workforce diversity will be indispensable for future organizations.

The above views are corroborated by the findings of the IBM CEO study presented briefly in Box 15.2.

BOX 15.2 IBM CEO Survey Findings

More than 1,500 Chief Executive Officers from 60 countries and 33 industries worldwide responded to the survey conducted by IBM. It is found that CEOs are confronted with massive shifts—new government regulations, changes in global economic power centers, accelerated industry transformation, growing volumes of data, and rapidly evolving customer preferences.

Eight in ten CEOs expect their environment to grow significantly more complex as the complexity of an interconnected world is being aggravated by a number of factors. The complexity is further intensified by geography—differences across the globe.

More than 60 per cent of CEOs said that industry transformation is the top factor, and companies need to discover more innovative ways of managing an organization's structure, finances, people and strategy. However, less than half of global CEOs believed their enterprises are adequately prepared to handle a highly volatile, increasingly complex business environment.

The CEOs emphasized one of their main jobs is to master complexity in all dimensions of their organizations:

- They have to constantly simplify operations, products and services.
- They have to experiment in the marketplace in close collaboration with their customers and partners.
- They have to standardize back-end operations and processes with customer- orientation to establish true competitive differentiation.
- They have to promote an entrepreneurial mindset in their organizations based on speed and flexibility.

The lessons from top-performing organizations support the perceived strategic and development approach of CEOs in facing the challenges:

- Top performing organizations made rapid decisions. The responding CEOs indicated they are learning to respond swiftly with new ideas to address the deep changes affecting their organizations.
- Top performing organizations became closer to customers as their most important strategic initiative—using Web, interactive, and social media channels to rethink how they engage with customers and citizens.
- Top performing organizations sought to capture 20 per cent more of their future revenue from new sources than their more traditional peers.

Source: IBM 2010 Global CEO Study: Constant Change Demands Creativity ... turbotodd.wordpress.com/ .../ibm-2010-global-ceo-study-constant-ch... 25 May 2010.

All these developments point out to the growth of OD as a critical discipline and practice in organizations. To remain competitive in today's global marketplace, one of the most effective tools is Organization Development (OD). As HR focusses on capacity building, and organizational learning, OD is becoming a broad HR competency. As organizations are increasingly employing OD to help achieve company business goals and strategies, OD is becoming a key strategic tool[6].

Burke (2004) identified five models of OD which defined status of OD in organizations[7].

1. *Traditional model:* OD is concerned with solving problems arising from mechanistic view of organization. It is a sub-function of HR.

2. *Independent model:* OD as a separate function of developing people in organization using socio-technical approach especially group development and team work. Reporting to operations head.

3. *Decentralized model:* OD elevated to organizational level from a unit level. OD practitioners in business units reporting to unit head and OD executive at headquarters.

4. *Integrated model:* Change is the primary responsibility of OD. Since adaptation has become a continuous process, OD is integrated into all aspects of HR.

5. *Strategy model:* OD is raised to strategic level and made an integral part of the strategic-planning function. OD executive directly reports to the CEO.

STRENGTH OF OD

The changes in global economy, technology and nature of workforce have significant implications for the practice of OD. It is interesting that OD practice is also growing strong and keeping pace with the changes[8]. First we will examine the practice environment of OD and identify its ability to work effectively.

Work Environment of OD Practitioners

What kind of situation do Organization Development practitioners face? Here is an illustrative list.

1. *Innovation:* OD has to focus on learning and innovation and its interdisciplinary nature will increase.

2. *Diverse clients:* OD practitioners have to work with diverse client organizations and cross-cultural teams. They will need to develop the required competence.

3. *Value dilemmas:* They have to resolve value dilemmas of modern organizations. Prior to solving them, OD practitioners will be required to resolve the dilemma within them regarding the focus of OD interventions.

4. *New organizational position:* As HR professionals are exploring the advantages of organization development and honing their respective OD competencies, OD is being regarded as a strategic HR tool. In the future, OD will become an integral part of organizational operations and OD skills will be acquired by employees at every level in the organization.

Ability to Meet Challenges

Can the OD practitioners meet the expectations? The answer is yes, because over the years, OD discipline and profession have acquired new strengths in terms of knowledge, approaches and values.

1. *Continuous innovations:* The research and practice in the field of OD has led to the emergence of new concepts and interventions. OD has been growing strong by evolving continuously to meet business needs.

2. *Democratic values:* OD by its nature depend on soundness of its processes, which emphasizes democratic values and procedures. For HR and OD professionals alike, change initiatives work best with a bottom-up approach.

3. *Holistic view:* OD focuses on the whole organization as well as work groups, departments and individuals.

4. *Action orientation:* Client-focused, OD is based in open-systems theory and approaches. It uses action research to focus on process and learns from doing. Based on the experience, OD practitioners develop the best pathway and rationale for change.

5. *Humanistic values:* OD is driven by humanistic values (respect, inclusion, authenticity, collaboration).

6. *Discipline of OD:* It is an education-based discipline, with the goal to develop values, norms, attitudes and management practices. It can be taught and people can be trained to be OD managers capable of creating a healthy organizational climate that rewards healthy behaviors.

ETHICS FOR OD

One of the important strength of an OD practitioner is ethical sensitivity and conduct. Developing a code of ethics or conduct of conduct, for practitioners to follow is an important challenge for OD educational institutes and professional organizations. In Chapter 2 of this book, a mention was made of International Organization Development Code of Ethics. Some OD consultants publicize the values they follow in their consulting practice. Box 15.3 presents the values of some OD consultants.

BOX 15.3   Values for OD
OD Synergy team subscribes to five core values that define the nature and quality of their relationships with their clients, customers and partners:
Integrity (moral wholeness), Excellence (technical standards), Professionalism (expertise), innovativeness (novelty) and Versatility (customized solutions).
OD Alternatives states that their values are:
Continuous Learning, Innovation, Bias for Action and Honesty (Its being straight forward).

BOX 15.3   Values for OD (*Contd.*)

The OD Network stands for the following values:

Social responsibility, Social justice, Appreciation of the interconnectedness of systems, Inclusion of people, Collaboration and Cooperation.

Source: Organizational Development Consulting Partnership, OD Professional www.odsynergy.com/od-synergy-partnership-terms.html, OD consultancy, interventions Leadership, coaching, Team building ... www.odalternatives.com/, and OD Network. www.odnetwork.org/.

RESEARCH ON OD

The journey of OD has begun when dehumanising effects of scientific management practices were recognized and remedial measures were required.

1. *Humanistic approach:*   The humanistic approach of OD used images of body and health to discuss the problem in organization and suggest the use of people, systems and technology framework. Several humanistic approaches like equality, ethics, shared values; training and development, employee feedback, systems thinking and action research were employed. Psychologists and social scientists brought a strongly values-driven approach to the study of OD.

2. *Group approach:*   Attention gradually shifted to relationships, teams and intergroup dynamics and 'T-group' had become the focus of OD.

3. *Employee engagement:*   From studies of fatigue, absenteeism, turnover, and unrest the focus shifted to employee engagement with staff survey becoming popular as employee feedback tool.

4. *Socio-technical systems perspectives:*   The view emerged when experiments with self-directed teams, became successful and the challenge of technology especially, IT was well recognized and adopted in organizations.

The focus of research relating to OD has been on the following:

1. *Organization design:*   Mechanistic to organic approaches with focus on efficiency to effectiveness.

2. *Systems thinking:*   Culture as an important vehicle for change; individual training vs organizational learning; holistic approach to organizational design, drawing on new sciences and metaphors to describe organizations as living systems and change.

3. *Leadership:*   The search for new styles of leadership and role in change, innovation and employee development.

4. *People:*   The attitudes, motivations, commitment, culture, climate and engagement aspects of people, etc.

ILLUSTRATIVE RESEARCH STUDIES

OD research as stated above has been contributing to the field of knowledge and providing tips to practitioners on how to make interventions more effective. Here is an illustrative coverage of the research themes.

Conceptual Base

Kahn examined the rapidly increasing body of OD literature and opined that much of the research was redundant and the term Organizational Development is scientifically undefined. He observed that OD literature as a whole was more autobiographical without organizational focus and scope. The author discussed a reconceptualization of organizational structure and process that permits clarification of key issues in the theory of organizational change[9].

Business Process Reengineering

Dey presented in his study how a radical improvement in materials management function of an Indian petroleum refinery was brought about through Business Process Re-engineering (BPR). The process involved analysis of current processes, identification of key issues, and development of re-engineered processes through customer value analysis. Two key processes—materials planning and procurement and warehousing and surplus disposal, were considered and projects were identified by the group of executives who took part in the re-engineering exercise. They were implemented in an integrated framework with the application of latest information technology tools[10].

Total Quality Management

Taylor and Wright, studied the perceived TQM success for a cohort of 109 firms over a 5-year period. It was found that about 42 small size firms, discontinued with TQM. The remaining 67 firms reported varying degrees of success. The success, however, was not influenced by: (i) the size of firm, (ii) the nature of the customer base (iii) ISO9000 series certification. The success was significantly associated with: (i) the time since adoption, (ii) the inclusion of quality objectives in the strategic planning process, and (iii) the need for initiatives from senior managers to involve employees in implementation[11].

Parallel Learning Structures

Bushe (1989) observed that parallel learning structures coexist with formal bureaucratic structures and show great promise as a techno-structural intervention to compensate for bureaucratic organization's inability to learn and adapt. From a case study of one manufacturing plant's efforts to implement such an innovation (statistical process control) he pointed out their advantages in implementation[12].

Organizational Learning

Khandekar and Sharma carried out a survey to analyze the role of organizational learning and strategic Human Resource Management (HRM) in sustainable competitive advantage. Data was collected from a random sample of 300 line or Human Resource (HR) managers from nine Indian and foreign global organizations, chosen purposefully from New Delhi (the national capital region of India). SPSS package 10 was used and descriptive statistics (percentages, means, cross tabulation) and testing tools, like Pearson's correlation, one-way analysis of variance, inter-item analysis and Cronbach alpha were computed. The results suggested that there is a positive relationship between organizational learning, strategic HRM and sustainable competitive advantage[13].

Process Consultation

Weir, Robin et al. through randomized controlled trial method was employed to test the efficacy of process consultation in improving the morale of nursing staff. Thirteen clinical in-patient units were randomly assigned to control and experiential treatments. The nurse managers from 7 experimental units were paired with outside nurse consultants in a cooperative form of retraining in problem solving through process consultation. The perceptions on work environment, attitudes on work alienation, personality measures, satisfaction and absenteeism were found out. Experimental groups reported positive results of satisfaction and morale[14].

Team Building

De Meuse and Liebowitz reviewed 36 published studies on, team building as an OD strategy. They examined the (1) research designs, (2) sample sizes, (3) dependent variables, and (4) the intervention time period. They found that team building is rated as an intervention with great potential for improving employee attitudes, perceptions, and behaviors as well as organizational effectiveness[15].

Kriek & Venter took a convenience sample of 314 first year students of Master of Business Leadership (MBL) at the Graduate School of Business Leadership (GSBL) of the University of South Africa and examined the team building effectiveness using ten hypotheses. The results of chi-square tests revealed that the following three hypotheses are acceptable:

- There is a relationship between the respondent's level in the organization and perception of teambuilding success.
- There is a relationship between the type of event and perception of teambuilding success.
- There is a relationship between facilitator affiliation and team building success[16].

Sensitivity Training

Tainsri and Axelson, investigated the effects of group sensitivity training on the inter- and intrapersonal relations and the work performance. They took a sample of 20 workers and 20 managers of the Petroleum Authority of Thailand. While significant improvement in both inter- and intrapersonal relations for the experimental workers group, experimental managers group, and experimental mixed workers/managers group, significant improvement in work performance was found for both experimental and control groups[17].

Appreciative Inquiry

The level of positive affect generated by the inquiry was not a predictor of the level of change. In all sites, and particularly post-identity ones, the generation of new, compelling ideas was central to the change process. This supports recent arguments that it is generativity, and not positivity, that is central to the AI change process. Appreciative inquiry was originally designed in response to Gergen's call for more generative theorizing in social science. Gergen defined generativity as the "...capacity to challenge the guiding assumptions of the culture, to raise fundamental questions regarding contemporary social life, to foster reconsideration of that which is 'taken for granted' and thereby furnish new alternatives for social actions". Bushe argues that, "AI can be generative in a number of ways. Using the concept of generative affect of AI, Bushe experimented AI in eight different sites in a large, Canadian urban school district. The process, training, facilitators and follow up resources were same for all the eight sites. During the initial two months of the 18 months period, the researcher designed AI process, facilitated the selection of the affirmative topic, provided advice and training to the District Management Team and the site teams. The author was a participant observer in all district level events. Results were mixed, four of the sites experienced transformational changes, two sites had incremental changes and two showed little or no change[18].

Conflict Resolution

Hotepo, et al. investigated the effect of organizational conflict on organizational performance. They employed descriptive research design and used a questionnaire to collect data from 96 managers in some selected Airlines, Road Transport and Insurance companies in Lagos Metropolis. They found that lack of resources and communication problems (24% and 18% respectively) are the major causes of conflict. Interpersonal conflict was top most followed by inter-group conflict according to 39.6% and 22.9% of the respondents. The major consequence is interference with organizational operations bargaining (29.2%), collaboration (19.8%), avoidance (15.6%), compromise (13.5%) and confrontation (11.5%) were the methods employed by organizations[19].

Visionary Leadership

Brown and Anfara, Jr. organized a study to explore the strategies that some middle school principals utilize for implementation of changes and understand what middle school principals do in the process of putting visionary leadership into practice. The exploratory, qualitative case study was part of a larger survey conducted over a period of 2 years. Data was collected through surveys and semi-structured interviews. Ninety-eight middle level principals were surveyed. Survey questions related to the principals' (a) educational, professional, and personal background, (b) knowledge of the middle school concept, (c) experience with and perceptions of school reform and change, (d) attitudes toward parent involvement in school and (e) knowledge of special education issues.

As many as 44 principals were interviewed. The questions focused on the following areas: (a) the principal's experiences with implementing reform in the school, (b) perceptions regarding the effect of the school's culture and climate on the change process, (c) experiences with successful and unsuccessful reform initiatives, (d) support from the school district in the process of reforming, (e) strategies used to bring about change, and (f) experience with reforms that have been bureaucratically imposed. Each interview took around 60 minutes. Findings indicate that visionary leadership in action involves an initial exploration of possible change areas and organizing discussions for educating people to buy support and commitment of followers[20].

Organizational Transformation

The thesis of Catherine focussed on providing insights into the transformation behavior of manufacturing SMEs. Using an exploratory case study methodology, she analyzed transformations of four manufacturing SMEs in Scotland, using the content, process, context framework. The findings suggest that transformation of manufacturing SMEs follow the punctuated equilibrium approach. Leadership, appropriate knowledge and skills, access to resources, and external collaboration are contextual enablers to transformation. Culture is found as a barrier if not managed[21].

Consultant–Client Relationships (CCR)

Noble conducted three case studies to examine consultant and client relationships. With the assistance of State and Regional Development (DSRD), three cases-one case as a successful CCR, one an unsuccessful CCR and one a typical CCR. In each case the client/owner of the SME was interviewed at the conclusion of the consultancy project to identify their perceptions and experience of the CCR. In the successful, case the business improved its financial position and retained the services of the consultant. In the typical case, though there is improvement in the financial performance, the client withdrew her support for the consultant. In the third case, client withdrew support much early. The findings suggested that trust and power are significant aspects of the CCR[22].

Future Outlook

Emerging from challenging times, organizations are today facing a new reality characterized by uncertainty and competition. The response for survival and success often takes shape of re-strategizing growth and development programs, restructuring organizations, reforming organization culture and climate, and revitalizing human capital and reorienting leadership. HR practitioners have rightly changed their focus from human problem perspective to business as a whole perspective, to enhance organizational effectiveness. As a result of all these changes, it is predicted that OD will soon emerge as an integral function of corporate enterprises and OD skills will become an important part of the leadership repertoire.

SUMMARY

OD has become an important field of study and research as demand has been growing for a variety of OD interventions in corporate as well as NGOs. New management viewpoints started emerging in the twenty first century with information revolution and consequent socio-psychological developments. E-commerce, knowledge management, lean production, Business Process Reengineering (BPR), TQM (Total Quality Management), and innovation management, like processes required knowledge workers and team spirit. Dominance of project structures and emergence of virtual organizations are visible in this era. Value-based Management is enriched by spiritual values like holistic view, self-realization, enlightened leadership, blissful satisfaction. Environmentalists and scientists also started advocating spiritual thoughts and green business concepts. Newer areas of attention are more usually linked to globalization, such as work quality, customer service and innovation and include: team work, creativity, empowerment, gender mainstreaming, performance management, training for updating knowledge and skills, etc., and Corporate Social Responsibility. In the coming decades, OD will have to find new interventions to tackle unforeseen and unusual problems which arise in the future environment.

All these developments point out to the growth of OD as a critical discipline and practice in organizations. To remain competitive in today's global marketplace, one of the most effective tools is Oganization Development (OD). Burke (2004) identified five models of OD which defined status of OD in organizations—Traditional model, independent model, decentralized model, integrated model, and strategy model. OD practitioners are required to offer innovative services, for diverse clients. They face value dilemmas and may occupy a new organizational position.

Can the OD practitioners meet the expectations? The answer is yes, because OD discipline and profession have acquired new strengths like continuous innovations, democratic values, holistic view, action orientation, humanistic values and rational discipline. One of the important strength of an OD practitioner is ethical sensitivity and conduct.

The journey of OD has begun when dehumanising effects of scientific management practices were recognized and remedial measures were required. The early humanistic approach, moved to analysis of groups and employee engagement. Socio-technical analysis presented 'human-technology integration' for holistic solutions with focus on effectiveness of structure, system, people, process and leadership. OD research has been contributing to the field of knowledge and providing tips to practitioners on how to make interventions more effective. As a result of all these changes, it is predicted that OD will soon emerge as an integral function of corporate enterprises and OD skills will become an important part of the leadership repertoire.

EXERCISES

I. Review Questions

1. Outline the changes in management philosophy.
2. What the emerging trends in OD?
3. What are the strong points of OD?
4. What in your view is the future of OD?

5. Why do you consider ethics is important to OD practitioners?

6. Briefly discuss the themes for OD research.

II. Discussion Questions

1. Discuss the factors that have led to changes in OD and outline the likely changes in OD consultancy in the next five years.

2. In the development of OD discuss the contribution of research by highlighting the major themes of research.

📖 MINI-PROJECT

Collect at least 10 research papers on any one of the OD interventions and prepare a research paper.

🖱 WEB ASSIGNMENT

From the following web sources, find out the work of OD consultant and explain the role of psychology in consulting.

i-studentadvisor | i-BEL | An Interview With... An Od Consultant
www.i-studentadvisor.com/.../an-interview-with-an-od-consultant and

Organization Development Consulting—Human Resources at MIT, hrweb.mit.edu/organizational.../organization-development-consulting

CASE STUDY

Socio-technical Analysis

Koustab Ghosh proposed to conduct a comparative socio-technical analysis of managerial level jobs in organizations that vary by ownership (public and private sector) and by operation (manufacturing and services) located in India. Socio-technical system is defined as follows:

- Social subsystem variables: (i) supervisory relationship, (ii) peer group interaction, and (iii) person-organization fit.
- Technical subsystem variables: (i) managerial job characteristics, (ii) work technology support, and (iii) received organizational support.

Six hypotheses were proposed for identifying: (i) relationships between variables, and (ii) differences between sectors (Table CS-1).

Methodology

Junior and middle level personnel at managerial category (both from technical and managerial background) from the manufacturing and service organizations formed the population. The population was stratified into two categories: those having the business turnover of ₹ 1,000 crore and above, and employed manpower of 1,000 and above.

TABLE CS-1 Hypotheses

Number	Hypotheses
1	Supervisory relationship, peer group interaction, and person–organization fit are significantly correlated with organizational social subsystem.
2	There is no significant difference in the social subsystem of the public and private sector organizations in the manufacturing industry.
3	There is no significant difference in the social subsystem of the public and private sector organizations in the service industry
4	Managerial job characteristics, work technology support, and received organizational support are significantly correlated with organizational technical subsystem.
5	There is no significant difference in the technical subsystem of the public and private organizations in the manufacturing industry.
6	There is no significant difference in the technical subsystem of the public and private organizations in the service industry.

Data collection was carried out using a structured questionnaire comprising scale items that had been drawn from previous studies had two parts: (a) background information of the respondents from different organizations, and (b) scale items related to the social and technical subsystem constructs of organizations. The pilot–test used a convenient sample of 93 company representatives from India. With the help of principal component factor analysis and Cronbach's alpha the reliability was tested and the scale items to be used in the final study were finalized. Box CS-1 shows the items.

BOX CS-1   Questionnaire Items

(a) Supervisory relationship

1. My supervisor gives me feedback that helps me improve my performance.
2. My supervisor consults and openly shares information on important matters with people working under him or her.
3. I feel my supervisor as reliable and trustworthy.
4. I receive credit from my supervisor for a job well done.
5. My supervisor tries to understand my point of view when he or she discusses problems or projects with me.
6. I feel my job performance is fairly evaluated.
7. My supervisor understands my job problems and needs well.

(b) Peer group interaction

1. I tell people in my department how the quality of their work affects me.
2. People in my department tell me how the quality of my work affects them.
3. I get cooperation from people in my department to do the job well.
4. We feel we can collectively influence many important issues in this department.
5. Members of the work group work closely together and during the same time-frame.
6. I am satisfied with the friendliness of the people I work with.
7. We interact informally with each other within our department.
8. I socialize with my co-workers even outside the job.

(c) Person organization fit

1. Individual differences (e.g. gender, race, physical disability, social background, etc.) are respected in my organization.
2. We discuss with people in other departments how the quality of their work affects us.
3. People outside my department discuss with us how the quality of our work affects them. Each department knows enough about other related departments within the company.
4. Sharing information freely information about the organization's long-range plan and financial status are shared with us.
5. Achievement and competence are more important than hierarchical status.
6. We are encouraged to try new ways of doing things, even if they always might not work out.

(d) Job characteristics

1. My Job is simple, repetitive and does not require a great deal of thought.
2. Staying on schedule and planning for the future are important for jobs in my area.
3. I have authority commensurate with my position to make the decisions necessary for accomplishing assigned task.
4. A number of employees diagnose, solve problem, and collaborate together to deal with the work in my department.
5. We are allowed to determine job sequence in our department.
6. To get the job done, I am required to coordinate my work with others in my department.
7. My job requires coordinating my work with people in other departments also.
8. My job requires expertise and specialized skills that may not be readily available with people.

(e) Work-technology support

1. The technology that I use makes it easy for me to work with others as part of a team.
2. The technology that I use in this department requires high level of technological skill.
3. The technology that I predominantly use is complex and advanced by nature.
4. The technology that I use helps to reduce the complexities of routine operating procedures.

(f) Received organizational support

1. Workstations in our department are comfortable.
2. I think I am fairly paid in this organization.
3. The amount of work I am expected to do on my job is reasonable.
4. There are opportunities available for me to develop career and learn new skills within this company.
5. There is good alignment between my department and others with whom we need to coordinate.
6. I believe that top management has high integrity and commitment to the growth of the organization.

(Contd.)

BOX CS-1	Questionnaire Items (*Contd.*)

7. Senior staff members are willing to extend cooperation in order to help me perform my job to the best of my ability.
8. This company really cares about employee well-being.
9. Time-off policies are flexible enough to let me take care of my personal and family needs.

Results

Hypotheses are tested by computing t-tests and Pearson's correlation coefficient. The results are presented in Table CS-2.

TABLE CS-2   Results of Hypothesis Testing

No.	Result	Reason
1	Accepted	Pearson's correlation coefficient was significant at 0 .01 level.
2	Rejected	Mean values of Private manufacturing firms (3.40) is higher than the public-manufacturing firms (3.17).
3	Rejected	Mean value of the organizational social subsystem was higher for public enterprizes (3.50) than the private enterprizes (3.26) in the service sector.
4	Accepted	Pearson's correlation coefficient was significant at 0 .01 level
5	Rejected	Mean value of the technical subsystem was higher for private manufacturing firms (3.36) than the public manufacturing firms (3.28).
6	Rejected	Mean value of the technical subsystem was higher for public enterprizes (3.36) than the private enterprizes (3.17) in the service sector.

Questions for Discussion

1. Is the study methodologically sound for taking decisions based on the results?
2. What kind of interventions are necessary and for which organizations?

Source: Adapted with permission from Ghosh, Koustab (2009), Socio-technical Analysis of Managerial Level Jobs: A Comparative Study in Indian Organizations, *TMC Academic Journal*, Vol. **4**(2), pp: 19-43. Available at www.tmc.edu.sg/.../Socio-analysis%20in%20India%20-%20Ghosh%...

REFERENCES

1. Adapted with permission from Centum Learning to Train Punjab National Bank Employees, August 06, 2012 available at Press releases, www.centumlearning.com.and Case studies: Welcome to Centum Learning www.centumlearning.com.

2. IBM—Global CEOs Expect New Forms of Innovation to Drive ... re-inventing-innovation.com/.../ibm-global-ceos-expect-new-forms-o...7 May 2007.

3. Value-based Management: A System for Building an Ownership ... www.cesj.org/vbm/ vbmsummary.htm.

4. Spencer, S., Rajah, T., Narayan, S., Mohan, S. and Latiri, G. (2007), *The Indian CEO: A Portrait of Excellence*. New Delhi: Response Books.

5. Chatterjee, S.R. and Pearson, C.A.L. (2000), Indian managers in transition: Orientations, work goals, values and ethics, *Management International Review*, Vol. **40**(1), pp. 81–95.

6. Dunn, J. (2006), Strategic human resources and strategic organization development: An alliance for the future? *Organization Development Journal*, Vol. **24**(4), pp. 69–77.

7. Burke (2004), Internal Organization Development Practitioners: Where do they belong? The Journal of Applied Behavioral Science, Vol. **40**(4), pp. 423–43.

8. Organization Development: A Strategic HR Tool, in Research Quarterly. www.shrm. org/Research/Articles/Articles/Pages/0907RQuartpdf.aspx. and McLean, G.N., and McLean, L.D. (2001), If we can't define HRD in one country, how can we define it in an international context? *Human Resource International*, Vol. **4**(3), pp. 313–326.

9. Robert L. Kahn, (1974), Organizational Development: Some Problems and Proposals, *Journal of Applied Behavioral Science*, October, Vol. **10**(4), pp. 485–502.

10. Dey, Prasanta Kumar (2001). Re-engineering materials management: A case study on an Indian refinery, *Business Process Management Journal*, Vol. **7**(5), 2001, pp. 394–408.

11. Taylor, W.A. and Wright G.H. (2003), A Longitudinal study of TQM implementation: factors influencing success and failure, *Omega*, Vol. **31**(2), April, pp. 97–111.

12. Bushe, Gervase, R. (1989), "Use of a Parallel Learning Structure to Implement System Transforming Innovations: The Case of Statistical Process Control", *Journal of Managerial Psychology*, Vol. **4**(4), pp. 25–31.

13. Khandekar, Aradhana, and Sharma, Anuradha (2005), "Organizational learning in Indian organizations: a strategic HRM perspective", *Journal of Small Business and Enterprise Development*, Vol. **12**(2), pp. 211–226.

14. Weir, Robin et al. (1997), The Efficacy and Effectiveness of Process Consultation in Improving Staff Morale and Absenteeism, *Medical Care*, Vol. **35**(4), April, pp. 334–353.

15. De Meuse, Kennet, P., and Liebowitz, S. Jay (1981), An Empirical Analysis of Team-Building Research, *Group Organization Management*, September, Vol. **6**(3), pp. 357–378.

16. Kriek, H.S. & Venter, P. (2009), The perceived success of teambuilding interventions in South African organizations, *Southern African Business Review*, Vol. **13**(1).

17. Tainsri, Rutchana and Axelson, John A. (1990), Group sensitivity training with Thai workers and managers as a process to promote inter- and intra-personal relations, and work performance, *International Journal for the Advancement of Counselling*, Vol. **13**(3), pp. 219–226.

18. Bushe, Gervase, R. (2010), A comparative case study of appreciative inquiries in one organization: Implications for practice, *Review of research and social intervention*, Vol. **29**, available at a comparative case study of appreciative inquiries in one ... www.gervasebushe.ca/comparative_case.pdf; Bright, D.S., Powley, E.H., Fry, R.E. and Barrett, F.J. (2010), The generative potential of cynical conversations; In Zandee, D., Cooperrider, D.L. and Avital, M. (Eds.), Generative Organization: Advances in Appreciative Inquiry, Vol. **3**. Bingley, England: Emerald Publishing; Bushe, G.R. (2007); Appreciative inquiry is not (just) about the positive. *Organization Development Practitioner*, Vol. **39**(4), pp. 30–35 and Gergen, K.J. (1978), Toward generative theory, *Journal of Personality and Social Psychology*, Vol. **36**(11), 1344–1360.

19. Hotepo, O.M., Asokere A.S.S., Abdul-Azeez I A and Ajemunigbohun S.S.A. (2010). Empirical Study of the Effect of Conflict on Organizational Performance in Nigeria, *Business and Economics Journal*, Vol. 2010: BEJ-15.

20. Brown, Kathleen M. and Anfara, Vincent A. Jr (2003), Paving the Way for Change: Visionary Leadership in Action at the Middle Level, NASSP Bulletin Vol. **87**(635), June, available at www.nassp.org/portals/0/content/48887.pdf

21. Maguire, Catherine (2010), *An exploratory study of organisational transformation in manufacturing SMEs*, PhD thesis, University of Strathclyde, An exploratory study of organisational transformation in ... strathprints.strath.ac.uk/18846/

22. Noble, G.I. (2000), Management consultant—client relationships: their impact on consultancy outcomes in SMEs; ANZAM(2000) Sydney, NSW: MGSM available at The critical success factors in the client-consulting relationship www.cas.umt.edu/dcs/faculty/bach/.../AppelbaumandSteed_000.pdf.

Index